Twenty Five Years of Financial Sector Reforms in India

1991-92 to 2016-17

Twenty Five Years of
Financial Sector Reforms in India

1991-92 to 2016-17

By

Sarika R. Lohana

UGC-Dr. Radhakrishnan Post-doctoral Fellow
in Humanities and Social Sciences,
School of Commerce and Management Sciences,
Swami Ramanand Teerth Marathwada University, Nanded

New Century Publications
New Delhi, India

NEW CENTURY PUBLICATIONS
4800/24, Bharat Ram Road,
Ansari Road, Daryaganj,
New Delhi – 110 002 (India)

Tel.: 011-2324 7798, 4358 7398, 4101 7798
E-mail: indiatax@vsnl.com • info@newcenturypublications.com
www.newcenturypublications.com

Editorial office:
LG–7, Aakarshan Bhawan
4754-57/23, Ansari Road, Daryaganj,
New Delhi – 110 002

Tel.: 011-4356 0919

First Published: **2017**

ISBN: **978-81-7708-452-8**

Published by New Century Publications and printed at Milan Enterprises, New Delhi

Designs: Patch Creative Unit, New Delhi

PRINTED IN INDIA

About the Book

A modern economy, characterised by acute specialisation and exchange, is unthinkable without financial intermediaries, financial markets and financial instruments. Developing appropriate financial institutions and financial markets is a pre-requisite for speedy economic growth.

Soon after Independence in 1947, Government of India followed a policy of social control of important financial institutions. The nationalisation of the Reserve Bank of India (RBI) in 1948 marked the beginning of this policy. This was followed by the takeover of the then Imperial Bank of India in 1956 which was rechristened as State Bank of India (SBI). In 1956 also, 245 life insurance companies were nationalised and merged into the newly created Life Insurance Corporation of India (LIC). In another significant development, Government nationalised 14 major commercial banks in 1969. The year 1972 saw the nationalisation of general insurance companies and the setting up of General Insurance Corporation (GIC). In 1980, 6 more commercial banks were nationalized and brought under public ownership.

As a result of state domination, India's monetary and financial system was characterised by barriers to entry, control over pricing of financial assets, high transaction costs and restrictions on movement of funds from one market segment to another. It was in this backdrop that wide-ranging financial sector reforms were introduced as an integral part of the economic reforms programme started in early 1990s. These reforms have paved the way for integration among various segments of the financial system. It is widely accepted that reduction/removal of financial repression has enhanced the efficiency and potential growth of the Indian economy.

Financial sector reforms since the early 1990s have focused on the following objectives: (a) elimination of segmentation across various markets in order to facilitate transmission of impulses across markets, (b) easing the liquidity management process and (c) making allocation of resources more efficient across the economy.

To achieve the above objectives, restrictions on pricing of assets have been removed along with the introduction of new instruments. Technological infrastructure has also been strengthened. The general approach to financial sector reforms has been a transparent, collaborative and consultative process aimed at resolving many possible dilemmas. The reform process itself has been characterised by caution with a tilt towards preserving stability, careful sequencing of measures, mutually reinforcing monetary initiatives and ensuring consistency and complementarity with other policies.

The present book explains and examines at length the changes which have swept India's financial sector since 1991. The book contains 35 chapters organized into 4 theme parts.

About the Author

Dr. Sarika R. Lohana is UGC-Dr. Radhakrishnan Post-doctoral Fellow in Humanities and Social Sciences, School of Commerce and Management Sciences, Swami Ramanand Teerth Marathwada (SRTM) University, Nanded. She received her M.Com. from SRTM University, Nanded; M.Phil. in commerce from Alaggappa University, Karaikudi; Ph.D. from the School of Commerce and Management Sciences, SRTM University and MBA in finance from Indira Gandhi National Open University (IGNOU), New Delhi.

She has co-authored 1 book titled, *Demonetization, Digital India and Governance* and also edited another book. She has published papers in *Indian Journal of Management Review; Global Journal of Multi-disciplinary Studies* and *Asian Journal of Management Sciences*. She is a member of the International Technical Committee on Social and Human Sciences, WASAT (USA). Her areas of research interest include financial and marketing management, entrepreneurship, corporate finance, and neuro and behavioural finance.

Contents

Part I: From Financial Repression to Financial Liberalization

Preface

A modern economy, characterised by acute specialisation and exchange, is unthinkable without financial intermediaries, financial markets and financial instruments. Developing appropriate financial institutions and financial markets is a pre-requisite for speedy economic growth. A financial system performs the following functions, *inter alia*, for the smooth conduct of an economy: (a) It facilitates trading and hedging of risks. Risk mitigation reduces uncertainty and enables resources to flow towards most profitable projects. Such a situation raises the efficiency of investments and the rate of growth. (b) By acting as an efficient conduit for allocating resources, the financial system enables improvement in technical progress. Technological innovations take place when entrepreneurs exploit the best chances of successfully imitating technologies in their production processes and introducing new products. (c) To the extent that financial development leads to the creation of financial infrastructure and enables better and more efficient provision of goods and services, costs of transactions are lowered with positive spill over on development efforts.

Soon after Independence in 1947, Government of India followed a policy of social control of important financial institutions. The nationalisation of the Reserve Bank of India (RBI) in 1948 marked the beginning of this policy. This was followed by the takeover of the then Imperial Bank of India in 1956 which was rechristened as State Bank of India. In 1956 also, 245 life insurance companies were nationalised and merged into the newly created Life Insurance Corporation of India (LIC). In another significant development, Government nationalised 14 major commercial banks in 1969. The year 1972 saw the nationalisation of general insurance companies and the setting up of General Insurance Corporation (GIC). In 1980, 6 more commercial banks were nationalized and brought under public ownership.

Thus, till the initiation of economic reforms in early 1990s, banking business in India was a near-monopoly of the Government of India. The underlying philosophy of this approach was to encourage growth—via availability of adequate credit at reasonable and/or concessional rates of interest—in areas where commercial considerations did not allow for disbursal of credit.

As a result of state domination, India's monetary and financial system was characterised by barriers to entry, control over pricing of financial assets, high transaction costs and restrictions on movement of funds from one market segment to another. It was in this backdrop that wide-ranging financial sector reforms were introduced as an integral part of the economic reforms programme started in early 1990s. These reforms have paved the way for integration among various segments of the financial system. It is widely accepted that reduction/removal of financial repression has enhanced the efficiency and potential growth of the Indian economy.

Nationalisation of commercial banks in 1969 and 1980 was a mixed blessing. After nationalisation there was a shift of emphasis from industry to agriculture. The country witnessed rapid expansion in bank branches, even in rural areas. However, bank nationalisation created its own problems like excessive bureaucratisation, red-tapism and disruptive tactics of trade unions of bank employees.

Being a near-monopoly of the Government, the banking sector suffered from lack of competition, low capital base, low productivity and high intermediation cost. The role of technology was minimal and the quality of service was not given adequate importance. Banks also did not follow proper risk management systems and the prudential standards were weak. All these resulted in poor asset quality and low profitability.

Financial markets were characterised by control over pricing of financial assets, barriers to entry, high transaction costs and restrictions in movement of funds between the market segments. This, apart from inhibiting the development of the markets, also affected their efficiency.

Likewise, capital market structure in India was subject to several controls and opaque procedures. The trading and settlement system was outdated and not in tune with international practices. Raising of capital from the market was regulated by the Capital Issues (Control) Act, 1947 which was administered by the Controller of Capital Issues (CCIs) in the Ministry of Finance, Government of India. The scheme of controls under the Act required all the companies to obtain prior consent for issues of capital to the public. Pricing as well as the features of the capital structure (such as debt-equity ratios), were controlled by the Government. The Securities Contracts (Regulation) Act, 1956 was administered by the Directorate of Stock Exchanges, also in the Ministry of Finance. It empowered the Government to recognise/derecognise stock exchanges, stipulate rules and by-laws for their functioning, compel listing of securities by public companies etc. Such a system of regulation and control was fragmented and inadequate in the context of liberalisation wave sweeping across the world. Urgent measures were needed to relax controls and modernise the functioning of capital market.

Furthermore, state monopoly of insurance business resulted in limited availability of insurance products, lack of information technology and poor quality of insurance services.

Thus, the environment in the financial sector up to the early 1990s was not particularly conducive for the development of deep and wide financial markets. In fact, it had resulted in segmented and under-developed markets characterised by paucity of instruments, and limited number of participants. Banks and financial institutions functioned in a highly regulated environment, characterised by an administered interest rate structure, quantitative restrictions on credit flows, fairly high reserve requirements and pre-emption of significant proportion of lendable resources for the priority and Government sectors. While the quantitative restrictions resulted in credit rationing for the private sector, interest rate controls led to sub-optimal use of credit resulting in low levels of investment and growth. These, coupled with other factors such as the absence of proper accounting, transparency and prudential norms, resulted in a large build-up of non-performing assets in the banking system. All this led to erosion of profitability in the banking sector, besides decline in productivity and efficiency. The bank-based and highly controlled regime turned out to be inimical to financial market development.

In short, until the early 1990s, the role of the financial system in India was primarily restricted to the function of channelling resources from surplus to deficit sectors. Although the financial system performed this role reasonably well, its operations came to be marked by some serious deficiencies over the years. The Indian Government determined the quantum, allocation and the price of credit, a situation referred to as *financial repression* and marked by: (a) high required reserve ratios, (b) subsidised or directed credit programmes, (c) credit rationing, (d) ceilings on deposit, and (e) fixing maximum interest rates on loans.

It was in this backdrop, that wide-ranging financial sector reforms in India were introduced as an integral part of the economic reforms process initiated in the early 1990s. Reforms in respect of financial intermediaries and financial markets have focused on creating a deregulated environment and enabling free play of market forces while at the same time strengthening the prudential norms and the supervisory system.

Financial sector reforms since the early 1990s have focused on the following objectives: (a) elimination of segmentation across various markets in order to facilitate transmission of impulses across markets, (b) easing the liquidity management process, and (c) making resource allocation more efficient across the economy.

To achieve the above objectives, restrictions on pricing of assets have been removed, new instruments have been introduced, and technological infrastructure has been strengthened.

Thus, financial repression has eased substantially with the deregulation of interest rates and substantial removal of directed credit allocation. It has paved the way for integration among various segments of the financial system. It can be said that reduction/removal of financial repression has enhanced the efficiency and potential growth of the Indian economy. The financial system has exhibited considerable dynamism in recent years. The system today is varied, with a well-diversified structure of financial institutions, financial companies and mutual funds. The setting up of some specialised financial institutions and refinance institutions has provided depth to financial intermediation outside the banking sector. These developments, coupled with increased financial market liberalisation, have enhanced competition. A number of existing financial institutions have diversified into several new activities, such as investment banking and infrastructure financing, providing guarantees for domestic and offshore lending for infrastructure projects.

Financial sector reforms since 1991 have supported the transition of the Indian economy to a higher growth path, while significantly improving the stability of the financial system. In comparison of the pre-reforms period, the Indian financial system today is more stable and efficient. However, these gains need to be consolidated, so that these could be translated to drive the institutions, markets and practices into a mature financial system that can meet the challenges of sustaining India on a higher growth trajectory. The financial system would, therefore, not only need to be stable, but would also need to support still higher levels of planned investments by channelling financial resources more efficiently from deficit to surplus sectors. The banks would need to reassess their core banking business to view how best they could undertake maturity transformation to step up the lendable resources in support of real economic activity.

The general approach to financial sector reforms has been a transparent, collaborative and consultative process aimed at resolving many possible dilemmas. The reform process itself was characterised by caution with a tilt towards preserving stability, careful sequencing of measures, mutually reinforcing monetary measures and ensuring consistency and complementarity with other policies.

Further, reforms in the financial markets have been undertaken within the overall monetary policy framework and in co-ordination with reforms in the money and foreign exchange markets. Many of the major reforms have been implemented in phases, allowing for transition so as not to destabilise market conditions or any group of participants or the financial system in general.

Financial sector reforms have paved the way for integration among various segments of the financial system. It is widely accepted that reduction/removal of financial repression has enhanced the efficiency and potential growth of the Indian economy.

2017

Sarika R. Lohana

Abbreviations/Acronyms

ACLF	Additional Collateralised Lending Facility
ADB	Asian Development Bank
ADR	Assets Development Reserve
ADRs	American Depository Receipts
ADs	Authorised Dealers
AIDBs	All India Development Banks
AIFIs	All India Financial Institutions
ALM	Asset Liability Management
AMC	Asset Management Company
AML	Anti-Money Laundering
AMS	Aggregate Measure of Support
APEC	Asia Pacific Economic Co-operation
ARC	Agricultural Refinance Corporation
ARC	Asset Reconstruction Company
ARDC	Agricultural Refinance and Development Corporation
ASEAN	Association of Southeast Asian Nations
ATM	Automated Teller Machine
BCs	Business Correspondents
BCBS	Basel Committee for Banking Supervision
BCSBI	Banking Codes and Standards Board of India
BFRS	Board for Financial Regulation and Supervision
BFS	Board for Financial Supervision
BIFR	Board for Industrial and Financial Reconstruction
BIS	Bank for International Settlements
BPSS	Board for Payment and Settlement Systems
BSE	Bombay Stock Exchange
CAAP	Capital Adequacy Assessment Process
CAC	Capital Account Convertibility
CAMELS	Capital Adequacy, Asset Quality, Management, Earnings, Liquidity and Systems Control
CAR	Capital to Assets Ratio
CBLO	Collateralised Borrowing and Lending Obligations
CBS	Core Banking System
CCFF	Compensatory and Contingency Financing Facility
CCIL	Clearing Corporation of India Ltd.
CDBMS	Centralised Database Management System
CDMA	Code Division Multiple Access
CDOs	Collateralised Debt Obligations
CDR	Corporate Debt Restructuring, Credit-Deposit Ratio
CDs	Certificates of Deposit

CFMS	Centralised Funds Management System
CFSs	Consolidated Financial Statements
CIBIL	Credit Information Bureau (India) Ltd.
COC	Controller of Currency
CP	Commercial Paper
CPC	Credit Planning Cell
CPR	Consolidated Prudential Reporting
CPSS	Committee on Payment and Settlement Systems
CPSUs	Central Public Sector Undertakings
CR	Contingency Reserve
CRAR	Capital to Risk-Weighted Assets Ratio
CRISIL	Credit Rating Information Services of India Ltd.
CRR	Cash Reserve Ratio
CSF	Consolidated Sinking Funds
CVPS	Currency Verification and Processing Systems
DBD	Department of Banking Development
DBO	Department of Banking Operations
DBOD	Department of Banking Operations and Development
DBS	Department of Banking Supervision
DCA	Department of Company Affairs
DCCBs	District Central Co-operative Banks
DCM	Department of Currency Management
DEIO	Department of External Investment and Operations
DFIs	Development Finance Institutions
DFS	Department of Financial Services
DIC	Deposit Insurance Corporation
DICGC	Deposit Insurance and Credit Guarantee Corporation
DoT	Department of Telecom
DPs	Depository Participants
DPSS	Department of Payment and Settlement Systems
DRI	Differential Rate of Interest
DRT	Debt Recovery Tribunals
DSB	Dispute Settlement Body
DSR	Debt Service Ratio
DSS	Debt Swap Scheme
DTH	Direct-to-Home
ECBs	External Commercial Borrowings
E-commerce	Electronic Commerce
ECR	Export Credit Refinance
ECS	Electronic Clearing Service
EDMU	External Debt Management Unit
EFF	Extended Fund Facility

EFT	Electronic Funds Transfer
EMEs	Emerging Market Economies
E-money	Electronic Money
EMU	European Monetary Union
EXIM Bank	Export Import Bank of India
FCA	Foreign Currency Assets
FCCBs	Foreign Currency Convertible Bonds
FCNR(A)	Foreign Currency Non-Resident (Accounts)
FCNR(B)	Foreign Currency Non-Resident Accounts (Banks)
FDI	Foreign Direct Investment
FEMA	Foreign Exchange Management Act
FERA	Foreign Exchange Regulation Act
FIIs	Foreign Institutional Investors
FRBM	Fiscal Responsibility and Budget Management
GDRs	Global Depository Receipts
GIC	General Insurance Corporation of India
GPRS	General Packet Radio Service
GSM	Global System for Mobile Communication
HDFC	Housing Development Finance Corporation
HFCs	Housing Finance Companies
IBA	Indian Banks' Association
IBRD	International Bank for Reconstruction and Development
ICAI	Institute of Chartered Accountants of India
ICDs	Inter-Corporate Deposits
ICICI	Industrial Credit and Investment Corporation of India
ICRA	Information and Credit Rating Agency
IDBI	Industrial Development Bank of India
IDBs	India Development Bonds
IDFC	Infrastructure Development Finance Company
IDRBT	Institute for Development and Research in Banking Technology
IFC	International Finance Corporation
IFCI	Industrial Finance Corporation of India
IFSC	Indian Financial System Code
IMF	International Monetary Fund
IMG	Inter-Ministerial Group
IRDA	Insurance Regulatory and Development Authority
IRS	Interest Rate Swaps
ISDA	International Swap and Derivatives Association
IT	Information Technology
IVR	Interactive Voice Response
KYC	Know Your Customer
LAF	Liquidity Adjustment Facility

LAN	Local Area Network
LERMS	Liberalised Exchange Rate Management System
LIBOR	London Inter-Bank Offered Rate
MFs	Mutual Funds
MMID	Mobile Money Identifier
MNCs	Multinational Companies
MNO	Mobile Network Operators
MoU	Memorandum of Understanding
MPFI	Mobile Payment Forum of India
M-PIN	Mobile PIN
NABARD	National Bank for Agriculture and Rural Development
NAIS	National Agricultural Insurance Scheme
NBFCs	Non-banking Financial Companies
NBFIs	Non-banking Financial Institutions
NEER	Nominal Effective Exchange Rate
NFA	Net Foreign Assets
NFEA	Net Foreign Exchange Assets
NFS	National Financial Switch
NHB	National Housing Bank
NLR	Net Liquidity Ratio
NPAs	Non-Performing Assets
NPCI	National Payments Corporation of India
NREGS	National Rural Employment Guarantee Scheme
NRI	Non-resident Indian
NSE	National Stock Exchange
NSSF	National Small Savings Fund
NSSO	National Sample Survey Organisation
ODs	Overdrafts
OGL	Open General License
OLTAS	Online Tax Account System
OMOs	Open-Market Operations
OMS	Open-Market Sales
ORFS	Online Return Filing System
OSS	Off-Site Surveillance System
OTA	Over the Air
OTC	Over the Counter
OTP	One Time Password
PACS	Primary Agricultural Credit Societies
PAN	Permanent Account Number
PDS	Public Distribution System
PLR	Prime Lending Rate
PSBs	Public Sector Banks

PSS	Payments and Settlement Systems
PSU	Public Sector Undertaking
QOS	Quality of Service
RBI	Reserve Bank of India
RBIA	Risk-Based Internal Audit
RBS	Risk-Based Supervision
REER	Real Effective Exchange Rate
REPO	Repurchase Agreement
RRBs	Regional Rural Banks
RTGS	Real Time Gross Settlement
SARFAESI	Securitisation and Reconstruction of Financial Assets and Enforcement of Security Interest Act
SBI	State Bank of India
SBS	Shredding and Briquetting System
SCBs	Scheduled Commercial Banks; State Cooperative Banks
SCICI	Shipping Credit and Investment Company of India
SDRs	Special Drawing Rights
SEBI	Securities and Exchange Board of India
SENSEX	Sensitive Index
SFC	State Finance Corporation
SHG	Self-help Group
SIDBI	Small Industries Development Bank of India
SIM	Subscriber Identity Module
SLR	Statutory Liquidity Ratio
SMS	Short Messaging Service
SPV	Special Purpose Vehicle
SRP	Supervisory Review Process
SSIs	Small-scale Industries
STCI	Securities and Trading Corporation of India
TBs	Treasury Bills
TRAI	Telecom Regulatory Authority of India
UCBs	Urban Co-operative Banks
UIDAI	Unique Identification Authority of India
UNCTAD	United Nations Conference on Trade and Development
UNDP	United Nations Development Programme
URL	Universal Resource Locator
USAID	United States Agency for International Development
USSD	Unstructured Supplementary Service Data
UTI	Unit Trust of India
VaR	Value at Risk
VAS	Value Added Services
VAT	Value-added Tax

WAP	Wireless Application Protocol
WMA	Ways and Means Advances
WTO	World Trade Organization
YTM	Yield-to-maturity

Unit and Currency Conversion Table

Unit Conversion
1 lakh   = 0.1 million
10 lakh   = 1.0 million
1 crore   = 10.0 million
100 crore = 1.0 billion

Currency Conversion
The unit of currency in India is Indian Rupee, symbolized as ₹. As per reference rate of Reserve Bank of India (RBI) for June 15, 2017:
US$ 1   = 64.31
UK£ 1   = 82.10
Euro (€) 1   = 72.12
Japanese Yen (¥) 100   = 58.45

Fiscal Year
Fiscal year in India runs from April 1 to March 31 of the following year

Pre- and Post-metric Systems of Currency and Measures in India
Metric system of currency in India was introduced from April 1, 1957
In the Pre-metric system, one Rupee was = 16 annas and one anna was = 4 paise
In the Post-metric system,
One Rupee = 100 paise
One mile = 1.6 kilometres
One yard = 0.9144 metre
One acre = 0.4046 hectare

Part I

From Financial Repression to Financial Liberalization

1

Financial System: An Overview

Finance is the pivot around which a modern economy revolves. A financial system helps to mobilise the financial surpluses of an economy and transfer them to areas of financial deficit. It is the linchpin of any development strategy. The financial system promotes savings by providing a wide variety of financial assets to the general public. Savings collected from the household sector are pooled together and allocated to various sectors of the economy for raising production levels. If the allocation of credit is judicious and socially equitable, it can help achieve the twin objectives of growth and social justice.

1.1 Meaning, Importance and Functions of Financial System

Financial sector of an economy is a multi-faceted term. It refers to the whole gamut of legal and institutional arrangements, financial intermediaries, markets and instruments with both domestic and external dimensions.

A well-functioning financial system is a pre-requisite for the pursuit of economic growth with stability. The core function of a financial system is to facilitate smooth and efficient allocation of resources from savers to the ultimate users. The financial infrastructure contributes to the effective functioning of institutions and markets and thereby to stability. Hence, it serves as the foundation for adequate access to financial services and sustained financial development.

In the context of relatively under-developed capital market and with little internal resources, firms or economic entities depend largely on financial intermediaries for their fund requirements. In terms of sources of credit, they could be broadly categorised as institutional and non-institutional. For example, the major institutional sources of credit in India are commercial banks, development finance institutions (DFIs) and non-banking financial companies (NBFCs) including housing finance companies (HFCs). The non-institutional or unorganised sources of credit include moneylenders, indigenous bankers and sellers for trade credit. However, information about unorganised sector is limited and not readily available.

The relationship between finance and development has been a crucial subject of public policy for long. As early as in the 19th century, a number of economists stressed the importance of financial development for the growth of an economy. The banking system was recognised to have important ramifications for the level and growth rate of national income via the identification and funding of productive investments. This, in turn, was expected to induce a more efficient allocation of capital and foster growth. A contrary view also prevailed at the same time suggesting that economic growth would create demand for financial services. This meant that financial development would follow growth more or less automatically. In other words, financial development could be considered as a by-product of economic development.

Following are some of the functions performed by a financial system:

1. It facilitates trading and hedging of risks. Risk mitigation reduces uncertainty and enables resources to flow towards most profitable projects. Such a situation raises the efficiency of investments and the rate of growth.
2. By acting as an efficient conduit for allocating resources, the financial system enables improvement in technical progress. Technological innovations take place when entrepreneurs exploit the best chances of successfully imitating technologies in their production processes and introducing new products.
3. To the extent that financial development leads to the creation of financial infrastructure and enables better and more efficient provision of goods and services, costs of transactions would be lower, with positive spill over on economic growth.

The role and importance of the financial sector in the process of economic growth has evolved over time along with the changing paradigms. Till the late 1960s, the role of financial intermediaries in general, and banks in particular, in the process of economic growth of a country was largely ignored.

1.2 Role of the Government in Financial Development

An important aspect of the process of financial development has been the role of the government. In many developing economies the governments traditionally played a significant role in fostering financial development. In the context of developing countries, this role is all the more important because financial systems in these countries are characterised by nascent accounting frameworks and inadequate legal mechanisms.

Several developing countries, therefore, undertook programmes for reforming their financial systems. In the initial stages of the development process, the financial sector in developing countries was characterised by directed credit allocation, interest rate restrictions and lending criteria based on social needs etc. These policies retarded the nature of financial intermediation in developing countries and the recognition of the same paved the way for financial sector reforms. Since the late 1970s and the 1980s, financial sector reforms encompassing deregulation of interest rates, revamping of directed credit and measures to promote competition in the financial services became an integral part of the overall structural adjustment programmes in many developing economies.

The interface between financial system and economic development revolves around on a wide range of issues, the following being more prominent.

1. Extant of state ownership of financial entities vis-à-vis private sector ownership.
2. Corporate governance in banks and other segments of the financial system.
3. Transparency of policies and practices of monetary and financial agencies.
4. Prudential requirements of market participants.
5. Maintenance of best practices in accounting and auditing.
6. Comprehensive and efficient regulation and supervision of the financial system.
7. Collection, processing and dissemination of information in order to meet the market needs.

The commonality among these concerns has given rise to a wide recognition and acceptance of having a set of international standards and best practices that every country should strive to foster and implement.

1.3 Determinants of Access to Financial Services

In the literature on finance, a number of factors have been mentioned which affect the access to financial services. Some important factors among these are as under:

1. **Level of Income:** Financial status of people is always important in gaining access to financial services. Extremely poor people find it difficult to access financial services even when the services are tailored for them.
2. **Type of Occupation:** Many banks have not developed the capacity to evaluate loan applications of small borrowers and unorganised enterprises and hence tend to deny loan requests by them.
3. **Legal Identity:** Lack of legal identities like identity cards, birth certificates or written records often exclude ethnic minorities, economic and political refugees and migrant workers from accessing financial services.
4. **Attractiveness of the Product:** Benefits of financial products offered and how their availability is marketed are crucial in accessing financial services.
5. **Terms and Conditions:** Terms and conditions attached to products such as minimum balance requirements and conditions relating to the use of accounts often dissuade people from using such products/services. Generally, transaction is free as long as the account has sufficient funds to cover the cost of transactions made. However, there is a range of other charges that have a disproportionate effect on people with low income.
6. **Socio-cultural Barriers:** Lack of financial literacy (basic accounting skills) and cultural and religious barriers to banking often constrain demand for financial services. Access to credit is often limited for women who do not have, or cannot hold title to assets such as land and property or must seek male guarantees to borrow.
7. **Living Conditions:** Factors like density of population, rural and remote areas, mobility of the population (i.e. highly mobile people with no fixed or formal address), insurgency in a location etc. also affect access to financial services.
8. **Age Factor:** Financial service providers usually target the middle of the economically active population, often overlooking older or younger customers.

1.4 Regulation and Supervision of Financial System

An efficient and robust regulatory structure is an essential pre-requisite for the stability of the financial system. The implications of increased cross-sectoral and cross-border conglomeration of financial companies highlight the need for increased focus on co-ordination and information sharing among regulators. The emergence of the holding company structure and its legal implications has given rise to concerns about their regulation and supervision. The recent international financial turbulence has shown that there is no single fail-proof method of financial regulation and that an ideal system would have elements of both principles-based and rules-based regulation.

The recent global financial crisis has highlighted the importance of liquidity management for institutions. In this context, it is imperative to have an adequate liquidity infrastructure in place. In the Indian context, active liquidity management has been an integral part of the Reserve Bank of India's monetary operations and it is being achieved through various instruments. However, the use of monetary policy requires to be further honed in order to deal with the impact of external capital flows.

1.5 Financial Neutrality versus Financial Activism

The views on neutrality of financial intermediaries to economic growth, however, came under attack during the late 1960s. It was pointed out that there exists a strong positive correlation between financial development and economic growth of a country. Financial experts started emphasising the negative impact of *financial repression*, under which the government determined the quantum, allocation and price of credit, on the growth process. They argued that credit is not just another input and instead, credit is the engine of growth.

The world of finance has changed markedly over the last 30 years or so. The change has been brought about by a number of events and circumstances. The growing dissatisfaction with the working of the fixed exchange rate system during the 1960s led many countries, especially of the industrialised world, to adopt a floating exchange rate system by the early 1970s. There was also a growing realisation that for achieving sustained growth with stability, it would be necessary to have freer trade, liberalised external capital movements, and a relatively flexible use of domestic monetary policy. With trade being subject to multilateral negotiations, industrialised countries and some of the emerging market economies took steps to liberalise capital movements across countries since about the middle of the 1970s. Simultaneously, efforts were made to remove distortions in the domestic financial sector through elimination or containment of reserve requirements and interest rate regulations. These initiatives coincided with the rapid technological improvements in electronic payments and communication systems. The interaction among these factors helped the process of internationalisation of financial markets.

Under the impact of economic liberalisation, the industrialised countries, as a group, improved their relative economic position in the world economy, and posted high growth rates in the 1980s and thereafter. This experience has confirmed the release of growth impulses following financial liberalisation.

Developing countries, on their part, have been adopting, since the early 1980s, market-oriented strategies of financial development, partly supported by international financial institutions, and partly to avail of the large pool of resources available in international financial markets. They either dismantled or sharply contained *financial repression* and undertook financial reforms with a view to enhancing allocative efficiency and competitiveness. Financial development required the deepening and widening of the existing financial markets as well as the introduction of new products and instruments to cater to the needs of savers and investors.

Financial development depends on market-based regulatory framework and incentives (disincentives) that promote market discipline. If market discipline is not well-understood or not complied with, there would arise possibilities of inefficiencies and/or volatilities in asset prices and capital movements. Financial stability, therefore, is a pre-requisite for sustained financial development which in turn would impact growth rate positively.

1.6 Financial Volatility versus Financial Stability

The process of deregulation and globalisation of financial markets gained momentum in the 1990s, and expanded the choices for investors, and helped to improve the prospects of reducing the costs of financial transactions and improving operational and allocative efficiency of the financial system. A number of developing countries, especially in Asia, that moved early on to the path of economic liberalisation had experienced large capital inflows through the 1980s and the first half of the 1990s. Large capital inflows, however, carry the risk of financial sector vulnerability, where the use of such flows is not administered by application of appropriate mix of macroeconomic measures. The currency and financial crises in Mexico and Thailand, followed by Korea and Indonesia, provide many insights about the problems that would arise when exchange rates are inflexible, and banking and financial systems are weak.

The experience of the crisis-affected countries highlights the need for setting in place regulatory and supervisory frameworks to ensure the safety and stability of financial systems. Their experience also underscores the premise that financial development is only a necessary condition for sustainable growth, and by no means a sufficient condition. In view of the costs of financial crises falling on the sovereign governments, financial stability has come to occupy a centre-stage in formulating public policy for economic development.

1.7 Financial Globalisation

No major economy in the world today can be viewed in isolation from the rest of the world. Given the size and the growing magnitude of interaction—in terms of trade, services, and capital flows—and the greater openness to globalisation, India is in a different economic milieu today than it was two decades ago. India is virtually part of the world of globalised finance and is learning to walk, negotiating the strong currents, both positive and negative, generated by the forces of financial globalisation.

The 1990s witnessed a paradigm shift towards market-oriented economic policies and a careful dismantling of obstacles in its wake. This has helped the smaller, emerging economies gain access to world markets, emergent technologies and collaborations. This has also given them a window to the developed world and helped them understand the significant role of globalisation as an instrument, which could be utilised not just to achieve economic efficiency, but also eradicate poverty.

Globalisation has also resulted in the creation of a new business framework. More changes can be expected in the business scenario specifically in terms of openness, adaptiveness and responsiveness. The most important dimensions of economic globalisation are: (a) breaking down of national barriers; (b) international spread of trade, financial and production activities, and (c) growing power of transnational corporations and international financial institutions in these processes. While economic globalisation is a very uneven process, with increased trade and investment being focused in a few countries, almost all countries are greatly affected by this process.

A major feature of globalisation is the growing concentration and monopolisation of economic resources and power by transnational corporations and by global financial firms and funds. This process has been termed transnationalisation, in which fewer and fewer transnational corporations are gaining a large and rapidly increasing proportion of world economic resources, production and market shares. Where a multinational company used to dominate the market of a single product, a big transnational company (TNC) now typically produces or trades in an increasing multitude of products, services and sectors. Through mergers and acquisitions, fewer and fewer of these TNCs now control a larger and larger share of the global market, whether in commodities, manufactures or services.

2

State Domination of the Financial Sector (1947-1990)

2.1 Pre-Independence Financial System

India has a long and chequered history of financial intermediation, particularly commercial banking. At the beginning of the 20th century, India had insurance companies (both life and general) and a functional stock exchange. Even before the setting up of the Reserve Bank of India in 1935, the country had market for money, Government securities and foreign exchange. The financial system was, however, characterised by paucity of funds and instruments, limited number of players and lack of depth and openness. It was primarily a bank-based system.

Till 1857, when India was under the rule of the East India Company, there was hardly any centralized or systematic financial administration in the country. After the events of 1857, the administration of India was taken over directly by the British Government in 1858. It established a highly centralized system of financial and administrative control with the purpose of consolidating its hold on the vast territory of India. The system of centralized financial control was exercised through the establishment of Finance Department which functioned rather well till the late 1930s. A Comptroller and Auditor General was appointed in 1860 by amalgamating audit and accounts functions. However, in the absence of a Government responsible to the legislature, he submitted his Annual Reports to the secretary of State for India in Britain.

In matters of rules, regulations, procedures, compilation of annual budgets, audit and accounts etc., the Indian system of financial administration was based on the pattern of treasury control prevalent in Britain. All revenues were required to be credited to a Public Account. Similarly, annual budgets included demands for grants and appropriation accounts as also taxation proposals. They were, however, passed with the Governor-General's approval instead of that of the legislature as was the practice in Britain.

The Government of India was also responsible for the financial administration of Provincial Governments till the introduction of Provincial Autonomy in 1937 when popularly elected Provincial governments responsible to legislatures were established. From 1921 onwards, the Central Legislative Assembly, with a non-official majority, was for the first time given the right to discuss and pass the Annual Budget of the Government of India in respect of *non-reserved* subjects, as also to pass the Finance Bill containing taxation proposals. A committee on Public Accounts, with 8 non-official members of the Central Legislative Assembly and 4 official members (including the Finance Member as chairman) was also constituted to receive and examine Annual Reports of the Auditor-General.

The system of financial control in accordance with the rules and orders in force prior to Independence was continued after August 15, 1947, pending the framing of the new constitution of India. When the new constitution was promulgated on January 26, 1950, the then prevailing system of financial control was permitted to continue, with necessary changes.

2.2 Post-Independence (1947-1990) Developments in the Financial Sector

At the time of Independence in 1947, India had a fairly well-developed banking system. The process of financial development in independent India has hinged effectively on the development of commercial banking, with impetus given to industrialisation based on the initiatives provided in the five year plans.

Soon after Independence in 1947, Government of India followed a policy of social control of important financial institutions. The nationalisation of the Reserve Bank of India (RBI) in 1948 marked the beginning of this policy. This was followed by the takeover of the then Imperial Bank of India in 1955 which was rechristened as State Bank of India. In 1956, 245 life insurance companies were nationalised and merged into the newly created Life Insurance Corporation of India (LIC). In another significant development, Government nationalised 14 major commercial banks in 1969. The year 1972 saw the nationalisation of general insurance companies and the setting up of General Insurance Corporation (GIC). In 1980, 6 more commercial banks were nationalized and brought under public ownership.

Trade and industrial activities during the 1950s, and the 1960s reflected the dominance of banking as the critical source. The number of banks and branches had gone up, notwithstanding the consolidation of small banks, and the support given to the community-operative credit movement. Functionally, banks catered to the needs of the organised industrial and trading sectors. The primary sector consisting of agriculture, forestry, and fishing had to depend largely on their own financing and on sources outside the commercial banks.

The course of development of financial institutions and markets during the post-Independence period has been largely guided by the process of planned development pursued in India with emphasis on mobilisation of savings and channelising investment to meet Plan priorities. The adoption of bank-dominated financial development strategy was aimed at meeting the sectoral credit needs, particularly of agriculture and industry. Towards this end, the RBI (nationalised in 1948) concentrated on regulating and developing mechanisms for institution building. The commercial banking network was expanded to cater to the requirements of general banking and for meeting the short-term working capital requirements of industry and agriculture. Specialised development finance institutions (DFIs) with majority ownership of the RBI were set up to meet the long-term financing requirements of industry and agriculture. To facilitate the growth of these institutions, a mechanism to provide concessional finance to these institutions was also put in place by the RBI.

2.2.1 Nationalisation of Imperial Bank of India (1955): Soon after Independence, India launched its First Five Year Plan (1951-56). The Plan accorded high priority to the development of rural India, particularly agriculture. The All India Rural Credit Survey

Committee recommended the creation of a State-partnered and State-sponsored bank by taking over the Imperial Bank of India and integrating with it the former State-owned or State-associated banks. Accordingly, an Act was passed in the Parliament in May 1955 and the State Bank of India was constituted on July 1, 1955. Later, the State Bank of India (Subsidiary Banks) Act was passed in 1959 enabling the State Bank of India to take over eight former State-associated banks as its subsidiaries.

2.2.2 Nationalisation of Life Insurance Business (1956): By the Life Insurance (Emergency Provisions) Ordinance, 1956, promulgated by the President of India on January 19, 1956, the management and control of life insurance business in India, including the foreign business of Indian insurers, and the Indian business of foreign insurers, vested with immediate effect in the Central Government. With this the life insurance business passed from the private sector to the public sector. This was a step never before attempted any where in the world on such a large scale.

Though the Ordinance was promulgated in January 1956, the Life Insurance Corporation Act was passed in the next session of parliament. According to this Act the Life Insurance Corporation of India came into existence on September 1, 1956.

2.2.3 Nationalisation of Commercial Banks (1969 and 1980): The process of state domination of financial sector was given impetus with the adoption of the policy of social control over banks in 1967, reinforced in 1969 by the nationalisation of 14 major scheduled commercial banks. In April 1980, government nationalised 6 more commercial banks. Driven largely by public sector initiative and policy activism, commercial banks have a dominant share in total financial assets and are the main source of financing for the private corporate sector. They also channel a sizeable share of household savings to the public sector. Besides, in recent years, they have been performing most of the payment system functions. With increased diversification in recent years, banks in both public and private sectors have been providing a wide range of financial services.

2.2.4 Nationalisation of General Insurance Business (1973): The general insurance business was nationalized with effect from January 1, 1973, through the General Insurance Business (Nationalization) Act, 1972. However, as a prelude to the above Act, the Government took over the management of all the operating companies in 1971 through General Insurance (Emergency Provision) Act, 1971. The emergency Act provided for the appointment of custodians who were empowered to exercise control over these companies subject to the directions of the Central Government. At the time of nationalization of these companies, there were a total of 107 companies underwriting general insurance business in India. All these companies were amalgamated and grouped into four, namely the National Insurance Company Limited, the New India Assurance Company Limited, the Oriental Insurance Company Limited, and the United India Insurance Company Limited with head offices at Kolkata, Mumbai, Delhi and Chennai respectively. The General Insurance Company (GIC) was formed as a holding company in November 1972. The GIC was constituted for the purpose of superintending, controlling and carrying out the business of general insurance. The entire capital of GIC was subscribed by the Government and that of four companies by the GIC on behalf of the Government of India.

Broadly speaking, financial development in India up to the early 1990s was, by and large, a state-induced activity.

2.3 Rethinking on State Domination of Financial Sector

Nationalisation of commercial banks in 1969 and 1980 was a mixed blessing. After nationalisation there was a shift of emphasis from industry to agriculture. The country witnessed rapid expansion in bank branches, even in rural areas. However, bank nationalisation created its own problems like excessive bureaucratisation, red-tapism and disruptive tactics of trade unions of bank employees.

Being a near-monopoly of the Government, the banking sector suffered from lack of competition, low capital base, low productivity and high intermediation cost. The role of technology was minimal and the quality of service was not given adequate importance. Banks also did not follow proper risk management systems and the prudential standards were weak. All these resulted in poor asset quality and low profitability.

Among non-banking financial intermediaries, development finance institutions (DFIs) operated in an over-protected environment with most of the funding coming from assured sources at concessional terms.

The mutual fund industry also suffered from lack of competition and was dominated for long by one institution, viz. the Unit Trust of India (UTI).

Non-banking financial companies (NBFCs) grew rapidly, but there was no regulation regarding their asset side. Financial markets were characterised by control over pricing of financial assets, barriers to entry, high transaction costs and restrictions in movement of funds between the market segments. This, apart from inhibiting the development of the markets, also affected their efficiency.

Similarly, capital market structure in India was subject to several controls and opaque procedures. The trading and settlement system was outdated and not in tune with international practices. Raising of capital from the market was regulated by the Capital Issues (Control) Act, 1947 which was administered by the Controller of Capital Issues (CCIs) in the Ministry of Finance, Government of India. The scheme of controls under the Act required all the companies to obtain prior consent for issues of capital to the public. Pricing as well as the features of the capital structure (such as debt-equity ratios), were controlled by the Government. The Securities Contracts (Regulation) Act was administered by the Directorate of Stock Exchanges also in the Ministry of Finance. It empowered the Government to recognise/derecognise stock exchanges, stipulate rules and bye-laws for their functioning, compel listing of securities by public companies etc. Such a system of regulation and control was fragmented and inadequate in the context of liberalisation wave sweeping across the world. Urgent measures were needed to relax controls and modernise the functioning of capital market.

Furthermore, state monopoly of insurance business resulted in limited availability of insurance products, lack of information technology and poor quality of insurance services. In this connection, the Committee on Reforms in Insurance Sector (Chairman: R.N. Malhotra), which was set up in April 1993 and which submitted its report in January 1994, remarked,

- "Indian insurance industry lacks depth, diversity and reach, both geographically as well as in terms of insurable population, as there was immensely vast potential yet to be tapped;
- It provides poor customer service in terms of pricing, adequacy and appropriateness of covers and the much needed and timely claims settlement;
- It lacks the global dimensions having remained in isolation too long".

In fact, the environment in the financial sector till the initiation of reforms in 1991 was not particularly conducive for the development of deep and wide financial markets. In fact, it had resulted in segmented and underdeveloped markets characterised by paucity of instruments, and limited number of participants. Banks and financial institutions functioned in a highly regulated environment, characterised by an administered interest rate structure, quantitative restrictions on credit flows, fairly high reserve requirements and pre-emption of significant proportion of lendable resources for the priority and Government sectors. While the quantitative restrictions resulted in credit rationing for the private sector, interest rate controls led to suboptimal use of credit resulting in low levels of investment and growth. These, coupled with other factors such as the absence of proper accounting, transparency and prudential norms, resulted in a large build-up of non-performing assets in the banking system. All this led to erosion of profitability in the banking sector, besides decline in productivity and efficiency. The bank-based and highly controlled regime turned out to be inimical to financial market development.

Thus, until the early 1990s, the role of the financial system in India was primarily restricted to the function of channelling resources from surplus to deficit sectors. Whereas the financial system performed this role reasonably well, its operations came to be marked by some serious deficiencies over the years. The Indian Government determined the quantum, allocation and the price of credit, a situation referred to as *financial repression* [1] by some experts.

It was in this backdrop, that wide-ranging financial sector reforms in India were introduced as an integral part of the economic reforms initiated in the early 1990s. [2]

Endnotes

1. Financial repression includes: (a) high required reserve ratios, (b) subsidised or directed credit programmes, (c) credit rationing, (d) ceilings on deposit, and (e) fixing maximum interest rates on loans.
2. As a matter of fact, the reform process started from the mid-1980s with initiation of several measures following the recommendations of the Committee to Review the Working of the Monetary System in India, 1985 (Chairman: Sukhamoy Chakravarty) and the Working Group on the Money Market, 1987 (Chairman: N. Vaghul). The process, however, gathered momentum in the early 1990s with wide ranging reforms in all segments (money, forex and Government securities) of the financial market. A gradual approach to market reform has been followed in India so as to avoid destabilising effects.

3

Financial Sector Reforms since 1991

Considering the strategic importance of the financial sector, the Government of India set up a Committee on Financial System (Chairman: M. Narasimham) in 1991. It was asked to examine all aspects relating to the structure, organisation, functions and procedures of the Indian financial system. The Committee submitted its report in November 1991. It was presented to Parliament in December 1991. The report focussed mainly on enabling and strengthening measures for the financial sector. The Committee on Banking Sector Reforms (Chairman: M. Narasimham), 1998 placed greater emphasis on structural measures and improvement in standards of disclosure and levels of transparency in order to align the Indian standards with international best practices. Pursuant to the recommendations of the two Committees, financial reforms introduced in India have brought about considerable improvements as reflected in various parameters relating to capital adequacy, asset quality, profitability and operational efficiency.

3.1 Focus of Financial Sector Reforms

Financial sector reforms since 1991 have focused on the following.

1. Elimination of segmentation across various markets in order to facilitate transmission of impulses across markets.
2. Easing the liquidity management process.
3. Making resource allocation more efficient across the economy.

For above purposes, restrictions on pricing of assets have been removed and new instruments introduced. Technological infrastructure has been strengthened. Liberalisation of the financial sector has included, among others, the following measures.

1. Deregulation of interest rates.
2. Introduction of new products.
3. Relaxation in investment norms for financial intermediaries, especially banks.
4. Lowering of restrictions on specialisation/diversification of banks.
5. Emergence of new institutions such as primary dealers and mutual funds.
6. Withdrawal of reserve requirements on inter-bank borrowings.
7. Withdrawal of credit controls and excessively high reserve requirements.
8. Deregulation and development of markets.
9. Moves toward privatisation of financial services.
10. Easing of restrictions in respect of banks' foreign currency investments.
11. Easing of restrictions on current and capital account convertibility.
12. Lowering of entry barriers/limits on participation of foreign banks.

These reforms have paved the way for integration among various segments of the financial system. It is widely accepted that reduction/removal of financial repression has enhanced the efficiency and potential growth of the Indian economy.

3.1.1 Banking Sector Reforms: The key objective of reforms in the banking sector has been to enhance the stability and efficiency of banks. To achieve this objective, various reform measures were initiated that could be categorised broadly into three main groups: (a) enabling measures, (b) strengthening measures, and (c) institutional measures.

Enabling measures were designed to create an environment where banks could respond optimally to market signals on the basis of commercial considerations. Salient among these included reduction in statutory pre-emptions so as to release greater funds for commercial lending, interest rate deregulation to enable price discovery, granting of operational autonomy to banks and liberalisation of the entry norms for financial intermediaries.

The strengthening measures aimed at reducing the vulnerability of banks in the face of fluctuations in the economic environment. These included, *inter alia*, capital adequacy, income recognition, asset classification and provisioning norms, exposure norms, improved levels of transparency, and disclosure standards.

Institutional measures focused on reforms in the legal framework pertaining to banks and creation of new institutions.

3.2 India's Approach to Financial Sector Reforms

Financial sector reforms in India have formed an important component of the overall economic reforms process initiated in the early 1990s. These reforms have followed a well calibrated approach.

The general approach to financial sector reforms has been a transparent, collaborative and consultative process aimed at resolving many possible dilemmas. The reform process itself was characterised by caution with a tilt towards preserving stability, careful sequencing of measures, mutually reinforcing monetary measures and ensuring consistency and complementarity with other policies.

Further, reforms in the financial markets have been undertaken within the overall monetary policy framework and in co-ordination with reforms in the money and foreign exchange markets. Many of the major reforms have been implemented in phases, allowing for transition so as not to destabilise market conditions or any group of participants or the financial system in general.

In the context of maximising benefits of financial integration and minimising the risks, the link with the real sector cannot be ignored. In India, reforms in the financial sector started early in the reform cycle which imparted efficiency and stability to the real sector. The financial sector can add competitive strength and growth if reforms in the financial and real sectors keep apace. A major agenda for reform at this juncture for India, given the impressive all-round confidence in the economy, relates to the structure and functioning of institutions and in particular lowering the high transaction costs prevalent in the system. There are several dimensions to the transaction costs—ranging from legal provisions, the judicial system and procedures to attitudes.

The policy of gradualism that has been followed by India focuses on evolution of appropriate institutional framework and the sequencing of reforms based on the experience gained so far. The sequencing and pace of reforms are also vital to safeguard monetary and financial stability and avoid reversals. The issues in this context include: (a) whether bank-based or market-based system of development should be adopted, (b) order of sequencing of reforms of various segments of the financial market to be followed, and (c) whether or not capital account liberalisation should precede domestic financial market reform.

3.2.1 Lessons from East Asian Crisis: By following a gradualist approach, India has successfully avoided financial disasters as were experienced by some East Asian countries. A number of developing countries especially in Asia that moved early on to the path of economic liberalization had experienced large capital inflows through the 1980s and the first half of the 1990s. Large capital inflows, however, carried the risk of financial sector vulnerability, where the use of such flows is not regulated by application of appropriate mix of macroeconomic and structural policy measures. The recent currency and financial crises in Mexico and Thailand, followed by Korea and Indonesia, provide many insights about the problems that would arise when exchange rates are inflexible, and banking and financial systems are weak.

The experience of the crisis-affected countries highlights the need for setting in place regulatory and supervisory frameworks to ensure the safety and stability of financial systems. Their experience also underscored the premise that financial development is only a necessary condition for sustainable growth, and by no means sufficient. In fact, with the incidence of the costs of financial crisis falling on the sovereign governments, financial stability has come to occupy a centre-stage in public policy making along with the requirement of ensuring that the efficiency of the financial sector is high.

Implementation of the reforms process has had several unique features. Financial sector reforms were undertaken early in the reform cycle. Notably, the reforms process was not driven by any banking crisis, nor was it the outcome of any external support package. Besides, the design of the reforms was crafted through domestic expertise, taking on board the international experiences in this respect. The reforms were carefully sequenced with respect to the instruments to be used and the objectives to be achieved. Thus, prudential norms and supervisory strengthening were introduced early in the reform cycle, followed by interest-rate deregulation and a gradual lowering of statutory pre-emptions. The more complex aspects of legal and accounting measures were ushered in subsequently when the basic tenets of the reforms were already in place.

3.3 Strategy of Financial Sector Reforms

Reforms in the financial sector are wide-ranging, encompassing institutional, legal and technological aspects of the functioning of financial intermediaries and financial markets.

3.3.1 Developing and Strengthening Financial Infrastructure: Measures to improve market infrastructure must be implemented at an early stage of reform alongside appropriate legal framework. These conditions facilitate growth of financial transactions including inter-bank transactions and active liquidity management.

Presence of well-established institutions, soundness of bank balance sheets, existence of adequate safety nets and vigilant supervision are the pre-requisites for successful financial liberalisation. The reform process in India within the banking system has sought to strengthen the balance sheets of individual banks, empower banks to respond in the most optimal manner to market stimuli and to establish institutions to ensure a level playing field for all market participants and provide a back-up system for contingencies.

Competition has been infused into the financial system by licensing new private banks since 1993. Foreign banks have also been given more liberal entry.

Progress has also been generated through demonstration and spread effects of advanced technology and risk management practices accompanying new private banks and foreign banks. Given the fiscal constraint being faced by the Government and in keeping with the evolving principles of corporate governance, the Government permitted public sector banks to raise fresh equity from markets to meet their capital shortfalls or to expand their lending. Several public and private sector banks have accessed the domestic equity market. Public sector banks have also raised capital through GDRs/ADRs while many banks have raised subordinated debt through the private placement route.

3.3.2 Financial Regulation and Supervision: The quality of financial regulation and supervision as well as of information and the legal system are important for reaping the benefits of globalisation. Hence, enactment of enabling legislation has been a priority area of the reforms. The Board for Financial Supervision (BFS) was constituted in 1994, with the mandate to exercise the powers of supervision and inspection in relation to the banking companies, financial institutions and non-banking financial companies.

With the switchover to international best practices on income recognition, asset classification and provisioning, the problem of non-performing assets (NPAs) assumed critical importance. It was widely perceived that the level of NPAs in India was high by international standards. The problem needed to be tackled urgently and from different fronts. A menu approach has been adopted to tackle this major constraint confronting the banking sector. These policy measures have resulted in reduction in gross NPAs in the banking system.

The need for monitoring and supervising becomes even more important systemically with the opening up of the economy. Thus, the prudential regulations were fortified by reorientation of *on-site inspections* and introduction of *off-site surveillance*. The focus of inspection has shifted from ensuring appropriate credit planning and credit allocation under a closed economy framework to assessment of the bank's safety and soundness and to identify areas where corrective action is needed to strengthen the institution and improve its performance.

In view of the growing liberalisation of the external sector and international banking by banks in India, monitoring of the cross-border flow of funds has assumed importance. RBI now compiles and disseminates international banking statistics (IBS) on the lines of the reporting system devised by the Bank for International Settlements (BIS). The locational banking statistics (LBS) provide the gross position of international assets and international liabilities of all banking offices located in India. They report exclusively banks' international transactions including the transactions with any of their own branches/subsidiaries/joint ventures located outside India.

3.3.3 Financial Openness: In India, opening up of the financial sector in terms of entry of foreign entities and easing of restrictions on international transactions took place within the broader process of reforms. The constant policy concern in this respect has been that of preparing the financial sector for global competition and taking preventive measures for the potential vulnerabilities that it might engender.

Despite their extensive branch network, the biggest banks in India are miniscule compared to most of the multinational banks, in terms of standard parameters like assets or deposits. Hence, the initial focus of reforms in the financial sector was to strengthen the domestic financial infrastructure, make it more competitive and to provide banks greater freedom in their foreign operations.

Since 1991, the presence of foreign entities within the Indian banking sector has increased and so also the international transactions of Indian banks.

International experience has shown that the cost of financial intermediation declines and quality of financial services improves with opening of the economy. However, openness should be preceded by deregulation and strengthening of institutional framework in order to limit contagious influences. The strategy adopted in India has been to maximise the beneficial effects of openness while minimising the adverse consequences. Financial crisis due to internal/external factors have been averted, while the financial system has been progressively deregulated and strengthened.

In short, India's financial sector has made rapid strides in reforming itself and aligning itself to the new competitive business environment. While the operational and supervisory practices in the sector have progressively approximated international best practices, the process of convergence is not yet complete. Greater conformity to prudential norms of international standards as also adoption of better systems of risk management will enhance the stability of the financial system even as banks expand the range and volume of their operations.

3.4 International Security Standards

There are at present a number of security standards available for different financial applications. Most of them are internationally accepted and part of the ISO standards. These international standards such as the BS7799 [1] have been accepted by the RBI. Banks, however, could also put in place measures which conform to their own policies and ensure regular and periodical audit.

The objectives of these standards are as listed below.

1. To provide management direction and support for information security which is a basic pre-requisite for BS7799.
2. To manage information security within the organisation, maintain the security of organisational information processing facilities and information assets accessed by third

parties, and to maintain the security of information when the responsibility for information processing has been outsourced to another organisation.

3. To maintain appropriate protection of corporate assets and ensure that information assets receive an appropriate level of protection.

4. To reduce risks of human error, theft, fraud or misuse of facilities and minimise the damage from security incidents and malfunctions and learn from such incidents.

5. To ensure the correct and secure operation of information processing facilities, minimise the risk of systems failures, to protect the integrity of software and information and maintain the integrity and availability of information processing and communication.

6. To control access to information, prevent unauthorised access, detect unauthorised activities and ensure information security when using mobile computing and tele-networking facilities.

7. To ensure security is built into operational systems, to prevent loss, modification or misuse of user data in application systems.

8. To counteract interruptions to business activities and critical business processes from the effects of major failures or disasters.

9. To prevent breaches of any criminal or civil law, statutory, regulatory or contractual obligations and of any security requirements, ensure compliance of systems with organisational security policies and standards and minimise interference to/from the system audit process.

3.5 Migration to Basel Norms

The banking systems worldwide have/are migrating to the Basel II regime. The Basel II framework is expected to promote adoption of stronger risk management practices by banks to address major risks. In the context of the Indian banking system's transformation to Basel II, some issues have arisen.

Though concurrent efforts are underway in India to refine and upgrade financial information monitoring, data dissemination and data warehousing in various banks, the magnitude of the task appears to be difficult as there are a large number of commercial banks in India, which are at various levels of development. As the new system is resource-intensive requiring large database and strong information technology architecture, it places heavy demand on banks and the regulator to improve their information base through appropriate tools. Implementation of various simplified approaches requires preparation on the part of the banks, banking regulator and the rating agencies. Inadequate historical data in conjunction with associated cost of developing and maintaining such data may also influence the speed of migration to advanced approaches of risk measurement under Basel II. As the implementation of Basel II gathers momentum, several banks in India may need additional capital to provide for capital charge for market risk and operational risk.

Despite these challenges, it appears that Indian banks would be able to migrate to Basel II norms as India has chosen to adopt simpler options for the transition initially. The RBI has adopted a consultative and participative approach for both designing and implementing the transition process. Many pubic sector banks and old private sector banks have already prepared a roadmap for migrating to Basel II.

See also section 11.9 of chapter 11 of this book.

3.6 Accounting and Auditing Standards

Indian accounting standards are generally in alignment with international accounting standards, except for some modifications to suit local customs, usages and level of development in the country. There has been significant progress in accounting standards though some issues remain to be addressed. There are suggestions that Institute of Chartered Accountants of India (ICAI) needs to be made an autonomous body with its own staff and independent funding. Need has also been felt to develop country-specific/sector-specific standards where similar standards are not developed by International Accounting Standards Board (IASB). Similarly, ICAI should make attempts to attain convergence with International Financial Reporting Standards (IFRS).

India is one of the earliest countries to have adopted International Standards on Auditing by amending them to suit Indian requirements. There has been significant progress since ROSC-2004. However, there are some areas which need attention. Auditing and Assurance Standards Board (AASB) needs to take steps to attain convergence with International Standards on Auditing. It needs to take proactive steps by bringing out more technical guidance and other literature to help small and medium practitioners to understand standards. There is a need to give functional independence to AASB.

3.6.1 Marking-to-market: The Indian accounting standards are generally aligned to the International Financial Reporting Standards, though there are some differences. India is yet to fully adopt the marking-to-market requirements as available in the international standards. The Indian standards are relatively conservative and do not permit recognition of unrealised gains in the profit and loss account or equity, though unrealised losses are required to be accounted. Banks are required to mark-to-market the investments in the held for trading (HFT) and available for sale (AFS) categories at periodical intervals, on a portfolio basis, and provide for the net losses and ignore the net gains. This has proved to be a stabilising factor, inasmuch as it has not induced an imbalance in the incentive structures and has also proved to be less pro-cyclical.

3.7 Technological Solutions for Financial Services

Most of the initiatives regarding technology are aimed at providing better and more efficient customer service by offering multiple options to the customer. The death of distance, which is a by-product of technology, has become a reality in the banking sector. Technology is also playing a key role in banks' strategy for gaining a competitive edge.

Many banks have commenced the process of setting up core banking solutions, which are at various stages of implementation. While such systems are already in place in respect of new private sector banks, a few old private sector banks and public sector banks are also quickly moving to set up such processes. This would benefit the customer in the banking sector. Computerisation of the business of banks has been receiving high importance. The public sector banks have already achieved a high level of computerisation of their business. The directive from the Central Vigilance Commission (CVC) to achieve 100 percent computerisation has resulted in renewed vigour towards computerisation of branches.

Networking has been receiving focused attention by banks. This activity is also being monitored by the RBI. Most banks have their own corporate networks to facilitate inter-branch and branch-controlling office communication in an electronic mode. Inter-bank and inter-city communication takes place through the Indian Financial Network (INFINET). As part of the INFINET, the terrestrial lines have been augmented to provide for increased data transfer capabilities. All these have resulted in the dependence of banks on network-based computing which has benefited the customer.

INFINET also provides for safe and secure transmission of electronic messages with the use of public key infrastructure (PKI) which has the legal backing of Information Technology Act, 2000. It also provides for messages to flow in a structured environment, using the structured financial messaging solutions (SFMS), which provides for inter-operability of messages so that straight through processing (STP) is achieved.

Another major development witnessed in recent years is the growth in multiple delivery channels to customers such as internet-based banking, mobile banking and anywhere banking. This has benefited the customers and the banks alike. While customers have now a wide variety of options to choose from, banks have been able to reduce costs which have had a positive impact on their profitability.

These developments have, however, also posed certain challenges. In a world where geographical barriers are losing significance, it is essential that security is given prime importance in a transnational scenario where large sums of money are at stake. While the challenges relating to physical security could be confronted with relative ease, the position is much more complicated in respect of IT security. The RBI has, therefore, provided guidelines on information system (IS) security as also IS audit which banks can use for their benefit. These are generic in nature and do not have any prescriptive tones.

3.8 Global Financial Crisis and India's Financial Sector

Beginning mid-September 2008, the Indian financial markets came under pressure owing to the knock-on effects of the global crisis through the monetary, financial, real and confidence channels. The contagion was initially felt in the equity markets due to the reversal of foreign institutional portfolio flows. With sharp tightening of global liquidity, Indian banks and corporates saw their overseas financing drying up. As a means of substitute financing, corporates withdrew their investments from domestic money market mutual funds, thereby putting redemption pressure on them and on NBFCs where the mutual funds had invested a significant portion of their funds. This substitution of overseas financing by domestic financing brought both money market and credit market under pressure.

Moreover, the foreign exchange market was impacted by the reversal of capital flows as part of the global de-leveraging process. Simultaneously, corporates were converting the funds raised locally into foreign currency to meet their external obligations. Both these factors put downward pressure on the rupee. In the foreign exchange market, the Indian rupee generally depreciated against major currencies. In the credit market, the lending rates of scheduled commercial banks (SCBs) have begun to exhibit some moderation since November 2008.

In response, RBI initiated several measures since September 16, 2008 to augment domestic and foreign exchange liquidity for proper functioning of the domestic markets and maintaining financial stability. While the overall policy approach has been able to mitigate the potential impact of the turmoil on domestic financial markets and the economy, with the increasing integration of the Indian economy and its financial markets with rest of the world, there is recognition that the country does face some downside risks from these international developments.

The risks arise mainly from the potential reversal of capital flows on a sustained medium-term basis from the projected slow down of the global economy, particularly in advanced economies, and from some elements of potential financial contagion. In India, the adverse effects have been mainly in the equity markets because of reversal of portfolio equity flows, and the concomitant effects on the domestic forex market and liquidity conditions. The macro effects have so far been muted due to the overall strength of domestic demand, the healthy balance sheets of the Indian corporate sector, and the predominant domestic financing of investment.

In short, the combined impact of the reversal of portfolio equity flows, the reduced availability of international capital both debt and equity, the perceived increase in the price of equity with lower equity valuations, and pressure on the exchange rate, growth in the Indian corporate sector is likely to feel some impact of the global financial turmoil. On the other hand, on a macro basis, with external savings utilisation having been low traditionally, between 1 to 2 percent of GDP, and the sustained high domestic savings rate, this impact can be expected to be at the margin. Moreover, the continued buoyancy of foreign direct investment suggests that confidence in Indian growth prospects remains healthy.

The process of de-leveraging and dysfunctional financial markets in the advanced economies accentuating a global financial crisis has highlighted the importance of orderly functioning of markets for achieving macroeconomic objectives. The equity markets followed the general global sentiments and market trends and after a phase of sharp downward movement, the market has shown recovery since March 2009.

3.9 Achievements of Financial Sector Reforms and Areas of Concern

Financial sector in the Indian economy since the early 1990s has undergone a transformation towards a vibrant, competitive and diversified system, with a multiplicity of financial institutions having different risk profiles intermediating in various segments of the market spectrum. The evolution of the Indian financial system from somewhat of a constricted and an undersized one to a more open, deregulated and market oriented one and its interface with the growth process are the major areas of reforms still underway.

The financial system has exhibited considerable dynamism in recent years. The system today is varied, with a well-diversified structure of financial institutions, financial companies and mutual funds. The setting up of some specialised financial institutions and refinance institutions has provided depth to financial intermediation outside the banking sector. These developments, coupled with increased financial market liberalization, have enhanced competition. A number of existing financial institutions have diversified into several new activities, such as, investment banking and infrastructure financing, providing guarantees for domestic and offshore lending for infrastructure projects.

Rapid expansion of non-banking financial companies (NBFCs) has taken place, providing avenues for depositors to hold assets and for borrowers to enhance the scale of funding of their activities. Various types of NBFCs have provided varied services that include equipment leasing, hire purchase, loans, investments, mutual benefit and chit fund activities. More recently, NBFCs activity has picked up in the area of housing finance.

Financial development is also reflected in the growing importance of mutual funds. In the 1990s, they enabled sizable mobilisation of financial surpluses of the households for investment in capital markets. Capital markets themselves have become an important source of financing corporate investments, especially after firms were permitted to charge share premium in a flexible manner.

An understanding of the organisational structure of markets for financial assets is vital for knowing the limitations and prospects with regards to efficiency, integration and stability. Financial markets in India comprise, in the main: the credit market, the money market, the foreign exchange market, the debt market and the capital market. Recently, the derivatives market has also emerged. With banks having already been allowed to undertake insurance business, bancassurance market is also likely to emerge in a big way.

Most of the financial markets were characterised, till the early 1990s, by controls over the pricing of financial assets, restrictions on flows or transactions, barriers to entry, low liquidity and high transaction costs. These characteristics came in the way of development of the markets and allocative efficiency of resources channelled through them.

The initiation of financial sector reforms in the early 1990s was essentially to bring about a transformation in the structure, efficiency and stability of financial markets, as also an integration of the markets.

In spite of the significant improvements in the banking industry as a result of reforms, several challenges lie ahead, the most important being the need to bring down the NPAs. Commercial banks continue to face the problem of non-performing assets (NPAs), attributable, *inter alia*, to factors such as weak debt recovery mechanism, non-realisation of collateral and poor credit appraisal techniques. Policy measures have not yielded the desired results. The recent enactment of the Securitisation and Reconstruction of Financial Assets and Enforcement of Security Interest Act, 2002 has increased the momentum for the recovery of NPAs. However, banks need to intensify their efforts to recover their overdues and prevent generation of fresh NPAs.

Co-operative banks constitute an important segment of the Indian banking system. They have an extensive branch network and reach out to people in remote areas. They have traditionally played an important role in creating banking habits among the lower and middle-income groups and in strengthening the rural credit delivery system. Unfortunately, financial reforms have not impacted the functioning of co-operative banks. Since the introduction of reforms, there has been very little perceptible improvement in either stability or efficiency of co-operative banks. In particular, the asset quality and profitability of co-operative banks has shown some deterioration in the reform period. Positive impact of reforms, as has been witnessed in the case of commercial banking sector, may take longer to get manifested for co-operative banks given the late start of the reform process in this sector.

Financial institutions, which constitute an important source of funds for the commercial sector, have been losing ground fast. The situation has come about as a result of the distinction between development and commercial banking getting blurred, high cost of funds and asset-liability mismatches. With reforms in the financial sector, the facility of low cost funds under long-term operations funds, funds from bilateral and multilateral agencies and bond issues under statutory liquidity ratio is no more available. Now the financial institutions are raising funds at market-related rates of interest. The Reserve Bank of India (RBI) has been advising financial institutions to chart a path for their evolution into universal banks. The merger of ICICI with the ICICI Bank was approved by the RBI in April 2002.

Competitive pressures as well as prudential regulatory requirements have made banks risk-averse, preferring their investment in relatively risk-free gilt instruments. The behaviour and strategies of bank business would need to change from the present so that they can factor in their own risk assessment even while performing their core activities. There is a need to ensure long term finance to support development and growth in the economy, even as restructuring takes place through mergers and universal banking.

True, there has been a significant progress towards globalisation in the recent past in India, the extent to which the country is globalised is considerably low as compared with other emerging economies. This indicates not only the existence of enormous opportunities but also challenges in terms of transition from a non-entity to a major player in the global financial system.

To sum up, in the context of the balance of payments crisis of 1991, a comprehensive structural and financial sector reform process was initiated in India as recommended by the Committee on the Financial System (Chairman: M. Narasimham, 1991) which became the starting point for gradual deregulation of the financial sector and development and integration of various segments of the financial market. Measures were initiated to streamline functioning of the financial system to create a sound, competitive and efficient banking system capable of meeting the increasing challenges of liberalisation and globalisation.

A safe and sound financial sector is a prerequisite for sustained growth of any economy. Globalisation, deregulation and advances in information technology in recent years have brought about significant changes in the operating environment for banks and other financial institutions. These institutions are faced with increased competitive pressures and changing customer demands. These, in turn, have engendered a rapid increase in product innovations and changes in business strategies. While these developments have enabled improvement in the efficiency of financial institutions, they have also posed some serious risks. The regulatory and supervisory policies are, accordingly, being reshaped and reoriented to meet the challenge of containing systemic risks. In this changing milieu, the main challenge for the supervisors has been to maintain the stability of the financial system and, at the same time, provide sufficient flexibility to financial institutions so that they can respond effectively to the growing competition while taking advantage of business opportunities and technological developments.

With the liberalisation of financial markets, policy authorities in India have also had to contend with episodes of financial volatility as were witnessed in some East Asian countries. Recognising the strong complementarity between financial stability and macroeconomic stability, the operational settings for policies are being geared to dampen excessive volatility and the possible impairment of the ability of financial institutions to handle fluctuations in financial asset prices. Current macroeconomic and financial developments in the Indian economy highlight the evolving role of the financial sector in the functioning of the economy and the growing integration across financial markets.

Although the financial sector in India has grown fairly rapidly in recent years, in terms of the conventional metrics of financial deepening—such as a ratio of total financial claims or bank loans to GDP—India appears to be considerably behind other emerging markets. One of the most important gaps in our existing financial structure is the lack of a sufficiently large venture capital and angel investor community, which play important role in financing start-ups, especially in areas where technology is the key to success and risk capital is needed.

The financial sector in the Indian economy is undergoing a transformation towards a vibrant, competitive and diversified system, with a multiplicity of financial institutions having different risk profiles intermediating in various segments of the market spectrum. The development of banking is a critical element in the agenda of financial sector reforms in India. Financial sector reforms in India are by no means complete. Plans are afoot to modernise the financial system to make it compatible with best international practices.

Endnote

1. BS7799 is comprehensive in its coverage of security issues, containing a significant number of control requirements. Hence, compliance with it is a major task for most organisations. By following this standard, financial institutions including banks can ensure compliance to most of the information security requirements.

4

Legislative and Institutional Measures for Strengthening Financial Sector

An efficient financial system requires a regulatory framework with well-defined objectives, adequate and clear legal framework and transparent supervisory procedure. This, in turn, requires comprehensive legislations to enable the regulatory authorities to discharge their responsibilities effectively. The RBI has, therefore, been making constant efforts to upgrade and strengthen the legal framework in tune with the changing environment.

Some recent Acts enacted by the Parliament are as under:

4.1 Prevention of Money Laundering Act (PMLA), 2002

Money laundering is the process of transforming the proceeds of crime and corruption into ostensibly legitimate assets. In a number of legal and regulatory systems, however, the term money laundering has become conflated with other forms of financial and business crime, and is sometimes used more generally to include misuse of the financial system, including terrorism financing and evasion of international sanctions. Most anti-money laundering laws openly conflate money laundering with terrorism financing when regulating the financial system.

Some countries define money laundering as obfuscating sources of money, either intentionally or by merely using financial systems or services that do not identify or track sources or destinations. Other countries define money laundering to include money from activity that *would have been* a crime in that country, even if it was legal where the actual conduct occurred. This broad brush of applying money laundering to incidental, extraterritorial or simply privacy-seeking behaviours has led some to label it *financial thought crime.*

PMLA, 2002 was enacted in January 2003. The Act along with the Rules framed thereunder came into force with effect from July 1, 2005. Section 3 of PMLA defines offence of money laundering as whosoever directly or indirectly attempts to indulge or knowingly assists or knowingly is a party or is actually involved in any process or activity connected with the proceeds of crime and projecting it as untainted property shall be guilty of offence of money-laundering. It prescribes obligation of banking companies, financial institutions and intermediaries for verification and maintenance of records of the identity of all its clients and also of all transactions and for furnishing information of such transactions in prescribed form to the Financial Intelligence Unit-India (FIU-IND). It empowers the Director of FIU-IND to impose fine on banking company, financial institution or intermediary if they or any of their officers fails to comply with the provisions of the Act.

PMLA empowers certain officers of the Directorate of Enforcement to carry out investigations in cases involving offence of money laundering and also to attach the property involved in money laundering. PMLA envisages setting up of an Adjudicating Authority to exercise jurisdiction, power and authority to confirm attachment or order confiscation of attached properties. It also envisages setting up of an Appellate Tribunal to hear appeals against the order of the Adjudicating Authority and the authorities like Director FIU-IND.

PMLA envisages designation of one or more courts of sessions as Special Court or Special Courts to try offences punishable under PMLA and offences with which the accused may, under the Code of Criminal Procedure, 1973, be charged at the same trial. PMLA allows Central Government to enter into an agreement with Government of any country outside India for enforcing the provisions of the PMLA, exchange of information for the prevention of any offence under PMLA or under the corresponding law in force in that country or investigation of cases relating to any offence under PMLA.

PMLA seeks to combat money laundering in India and has three main objectives:
1. To prevent and control money laundering.
2. To confiscate and seize the property obtained from the laundered money.
3. To deal with any other issue connected with money laundering in India.

Special Courts have been set-up in a number of States/UTs by the Central Government to conduct the trial of the offences of money laundering. The authorities under the Act, like the director, adjudicating authority and the appellate tribunal, have been constituted to carry out the proceedings related to attachment and confiscation of any property derived from money laundering.

In order to enlarge the scope of this Act and to achieve the desired objectives, the Act provides for bilateral agreements between countries to cooperate with each other and curb the menace of money laundering. These agreements shall be for the purpose of either enforcing the provisions of this Act or for the exchange of information which shall help in the prevention in the commission of an offence under this Act or the corresponding laws in that foreign State.

In certain cases the Central Government may seek/provide assistance from/to a contracting State for any investigation or forwarding of evidence collected during the course of such investigation. The Act provides for reciprocal arrangements for processes/assistance with regard to accused persons.

The Government constituted the Financial Intelligence Unit-India, in November, 2004. The organization has started receiving Cash Transaction Reports and Suspicious Transaction Reports from the banking companies etc. in terms of Section 12 of the PMLA.

4.2 Credit Information Companies (Regulation) Act, 2005

It is aimed at providing for regulation of credit information companies and to facilitate efficient distribution of credit. No company can commence or carry on the business of credit information without obtaining a certificate of registration from the RBI. The Act sets out procedures for obtaining certificate of registration, the requirements of minimum capital and management of credit information companies. The Act also empowers the RBI to determine policy in relation to functioning of credit information companies and to give directions to such companies, credit institutions and specified users.

The Act also lays down the functions of credit information companies, powers and duties of auditors, obtaining of membership by credit institutions in credit information companies, information privacy principles, alterations of credit information files and credit reports, regulation of unauthorised access to credit information, offences and penalties, obligations as to fidelity and secrecy.

Other salient features of the Act include settlement of disputes between credit institutions and credit information companies or between credit institutions and their borrowers. The Act also provides for amendment of certain enactments so as to permit disclosure of credit information.

4.3 Government Securities Act, 2006

This Act was enacted by the Parliament with a view to consolidating and amending the law relating to Government securities and its management by the Reserve Bank of India. The Act applies to Government securities created and issued, whether before or after the commencement of the Act, by the Central or a State Government. Accordingly, the Public Debt Act, 1944 ceased to apply to the Government securities. The Indian Securities Act, 1920 was repealed.

The new Act would facilitate widening and deepening of the Government securities market and its more effective regulation by the Reserve Bank in various ways, such as:

1. Stripping or reconstitution of Government securities.
2. Legal recognition of beneficial ownership of the investors in Government securities through the constituents' subsidiary general ledger (CSGL).
3. Statutory backing for the Reserve Bank's power to debar subsidiary general ledger (SGL) account holders from trading, either temporarily or permanently, for misuse of SGL account facility.
4. Facility of pledge or hypothecation or lien of Government securities for availing of loan.
5. Extension of nomination facility to hold the securities or receive the amount thereof in the event of death of the holder.
6. Recognition of title to Government security of the deceased holder on the basis of documents other than succession certificate such as will executed by the deceased holder, registered deed of family settlement, gift deed, deed of partition, etc., as prescribed by the Reserve Bank of India.
7. Recognition of mother as the guardian of the minor for the purpose of holding Government Securities.
8. Statutory powers to the Reserve Bank to call for information, cause inspection and issue directions in relation to Government securities.

4.4 Payment and Settlement Systems Act, 2007

This Act, along with Payment and Settlement Systems Regulations, 2008, stipulates that no person other than the Reserve Bank of India (RBI), shall commence or operate a payment system except under and in accordance with an authorisation issued by the RBI under the provisions of the Act.

All persons currently operating a payment system or desirous of setting up a payment system, as defined in Section 2(1)(i) of the Act should apply for authorisation to the Reserve Bank, unless specifically exempted in terms of the Act. Existing payment systems will cease to have the right to carry on their operations, unless they obtain an authorisation within six months from the commencement of the Act (i.e. August 12, 2008).

The Payment and Settlement Systems Regulations, 2008 detail the form and manner in which the application is to be made to the Reserve Bank for grant of authorisation.

4.5 Black Money (Undisclosed Foreign Income and Assets) and Imposition of Tax Act, 2015

Individuals and institutions globally are engaged in evading taxes and generating surplus which do not get accounted for in the formal economy. These funds are generated from activities which may be legal or illegal by nature. However, the mere fact that taxes have not been paid on such incomes, as per the rules of the land, converts such funds to form a part of the parallel economy or black money generation. The Government has been focused on the black money peril both within the confines of India and the sums of money parked abroad. To tackle the complex issue of black money abroad which has been in the headlines, a separate regime for taxation of The Black Money (Undisclosed Foreign Income and Assets) and Imposition of Tax Act, 2015 has been introduced.

The Act was passed by Lok Sabha on May 11, 2015 and by the Rajya Sabha on May 13, 2015. It received President's assent on May 26, 2015 and came into force on July 1, 2015. The Act extends to the whole of India.

The Act makes provisions to deal with the problem of the black money (i.e. undisclosed foreign income and assets), to frame procedures for dealing with such income and assets and to provide for imposition of tax on any undisclosed foreign income and asset held outside India and for matters connected therewith or incidental thereto.

4.6 Benami Transactions (Prohibition) Amendment Act, 2016

It came into force from November 1, 2016. The new law seeks to give more teeth to the authorities to curb benami transactions and hence black money. The Act is an amendment of the existing Benami Transactions (Prohibition) Act, 1988. After coming into force, it was renamed as Prohibition of Benami Property Transactions Act, 1988 (PBPT Act). The Act defines *benami* transactions and also provides imprisonment up to 7 years and fine for violation of the Act. The earlier law provided for up to 3 years of imprisonment or fine or both.

The PBPT Act prohibits recovery of the property held benami from benamidar by the real owner. Properties held benami are liable for confiscation by the government without payment of compensation. The new law also provides for an appellate mechanism in the form of an adjudicating authority and appellate tribunal.

The amendments aim to strengthen the Act in terms of legal and administrative procedure. The *benami* (without a name) property refers to property purchased by a person in the name of some other person. The person on whose name the property is purchased is called the *benamdar* and the property so purchased is called the *benami* property. The person who finances the deal is the real owner.

The PBPT Act prohibits recovery of the property held benami from benamdar by the real owner. As per the Act, properties held benami are liable for confiscation by the government, without payment of compensation. An appellate mechanism has been provided under the act, in the form of an adjudicating authority and appellate tribunal.

The four authorities who will conduct inquiries or investigations are the initiating officer, approving authority, administrator and adjudicating authority.

In the case of charitable or religious organisation properties, the government has the power to grant exemption.

4.7 High Level Committee on Financial Sector Reforms, 2008

With a view to outlining a comprehensive agenda for the evolution of the financial sector—indicating especially the priorities and sequencing decisions which the Government of India must keep in minds—a High Level Committee on Financial Sector Reforms was set up by the Planning Commission of India in August 2007. The Committee (Chairman: Raghuram G. Rajan) submitted its report in September 2008, and made the following main recommendations:

1. Allow more entry to private well-governed, deposit-taking small finance banks.
2. Liberalise the banking correspondent regulation so that a wide range of local agents can serve to extend financial services. Use technology both to reduce costs and to limit fraud and misrepresentation.
3. Offer priority sector loan certificates (PSLC) to all entities that lend to eligible categories in the priority sector. Allow banks that undershoot their priority sector obligations to buy the PSLC and submit it towards fulfilment of their target.
4. Sell small under-performing public sector banks, possibly to another bank or to a strategic investor, to gain experience with the process and gauge outcomes.
5. Create stronger boards for large public sector banks, with more power to outside shareholders (including possibly a private sector strategic investor), devolving the power to appoint and compensate top executives to the board.
6. After starting the process of strengthening boards, delink the banks from additional government oversight, including by the Central Vigilance Commission and Parliament, with the justification that with government-controlled boards governing the banks, a second layer of oversight is not needed.
7. Be more liberal in allowing takeovers and mergers, including by domestically incorporated subsidiaries of foreign banks.

8.   Free banks to set up branches and ATMs anywhere.

4.8 Committee on Financial Sector Assessment (CFSA), 2009

In March 2009, the Government and RBI jointly released the report of the Committee on Financial Sector Assessment (CFSA) that was co-chaired by Deputy Governor Rakesh Mohan and Finance Secretary Ashok Chawla. The report is the culmination of work started in September 2006 to undertake a comprehensive self-assessment of India's financial sector, particularly focusing on stability assessment and stress testing and compliance with all financial standards and codes.

CFSA owed its origins to the Financial Sector Assessment Programme (FSAP) that was initiated in 1999 and carried out jointly by the IMF and the World Bank after the Asian crisis. Several countries, including India, participated in this long- drawn and resource-intensive exercise. This programme so far has been conducted by the IMF and the World Bank using experts from around the world to carry out the assessment with participation from the host country.

The CFSA followed a forward-looking and holistic approach to self-assessment, based on three mutually reinforcing pillars:
1.   Financial stability assessment and stress testing.
2.   Legal, infrastructural and market development issues.
3.   Assessment of the status of implementation of international financial standards and codes.

The first pillar is essentially concerned with stability assessment. Taking into account the legal, regulatory and supervisory architecture in India, the CFSA felt the need for involving, and associating closely, all the major regulatory institutions in the financial sector—RBI, SEBI and IRDA [1], besides the relevant government departments. Direct official involvement at different levels brought about enormous responsibility, ownership, and commitment to the process, ensuring constructive pragmatism when faced with contentious issues.

Since the assessment required comprehensive domain knowledge in the various technical areas examined, the CFSA initially constituted Technical Groups comprising officials with first-hand experience in handling the respective areas from the regulatory agencies concerned as well as the government to undertake the preliminary assessment and to prepare technical notes and background material in the concerned areas. This ensured that officials who are well-conversant with their own systems and are aware of the existing strengths and weaknesses could identify the best alternative solutions.

To ensure an impartial assessment, the CFSA constituted four external independent advisory panels, comprising non-official experts drawn from within the country. These Panels made their assessments after thorough debate and rigorous scrutiny of inputs provided by the technical groups. To further strengthen the credibility of this assessment, the advisory panels' assessments were reviewed by eminent international experts.

The CFSA then drew up its own overview report at the final stage, drawing upon the assessments, findings and recommendations of the advisory panels and the comments of the peer reviewers. The assessments and recommendations comprise six volumes.

Overall, the CFSA found that India's financial system is essentially sound and resilient, and that systemic stability is by and large robust. India is broadly compliant with most of the standards and codes though gaps were noted in the timely implementation of bankruptcy proceedings.

Of immediate interest, and related closely to the current macroeconomic conditions, the CFSA also carried out single-factor stress-tests for credit and market risks and liquidity ratio and scenario analyses. These tests show that there are no significant vulnerabilities in the banking system. This does not mean that NPAs will not rise in this economic slowdown. NPAs may indeed rise. However, given the strength of the banks' balance sheets, that rise is not likely to pose any systemic risks, as it might in many advanced countries.

Risk assessment, however, is a continuous process and the stress tests need to be conducted taking into account the macroeconomic linkages as also the second round and contagion risks.

4.9 Financial Sector Legislative Reforms Commission (FSLRC), 2013

The Indian financial system is increasingly out of touch with the requirements of the economy today and the even greater requirements of the economy in the future. Most changes in the framework of financial regulation in India have been made in response to the need of the hour. This has meant piecemeal changes to the various laws that give powers to regulators to regulate finance.

In recent years, a consensus has emerged about the direction of reforms through a series of expert committees, which have drawn on hundreds of independent experts and a body of research on the failings of Indian finance. However, many of the changes proposed are incompatible with the basic structure of existing laws.

With a view to revamping financial sector laws to bring them in tune with current requirements, the Government set up the FSLRC (Chairman: B.N. Srikrishna) on March, 24, 2011. [2] FSLRC in its Report, submitted in March 2013, gave wide-ranging recommendations, both legislative and non-legislative, on the institutional, legal, and regulatory framework and operational changes in the Indian financial sector. The draft Indian Financial Code (IFC) was proposed by FSLRC has provisions that aim at replacing a large numbers of existing financial laws. FSLRC has designed a modified financial regulatory architecture which would increase accountability by achieving clarity of purpose for each organization and avoid conflicts of interest. The modified arrangements also facilitate achieving economies of scope and scale of related activities, for the private sector and for the government.

The FSLRC was set up to review and redraft the laws so that Indian finance can be reformed to prepare India for growing into a modern economy, without having to constantly amend existing laws to incorporate each new step for the financial system.

The task for FSLRC was to question the fundamental arrangements between regulators, the Government, the regulated, and the consumer for whose protection regulation is ultimately being done. FSLRC proposed a new draft law, viz. the Indian Financial Code. This law puts consumer protection at the heart of all financial regulations. In order to protect the consumer without putting a burden on the taxpayer, regulators do micro-prudential regulation and reduce the risk of failure of financial firms. They protect policy holders and prevent unsuitable products from being sold through regulations about consumer protection and through redressal forums. When financial firms fail, shareholders should bear the full brunt of the failure, but consequences for consumers and the economy should be blocked using a resolution corporation. Through systemic risk regulation, the regulators and the government prevent a large-scale disruption of financial services. This adds up to a rational approach to interventions by financial agencies in the financial system, as opposed to the existing approach of command and control.

A major theme of many of the recommendations of previous committee reports in India has been the impediments placed by financial agencies against progress. This issue has been addressed by FSLRC by giving regulators clear objectives and enumerated powers. The regulator in this scenario needs to demonstrate that the regulation is required to meet the objectives assigned to him, and it lies within his powers, and that a cost-benefit analysis of the regulation shows that the additional cost, monetary or otherwise, of complying with this regulation is going to bring clear benefits to the economy.

4.10 Indian Financial Code (IFC)

The Report of FSLRC contained the Draft Indian Financial Code. IFC replaces most existing Indian financial laws. It seeks to address present weaknesses of the Indian financial system, and meet the requirements of the Indian economy over the coming 30 years.

IFC articulates clear objectives for financial regulation where Government intervention is required. These include: (a) consumer protection, (b) micro-prudential regulation, (c) systemic risk reduction, (d) market abuse in organized financial trading, (e) consumer redress, (f) debt management, (g) capital controls, and (h) monetary policy. In each area, precise objectives are stated and precise powers given to financial agencies.

IFC lays great emphasis on the formal process through which the legislative, executive, and judicial functions take place in financial regulation. The principles of rule of law and accountability are emphasized to create a better environment of checks and balances around regulators.

The present financial regulatory architecture has come about through numerous episodes in the past decades, without a coherent design. FSLRC has designed a modified financial regulatory architecture, which would increase accountability by achieving clarity of purpose for each organization and avoid conflicts of interest. The modified arrangements also facilitate achieving economies of scope and scale.

Financial Stability and Development Council (FSDC) decided that while the draft IFC is a bill that requires Parliamentary action, a number of changes proposed by the FSLRC can be implemented voluntarily, without any legislative changes. To provide examples of best practices, and to guide regulators on compliance with the measures recommended by the FSLRC, the Ministry of Finance has published a handbook on adoption of governance enhancing and non-legislative elements of the draft Indian Financial Code.

IFC is on the legislative agenda. This legislative and non-legislative work is now the centrepiece of financial reforms in India.

4.11 Financial Stability and Development Council (FSDC)

Following the recent global financial crisis, several nations have been revisiting their regulatory architecture. India has also been prompt to act on this front. In pursuance of the announcement made in the Budget 2010-11, an apex-level Financial Stability and Development Council was set up under the Chairmanship of the Finance Minister for strengthening and institutionalizing the mechanism for maintaining financial stability and enhancing inter-regulatory coordination. FSDC is a non-statutory apex council for coordination among various regulatory bodies, since in India's increasingly complex economy, issues arise that straddle multiple financial jurisdictions.

FSDC monitors macro-prudential supervision of the economy, including functioning of large financial conglomerates, and addresses inter-regulatory coordination and financial-sector development issues. It also focuses on financial literacy and financial inclusion.

A sub-committee of the FSDC has also been set up under the chairmanship of the Governor of Reserve Bank of India (RBI). Under the aegis of the FSDC, two empowered technical groups (i.e. Technical Group on Financial Literacy and Financial Inclusion and Inter-Regulatory Technical Group) have been formed.

4.12 Financial Action Task Force (FATF)

FATF is an inter-governmental policy-making body established in 1989 by the Ministers of its Member jurisdictions. The objectives of the FATF are to set standards and promote effective implementation of legal, regulatory and operational measures for combating money laundering, terrorist financing and other related threats to the integrity of the international financial system. The FATF is therefore a *policy-making body* which works to generate the necessary political will to bring about national legislative and regulatory reforms in these areas.

The FATF has a ministerial mandate to establish international standards for combating money laundering and terrorist financing. India joined the FATF as its 34th member in June 2010. At present the FATF has 37 members comprising 35 countries and two organizations, namely the European Commission and Gulf Cooperation Council. India participated in the FATF plenary and Working Group Meetings held in Mexico from June 20-24, 2011.

FATF has developed a series of Recommendations that are recognised as the international standard for combating of money laundering and the financing of terrorism and proliferation of weapons of mass destruction. They form the basis for a co-ordinated response to these threats to the integrity of the financial system and help ensure a level playing field. First issued in 1990, the FATF Recommendations were revised in 1996, 2001, 2003 and

2012 to ensure that they remain up to date and relevant, and they are intended to be of universal application.

FATF monitors the progress of its members in implementing necessary measures, reviews money laundering and terrorist financing techniques and counter-measures, and promotes the adoption and implementation of appropriate measures globally. In collaboration with other international stakeholders, the FATF works to identify national-level vulnerabilities with the aim of protecting the international financial system from misuse.

FATF's decision making body, the FATF Plenary, meets three times per year.

4.13 Financial Stability Board (FSB)

FSB was established in 2009 under the aegis of the G20 bringing together the national authorities, standard-setting bodies, and international financial institutions to address vulnerabilities and to develop and implement strong regulatory, supervisory, and other policies in the interest of financial stability. India is an active Member of the FSB. Financial Stability and Development Council (FSDC) Secretariat in the Department of Economic Affairs, Ministry of Finance coordinates with the various financial sector regulators and other relevant agencies to represent India's views with the FSB. As a member of the FSB, Basel Committee on Banking Supervision (BCBS), and International Monetary Fund (IMF), India actively participates in post-crisis reforms of the international regulatory and supervisory framework under the aegis of the G20. India remains committed to adoption of international standards and best practices, in a phased manner and calibrated to local conditions, wherever necessary.

Endnotes

1. The supervisory control of insurance companies is exercised by Insurance Regulatory and Development Authority (IRDA) and these powers flow from Insurance Act, 1938 as well as from IRDA Act, 1999. IRDA Act 1999 states: "Subject to the provisions of this Act and any other law for the time being in force, the Authority shall have the duty to regulate, promote and ensure orderly growth of insurance business and reinsurance business". Regulatory and supervisory powers of the IRDA are wide and pervasive.

2. Government of India, Ministry of Finance, *Report of the Financial Sector Legislative Reforms Commission* (Chairman: B.N. Srikrishna), March 2013.

5

Financial Regulators in India

Financial regulators in India are multiple. There is a plethora of legislations, rules and regulations to regulate and supervise the financial sector. In this context, the Report of the Financial Sector Legislative Reforms Commission (Chairman: B.N. Srikrishna), 2013 remarked, "The institutional framework governing the financial sector has been built up over a century. There are over 60 Acts and multiple rules and regulations that govern the financial sector. Many of the financial sector laws date back several decades, when the financial landscape was very different from that seen today. For example, the Reserve Bank of India (RBI) Act and the Insurance Act are of 1934 and 1938 vintage respectively. Financial economic governance has been modified in a piecemeal fashion from time to time, without substantial changes to the underlying foundations. Over the years, as the economy and the financial system have grown in size and sophistication, an increasing gap has come about between the requirements of the country and the present legal and regulatory arrangements". [1]

The Commission further observed, "The existing regulatory environment in India is fragmented and complex. There are multiple regulators, each one tasked with a silo within the financial sector. Given the fluidity and the fungibility of financial markets, such a fragmented approach cannot possibly achieve the results desired in terms of providing an organicunity to the sector in addressing domestic and global co-ordination, addressing financial development and inclusion, and dealing with systemic stability and other concerns. In fact, the experience of regulatory co-operation in India has not been very encouraging and has witnessed escalation of conflicts in the recent past. The Commission, therefore, feels that the fragmented approach to financial sector regulation in India has failed on many grounds, which need to be corrected. But at the same time, learning from the global crisis and the consequential regulatory rethinking in multiple jurisdictions, and the need for aligning the regulatory requirements to our own milieu, the Commission deliberated the issue of appropriate regulatory structure in detail". [2]

See also section 4.9 of chapter 4 of this book.

The chief regulators and supervisors of the Indian financial system are described below.

5.1 Ministry of Finance, Government of India

The work of the Ministry is divided into 5 departments.

5.1.1 Department of Economic Affairs (DEA): DEA is the nodal agency of the Union Government to formulate and monitor country's economic policies and programmes having a bearing on domestic and international aspects of economic management. A principal responsibility of this Department is the preparation of the

Union Budget annually (excluding the Railway Budget). Other main functions include the following:

1. Formulation and monitoring of macroeconomic policies, including issues relating to fiscal policy and public finance, inflation, public debt management and the functioning of capital market including stock exchanges. In this context, it looks at ways and means to raise internal resources through taxation, market borrowings and mobilization of small savings.
2. Monitoring and raising of external resources through multilateral and bilateral official development assistance (ODA), sovereign borrowings abroad, foreign investments and monitoring foreign exchange resources including balance of payments.
3. Production of bank notes and coins of various denominations, postal stationery, postal stamps; and cadre management, career planning and training of the Indian Economic Service (IES).

5.1.2 Department of Expenditure: It is the nodal Department for overseeing the public financial management system in the Central Government and matters connected with State finances. The principal activities of the Department include the following:

1. Pre-sanction appraisal of major schemes/projects (both Plan and non-Plan expenditure).
2. Handling the bulk of the Central budgetary resources transferred to States.
3. Implementation of the recommendations of the Finance Commission and Central Pay Commission.
4. Overseeing the expenditure management in the Central Ministries/Departments through the interface with the financial advisors and the administration of the financial rules, regulations and orders through monitoring of audit comments and observations.
5. Preparation of Central Government Accounts.
6. Managing the financial aspects of personnel management in the Central Government.
7. Assisting Central Ministries/Departments in controlling the costs and prices of public services.
8. Assisting organizational re-engineering through review of staffing patterns and reviewing systems and procedures to optimize outputs and outcomes of public expenditure.

The Department also coordinates matters concerning the Ministry of Finance including Parliament-related work of the Ministry. The Department has under its administrative control the National Institute of Financial Management (NIFM), Faridabad.

5.1.3 Department of Revenue: It exercises control in respect of matters relating to all the Direct and Indirect Union Taxes through two statutory Boards namely, the Central Board of Direct Taxes (CBDT) and the Central Board of Excise and Customs (CBEC). Each Board is headed by a Chairman who is also ex-officio Special Secretary to the Government of India. Matters relating to the levy and collection of all Direct taxes are looked after by the CBDT whereas those relating to levy and collection of Customs and Central Excise duties and other Indirect taxes fall within the purview of the CBEC. The two Boards were constituted under the Central Board of Revenue Act, 1963.

5.1.4 Department of Financial Services: It looks after the following matters:
1. Citizen's Charter.
2. Banking.
3. Industrial finance and micro small and medium enterprise sector.
4. Insurance.
5. Pension reforms.
6. Work allocation.
7. Advertisements.

5.1.5 Department of Disinvestment: It promotes people's ownership of Central Public Sector Enterprises to share in their prosperity through disinvestment. The Mission of the Department is as follows:
1. List all profitable Central Public Sector Enterprises (CPSEs) on stock exchanges.
2. Listing to result in: (a) improvement in corporate governance, (b) higher disclosure levels due to listing to bring about greater transparency and accountability in the functioning of the CPSEs, and (c) adding market discipline to the functioning of CPSEs
3. Disinvestment process to facilitate unlocking the true value of the CPSEs for all stakeholders—investors, employees, company and the Government.

5.2 Reserve Bank of India (RBI)

There is only one central bank in a country whose main function is to control the operations of the rest of the banking system. Reserve Bank of India (RBI), the central bank of India, is the apex institution responsible for managing and supervising the monetary and financial system of the economy.

5.2.1 Changing Role of RBI in the Financial Sector: Since the setting up of the Reserve Bank of India in 1935, its role in the financial sector and financial market development has undergone significant changes. Emerging primarily as a bank-based financial system, the development of financial structure in India has been to finance the planned development efforts. To this end, institutional development received considerable attention of the RBI. The broad-based development of the banking sector to meet short-term financing needs was supplemented by the setting up of specialised development finance institutions by the RBI to cater to long-term financing needs. Since the early 1990s, the introduction of financial sector reforms has provided a strong impetus to the development of financial markets. The introduction of market-based monetary policy instruments, the liberalisation of capital controls and integration of the Indian economy with global markets have exposed the country to potentially volatile capital inflows, posing new challenges and dilemmas for the RBI in monetary and exchange rate management.

The RBI has been suitably reorienting the regulatory and supervisory framework so as to meet the challenges of a new environment. It has been the endeavour of the RBI to develop a competitive, strong and dynamic banking system so that it plays an effective role in supporting the growth process of the economy. The emphasis has been on safeguarding the financial stability of the overall system through increased emphasis on prudential guidelines and effective monitoring, improving institutional soundness, strengthening the regulatory and supervisory processes by aligning with international best practices and by developing the necessary technological and legal infrastructure. While the approach towards the reforms has essentially been gradual and relevant to the context, consultative processes and appropriate timing and sequencing of measures have succeeded in aiding growth, enhancing efficiency, avoiding crises and imparting resilience to the financial system.

5.2.2 Global Financial Crisis and the RBI: Though adversely affected by global meltdown, Indian economy has shown considerable absorption capacity and resilience. Soon after the start of the crisis, net portfolio flows to India turned negative as foreign institutional investors (FIIs) rushed to sell equity stakes in a bid to replenish overseas cash balances. This had a knock-on effect on the stock market which nosedived to record levels. Supply and demand imbalance in the foreign exchange market led to depreciation of rupee, vis-à-vis other currencies. The current account was affected mainly after September 2008 through slowdown in exports. Despite setbacks, however, the balance of payments situation of the country has remained comfortable.

India has remained relatively immune from the fallout of the crisis due to several reasons including prudential, supervisory and regulatory framework of the Reserve Bank of India (RBI). Moral suasions on the part of Government of India, RBI and Securities and Exchange Board of India (SEBI) have also worked. More importantly, the Indian banking system has shown remarkable market discipline, docility, and sincerity of purpose as against the financial gimmicks and dubious practices of the financial institutions in the US. It is heartening to note that in India, complex structures like synthetic securitisations have not been permitted so far.

RBI has the necessary framework for provision of liquidity to the banking system, in terms of Sections 17 and 18 of the Reserve Bank of India Act, 1934. RBI can undertake purchase/sale of securities of the Central or State Governments and can purchase, sell and rediscount bills of exchange and promissory notes drawn on and payable in India and arising out of bonafide commercial or trade transactions for provision/absorption of liquidity for normal day-to-day liquidity management operations as also for provision of emergency liquidity assistance to the banks under the lender-of-last-resort function.

RBI is empowered under the existing legal framework to deal with the resolution of weak and failing banks. The Banking Regulation Act provides the legal framework for voluntary amalgamation and compulsory merger of banks under Sections 44 (A) and 45, respectively. The Deposit Insurance and Credit Guarantee Corporation (DICGC) offers deposit insurance cover in India. The mergers of many weak private sector banks with healthy banks have improved overall stability of the system. Not a single scheduled commercial bank in the country has capital adequacy ratio which is less than the minimum regulatory requirement of 9 percent.

RBI took a number of monetary easing and liquidity enhancing measures including reduction in cash reserve ratio (CRR), statutory liquidity ratio (SLR) and key policy rates. The objective has been to facilitate flow of funds from the financial system to meet the needs of productive sectors. RBI's monetary policy stance has consistently been to balance growth, inflation and financial stability concerns. It has taken a slew of measures aimed at infusing rupee as well as foreign exchange liquidity into the system and to maintain credit flow to productive sectors of the economy.

In tune with the national economic objectives, RBI has followed a monetary policy usually called the policy of *controlled expansion.* The money supply has expanded sufficiently to meet the growing needs of industry and trade. However, it has been ensured that the expansion is not reckless. Broadly speaking, the expansion of money supply has been somewhat more than the increase in output thereby allowing a reasonable increase in the price level.

5.3 Ministry of Corporate Affairs

The Ministry is primarily concerned with administration of the Companies Act, 2013 for regulating the functioning of the corporate sector in accordance with law. The Ministry is also responsible for administering the Competition Act, 2002. Besides, it exercises supervision over the three professional bodies—Institute of Chartered Accountants of India (ICAI), Institute of Company Secretaries of India (ICSI) and the Institute of Cost and Works Accountants of India (ICWAI)—which are constituted under three separate Acts of the Parliament for proper and orderly growth of the professions concerned. The Ministry also has the responsibility of carrying out the functions of the Central Government relating to administration of Partnership Act, 1932, the Companies (Donations to National Funds) Act, 1951 and Societies Registration Act, 1980.

5.3.1 Companies Act, 2013

A. Background: The Companies Act, 1956 Act was in need of a substantial revamp for quite some time, to make it more contemporary and relevant to corporates, regulators and other stakeholders in India. While several unsuccessful attempts were made in the past to revise the 1956 Act, the most recent attempt was the Companies Bill, 2009 which was introduced in the Lok Sabha on August 3, 2009. This Companies Bill, 2009 was referred to the Parliamentary Standing Committee on Finance, which submitted its report on August 31, 2010 and was withdrawn after the introduction of the Companies Bill, 2011. The Companies Bill, 2011 was also considered by the Parliamentary Standing Committee on Finance which submitted its report on June 26, 2012. Subsequently, the Bill was considered and approved by the Lok Sabha on December 18, 2012 as the Companies Bill, 2012. The Bill was then considered and approved by the Rajya Sabha too on August 8, 2013. After having obtained the assent of the President of India on August 29, 2013, it came into effect.

B. Significance: The 2013 Act introduces significant changes in the provisions related to governance, e-management, compliance and enforcement, disclosure norms, auditors and mergers and acquisitions. Also, new concepts such as one-person company, small companies, dormant company, class action suits, registered valuers and corporate social responsibility have been included.

An attempt has been made to reduce the content of the substantive portion of the related law in the Companies Act, 2013 as compared to the Companies Act, 1956. In the process, much of the aforesaid content has been left, *to be prescribed*, in the Rules which are yet to be finalised and notified.

The changes in the 2013 Act have far-reaching implications that are set to significantly change the manner in which corporates operate in India. The 2013 Act has introduced several new concepts and has also tried to streamline many of the requirements by introducing new definitions.

C. Main Provisions:
(a) Types of Companies:

1. **One-person Company:** The 2013 Act introduces a new type of entity to the existing list i.e. apart from forming a public or private limited company, the 2013 Act enables the formation of a new entity a 'one-person company' (OPC). An OPC means a company with only one person as its member [Section 3(1) of 2013 Act].

2. **Private Company:** The 2013 Act introduces a change in the definition for a private company, *inter alia*, the new requirement increases the limit of the number of members from 50 to 200 [Section 2(68) of 2013 Act].

3. **Small Company:** A small company has been defined as a company, other than a public company.

- Paid-up share capital of which does not exceed ₹ 50 lakh or such higher amount as may be prescribed which shall not be more than ₹ 5 crore.

- Turnover of which as per its last profit-and-loss account does not exceed ₹ 2 crore INR or such higher amount as may be prescribed which shall not be more than ₹ 20 crore:

  As set out in the 2013 Act, this section will not be applicable to the following: (a) a holding company or a subsidiary company, (b) a company registered under Section 8, and (c) a company or body corporate governed by any special Act [Section 2(85) of 2013 Act].

4. **Dormant Company:** The 2013 Act states that a company can be classified as dormant when it is formed and registered under this 2013 Act for a future project or to hold an asset or intellectual property and has no significant accounting transaction. Such a company or an inactive one may apply to the ROC in such manner as may be prescribed for obtaining the status of a dormant company [Section 455 of 2013 Act].

(b) Mergers and Acquisitions: The 2013 Act features some new provisions in the area of mergers and acquisitions, apart from making certain changes from the existing provisions. While the changes are aimed at simplifying and rationalising the procedures involved, the new provisions are also aimed at ensuring higher accountability for the company and majority shareholders and increasing flexibility for corporates. The 2013 Act has streamlined as well as introduced concepts such as reverse mergers (merger of foreign companies with Indian companies) and squeeze-out provisions, which are significant. The 2013 Act has also introduced the requirement for valuations in several cases, including mergers and acquisitions, by registered valuers.

(c) Prohibition of Association or Partnership of Persons Exceeding Certain Number: The 2013 Act puts a restriction on the number of partners that can be admitted to a partnership at 100. To be specific, the 2013 Act states that no association or partnership consisting of more than the given number of persons as may be prescribed shall be formed for the purpose of carrying on any business that has for its object the acquisition of gain by the association or partnership or by the individual members thereof, unless it is registered as a company under this 1956 Act or is formed under any other law for the time being in force.

As an exception, the aforesaid restriction would not apply to the following: (a) A Hindu undivided family carrying on any business, and (b) an association or partnership, if it is formed by professionals who are governed by special acts like the Chartered Accountants Act etc. [Section 464 of 2013 Act].

(d) Insider Trading and Prohibition on Forward Dealings: The 2013 Act for the first time defines insider trading and price-sensitive information and prohibits any person including the director or key managerial person from entering into insider trading [Section 195 of 2013 Act]. Further, the Act also prohibits directors and key managerial personnel from forward dealings in the company or its holding, subsidiary or associate company [Section 194 of 2013 Act].

(e) Corporate Governance: The 2013 Act intends to improve corporate governance by requiring disclosure of nature of concern or interest of every director, manager, any other key managerial personnel and relatives of such a director, manager or any other key managerial personnel and reduction in threshold of disclosure from 20 percent to 2 percent. The term 'key managerial personnel' has now been defined in the 2013 Act and means the chief executive officer, managing director, manager, company secretary, whole-time director, chief financial officer and any such other officer as may be prescribed.

(f) Accounts and Audit: The 2013 Act has introduced certain significant amendments in this chapter. It has also introduced several additional requirements such as preparation of consolidated financial statements, additional reporting requirements for the directors in their report such as the development and implementation of the risk management policy, disclosures in respect of voting rights not exercised directly by the employees in respect of shares to which the scheme relates, etc., in comparison with the requirements of the 1956 Act.

The 2013 Act features extensive changes within the area of audit and auditors with a view to enhance audit effectiveness and accountability of the auditors. These changes undoubtedly, have a considerable impact on the audit profession. However, it needs to be noted that these changes will also have a considerable impact on the company in terms of time, efforts and expectations involved. Apart from introducing new concepts such as rotation of audit firms and class action suits, the 2013 Act also increases the auditor's liability substantially in comparison with the 1956 Act.

Unlike the appointment process at each annual general meeting under the 1956 Act, the auditor will now be appointed for a period of 5 years, with a requirement to ratify such an appointment at each annual general meeting [Section 139(1) of 2013 Act].

(g) Dividend: The 2013 Act proposes to introduce significant changes to the existing provisions of the 1956 Act in respect of declaration of dividend. The changes are likely to affect the existing practices followed by companies with regard to the declaration of dividend.

The existing provisions of the 1956 Act in relation to the transfer of a specified percentage of profit to reserve is no longer applicable and thus, companies will be free to transfer any or no amount to its reserves.

(h) Revival and Rehabilitation of Sick Companies: Chapter XIX of the 2013 Act lays down the provisions for the revival and rehabilitation of sick companies. The chapter describes the circumstances which determine the declaration of a company as a sick company, and also includes the rehabilitation process of the same. Although it aims to provide comprehensive provisions for the revival and rehabilitation of sick companies, the fact that several provisions such as particulars, documents as well as content of the draft scheme in respect of application for revival and rehabilitation, etc. have been left to substantive enactment, leaves scope for interpretation.

The coverage of this chapter is no longer restricted to industrial companies, and the determination of the net worth would not be relevant for assessing whether a company is a sick company.

(i) Corporate Social Responsibility: The 2013 Act makes an effort to introduce the culture of corporate social responsibility (CSR) in Indian corporates by requiring companies to formulate a corporate social responsibility policy and at least incur a given minimum expenditure on social activities.

5.4 Securities and Exchange Board of India (SEBI)

SEBI is an autonomous and independent statutory body. Its legally mandated objectives are the following: (a) protection of the interests of investors in securities, (b) development of the securities market, (c) regulation of the securities market, and (d) matters connected therewith and incidental thereto.

For details, see section 26.3 of chapter 26 of this book.

5.5 Pension Fund Regulatory and Development Authority (PFRDA)

PFRDA was established by Government of India on August 23, 2003. The Government has, through an executive order dated October 10, 2003, mandated PFRDA to act as a regulator for the pension sector. The mandate of PFRDA is development and regulation of pension sector in India.

For details, see section 20.2 of chapter 20 of this book.

5.6 Insurance Regulatory and Development Authority (IRDA)

Regulatory and supervisory control of insurance companies in India is exercised by IRDA and its powers flow from Insurance Act, 1938 as well as from IRDA Act, 1999. IRDA Act, 1999 states: "Subject to the provisions of this Act and any other law for the time being in force, the Authority shall have the duty to regulate, promote and ensure orderly growth of insurance business and reinsurance business".

For details, see section 21.5 of chapter 21 of this book.

5.7 Monitoring Framework for Financial Conglomerates (FCs)

The quickening pace of technological innovations coupled with blurring of sectoral distinctions has enabled financial intermediaries to effectively compete in sectors beyond their domain by deconstructing and recombining risks. Financial liberalisation has led to the emergence of financial conglomerates, cutting across not only various financial sectors such as banking, insurance and securities but across geographical boundaries as well.

These developments have also ushered in the attendant risks like that of contagion whereby the problems of different sectors and different geographies could have an adverse impact upon the balance sheets of parent regulated entity viz. the bank, insurance company or the securities company. Supervisors have realised the inadequacy of the sectoral regulations to deal with the complexities interwoven into operations of financial conglomerates.

In order to address the limitations of the segmental approach to supervision, the Reserve Bank, in consultation with SEBI and IRDA, decided upon putting in place a special monitoring system for systemically important financial intermediaries (SIFIs) or Financial Conglomerates. Accordingly, a financial conglomerates (FCs) monitoring mechanism was put in place in June 2004.

For the purpose of monitoring of FCs, the above three regulators are designated as the principal regulators to whom the identified FCs submit the FC Returns through their designated entities. The mechanism involves a quarterly reporting of relevant data by the identified FCs to their respective principal regulators with a focus on the extent of intra-group transactions and exposures of the identified groups. Primarily, the review of the intra-group transactions is conducted with a view to track build-up of large exposures to entities within the Group, to outside counterparties and to various financial market segments (equity, debt, money market, and derivatives markets), identify cases of migration/transfer of 'losses' and detecting situations of regulatory/supervisory arbitrage. The monitoring mechanism, thus, seeks to capture the 'contagion risk' within the group as also its cumulative exposure to specific outside entities, sectors and market segments.

The identification of financial groups for specialized monitoring under the FC framework is incumbent upon the scale of their operations in respective financial market segments (banking, insurance, securities, and non-banking finance). The size of the off-balance sheet position of the entities is also being additionally included as a parameter for determining the size of operations of the entities in respective market segments. While a group having a significant presence in two or more of these financial market segments qualifies to be an *identified FC*, few other financial groups which are otherwise important from a *systemic* standpoint (mainly on account of their size, involvement in specialised transactions like derivatives and securitisation and on account of market feedback), also get identified as FCs and are subjected to focused monitoring.

Since the monitoring framework also covers the housing finance segment which falls under the jurisdiction of the National Housing Bank (NHB), it has been named as a specified regulator.

The High Level Co-ordination Committee on Financial Markets (HLCCFM) Technical Committee on RBI Regulated Entities has been designated as the inter-regulatory forum for having an overarching view of the FC monitoring mechanism and for providing guidance/directions on concerns arising out of analysis of FC data and for sharing of other significant information in the possession of the Principal Regulators, which might have a bearing on the Group as a whole.

Thus, the FC monitoring framework endeavours to identify contagion like situations at the incipient stage, which could snowball into a systemic concern unless addressed promptly. The framework also aims at addressing market disruptions issues by undertaking assessments of sources of liquidity for the group which is quite critical from a financial stability angle.

Endnotes

1. Government of India, Ministry of Finance, *Report of the Financial Sector Legislative Reforms Commission* (Chairman: B.N. Srikrishna), Volume I, March 2013, p. xiii.
2. Ibid., p. 9.

Financial Inclusion Policies and Initiatives

6.1 Origins of the Current Approach to Financial Inclusion

The present concern for financial inclusion can be traced to the United Nations Capital Development Fund (UNCDF) initiatives [1], which broadly underlined the main goals as also the broad frameworks and parameters of inclusive finance, as access to a range of financial services, including savings, credit, insurance, remittance and other banking/payment services to all 'bankable' households and enterprises at a reasonable cost.

According to UNCDF the main goals of inclusive finance are as under:

1. Access at a reasonable cost of all households and enterprises to the range of financial services for which they are 'bankable', including savings, short and long-term credit, leasing and factoring, mortgages, insurance, pensions, payments, local money transfers and international remittances.
2. Sound institutions, guided by appropriate internal management systems, industry performance standards, and performance monitoring by the market, as well as by sound prudential regulation where required.
3. Financial and institutional sustainability as a means of providing access to financial services over time.
4. Multiple providers of financial services, wherever feasible, so as to bring cost-effective and a wide variety of alternatives to customers (which could include any number of combinations of sound private, non-profit and public providers).

The Report of the Centre for Global Development (CGD) Task-Force on Access to Financial Services further laid down the broad policy principles for expanding financial access, including the implicit institutional mechanisms, with particular emphasis on the need for ensuring data collection, monitoring and evaluation. [2]

G-20 Toronto Summit [3] had also outlined the "Principles for Innovative Financial Inclusion", which serves as a guide for policy and regulatory approaches aimed at fostering safe and sound adoption of innovative, adequate, low-cost financial delivery models, helping provide conditions for fair competition and a framework of incentives for the various bank, insurance, and non-bank actors involved in the delivery of a full-range of affordable and quality financial services. The G-20's highest priority, as declaration goes, is to safeguard and strengthen the recovery and lay the foundation for strong, sustainable and balanced growth, and strengthen our financial systems against risks.

6.2 Financial Exclusion and Financial Inclusion Defined

In most developing countries, a large segment of society, particularly low-income people, has very little access to financial services, both formal and semi-formal. As a consequence, many of them have to necessarily depend either on their own or high cost informal sources of finance such as moneylenders. This is particularly true for the sporadic financing requirements of low income households for non-productive consumption purposes and other emergency requirements such as medical expenditure. Benefits of growth, therefore, tend to concentrate in the hands of those already served by the formal financial system.

Despite the rapid spread of banking over the years, a significant segment of the population, predominantly in the rural areas, is excluded from the formal financial system. It is well-known that poor people, potential entrepreneurs, small enterprises and others are excluded from the financial sector, which leads to their marginalisation and denial of opportunity for them to grow and prosper. Therefore, access to a greater proportion of the population to the organised financial system should be high on the agenda of the Government of India. The key issue, however, is how to mainstream the institutional sources so as to achieve wider coverage in terms of extending credit. There are also a large number of households with low income and small savings, which need to be mobilised.

Apart from the rural areas, there is significant degree of financial exclusion in urban areas as well. The cost of financial exclusion is recognised to be enormous for the society as well as for individuals, particularly in terms of inability to realise full potential due to financial constraints.

The recent developments in banking technology have transformed banking from the traditional brick-and-mortar infrastructure like staffed branches to a system supplemented by other channels like automated teller machines (ATMs), credit/debit cards, internet banking, online money transfers etc. However, the access to such technology is restricted only to certain segments of the society. Indeed, some trends, such as increasingly sophisticated customer segmentation technology—allowing, for example, more accurate targeting of sections of the market—have led to restricted access to financial services for some groups. There is a growing divide, with an increased range of personal finance options for a segment of high and upper middle income population and a significantly large section of the population who lack access to even the most basic banking services. This is termed *financial exclusion*. These people, particularly, those living on low incomes, cannot access mainstream financial products such as bank accounts, credit, remittances and payment services, financial advisory services, insurance facilities etc.

Merely having a bank account may not be a good indicator of financial inclusion. The ideal definition should look at people who want to access financial services but are denied the same. If genuine claimants for credit and financial services are denied the same, then that is a case of exclusion. As this aspect would raise the issue of credit worthiness or bankability, it is also necessary to dwell upon what could be done to make the claimants of institutional credit bankable or creditworthy. This would require re-engineering of existing financial products or delivery systems and making them more in tune with the expectations and absorptive capacity of the intended clientele.

According to the Committee on Financial Inclusion (Chairman: C. Rangarajan), 2008, "Financial inclusion may be defined as the process of ensuring access to financial services and timely and adequate credit where needed by vulnerable groups such as weaker sections and low income groups at an affordable cost".

The essence of financial inclusion is in trying to ensure that a range of appropriate financial services is available to every individual and enabling them to understand and access those services. Apart from the regular form of financial intermediation, it may include a basic no-frills banking account for making and receiving payments, a savings product suited to the pattern of cash flows of a poor household, money transfer facilities, small loans and overdrafts for productive, personal and other purposes, insurance (life and non-life) etc. While financial inclusion, in the narrow sense, may be achieved to some extent by offering any one of these services, the objective of *comprehensive financial inclusion* would be to provide a holistic set of services encompassing all of the above.

6.3 Advantages of Financial Inclusion

The objective of financial inclusion is to extend financial services to the large hitherto unserved population of the country to unlock its growth potential. In addition, it strives towards a more inclusive growth by making financing available to the poor in particular. Government of India has been actively pursuing the agenda of financial inclusion, with key interventions in four groups, viz. expanding banking infrastructure, offering appropriate financial products, making extensive and intensive use of technology and through advocacy and stakeholder participation.

Access to safe, easy and affordable credit and other financial services by the poor and vulnerable groups, disadvantaged areas and lagging sectors is recognised as a pre-condition for accelerating growth and reducing income disparities and poverty. A developing country can benefit from financial inclusion in the following ways:

1. Access to a well-functioning financial system—by creating equal opportunities—enables economically and socially excluded people to integrate effectively into the economy and contribute to development and protect themselves against economic shocks.
2. Availability of external finance to potential entrepreneurs and small firms enables new entrants, leading to increased competition to incumbents. This, in turn, encourages entrepreneurship and productivity.
3. Inclusive finance—including safe savings, appropriately designed loans for poor and low-income households and for micro, small and medium-sized enterprises, and appropriate insurance and payments services—can help people to enhance incomes, acquire capital, manage risk, and come out of poverty.
4. Access to financial services contributes to higher production and social protection, as the financial sector—through stored savings, credit and insurance—serves as a measure of crisis mitigation.
5. Financial inclusion can improve the efficiency of the process of intermediation between savings and investments while facilitating change in the composition of the financial system with regard to the transactions that take place, the clients that use the various services, the new risks created, and possibly the institutions that operate in newly created or expanded markets. As the balance sheet of the financial sector grows more diversified and encompasses a broader spectrum of economic agents, its contribution to a more

resilient economy is commensurately higher.

6. For financial institutions, especially banks, financial inclusion helps provide a more stable retail base of deposits. As the recent global crisis also demonstrated, stable retail sources of funding, as against reliance on borrowed funds, can greatly enhance the soundness and resilience of financial institutions and can reduce volatility in earnings. It has been well-recognised that access to financial services facilitates making and receiving financial payments and reduces transaction costs. Financial inclusion enables to finance activities or firms or individuals that are at the margin, thereby promoting their growth-inducing productive activities.

7. Financial inclusion facilitates greater participation by different segments of the economy in the formal financial system. The presence of a large informal sector can impair the transmission of monetary policy as a significant segment of financially excluded households and small businesses make financial decisions independent of and un-influenced by, the monetary policy actions of the central bank. As the share of the formal financial sector increases through greater financial inclusion, it yields an important positive externality by making monetary policy transmission more effective.

8. To the extent that financial inclusion helps people move from the cash economy to bank accounts which can be monitored, it helps facilitate implementation of anti-money laundering and combating the financing of terrorism.

9. Financial inclusion can contribute to enhanced financial stability through contributing to the improved health of the household sector, of small businesses and, to some extent, that of the corporate sector. The health of the household sector is improved through improved economic linkages, reducing reliance on the costly informal sector and through improved ability to make and receive payments.

10. Financial inclusion can improve the access to finance and the social quality (including gender equality) and cost of the service that small businesses receive from banks. These factors are a key to the profitability and prosperity of these businesses and that are the backbones of the growing economy. Therefore, achieving greater financial inclusion and maintaining financial stability are now complementary policy compulsions in so far as India is concerned.

6.4 Measures Taken by Reserve Bank of India (RBI) for Financial Inclusion

Given the socio-demographic complexities in India, the policy endeavour of the RBI has been to adopt a multi-institutional and multi-instrument approach to comprehensively address the issue of financial inclusion in all its dimensions, going beyond mere availability of credit to the masses. The term *financial inclusion* needs to be understood in a broader perspective to mean the provision of the full range of affordable financial services, viz. access to payments and remittance facilities, savings, loans and insurance services by the formal financial system to those who tend to be excluded from these services. The RBI, while recognising the concerns in regard to the banking practices that tend to exclude rather than attract vast sections of population, has been urging the banks to review their existing practices to align them with the objective of achieving greater financial inclusion. The RBI too has taken a number of measures with the objective of attracting the financially excluded population into the formalised financial system. Some of the measures taken in this direction are as follows.

6.4.1 No Frills Account: RBI vide Mid-term Review of Annual Policy Statement for the year 2005-2006, advised banks to align their policies with the objective of financial inclusion. Banks were advised to make available a basic banking *No frills* account either with *nil* or very minimum balances as well as charges that would make such accounts accessible to vast sections of population. Besides, it was emphasized upon by the RBI for deepening and widening the reach of financial services so as to cover a large segment of the rural and poor sections of population.

All the public and the private sector banks as well as the foreign banks, except those not having significant retail presence, are reported to have introduced the basic banking 'no-frills' account.

6.4.2 General Credit Card (GCC): With the objective of providing hassle-free credit to the banks' constituents in rural and semi urban areas, the banks were advised in December 2005, to consider introduction of a *General Credit Card* (GCC) to such constituents. The card was to have a credit limit of up to ₹ 25,000, based on the assessment of income and cash flows of the household without insistence on security or purpose or end-use of credit. The credit facility was to be in the nature of revolving credit entitling the holder to withdraw up to the limit sanctioned. The banks are required to charge appropriate and reasonable Interest rate on the facility.

6.4.3 Business Facilitator and Business Correspondent (BC) Models: In January 2006, banks were permitted to utilise the services of non-governmental organisations (NGOs/SHGs), micro finance institutions and other civil society organisations as intermediaries in providing financial and banking services through the use of *business facilitator* and *business correspondent (BC) models*. The BC model allows banks to do *cash in-cash out* transactions at the location of the BC and allows branchless banking.

6.4.4 Passbook Facility: The matter of issuing passbooks to the small depositors has been a nagging issue for sometime past. Pass books provide the account holders a ready reckoner of the transactions in their accounts and is a convenient reference document— which can not be substituted by periodical bank account statements, particularly by the small account holders. Since non-issuance of the passbooks to the small customers could indirectly lead to their financial exclusion, the RBI had advised the banks in October 2006 to invariably offer the passbook facility to all its savings bank account holders (individuals) and not to levy any charge on the customers thereof.

6.4.5 Simplified KYC Procedure: With a view to facilitating the opening of bank accounts by the common man through a simplified KYC procedure, in the Mid-Term Review of the Annual Policy of the RBI for the year 2006-07, it was announced that the "banks could open accounts of low balance/turnover (where the balance does not exceed ₹ 50,000 in all the accounts taken together and the total credit in all the accounts taken together is not expected to exceed rupees two lakh in a year) only with self certification of address by the customers and his photograph". However, this policy announcement is yet to be operationalised as the matter is under consideration of the Government in the light of the provisions of the Rules framed under Prevention of Money Laundering Act.

6.4.6 Credit Counselling and Financial Education: Promoting *credit counselling and financial education* of the clientele of the banks is also an area that deserves due attention of the banking community. Towards this objective, the banks were also advised by the RBI to make available all printed material used by retail customers in the concerned regional language. As far as RBI itself is concerned, it has launched on June 18, 2007, a multilingual website in 13 Indian languages on all matters concerning banking and the common person so that the language does not become a barrier to acquiring financial education by the public at large.

6.4.7 Use of Technology: Recognizing that technology has the potential to address the issues of outreach and credit delivery in rural and remote areas in a viable manner, banks have been advised to make effective use of information and communications technology (ICT), to provide doorstep banking services through the business communication (BC) model where the accounts can be operated by even illiterate customers by using biometrics, thus ensuring the security of transactions and enhancing confidence in the banking system.

6.4.8 Simplified Branch Authorization: To address the issue of uneven spread of bank branches, in December 2009, domestic scheduled commercial banks were permitted to freely open branches in tier III to tier VI centres with a population of less than 50,000 under general permission, subject to reporting.

6.4.9 Banking Services in Unbanked Villages: Banks were advised to draw up a road map to provide banking services in every unbanked village having a population of over 2,000 by March 2012. RBI advised banks that such banking services need not necessarily be extended through a bricks and mortar branch, but could also be provided through any of the various forms of ICT-based models. About 73,000 such unbanked villages were identified and allotted to various banks through state-level bankers' committees.

6.4.10 Financial Inclusion Plans of Banks for Three Years: RBI advised all public and private sector banks to submit a board-approved, three-year financial inclusion plan (FIP) starting April, 2010. These plans broadly include self-set targets in respect of rural bricks and mortar branches opened, BCs employed, coverage of unbanked villages with a population above 2,000 as also other unbanked villages with population below 2,000 through branches.

Government of India had set up the Financial Stability and Development Council (FSDC), which is mandated, *inter alia,* to focus on financial inclusion and financial literacy issues. In order to further strengthen the ongoing financial inclusion agenda in India, a high level Financial Inclusion Advisory Committee has been constituted by RBI. The Committee would pave the way for developing a viable and sustainable banking services delivery model focusing on accessible and affordable financial services, developing products and processes for rural and urban consumers presently outside the banking network and for suggesting appropriate regulatory framework to ensure that financial inclusion and financial stability move in tandem. India has, for a long time, recognized the social and economic imperatives for broader financial inclusion and has made an enormous contribution to economic development by finding innovative ways to empower the poor.

6.5 Financial Inclusion Measures by NABARD

Set up in 1982, National Bank for Agriculture and Rural Development (NABARD) is the apex institution accredited with all matters concerning policy, planning and operations in the field of credit for agriculture and other economic activities in rural areas in India.

NABARD serves as an apex refinancing agency for the institutions providing investment and production credit in rural areas.

NABARD has been instrumental in facilitating various activities under micro finance sector, involving all possible partners at the ground level in the field. NABARD has been encouraging voluntary agencies, bankers, socially spirited individuals, other formal and informal entities and also government functionaries to promote and nurture self-help groups (SHGs).

The focus in this direction has been on training and capacity building of partners, promotional grant assistance to self-help promoting institutions (SHPIs), revolving fund assistance (RFA) to MFIs, equity/capital support to MFIs to supplement their financial resources and provision of 100 percent refinance against bank loans provided by various banks for microfinance activities.

In view of the large outreach and pre-dominant position of the micro finance programme, it is important to keep a continuous track of the status, progress, trends, qualitative and quantitative performance comprehensively. To achieve this objective, Reserve Bank of India and NABARD issued guidelines in the year 2006-07 to commercial banks, regional rural banks and co-operative banks to furnish data on progress under micro finance.

The data so collected covers various parameters like savings of SHGs with banks, bank loan disbursed to SHGs, bank loan outstanding against SHGs, gross non-performing assets of bank loans to SHGs, recovery performance of loans to SHGs. Further, the banks also furnish the data regarding bank loans provided to micro finance institutions (MFIs). NABARD has been bringing out the consolidated document annually.

The data furnished by the banks have been analysed on a region-wise, state-wise, agency-wise, bank-wise and also for SHGs exclusively under Swarnajayanti Gram Swarojgar Yojana and exclusive women SHGs.

The major support provided by NABARD under Micro Finance Development and Equity Fund relates to promotion and nurturing of SHGs by self-help promoting institutions and training and capacity building of the stakeholders in the sector. NABARD is also experimenting innovative projects for further developing the micro finance through Joint Liability Groups.

Since 2006-07, NABARD has been compiling and analysing the data on progress made in micro finance sector, based on the returns furnished by commercial banks (CBs), regional rural banks (RRBs) and co-operative banks operating in the country.

Most of the banks participating in the process of microfinance have reported the progress made under the programme.

6.6 Committee on Financial Inclusion

Committee on Financial Inclusion (Chairman: C. Rangarajan) [4] was constituted by the Government of India on June 26, 2006 to prepare a strategy of financial inclusion. The Committee submitted its Final Report on January 4, 2008.

As is evident from the preamble of the report, the Committee interpreted financial inclusion as an instrumentality for social transformation: "Access to finance by the poor and vulnerable groups is a prerequisite for inclusive growth. In fact, providing access to finance is a form of empowerment of the vulnerable groups. Financial inclusion denotes delivery of financial services at an affordable cost to the vast sections of the disadvantaged and low-income groups.

The various financial services included credit, savings, insurance and payments and remittance facilities. The objective of financial inclusion is to extend the scope of activities of the organized financial system to include within its ambit people with low incomes. Through graduated credit, the attempt must be to lift the poor from one level to another so that they come out of poverty".

The Report viewed financial inclusion as a comprehensive and holistic process of ensuring access to financial services and timely and adequate credit, particularly to vulnerable groups such as weaker sections and low income groups at an affordable cost.

Financial inclusion, therefore, according to the Committee, should include access to mainstream financial products such as bank accounts, credit, remittances and payment services, financial advisory services and insurance facilities.

The Report observed that in India, 51.4 percent of farmer households are financially excluded from both formal/informal sources and 73 percent of farmer households do not access formal sources of credit.

Exclusion is most acute in Central, Eastern and North Eastern regions with 64 percent of financially excluded farmer households. According to the Report, the overall strategy for building an inclusive financial sector should be based on the following policy measures:
1. Effecting improvements within the existing formal credit delivery mechanism.
2. Suggesting measures for improving credit absorption capacity especially amongst marginal and sub-marginal farmers and poor non-cultivator households.
3. Evolving new models for effective outreach.
4. Leveraging on technology based solutions.

Keeping in view the enormity of the task involved, the Committee recommended the setting up of a mission mode National Rural Financial Inclusion Plan (NRFIP) with a target of providing access to comprehensive financial services to at least 50 percent (55.77 million) of the excluded rural households by 2012 and the remaining by 2015. This would require semi-urban and rural branches of commercial banks and RRBs to cover a minimum of 250 new cultivator and non-cultivator households per branch per annum. The Committee also recommended that the Government should constitute a National Mission on Financial

Inclusion (NaMFI) comprising representatives of all stakeholders for suggesting the overall policy changes required, and supporting stakeholders in the domain of public, private and NGO sectors in undertaking promotional initiatives.

The major recommendations relating to commercial banks included: (a) target for providing access to credit to at least 250 excluded rural households per annum in each rural/semi-urban branches, (b) targeted branch expansion in identified districts in the next three years, (c) provision of customised savings, credit and insurance products, (d) incentivising human resources for providing inclusive financial services, and (e) simplification of procedures for agricultural loans.

The major recommendations relating to regional rural banks (RRBs) included: (a) extending their services to unbanked areas and increasing their credit-deposit ratios, (b) no further merger of RRBs, (c) widening of network and expanding coverage in a time-bound manner, and (d) separate credit plans for excluded regions and strengthening of their boards.

In the case of co-operative banks, the major recommendations were: (a) early implementation of Vaidyanathan Committee Revival Package, (b) use of primary agricultural credit societies (PACS) and other primary co-operatives as business correspondents, and (c) co-operatives to adopt group approach for financing excluded groups.

Other important recommendations of the Committee included: (a) encouraging self-help groups (SHGs) in excluded regions, (b) legal status for SHGs, and (c) measures for urban micro-finance and separate category of micro finance institutions (MFIs).

The Committee recommended setting up of two funds: Financial Inclusion Fund (FIF) and Financial Inclusion Technology Fund (FITF). Each of the Funds shall consist of an overall corpus of ₹ 500 crore, with initial funding to be contributed by the Government of India, Reserve Bank of India (RBI) and NABARD in the ratio of 40:40:20.

The two funds have been established with NABARD which is the coordinating agency for financial inclusion initiatives with its Financial Inclusion Department (FID) as the nodal department. The core activities of the FID are to carry forward the agenda of financial inclusion of the excluded population at the national level as per the framework described by the Committee on Financial Inclusion in general and operationalising the Financial Inclusion Fund (FIF) and Financial Inclusion Technology Fund (FITF), in particular. The implementation is under the guidance of the two Advisory Boards set up for FIF and FITF respectively.

6.7 Committee on Comprehensive Financial Services for Small Businesses and Low-income Households (CCFS), 2014

On September 23, 2013, the Reserve Bank of India (RBI) constituted a Committee on Comprehensive Financial Services for Small Businesses and Low Income Households (Chairman: Nachiket Mor). On January 7, 2014, the Committee submitted its final report.

CCFS emphasized that in order to achieve the task of financial inclusion in a manner that enhances both financial inclusion and stability, there was need to move away from an exclusive focus on any one model to an approach where multiple models and partnerships were allowed to thrive, particularly between national full-service banks, regional banks of various types, non-banking financial companies (NBFCs), and financial markets. The common theme of all the recommendations made by the CCFS was that instead of focusing only on large generalist institutions, specialization and partnerships between specialists must be encouraged. Such an approach, in its view, would be far more effective at delivering high quality financial inclusion, without compromising financial stability or responsibility towards customers.

Some of the key recommendations of the CCFS included the following:

1. Universal Electronic Bank Account for every resident to be made available at the time of issuing the Aadhaar number.
2. Licensing, with lowered entry barriers but otherwise equivalent treatment, more functionally focused banks, including payment banks, wholesale consumer banks, and wholesale investment banks.
3. Developing risk-based supervision processes for regional banks and strengthening existing ones before creating new regional banks.
4. Reorienting the focus of NABARD, SIDBI, and NHB to be market-makers and providers of risk-based credit enhancements.
5. Consolidating NBFC definitions into two categories: core investment companies and other NBFCs.
6. On priority sector lending, while the CCFS acknowledged that the current focus of the policy, on small farmers, small businesses, and weaker sections, was well placed, it recommended an approach that incentivizes each provider to specialise in one or more sectors of the economy and regions of the country. Government subsidies should be channelled as direct benefit transfers (DBTs) rather than as subventions or waivers.
7. All financial firms regulated by the RBI should be required to have an internal process to assess suitability of products prior to advising clients with regard to them.

6.8 Pradhan Mantri Jan-Dhan Yojana (PMJDY), 2014

Exclusion from the banking system excludes people from all benefits that come from a modern financial system. Thus, financial inclusion is a national priority of the Government of India as it is an enabler for inclusive growth. Financial inclusion is important as it provides an avenue to the poor for bringing their savings into the formal financial system, a means to remit money to their families in villages besides taking them out of the clutches of the usurious money lenders.

6.8.1 Background: The efforts to include the financially excluded segments of the society in India are not new. The concept was first mooted by the Reserve Bank of India in 2005 and branchless banking through banking agents called *Bank Mitras* [Business Correspondents (BCs)] was started in the year 2006. In the year 2011, banks covered 74,351 villages, with population of more than 2,000 (as per 2011 Census), with banking facilities under the *Swabhimaan* campaign. However, the programme had a very limited reach and impact.

This campaign was limited in its approach in terms of reach and coverage. Convergence of various aspects of comprehensive financial inclusion like opening of bank accounts, access to digital money, availing of micro credit, insurance and pension was lacking.

The campaign focused only on the supply side by providing banking facility in villages of population greater than 2,000 but the entire geography was not targeted. There was no focus on the households. Also, some technology issues hampered further scalability of the campaign. Consequently, the desired benefits could not be achieved and a large number of bank accounts remained dormant. A comprehensive plan was felt necessary to keep the accounts active and use them as an instrument of some economic activity leading to livelihoods.

In order to provide the much needed thrust, a flagship programme called the Pradhan Mantri Jan-Dhan Yojana (PMJDY) was announced by the Prime Minister Narendra Modi in his Independence Day address to the nation on August 15, 2014. PMJDY was launched on August 28, 2014, across the country simultaneously. PMJDY lies at the core of development philosophy of *Sab Ka Sath Sab Ka Vikas* (inclusive growth).

6.8.2 PMJDY: Brief Introduction: PMJDY is a National Mission on financial inclusion. This Mission would enable all households—urban and rural—to gain easy and universal access to financial services. In this Mission, households will not only have bank accounts with indigenous RuPay debit cards but will also gain access to credit for economic activity and to insurance and pension services for their social security. The Mission has a strong focus on the use of technology and incorporates lessons learnt from earlier efforts.

PMJDY encompasses an integrated approach to bring about comprehensive financial inclusion of all the households in the country. The Plan envisages universal access to banking facilities with at least one basic banking account for every household, financial literacy, access to credit, insurance and pension facility. In addition, the beneficiaries would get RuPay Debit card having in-built accident insurance cover of ₹ 1 lakh. The plan also envisages channelling all Government benefits (from Centre/State/Local Body) to the beneficiaries' accounts and pushing the direct benefits transfer (DBT) scheme of the Union Government. The technological issues like poor connectivity, online transactions would also be addressed. Mobile transactions through telecom operators and their established centres as Cash Out Points are also planned to be used for financial inclusion under the Scheme. Also, an effort is being made to reach out to the youth of the country to participate in this Mission Mode Programme.

PMJDY aims to provide bank account to every household in the country and make available the following basic banking services facilities:

- Opening of bank account with RuPay debit card and mobile banking facility.
- Cash withdrawal and deposits.
- Transfer.
- Balance enquiry.
- Mini statement.

Other services are also to be provided in due course in a time-bound manner apart from financial literacy which is to be disseminated side by side to make citizens capable to use optimum utilization of available financial services. To provide these banking services, banking outlets are to be provided within 5 kilometres distance of every village. Necessary infrastructure also needs to be placed to enable e-KYC for account opening and AEPS for withdrawal of cash-based biometric authentication from UIDAI database.

6.8.3 Six Pillars of PMJDY: PMJDY, to be executed in the Mission Mode, envisages provision of affordable financial services to all citizens within a reasonable distance. It comprises of the following six pillars:

1. **Universal Access to Banking Facilities:** Mapping of each district into sub service area (SSA) catering between 1,000-1,500 households in a manner that every habitation has access to banking services within a reasonable distance, say 5 km. by August 14, 2015. Coverage of parts of J&K, Himachal Pradesh, Uttarakhand, North East and the Left Wing Extremism affected districts which have telecom connectivity and infrastructure constraints would spill over to the Phase II of the programme (August 15, 2015 to August 15, 2018).

2. **Providing Basic Banking Accounts with Overdraft Facility and RuPay Debit Card to all Households:** The effort would be to first cover all uncovered households with banking facilities by August 2015, by opening basic bank accounts. Account holder would be provided a RuPay debit card. Facility of an overdraft to every basic banking account holder would be considered after satisfactory operation/credit history of six months.

3. **Financial Literacy Programme:** Financial literacy would be an integral part of the Mission in order to let the beneficiaries make best use of the financial services being made available to them.

4. **Creation of Credit Guarantee Fund:** Creation of a Credit Guarantee Fund would be to cover the defaults in overdraft accounts.

5. **Micro Insurance:** To provide micro insurance to all willing and eligible persons by August 14, 2018, and then on an ongoing basis.

6. **Unorganized Sector Pension Schemes like Swavalamban:** By August 14, 2018 and then on an ongoing basis.

   Under the Mission, the first three pillars would be given thrust in the first year.

22.8.4 Timeline for Financial Inclusion Plan: Comprehensive financial inclusion of the excluded sections is proposed to be achieved by August 14, 2018 in two phases as under:

Phase I - (August 15, 2014 to August 14, 2015):

- Universal access to banking facilities in all areas except areas with infrastructure and connectivity constrains like parts of North-East, Himachal Pradesh, Uttarakhand, J&K and 82 Left Wing Extremism (LE) districts.

- Providing basic banking accounts and RuPay debit card which has an in-built accident insurance cover of ₹ 1 lakh. Aadhaar number will be seeded to make account ready for DBT payment.

- Financial Literacy Programme.

Phase II - (August 15, 2015 to August 14, 2018):

- Overdraft facility up to ₹ 5,000 after six months of satisfactory operation/history.

- Creation of Credit Guarantee Fund for coverage of defaults in accounts with overdraft limit up to ₹ 5,000.
- Micro insurance.
- Unorganized sector pension schemes like Swavalamban.

Some of the Phase II activities would also be carried out in Phase I. In addition, in this phase, coverage of households in hilly, tribal and difficult areas would be carried out. Moreover, this phase would focus on coverage of remaining adults in the households and students.

To sum up, the banking industry in India has grown both horizontally and vertically but the branch penetration in rural areas has not kept pace with the rising demand and the need for accessible financial services. Even after decades of bank nationalization—whose rationale was to shift the focus from class banking to mass banking—usurious money lenders in rural areas and urban slums continue to exploit the poor. After economic reforms initiated in 1991, the country can ill-afford not to include the poor in the growth paradigm. Financial inclusion of the poor will help in bringing them to the mainstream of growth and would also provide the financial institutions an opportunity to be partners in inclusive growth.

The Indian experience has proved that financial inclusion can work within the framework of financial stability given an enabling regulatory environment. A combination of viable business strategies targeted towards the population at the bottom of the pyramid, lower transactions costs with technological innovations and appropriate regulatory environment have helped foster greater financial inclusion with stability. The twin objectives of financial stability and financial inclusion are arguably two sides of a coin but it is imperative that a robust risk-mitigating framework which exploits their complementarities while minimizing the conflicts is adopted to ensure that they do not work at cross purposes. Looking to the immense potential lying ahead, rapid progress of financial inclusion efforts in India is the need of the hour. The stakeholders have come to realize the need for viable and sustainable business models which can sharply focus on accessible and affordable financial services, products and processes, synergistic partnerships with non-bank entities including the technology service providers.

There is substantial progress towards opening of accounts, providing basic banking services during the recent years. However, it is essential that all the sections be financially included in order to have financial stability and sustainability of the economic and social order. There is urgent need to push forward the financial inclusion agenda to ensure that people at the bottom of the pyramid join the mainstream of the formal financial system.

Endnotes

1. United Nations Capital Development Fund (UNCDF), *Building Inclusive Financial Sectors for Development*, UNCDF, May 2006. UNCDF is the UN's capital investment agency for the world's 48 least developed countries. It creates new opportunities for poor people and their communities by increasing access to micro finance and investment capital.

    UNCDF focuses on Africa and the poorest countries of Asia, with a special commitment to countries emerging from conflict or crisis. It provides seed capital—grants and loans—and technical support to help micro finance institutions reach more poor households and small businesses, and local governments finance the capital investments—water systems, feeder roads, schools, irrigation schemes—that will improve poor peoples' lives.

UNCDF works to enlarge peoples' choices. It believes that poor people and communities should take decisions about their own development. Its programmes help to empower women—over 50 percent of the clients of UNCDF-supported micro finance institutions are women—and its expertise in micro finance and local development is shaping new responses to food insecurity, climate change and other challenges. All UNCDF support is provided via national systems, in accordance with the Paris Principles. UNCDF works in challenging environments—remote rural areas, countries emerging from conflict—and paves the way for others to follow. Established by the General Assembly in 1966 and with headquarters in New York, UNCDF is an autonomous UN organization affiliated with UNDP.

2. Report of the Taskforce set up by the Centre for Global Development, October 2009.
3. G-20 Toronto Summit Declaration, June 26-27, 2010.
4. Government of India, Planning Commission, *Report of the Committee on Financial Inclusion* (Chairman: C. Rangarajan), 2008.

Micro Finance and Self-help Groups (SHGs)

7.1 Micro Finance

Micro finance is a movement whose objective is a world in which as many poor and near-poor households as possible have permanent access to an appropriate range of high quality financial services, including not just credit but also savings, insurance, and fund transfers. Many of those who promote micro finance believe that such access will help poor people get out of poverty. For others, micro finance is a way to promote economic development, employment and growth through the support of micro entrepreneurs and small businesses.

7.1.1 Micro Finance Defined: Micro finance is the provision of a diverse range of financial services and products including small loans (micro credit), savings accounts, insurance, pensions and money transfers. These are designed to assist people living in poverty who are not able to access financial services in the mainstream banking sector because they have no collateral, formal identification or steady income.

Poor people borrow from informal moneylenders and save with informal collectors. They receive loans and grants from charities. They buy insurance from state-owned companies. They receive funds transfers through formal or informal remittance networks. It is not easy to distinguish micro finance from similar activities. It could be claimed that a government that orders state banks to open deposit accounts for poor consumers, or a moneylender that engages in usury, or a charity that runs a heifer pool are engaged in micro finance. Ensuring financial services to poor people is best done by expanding the number of financial institutions available to them, as well as by strengthening the capacity of those institutions. In recent years there has also been increasing emphasis on expanding the diversity of institutions, since different institutions serve different needs.

7.1.2 Role of Micro Finance: Micro finance is the provision of financial services to low-income clients or solidarity lending groups including consumers and the self-employed, who traditionally lack access to banking and related services.

A. Micro Finance and Individuals/Households: Micro finance is the provision of financial services to people who would not usually qualify for traditional banking services because they have no form of collateral or formal identification. Even a small loan of ₹ 5,000 can help someone living in poverty to start or grow his own small business. This enables them to earn an income so they no longer have to struggle to afford food, clean water, healthcare and an education for their children.

By helping a mother buy a sewing machine to start a tailoring business or a father buy seeds to plant a vegetable garden, small loans enable people in poverty to earn an income and provide for their families. As each business grows, loans are paid back and lent out again. With loans repaid, the cycle continues, year after year. Each successful business can feed a family, employ more people and eventually help empower a whole community.

Various studies of the impact of micro finance have been carried out over the past 20 years, including large-scale studies by the World Bank. These studies have established that micro finance can improve the living standards of poor households and the communities in which they live. The benefits of micro finance include:

1. Higher and more reliable income and savings.
2. Improved access to healthcare and better nutrition.
3. Greater female empowerment.
4. Better housing.
5. More children being placed in school.

Experience shows that micro finance can help people living in poverty to increase their income, build viable businesses and reduce their vulnerability to external shocks. It can also be a powerful instrument for self-empowerment by enabling the poor, especially women, to become agents of change, not just economically, but also socially as they emerge as influential leaders in their community.

Income generation from a business helps not only the business activity expand, but also contributes to household income, resulting in better food, shelter, education, sanitation, healthcare and so on.

Families living in poverty are often vulnerable to shocks such as the illness of a wage earner, extreme weather, theft or other such events. These shocks place a huge burden on the limited financial resources of a family, and can drive a family deeper into poverty if they do not have access to financial services like credit, insurance and savings.

It should be noted that although a large number of studies undertaken so far on the impact of micro credit programmes on household income show that participants of such programmes usually have higher and more stable incomes than they did before they joined the programmes, some practitioners still have reservations about the findings of these studies. Moreover, not many micro credit programmes can afford to undertake impact assessments because they are generally expensive and time-consuming. There are serious disagreements among experts on the validity of methodologies used in some of the published studies. In some cases, even the more rigorous studies have produced inconclusive results. Some studies show that there are limits to the use of credit as an instrument for poverty eradication, including difficulties in identifying the poor and targeting credit to reach the poorest of the poor. Added to this is the fact that many people, especially the poorest of the poor, are usually not in a position to undertake an economic activity, partly because they lack business skills and even the motivation for business.

B. Micro Finance and Women: Micro finance experts generally agree that women should be the primary focus of service delivery. Evidence shows that they are less likely to default on their loans than men. Because operating margins become tighter the smaller the loans delivered, many MFIs consider the risk of lending to men to be too high.

Women are typically poorer than men and have fewer options for earning a livelihood to provide adequate food, housing and education for their children. They are also the *change agents* of the family. Women are more likely to invest their earnings into improving the lives of the families. By encouraging women to take charge of their futures, MFIs can impact families and whole communities.

In developing countries, more women are involved in the informal labour sector. Men are more likely to be employed in contract work as labourers or overseas workers. Women are often left to support their families or supplement their husband's income by using any skills they possess. With limited resources to start or expand a small business, micro finance is attractive to women who are prepared to work hard to give their children a brighter future.

Micro finance generally targets poor women because they have proven to be reliable credit risks and when they have the financial means, they invest that money back into their families, resulting in better health and education and stronger local economies.

C. Micro Finance and Social Interventions: There are currently a few social interventions that have been combined with micro finance to increase awareness of HIV/AIDS, and gender equity. Such interventions educate on different gender roles, gender-based violence, and HIV/AIDS infections to strengthen the communication skills and leadership of women. Micro finance has also been combined with business education and with other packages of health interventions.

Micro finance programmes have been instrumental in generating employment, income and enhancing living standards of poor in underdeveloped and developing countries. They have good potential for uplifting the economic conditions of assetless poor people through group approach. Micro finance through self-help groups ensures active participation and involvement of the beneficiaries in effective implementation of the programmes for socio-economic development.

In India, micro finance programme has a crucial role to play in uplifting people living below poverty line. Poor people have less access to financial services because of their inability to provide collateral security which is demanded by the banks.

D. Micro Finance and the Economy: Micro finance is a form of financial services for entrepreneurs and small businesses lacking access to banking and related services. The two main mechanisms for the delivery of financial services to such clients are: (a) relationship-based banking for individual entrepreneurs and small businesses, and (b) group-based models, where several entrepreneurs come together to apply for loans and other services as a group. There is a rich variety of financial institutions in India which serve micro entrepreneurs and small businesses.

A significant proportion of the working population in many developing countries survives through involvement in the informal sector. By offering people a means to grow their small businesses to the point where many employ other people, micro finance has flow-on effects for local economies, decreasing unemployment and providing incomes for other poor families in the community.

With an increased income and therefore more money spent on items such as food, clothing and transport, micro finance clients become active participants in their local economies, also benefiting the providers of those products and services. By boosting local economies, micro finance benefits the developing world.

7.1.3 Micro Finance Institutions (MFIs): In India micro finance operates through the following two channels:

1. Micro finance institutions (MFIs).
2. Self-help Group (SHG)-Bank Linkage Programme (SBLP).

Those institutions which have micro finance as their main operation are known as micro finance institutions. Micro finance institutions (MFIs) offer financial services to underprivileged and impoverished communities. A micro finance institution (MFI) is a registered organisation that offers financial services to people living in poverty. Within the micro finance industry, the term *micro finance institution* has come to refer to a wide range of organisations dedicated to providing these services, such as non-governmental organisations (NGOs), credit unions, cooperatives, private commercial banks and non-banking financial institutions.

Not all MFIs are socially motivated, i.e. with the aim to help people out of poverty above all else. Some MFIs primarily exist to make a profit and seek commercial returns over social outcomes.

Clients of MFIs are typically self-employed, often household-based entrepreneurs, who do not have access to financial services in the traditional banking sector.

Forbes magazine named 7 micro finance institutions in India in the list of world's top 50 micro finance institutions. These are as under:

1. Bandhan.
2. Micro Credit Foundation of India.
3. Saadhana Microfin Society.
4. Grameen Koota.
5. Sharada's Women's Association for Weaker Section.
6. Asmitha Microfin Ltd.
7. SKS Microfinance Private Ltd.

To administer these services, MFIs need to develop and grow so that funds can be effectively managed on an on-going basis. MFIs need to develop strong leadership, train and equip staff, build new branches, and create efficient systems and processes that meet the needs of clients. Instead of funds having a one-time impact as with many humanitarian aid groups, MFIs leverage and recycle funds over and over, having a greater impact over a longer period of time.

Most MFIs lend on the basis of the past record of the group, i.e. self-help group (SHG) or joint liability group (JLG) and also on the individuals repayment performance. In the absence of a decent past record, members are deprived of getting bigger loan amounts and additional services.

MFIs also provide non-financial services such as business development to strengthen enterprises, and financial literacy training to empower families to look after their own finances. Access to these kinds of services helps empower families to become active participants in society, building self-confidence and dignity.

NABARD has been supporting the SHG-Bank Linkage Programme since 1992. In the context of growing demand for micro finance by self-help groups, RBI made linkage of self-help groups with banks as a priority sector activity in 1996. The Government of India has been supporting the programme by making special budgetary provision for promotion of self-help groups since 1999.

7.1.4 Legal Status: A number of organizations with varied size and legal forms offer micro finance service. MFIs in India exist as NGOs (registered as societies or trusts), Section 25 companies and non-banking financial companies (NBFCs) [Table 7.1]. Commercial banks, regional rural banks (RRBs), cooperative societies and other large lenders have played an important role in providing refinance facility to MFIs. Banks have also leveraged the self-help group (SHG) channel to provide direct credit to group borrowers.

Table 7.1: Legal Pattern of Micro Finance Institutions (MFIs) in India

Type of MFI	Legal Registration
MFIs Not-for profit	
Non-governmental Organizations (NGOs)	Society Registration Act, 1860 Indian Trust Act, 1882
Non-profit Companies	Section 25 of Indian Companies Act, 1956
MFIs for Mutual Benefits	
Mutually-aided Co-operative Societies (MACS)	Mutually-aided Co-operative Societies (MACS) Acts enacted by State Governments
MFIs for Profit	
Non-banking Financial Companies (NBFCs)	Indian Companies Act, 1956 Reserve Bank of India Act, 1934

A non-banking financial company (NBFC) in India is a company registered under the Companies Act, 1956. It engages in the business of loans and advances, acquisition of shares, stock, insurance business, and chit fund business. NBFCs perform functions similar to that of banks. However, there are a few differences: (a) an NBFC cannot accept demand deposits, (b) an NBFC is not a part of the payment and settlement system and as such, an NBFC cannot issue cheques drawn on itself, and (c) deposit insurance facility of the Deposit Insurance and Credit Guarantee Corporation is not available for NBFC depositors, unlike banks.

Although the SHG-Bank Linkage model is well managed in India by NABARD, currently there is no proper regulatory body for the supervision of MFIs. The presence of institutions with a variety of legal forms makes it difficult for the regulation of all such institutions by a single regulatory body in the current Indian legal structure. Though NBFCs, which cover the major part of the outstanding loan portfolio by the micro finance channel, are regulated by Reserve Bank of India, other MFIs like societies, trusts, Section 25 companies and cooperative societies fall outside the purview of RBI's regulation.

The Micro Finance Institutions (Development and Regulation) Bill, 2011 is a major step taken by the Government of India in the micro finance sector. The proposed bill clarifies all doubts pertaining to regulation of the MFIs by appointing RBI as the sole regulator for all MFIs.

7.1.5 Problem Areas of Micro Finance: While much progress has been made in developing a viable, commercial micro finance sector in the last few decades, several issues remain that need to be addressed. The obstacles or challenges to building a sound commercial micro finance industry include the following.

1. High cost of loans.
2. Repayment problems.
3. Financial illiteracy of the clients.
4. Inability of MFIs to generate sufficient funds
5. Dropout and migration of members
6. Cluster formation to grab established market.
7. Multiple lending and over-indebtedness.
8. Poor regulation and supervision.
9. Incomplete range of products.

7.1.6 Micro Finance and Central Government: It was announced in the Union Budget for 2005-06 that the Government of India intends to promote micro finance institutions (MFIs) in a big way. For this purpose, the Micro-Finance Development Fund (MFDF) was re-designated as Micro-Finance Development and Equity Fund (MFDEF) and the corpus of the fund was increased from ₹ 100 crore to ₹ 200 crore. MFDEF is expected to play a vital role in capitalising the MFIs and thereby improving their access to commercial loans.

The Central Government is considering the need to identify and classify the MFIs and rate such institutions to empower them to intermediate between the lending banks and the clients. To facilitate the process of rating of MFIs, NABARD has decided to extend financial assistance to commercial banks and RRBs by way of grant to enable them to avail the services of credit rating agencies for rating of MFIs.

A. Micro Finance Development and Equity Fund (MFDEF): Recognising the need for up-scaling the micro finance interventions in the country, the Union Finance Minister, while presenting the budget for the year 2000-01, had created Micro Finance Development Fund (MFDF) with an initial contribution of ₹ 100 crore, to be funded by Reserve Bank of India, NABARD and commercial Banks in the ratio of 40:40:20. In the Union Budget for 2005-06, the Government of India decided to re-designate the MFDF into MFDEF and raised its corpus from ₹ 100 crore to ₹ 200 crore.

To strengthen the efforts of NABARD towards promotional support for micro finance, the Government of India in the Union Budget for 2010-11 further increased the corpus of MFDEF to ₹ 400 crore.

The MFDEF is managed and administered by NABARD under the guidance of an MFDEF Advisory Board. The objective of MFDEF is to facilitate and support the orderly growth of the micro finance sector through diverse modalities for enlarging the flow of financial services to the poor, particularly for women and vulnerable sections of society consistent with sustainability.

The Fund is utilised to support interventions to eligible institutions and stakeholders. The major components of the assistance include promotional grant assistance to self-help promoting agencies, training and capacity building for microfinance clients and stakeholders of SHG-Bank Linkage Programme, funding support to MFIs, management information system (MIS) for microfinance, research, studies and publications.

7.1.7 Micro Finance and Reserve Bank of India (RBI): The RBI has been taking a pro-active role in promoting micro-finance. It set up four Groups in 2002 to look into various aspects of micro-financing. Based on the recommendations made by these Groups, the RBI announced that banks should provide adequate incentives to their branches in making the procedures for financing the SHGs simple and easy.

Based on the recommendations of the Vyas Committee, the RBI, in its annual policy statement for 2004-05, indicated that micro finance institutions would not be permitted to accept public deposits, unless they comply with the extant regulatory framework.

In view of the new paradigm shift in micro finance, the RBI is reviewing the issue of micro finance in a comprehensive manner. Accordingly, several initiatives have been taken in the recent period.

A Technical Paper on Policy relating to Development, Regulation and Supervision of Micro finance Services was prepared and discussed with the representatives of MFIs on July 18, 2005. Similarly, an Internal Group of the RBI on Rural Credit and Micro-Finance (Chairman: H.R. Khan) was set up to examine the issues relating to micro-finance. The final version of the Report was released to the public in July 2005.

The SHG-Bank linkage programme is now considered by the banking system as a commercial proposition, with advantages of lower transaction cost, near zero NPAs and coverage of maximum number of the rural clientele by the bank branches. It has also led to other quantifiable benefits in business expansion.

A. Priority-sector Status for Bank Loans to Micro Finance Institutions (MFIs): The RBI set up a committee to study issues and concerns in the micro finance sector (Chairman: Y.H. Malegam). Based on its recommendation, all SCBs have been advised by the RBI that bank credit to MFIs extended on, or after April 1, 2011 for on-lending to individuals and also to members of SHGs/joint-liability groups (JLGs) will be eligible for categorization as priority-sector advance under the categories agriculture, MSE, and micro credit (for other purposes), as indirect finance, provided not less than 85 percent of total assets of the MFI (other than cash balances with banks and financial institutions, government securities, and money market instruments) are in the nature of 'qualifying assets'. In addition, the aggregate amount of loan, extended for income-generating activity, should not be less than 75 percent of the total loans given by MFIs.

B. Exemptions Granted to NBFCs Engaged in Micro Finance Activities: The Task Force on Supportive Policy and Regulatory Framework for Micro finance set up by NABARD in 1999 provided various recommendations. Accordingly, it was decided to exempt NBFCs which are engaged in micro financing activities, licensed under Section 25 of the Companies Act, 1956, and which do not accept public deposits, from the purview of Sections 45-IA (registration), 45-IB (maintenance of liquid assets) and 45-IC (transfer of profits to the Reserve Fund) of the RBI Act, 1934.

Hence, an increasing number of micro finance institutions (MFIs) is seeking non-banking finance company (NBFC) status from RBI to get wide access to funding, including bank finance.

RBI has been playing a supportive role for strengthening micro credit movement in India. As per notification issued by the RBI dated January 13, 2000, relevant provisions of RBI Act, 1934 as applicable to NBFCs do not apply to NBFCs: (i) licensed under section 25 of Companies Act, 1956, (ii) providing credit not exceeding ₹ 50,000 for a business enterprise and ₹ 1,25,000 for meeting the cost of a dwelling unit to any poor person, and (iii) not accepting public deposits. This provision certainly encourages NBFCs to participate in micro finance programme.

7.2 Self-help Groups (SHGs)

Micro finance is routed through self-help groups (SHGs). Over the years, SHG-Bank Linkage Programme—which includes commercial banks, regional rural banks and co-operative banks—has emerged as the major micro finance programme in the country. The focus under SHG-Bank Linkage Programme is largely on those rural poor who have no sustainable access to the formal banking system. The target groups, therefore, broadly comprise small and marginal farmers, agricultural and non-agricultural labourers, artisans and craftsmen and other poor engaged in small businesses like vending, and hawking.

The programme has been providing the rural poor access to the formal banking system and has achieved several milestones in terms of gender sensitisation, empowerment and poverty alleviation. The programme provides thrift linked credit support to the members of SHGs. While the programme directly benefits the members, it also helps banks in reducing their transaction costs as well as risk in delivering small loans.

The programme has now assumed the form of a micro finance movement in many parts of the country and has started making inroads in the resource poor regions of the country as well.

7.2.1 Self-help Group (SHG) Defined: A self-help Group (SHG) is a small voluntary association of 10-20 poor people from the same socio-economic background who come together for the purpose of addressing their common socio-economic problems through self-help and mutual-help. They collect small savings (thrift) on regular basis. Out of the pooled money, small interest bearing loans are given to the members and some amount is deposited with a bank regularly. The bank lends money for economic activities of the group without collateral security and at market rates. The savings of poor members are pooled resources saved with great difficulty. This hard-earned money is termed as *warm money*. The money obtained by the group from outsiders, i.e. banks, MFIs is termed as *cold money*.

Most self-help groups are located in India, though SHGs can also be found in other countries, especially in South Asia and Southeast Asia.

Members make small regular contributions over a few months until there is enough capital with the group to begin lending. Funds may then be lent back to the members or to others in the village for any purpose. In India, many SHGs are *linked* to banks for the delivery of micro credit.

SHGs are started by non-governmental organizations (NGOs) that generally have broad anti-poverty agendas. SHGs are seen as instruments for a variety of goals including empowering women, developing leadership abilities among poor people, increasing school enrolments, and improving nutrition and the use of birth control. Financial intermediation is generally seen more as an entry point to these other goals, rather than as a primary objective.

7.2.2 Benefits of SHGs: There are many advantages of financing through SHGs: (a) an economically poor individual gains strength as part of a group, (b) financing through SHGs reduces transaction costs for both lenders and borrowers, (c) Lenders have to handle only a single SHG account instead of a large number of small-sized individual accounts, and (d) borrowers, as part of an SHG, cut down expenses on travel (to and from the branch and other places) for completing paper work and on the loss of workdays in canvassing for loans.

A. Benefits of SHG to the Members: A self-help group benefits its members in a number of ways.
1. Members are benefited with regular saving habits.
2. Easy availability of micro credit.
3. Creation of productive assets.
4. Financial discipline.
5. Status as an economic person.
6. Unity, fraternity and co-operation.
7. Development of entrepreneurship and leadership.
8. Employment to self and others.
9. Joint action for education, health, drinking water, housing, rural roads, family welfare and planning, sanitation, village cleanliness etc.
10. Exposure to the schemes for development, awareness about environment protection, prevention of social evils such as alcoholism, dowry, child marriages.

B. Benefits of SHGs to Banks: Due to group deposits and finance there is benefit of less paperwork and naturally it results in reduction of transaction cost. Loan recovery improves due to peer pressure. The banks have a huge scope for expansion of their business because of fast growing SHG-Bank Linkage Programme.

SHGs are seen as an effective tool for eradicating poverty. It is noteworthy that the SHGs-Bank Linkage Programme in India is the fastest and largest micro finance initiatives in the world having participation of Government organisations, non-government organizations, social workers, health workers and village level workers. NABARD, RBI, commercial banks, regional rural banks, co-operative banks and other financial institutions provide institutional support to SHGs.

The target groups of SHG-Bank Linkage Programme are poorest of the poor. Homogeneous groups of the same socio-economic background are preferred to avoid conflicting interests. However, mixed groups can be formed and no discrimination is allowed on the basis of gender, caste or religion. SHGs are formed and nourished by self-help promoting institutions (SHPIs), financed by MFIs for undertaking micro entrepreneurial activities.

It has been observed that small groups of 10-20 members are more participative and active as they are well-acquainted with each other and a good interaction is possible among them. Group meetings at regular intervals give opportunity to the members to express their views on financial and non-financial matters. Transparency at all levels of activities promotes trust and mutual understanding among the members of the group.

The Reserve Bank of India (RBI) has issued instructions to all banks permitting them to open savings bank accounts in the name of registered or unregistered SHGs. By initially managing their own common fund for some time, SHG members not only take care of the financing needs of each other, but develop their skills of financial management and intermediation as well. Lending to members also enhances the knowledge of SHG members in setting the interest rate and periodic loan instalments.

In order to have participation of cooperative societies in micro finance programme, various State Governments have amended their respective cooperative acts for the promotion of mutually-aided co-operative societies (MACS) based on thrift and self-help.

7.2.3 SHG-Bank Linkage Programme: This is the bank-led micro finance channel which was initiated by NABARD in 1992. Under the SHG model the members, usually women in villages, are encouraged to form groups of around 10-15. The members contribute their savings in the group periodically and from these savings small loans are provided to the members. In the later period, these SHGs are provided with bank loans generally for income generation purpose. Members of the group meet periodically when the new savings come in, recovery of past loans are made from the members and also new loans are disbursed. This model has been very much successful in the past and with time it is becoming more popular. The SHGs are self-sustaining and once the group becomes stable it starts working on its own with some support from NGOs and institutions like NABARD and SIDBI.

Many self-help groups, especially in India, under NABARD's SHG-bank-linkage programme, borrow from banks once they have accumulated a base of their own capital and have established a track record of regular repayments.

This model has attracted attention as a possible way of delivering micro finance services to poor people that have been difficult to reach directly through banks or other institutions. By aggregating their individual savings into a single deposit, self-help groups minimize the bank's transaction costs and generate an attractive volume of deposits. Through self-help groups the bank can serve small rural depositors while paying them a market rate of interest.

The SHG-Bank Linkage Programme since its beginning has been predominant in certain states, showing spatial preferences especially for the southern region–Andhra Pradesh, Tamil Nadu, Kerala and Karnataka.

7.2.4 Problems of SHGs: SHG programme is not without difficulties and challenges.

Some of these are mentioned below.

A. Lack of Support from Family Members: Lack of support from family members discourage woman to join the SHG. In case of mixed groups, male members do not extend support to female members. So, the essential objective of SHGs programme is defeated.

B. Low Income Generating Activities: Economic activities undertaken by the members are traditional. Obviously, the activities generate lower income. Therefore, the micro finance movement is losing its main objective of empowering poor people.

C. Political Interference: Political affiliations of group members disturb group activities. Actually, the concept of self-help group is based on the principle of co-operation, i.e. equality, mutual help, democracy and thrift. It has been observed that political leaders are taking interest in the formation of SHGs to add to their vote bank. Political interference might have adverse impact on the progress of self-help group movement.

The micro finance initiative of NABARD, i.e. SHG-Bank Linkage Programme has passed through various phases over the two and half decades, *viz.* pilot testing during 1992 to 1995, mainstreaming during 1996 to 1998 and expansion from 1998 onwards. A self-help group is a group of about 15 to 20 people from a homogenous class who join together to address common issues. They involve voluntary thrift activities on a regular basis, and use of the pooled resource to make interest-bearing loans to the members of the group. In the course of this process, they imbibe the essentials of financial intermediation and also the basics of account keeping. The members also learn to handle resources of size, much beyond their individual capacities. They begin to appreciate the fact that the resources are limited and have a cost.

To sum up, micro credit programme has made rapid strides in India exhibiting considerable democratic functioning and group dynamism. The micro credit programme in India is now the largest in the world. Since Independence, the Government of India and the RBI have made concerted efforts to provide the poor with access to credit. Despite the phenomenal increase in the physical outreach of formal credit institutions in the past several decades, the rural poor continue to depend on informal sources of credit. Institutions have also faced difficulties in dealing effectively with a large number of small borrowers, whose credit needs are small and frequent and their ability to offer collaterals is limited. Besides, cumbersome procedures and risk perceptions of the banks left a gap in serving the credit needs of the rural poor.

8

Demonetization of High Denomination Currency Notes in November 2016

In a historical move to fight against the evils of black money, corruption, money laundering, financing of terrorists and counterfeit notes, the Government of India decided to withdraw the legal tender character of ₹ 500 and ₹ 1,000 banknotes of the Mahatma Gandhi Series from the midnight of November 8, 2016. The announcement was made by no less a person than the Prime Minister Shri Narendra Modi himself in an unscheduled live televised address to the nation on the evening of November 8, 2016.

8.1 Demonetization Defined

Demonetization is the act of stripping a currency unit of its status as legal tender. [1] Demonetization is necessary whenever there is a change of national currency. The old unit of currency must be retired and replaced with a new currency unit. The process of demonetization involves either introducing new notes or coins of the same currency or completely replacing the old currency with new currency. The opposite of demonetization is remonetization where a form of payment is restored as legal tender. There are multiple reasons why nations demonetize their local units of currency. Some reasons include combating inflation, curbing corruption, and discouraging a cash system.

8.2 History and Background

Historically, previous Indian governments had demonetised bank notes. In January 1946, banknotes of ₹ 1,000 and ₹ 10,000 were withdrawn and new notes of ₹ 1,000, ₹ 5,000 and ₹ 10,000 were introduced in 1954. The Janata Party coalition government had again demonetised banknotes of ₹ 1,000, ₹ 5,000 and ₹ 10,000 on January 16, 1978 as a means of curbing counterfeit money and black money. However, it did not have any significant effect on cash.

In 2012, the Central Board of Direct Taxes had recommended against demonetization, saying in a report that "demonetization may not be a solution for tackling black money in the economy, which is largely held in the form of *benami* properties, bullion and jewellery". According to data from income tax probes, black money holders keep only 6 percent or less of their ill-gotten wealth as cash, hence targeting this cash may not be a successful strategy.

Prior to the announcement, Prime Minister Shri Narendra Modi had, time and again, reiterated his commitment to eradicate the menace of black money. The action followed a series of earlier efforts to curb such illicit activities, including the following:

- Creation of the Special Investigation Team (SIT) in 2014.
- Black Money (Undisclosed Foreign Income and Assets) and Imposition of Tax Act, 2015. [2]

- Benami Transactions (Prohibition) Amendment Act, 2016. [3]
- Income Declaration Scheme (IDS), 2016. [4]
- Information exchange agreement with Switzerland.
- Changes in the tax treaties with Mauritius and Cyprus.

Prime Minister raised the issue of black money at the global forums, including multilateral summits and bilateral meetings with the world leaders.

8.3 Prime Minister's Historic Announcement

Various policies and programmes announced by Prime Minister Shri Narendra Modi, from time to time, have led to India emerging as a bright spot in the global economy. India is a preferred destination for investment and India is also an easier place to do business in. Leading financial agencies have shared their optimism about India's growth as well. Combined with this, Indian enterprise and innovation has received a fillip due to the *Make-in-India, Start-up India* and *Stand-up India* initiatives that seek to encourage enterprise, innovation and research in India. However, the problems of black money and corruption have been plaguing the economy.

A radical governance-cum-social engineering measure was enacted on November 8, 2016 when the Prime Minister announced the demonetization of two largest denomination notes—₹ 500 and ₹ 1,000—together comprising 86 percent of all the cash in circulation. These notes ceased to be legal tender with immediate effect, except for a few specified purposes (such as paying utility bills). These notes were to be deposited in the banks by December 30, 2016 while restrictions were placed on cash withdrawals. In other words, restrictions were placed on the convertibility of domestic money and bank deposits.

In terms of value, the annual report of the Reserve Bank of India (RBI) of March 31, 2016 stated that total bank notes in circulation valued to ₹ 16.42 trillion of which nearly 86 percent (around ₹ 14.18 trillion) were ₹ 500 and ₹ 1,000 banknotes.

Government also announced the issuance of new ₹ 500 and ₹ 2,000 banknotes of the Mahatma Gandhi New Series in exchange for the old banknotes. Banknotes of ₹ 100, ₹ 50, ₹ 20, ₹ 10, ₹ 5, ₹ 2 and ₹ 1 remained as legal tenders and thus unaffected by the decision of the Government.

Persons holding old notes of ₹ 500 or ₹ 1,000 could deposit these notes in bank or post offices from November 10, 2016 onwards till December 30, 2016. There were also some limits placed on the withdrawals of new notes from ATMs and banks.

The Government's move was aimed at eradicating counterfeit currency, fighting tax evasion, eliminating black money, curbing terrorist financing and promoting a cashless economy.

Prime Minister assured the people that these decisions would fully protect the interests of honest and hard-working citizens of India and that those ₹ 500 and ₹ 1,000 notes hoarded by anti-national and anti-social elements would become worthless pieces of paper. He reiterated that the steps taken by the Government would strengthen the hands of the common citizens in the fight against corruption, black money and counterfeit notes.

Fully sensitive to some of the difficulties the common citizens may face in the coming days, the Prime Minister announced a series of steps to help overcome the potential problems. He stated that on humanitarian grounds, ₹ 500 and ₹ 1,000 notes would be accepted at government hospitals, pharmacies in government hospitals (with prescription of a doctor), booking counters for railway tickets, government buses, airline ticket counters, petrol, diesel and gas stations of oil companies of public sector undertakings (PSUs), consumer co-operative stores authorized by the Central or State Government, milk booths authorized by State Governments, and crematoria and burial grounds.

He emphasized that there was no restriction on any kind of non-cash payments by cheques, demand drafts, debit or credit cards and electronic funds transfer.

In his address, the Prime Minister shared the insight into how the magnitude of cash in circulation was linked to inflation and how the inflation situation has worsened due to the cash deployed through corrupt means. He added that it adversely affected the poor and the neo-middle class people. He cited the example of the problems being faced by the honest citizens while buying houses.

By making the high denomination notes worthless, individuals and entities with huge sums of black money were forced to convert the money at a bank which is by law required to acquire tax information from the entity. If the entity could not provide proof of making any tax payments on the cash, a tax penalty of 200 percent of the tax owed was imposed.

After the official announcement by Prime Minister Modi, the Governor of the Reserve Bank of India, Urjit Patel, and Economic Affairs secretary, Shaktikanta Das explained at a press conference that while the supply of notes of all denominations had increased by 40 percent between 2011 and 2016, the ₹ 500 and ₹ 1,000 banknotes increased by 76 percent and 109 percent respectively during this period, owing to forgery. This forged cash was then used to fund terrorist activities against India. As a result, the decision to eliminate the notes had been taken.

Patel also informed that the decision had been made about six months ago, and the printing of new banknotes of denomination ₹ 500 and ₹ 2,000 had already started. However, only the top members of the government, security agencies and the central bank were aware of the move.

8.4 Objectives of the Scheme: These were as under:

8.4.1 Eliminating Black Money: In recent years, the issue of corruption and black money has come to the forefront after a series of financial scandals. Generation of black money—and its stashing abroad in tax havens and offshore financial centres—has dominated discussions and debates in public fora during the recent past. Members of the Parliament, the Supreme Court of India and the public at large have unequivocally expressed concern on the issue, particularly after some reports suggested enormous estimates of such unaccounted wealth being held abroad.

After uproar in the Parliament, the Government of India came out with a *White Paper* on Black Money in May 2012. The *White Paper* presented the different facets of black money and its complex relationship with policy and administrative regime in the country. It also reflected upon the policy options and strategies that the Government had been pursuing to address the issue of black money and corruption in public life.

To meet the deadline set by the Honourable Supreme Court for the previous Government, the new Government of Prime Minister Narendra Modi constituted a Special Investigation Team (SIT), soon after assuming office on May 26, 2014. Headed by Justice M.B. Shah, a former judge of the Supreme Court, SIT was notified on May 27, 2014 to look into the issue of black money.

8.4.2 Curbing Corruption: Corruption is both morally abhorrent and imposes economic costs. Corruption distorts the decision-making mechanism and leads to an inefficient distribution of resources. Improving anti-corruption efforts is one of the highest rated priorities of the Government of India.

8.4.3 Preventing Money Laundering: *Money laundering* is the process of transforming the proceeds of crime and corruption into ostensibly legitimate assets. In recent years, prevention of money laundering has assumed importance in international financial relationships. [5]

8.4.4 Eradicating Counterfeit Currency: The incidence of fake Indian currency notes in higher denomination had increased. For ordinary persons, the fake notes looked similar to genuine notes, even though no security feature had been copied. The fake notes were used for anti-national and illegal activities. High denomination notes had been misused by terrorists and for hoarding black money. In the cash-based economy of India, circulation of fake Indian currency notes was a menace.

8.4.5 Fighting Tax Evasion: Black money and tax evasion have been eating into the social and moral fabric of the Indian society. They are undermining the socio-economic objectives of national policies. They are responsible for conspicuous and wasteful consumption, reduced savings, and increasing gap between the rich and the poor. Black money in social, economic and political space of the country has a debilitating effect on the institutions of governance and conduct of public policy in the country. Governance failure adversely affects the interests of vulnerable and disadvantaged sections of the society. The success of an inclusive growth strategy critically hinges on the capacity of society to root out the evil of corruption and black money from its very foundations.

The effects of tax evasion, resulting in black money, on an economy are indeed disastrous. Tax evasion leads to the creation of black money which in turn is a menace to the economy in its own way. Tax evasion and black money encourage concentration of economic power in the hands of undesirable groups in the country.

8.4.6 Combating Terrorist Financing: India has been a victim of terrorist attacks time and again. Demonetization scheme is expected to choke funding for arms smuggling, espionage, and terrorism through *hawala* transactions. [6]

8.4.7 Promoting a Cashless Economy: The benefits of a cashless economy include: (a) reduced cash and hence more safety, (b) faster payment, (c) reduced number of visits to banks, (d) interest earning on money in the bank, (e) quick settlement of transactions, and (f) improved accounting and book keeping.

In order to promote the above objectives, the scheme to withdraw legal tender character of old bank notes in the denominations of ₹ 500 and ₹ 1,000 was introduced. Demonetization was aimed at signalling a regime change, emphasizing the government's determination to penalize illicit activities and the associated wealth. In effect, the tax on illicit activities as well as on legal activities that were not disclosed to the tax authorities was sought to be permanently and punitively increased.

8.5 Main Features of the Demonetization Scheme

8.5.1 Deposit of Demonetized Bank Notes: Demonetized notes could be deposited in banks and post offices from November 10, 2016 to December 30, 2016 without any limit.

8.5.2 Exchange of Demonetized Bank Notes: The legal tender character of the demonetized notes was withdrawn, they could not be used for transacting business and/or store of value for future usage. Demonetized notes could be exchanged for value at any of the 19 offices of the Reserve Bank of India and deposited at any of the bank branches of commercial banks/regional rural banks/co-operative banks (only urban co-operative banks and state co-operative Banks) or at any head post office or sub-post office.

8.5.3 Cash in Exchange for Demonetized Notes over the Bank Counter: From November 10, 2016 to November 24, 2016, over the counter exchange (in cash) of demonetized notes was permitted up to prescribed limits. However, the facility was withdrawn from November 25, 2016 in view of its misuse by unscrupulous elements.

8.5.4 Withdrawal of Cash against Cheque: Depositors were allowed to withdraw cash against withdrawal slip or cheque subject to a weekly limit of ₹ 24,000 (including withdrawals from ATMs) from their bank accounts.

Business entities having current accounts which were operational for the last 3 months or more were allowed to withdraw ₹ 50,000 per week. This could be done in a single transaction or multiple transactions.

8.5.5 Withdrawal from ATMs: The ATMs were progressively recalibrated. As and when they were recalibrated, the cash limit of such ATMs was ₹ 2,500 per day. This enabled dispensing of lower denomination currency notes for about ₹ 500 per withdrawal. Other ATMs which were yet to be recalibrated, continued to dispense ₹ 2,000 till they were recalibrated.

8.5.6 Withdrawal Limits for Farmers: Farmers were allowed to draw up to ₹ 25,000 per week in cash from their loan (including Kisan Credit Card limit) or deposit accounts subject to their accounts being compliant with the extant KYC norms. Demonetized bank notes could be used for making payments towards purchase of seeds from the centres, units or outlets belonging to the Central or State Governments, public sector undertakings, National or State Seeds Corporations, Central or State Agricultural Universities and the Indian Council of Agricultural Research, on production of proof of identity.

Rules regarding deposits and withdrawals were changed frequently depending upon the feedback received from the banking system.

8.6 Package for Promotion of Digital and Cashless Economy

In the aftermath of the cancellation of the legal tender character of old ₹ 500 and ₹ 1,000 notes, there has been a surge in the digital transactions through the use of credit/debit cards and mobile phone applications/e-wallets etc. To further accelerate this process, the Central Government has announced from time-to-time, various incentives and measures for the promotion of digital and cashless economy in the country. These incentives/measures have included the following:

1. The Central Government petroleum PSUs (public sector undertakings) shall give incentive by offering a discount at the rate of 0.75 percent of the sale price to consumers on purchase of petrol/diesel if payment is made through digital means.

2. To expand digital payment infrastructure in rural areas, the Central Government through NABARD will extend financial support to eligible banks for deployment of 2 PoS devices each in 1 lakh villages with a population of less than 10,000. These PoS machines are intended to be deployed at primary co-operative societies, milk societies, agricultural input dealers to facilitate agri-related transactions through digital means. This will benefit farmers of 1 lakh village covering a total population of nearly 75 crore who will have the facility to transact cashless in their villages for their agri needs.

3. The Central Government through NABARD will also support rural regional banks and co-operative banks to issue "Rupay Kisan Cards" to 4.32 crore Kisan Credit Card holders to enable them to make digital transactions at PoS machines/micro ATMs/ATMs.

4. Railway, through its sub-urban railway network, shall provide incentive by way of discount up to 0.5 percent to customers for monthly or seasonal tickets from January 1, 2017, if payment is made through digital means.

5. All railway passengers buying online ticket shall be given free accidental insurance cover of up to ₹ 10 lakh.

6. For paid services, e.g. catering, accommodation, retiring rooms etc. being offered by the railways through its affiliated entities/corporations to the passengers, it will provide a discount of 5 percent for payment of these services through digital means. All the passengers travelling on railways availing these services may avail the benefit.

7. Public sector insurance companies will provide incentive, by way of discount or credit, up to 10 percent of the premium in general insurance policies and 8 percent in new life policies of Life Insurance Corporation sold through the customer portals, in case payment is made through digital means.

8. The Central Government departments and PSUs will ensure that transactions fee/MDR charges associated with payment through digital means shall not be passed on to the consumers and all such expenses shall be borne by them. State Governments have been advised that the State Governments and its organizations should also consider absorbing the transaction fee/MDR charges related to digital payments to them and consumers should not be asked to bear it.

9. Public sector banks are advised that merchant should not be required to pay more than ₹ 100 per month as monthly rental for PoS terminals/micro ATMs/mobile PoS

from the merchants to bring small merchants on board the digital payment eco-system. Nearly 6.5 lakh machines by public sector banks have been issued to merchants who will be benefited by the lower rentals while promoting digital transactions. With lower rentals, more merchants will install such machines and promote digital transactions.

10. No service tax will be charged on digital transaction charges/MDR for transactions up to ₹ 2,000 per transaction.

11. For the payment of toll at toll plazas on national highways using RFID card/fast tags, a discount of 10 percent will be available to users during the year 2016-17.

12. Launch of the BHIM (Bharat Interface for Money) app for smartphones. This is based on the new Unified Payments Interface (UPI) which has created inter-operability of digital transactions. As of May 31, 2017, there had been 14.54 million downloads, and close to 4 million transactions had been conducted. The 250 million digital-haves can use their smartphone to make simple and quick payments.

13. Launch of BHIM USSD 2.0, a product that allows the 350 million feature phone users to take advantage of the UPI.

14. Launch of Aadhaar Merchant Pay, aimed at 350 million who do not have phones. This enables anyone with just an Aadhaar number and a bank account to make a merchant payment using his biometric identification. Aadhar Merchant Pay will soon be integrated into BHIM and the necessary POS devices will soon be rolled out.

15. Reductions in fees (Merchant Discount Rate) paid on digital transactions and transactions that use the UPI. There have also been relaxations of limits on the use of payment wallets. Tax benefits have also been provided for to incentivize digital transactions.

16. Encouraging the adoption of POS devices beyond the current 1.5 million, through tariff reductions.

8.7 Pradhan Mantri Garib Kalyan Deposit Scheme, 2016

Prime Minister Shri Narendra Modi is trying his level best to eliminate the black money from the Indian economy. Those who have not declared their unaccounted money were given the last chance through this scheme.

This scheme was announced by the Government of India on December 16, 2016. It came into force from December 17, 2016 and was valid till March 31, 2017.

The salient features of the Scheme are as under:

- Declaration under the Scheme can be made by any person in respect of undisclosed income in the form of cash or deposits in an account with bank or post office or specified entity.

- Tax at the rate of 30 percent of the undisclosed income, surcharge at the rate of 33 percent of tax and penalty at the rate of 10 percent of such income is payable besides mandatory deposit of 25 percent of the undisclosed income in Pradhan Mantri Garib Kalyan Deposit Scheme, 2016. The deposits are interest free and have a lock-in period of 4 years.

- The income declared under the Scheme shall not be included in the total income of the declarant under the Income-tax Act for any assessment year.

Non-declaration of undisclosed cash or deposit in accounts under the Scheme will render such undisclosed income liable to tax, surcharge and cess totalling to 77.25 percent of such income, if declared in the return of income. In case the same is not shown in the return of income, a further penalty at the rate of 10 percent of tax shall also be levied followed by prosecution. It may be noted that the provisions for levy of penalty for misreporting of income at the rate of 200 percent of tax payable under Section 270A of the Income-tax Act have not been amended and shall continue to apply with respect to cases falling under the said section.

The Taxation Laws (Second Amendment) Act, 2016 has also amended the penalty provisions in respect of search and seizure cases. The existing slab for penalty of 10 percent, 20 percent and 60 percent of income levied under Section 271AAB has been rationalised to 30 percent of income, if the income is admitted and taxes are paid. Otherwise, a penalty at the rate of 60 percent of income shall be levied.

8.8 Gains from Demonetization

Demonetisation generated long-term benefits in terms of reduced corruption, greater digitalization of the economy, increased flows of financial savings, and greater formalization of the economy, all of which can eventually lead to higher GDP growth, better tax compliance and greater tax revenues.

The government claimed that the demonetization was an effort to stop counterfeiting of the current banknotes allegedly used for funding terrorism, as well as a crack down on black money in the country. The move was also described as an effort to reduce corruption, use of drugs, and smuggling.

8.8.1 Tax on Black Money: Demonetisation was designed to tax holdings of black money. Some cash holdings were perfectly *white*, the result of incomes on which taxes had either been paid or had not been applicable in the first place (e.g. agricultural income). Accordingly, the scheme included a screening mechanism, aimed at separating *white income* from *black income*. Cash holdings arising from income that had been declared could readily be deposited at banks and ultimately exchanged for new notes. However, those with black money faced three difficult choices. They could: (a) declare their unaccounted wealth and pay taxes at a penalty rate, (b) continue to hide it, not converting their old notes and thereby suffering a tax rate of 100 percent or (c) launder their black money, paying a cost for converting the money into white.

There was, indeed, active laundering. Some black money holders did pay a percentage to private intermediaries as a price for converting it into white. For example, some holders reportedly paid individuals to queue up at banks to exchange or deposit money for them. It was also widely reported that Jan Dhan accounts witnessed a surge in deposits during the 50-day window between November 8 and December 30, 2016.

In all these cases, black money holders still suffered a substantial loss, in taxes or *conversion fees*. Moreover, bank accounts are still being screened for suspicious transactions, which means that those who engaged in laundering run the risk of punitive taxes and prosecution, in addition to the fees or taxes already paid.

8.8.2 Tax Compliance: Demonetization could also be interpreted as a regime shift on the part of the government. It was a demonstration of the government's resolve to crack down on black money, showing that tax evasion would no longer be tolerated or accepted as an inevitable part of life. Since this action commanded support amongst the population, demonetization showed that black money would no longer be tolerated by the wider public, either.

These two sanctions—financial penalty and social condemnation—can have a powerful and long-lasting effect on behaviour, especially if they are combined with other incentive-compatible measures. In this case, evaders might decide in the years to come that it would be better to pay a moderate regular tax, rather than risk having to pay a sudden penal tax. Corruption and compliance can be permanently affected.

Demonetization aided tax administration in another way, by shifting transactions out of the cash economy and into the formal payments system. Households and firms have begun to shift from cash to electronic payment technologies.

As the Finance Minister Shri Arun Jaitley in his 2017-18 Budget Speech observed, "Demonetization of high denomination bank notes was in continuation of a series of measures taken by our Government during the last two years. It is a bold and decisive measure. For several decades, tax evasion for many has become a way of life. This compromises the larger public interest and creates unjust enrichment in favour of the tax evader, to the detriment of the poor and deprived. This has bred a parallel economy which is unacceptable for an inclusive society. Demonetization seeks to create a new 'normal' wherein the GDP would be bigger, cleaner and real. This exercise is part of our Government's resolve to eliminate corruption, black money, counterfeit currency and terror funding. Like all reforms, this measure is obviously disruptive, as it seeks to change the retrograde status quo. Drop in economic activity, if any, on account of the currency squeeze during the remonetisation period is expected to have only a transient impact on the economy. I am reminded here of what the Father of the Nation, Mahatma Gandhi, had said: *A right cause never fails*". [7]

8.8.3 Digitalisation: One intermediate objective of demonetization was to create a less-cash economy, as this is key to channelling more savings through the formal financial system and improving tax compliance. Currently, India is far away from this objective.

Digitalisation can broadly impact three sections of society: the poor, who are largely outside the digital economy; the less affluent, who are becoming part of the digital economy having acquired Jan Dhan accounts and RuPay cards; and the affluent, who are fully digitally integrated via credit cards.

8.8.4 Real Estate: Demonetization could have particularly profound impact on the real estate sector. In the past, much of the black money was accumulated by evading taxes on property sales. To the extent that black money is reduced and financial transactions increasingly take place through electronic means, this type of tax evasion will also diminish. A reduction in real estate prices is desirable as it will lead to affordable housing for the middle class, and facilitate labour mobility across India currently impeded by high and unaffordable rents.

8.8.5 Redistribution of Resources: Demonetisation redistributed resources to some extent. For example, to the extent that black money holders laundered their money by employing people to stand in queues, there was a positive wealth effect because cash went from rich to the poor.

However, the most important redistributive effect was that it shifted resources from the private sector to the government. The December 30, 2016 Ordinance declared the unreturned notes as no longer constituting legal tender. Thus, the associated liability of RBI—amounting to the value of unreturned notes—was extinguished, and the RBI's net worth increased to the same extent. In this sense, demonetisation effected a transfer of wealth from holders of illicit black money to the Government, which can now be redeployed in various productive ways.

8.9 Problems Created by Demonetization

Short-term costs took the form of inconvenience and hardships, especially to those in the informal and cash-intensive sectors of the economy who lost income and employment. These costs were transitory. There were reports of job losses, declines in farm incomes, and social disruption, especially in the informal, cash-intensive parts of the economy.

In the days following the demonetization, banks and ATMs across the country faced severe cash shortages affecting small businesses, agriculture sector, and the transportation sector. People seeking to exchange their notes had to stand in queues due to the rush to exchange cash. The move was severely criticized by members of the opposition parties, leading to debates in both houses of the Parliament and triggering organized protests against the government at several places across India. The Government opined that the queues due to demonetization were the last queues that would end all other queues.

Analysts were unanimous in holding the view that the demonetization move of the Government would hit the economy hard in the short-term albeit benefiting the country in the long-run. Consumers refrained from making any purchases except essential items from the consumer staples, healthcare, and energy segments. Activity in the real estate sector, which includes a lot of cash and undocumented transactions, slowed down significantly.

To sum up, India's demonetization was unprecedented in international economic history, in that it combined secrecy and suddenness amidst normal economic and political conditions. All other sudden demonetizations have occurred in the context of hyperinflation, wars, political upheavals, or other extreme circumstances. It is too early to quantify the direction and magnitude of long-term changes. It will take several years to see the impact of demonetization on illicit transactions, on black money, and on financial savings. But there are some signs pointing to change.

Endnotes

1. Legal tender is any official medium of payment recognized by law that can be used to

extinguish a public or private debt, or meet a financial obligation. National currency is legal tender in practically every country. A creditor is obligated to accept legal tender toward repayment of a debt. Legal tender can only be issued by the national body that is authorized to do so, such as the RBI in the case of India. Widely accepted currencies such as the US dollar and Euro are accepted as legal tender in many nations, especially those where foreign currencies are in short supply. Countries with extensive business and cultural ties may also accept each other's currencies as legal tender in limited amounts.

2. This Act makes provisions to deal with the problem of the black money that is undisclosed foreign income and assets, the procedure for dealing with such income and assets and to provide for imposition of tax on any undisclosed foreign income and asset held outside India and for matters connected therewith or incidental thereto.

3. This Act came into force from November 1, 2016. The new law seeks to give more teeth to the authorities to curb benami transactions and hence black money.

4. The Government of India devised an Income Declaration Scheme (IDS), which opened on June 1, 2016 and ended on September 30, 2016. Under the scheme, the black money holders could come clean by declaring the assets, paying the tax and a penalty of 45 percent thereafter.

5. Prevention of Money Laundering Act (PMLA), 2002 was enacted to prevent money laundering and provide for confiscation of property derived from, or involved in, money laundering and for matters connected therewith or incidental thereto. The Act also addresses international obligations under the Political Declaration and Global Programme of Action adopted by the General Assembly of the United Nations to prevent money laundering.

6. **Hawala Transactions:** The hawala system has existed since the 8th century between Arabic and Muslim traders alongside the Silk Road and beyond as a protection against theft. It is believed to have arisen in the financing of long-distance trade around the emerging capital trade centres in the early medieval period.

    Meaning: Hawala (reference/trust) is a popular and informal value transfer system based on the past record and honour of a huge network of money brokers—primarily located in the Middle East and the Indian subcontinent—operating outside of, or parallel to, traditional banking, financial channels, and remittance systems. Dubai has been standing out for decades as a welcoming hub for hawala transactions worldwide.

    Working Mechanism: In the most basic variant of the hawala system, money is transferred via a network of hawala brokers. It is the transfer of money without actually moving it or money transfer without money movement.

    Let us suppose a customer (named A) approaches a hawala broker (named B) in New York and gives a sum of money (US$ 1,000) that is to be transferred to a recipient (named C) in New Delhi. Along with the money, A specifies something like a password (e.g. red rose) that will lead to the money being paid out. The hawala broker B calls another hawala broker (named D) in New Delhi—the recipient's city—and informs D about the agreed password and other details regarding funds and meeting place and time. Now, the intended recipient (C)—who also has been informed by A about the password etc. approaches D and tells him the agreed password. If the password is correct, then D releases the transferred sum to C in Indian rupees (₹ 70,000 if 1 US$ = ₹ 70), usually minus a small commission. B now basically owes D the money that D had paid out to C. Thus, D has to trust B's promise to settle the debt at a later date.

    Apparently, hawala mechanism can work in the reverse also if funds are to be transferred from New Delhi to New York.

    Features: The unique feature of the system is that no promissory instruments are exchanged between the hawala brokers. The transaction takes place entirely on the trust/honour system. As the system does not depend on the legal enforceability of claims, it can operate even in the absence of a legal and juridical environment. Trust and extensive use of connections, such as family relations and regional affiliations, are the components that distinguish it from other remittance systems.

Informal records are kept of individual transactions, and a running tally of the amount owed by one broker to another is kept. Settlements of debts between hawala brokers can take a variety of forms (such as goods, services, properties etc.) and need not take the form of direct cash transactions.

In addition to commissions, hawala brokers often earn their profits through bypassing official exchange rates. Generally, the funds enter the system in the source country's currency (in this example, US$) and leave the system in the recipient country's currency (in this example, Indian rupees). As settlements often take place without any foreign exchange transactions, they can be made at other than official exchange rates.

Hawala is attractive to customers because it provides a fast and convenient transfer of funds, usually with a far lower commission than that charged by banks. Its advantages are most pronounced when the receiving country applies unprofitable exchange rate regulations or when the banking system in the receiving country is less efficient. Hawala is often used for migrant workers' remittances to their countries of origin.

Hawala route can be used to facilitate drug smuggling, money laundering, tax evasion, and anonymously movement of fund for terrorist activities. Hence, it is illegal in many countries including India.

7. Government of India, Ministry of Finance, Budget Papers, 2017-18, *Speech of the Finance Minister*, para 11.

Part II

Reforms Impacting Financial Institutions

9

Classification, Regulation and Supervision of Financial Institutions in India

Financial institutions in India have transited since the mid-1990s from an environment of an administered regime to a system dominated by market-determined interest and exchange rates, and migration of the central bank from direct and quantitative to price-based instruments of monetary policy and operations. However, increased globalisation has resulted in further expansion and sophistication of the financial sector, which has posed new challenges to regulation and supervision, particularly of the banking system. In this context, the capabilities of the existing regulatory and supervisory structures also need to be assessed by benchmarking them against the best international practices.

Emphasizing the need for an efficient financial intermediation, the Twelfth Five Year Plan (2012-17) observed, "While availability of savings in the aggregate is an important part of macroeconomic balance, it is also important to have an efficient financial system that can channel savings to the most productive uses, and also ensure inclusiveness. The past two decades have seen far-reaching change in the character and structure of the country's banking system and the capital markets. These changes have addressed the management of credit risk, provisioning against delinquent loans and a greater focus on fee-based income. The interest rate regime that used to be highly regulated was systematically replaced by a commercially determined framework that helped price-in credit quality, duration and diversification of risk. The kind of loan products available and the servicing of these for the commercial sector have also become more efficient. Retail banking, that is, personal loans for buying homes and other durable assets, and payment and settlement facilities, have become an important and rapidly growing component of banking. Lending to small borrowers typified by the self-help group (SHG) and micro finance has come some distance towards making financial inclusion meaningful.

These changes have also changed the behaviour of corporate borrowers. In many ways, financial risk was not meaningful in the years before 1991. It changed subsequently, and with it the incentives to maintain a clean credit record and a lower leverage. Dismantling of the production licensing system, lower import tariffs and the end of quantitative restrictions on imports made competition a reality in India, that is, both domestic competition and competition vis-à-vis the global producers. Finally, the decline in the ownership functions of government and quasi-governmental agencies, and the enhanced role of capital markets in raising finance has given new importance to the interests of shareholders, especially minority shareholders. Associated with this is the challenge of corporate control, which now has to face up to proactive mergers, acquisition and sale". [1]

9.1 Classification of Financial Institutions in India

Financial institutions in India can be classified as given in Table 9.1.

Table 9.1: Classification of Financial Institutions in India

1. Reserve Bank of India (RBI)
2. Commercial Banks
2.1 Scheduled Commercial Banks
2.1.1 Public Sector Banks: (a) State Bank group, (b) Nationalised banks, and (c) Other public sector banks
2.1.2 Private sector banks: (a) Old private banks, and (b) New private banks
2.1.3 Foreign banks
2.1.4 Regional rural banks
2.2 Non-scheduled commercial banks (Local area banks)
2.3 Payment banks
3. Co-operative Banks
3.1 Urban co-operative banks
3.1.1 Scheduled
3.1.2 Non-scheduled
3.2 Rural co-operative banks
3.2.1 Short-term structure: (a) State co-operative banks (SCBs), and (b) District central co-operative banks (DCCBs)
3.2.2 Primary agricultural credit societies (PACS)
3.2.3 Long-term structure: (a) State co-operative agriculture and rural development banks (SCARDBs), and (b) Primary co-operative agriculture and rural development banks (PCARDBs)
4. State Financial Corporations (SFCs)
5. Development Finance Institutions (DFIs)
6. Non-banking Financial Companies (NBFCs)
6.1 NBFCs (Deposit-taking)
6.2 NBFCs (Non-deposit-taking)
6.3 Residuary non-banking companies (RNBCs)
6.4 Primary dealers
6.5 Housing finance companies
7. Mutual Funds
7.1 Bank-sponsored
7.2 Institution-sponsored
7.2.1 Indian
7.2.2 Foreign

7.3 Joint ventures (predominantly Indian)	
7.4 Joint ventures (predominantly foreign)	
8. Pension Funds	
9. Insurance Institutions	

9.1 Life insurance
   9.1.1 Public
   9.1.2 Private	

9.2 Non-life insurance
   9.2.1 Public
   9.2.2 Private
   9.2.3 Others [Deposit Insurance and Credit Guarantee Corporation (DICGC)
      and Reinsurance Corporation of India Ltd.]	

10. Other Institutions	
Other institutions established to meet specific financing needs include Power Finance Corporation (PFC) and Rural Electrification Corporation (REC) (financial assistance to the power sector) and Indian Railway Finance Corporation (IRFC), which is the capital market financing arm of Indian Railways. These institutions have been notified as public financial institutions (PFIs) under the Companies Act, 1956 and enjoy less stringent compliance and regulatory norms. In addition, at the state-level, there exists the North Eastern Development Finance Corporation (NEDFC) extending credit to industry and agricultural concerns in the North Eastern region, and Technical Consultancy Organisations, providing technical inputs for feasibility studies on viability of projects. Besides, the State Industrial Development Corporations (SIDCs), registered under the Companies Act, 1956 also provide credit to industries at the state level.	
Financial Institutions (1 to 10)	
Banking Sector (1+2+3)	

9.2 Regulation and Supervision of Financial Institutions in India

Financial institutions in India are regulated and supervised by various authorities and legislations (Table 9.2).

Table 9.2: Regulation and Supervision of Financial Institutions in India

Institutions	Regulator(s)	Act(s)
Commercial Banks	- Reserve Bank of India (RBI)	- Banking Regulation Act, 1949 - Reserve Bank of India Act, 1934 - State Bank of India Act, 1955 - State Bank of India (Subsidiary) Banks Act, 1959 - Banking Companies (Acquisition and Transfer of Undertaking) Acts, 1970 and 1980 - Deposit Insurance and Credit Guarantee Co-operation (DICGC) Act, 1961

Urban Co-operative Banks	- RBI - Registrar of Co-operative Societies	- Banking Regulation Act, 1949 - Co-operative Societies Act of various State Governments - Multi-State Co-operative Societies Act, 2002 - DICGC Act, 1961
Regional Rural Banks (RRBs)	- RBI - National Bank for Agriculture and Rural Development (NABARD)	- Banking Regulation Act, 1949 - DICGC Act, 1961 - Regional Rural Banks Act, 1976 - Reserve Bank of India, Act, 1934
State Co-operative Banks/District Central Co-operative Banks	- RBI - Registrar of Co-operative Societies - NABARD	- Banking Regulation Act, 1949 - Co-operative Societies Act of various State Governments - DICGC Act, 1961
Development Finance Institutions (DFIs)/Non-banking Financial Companies (NBFCs)	- RBI - Ministry of Corporate Affairs	- Reserve Bank of India, Act, 1934 - Companies Act, 1956
Housing Finance Companies	- National Housing Bank (NHB) - Ministry of Corporate Affairs	- Reserve Bank of India, Act, 1934 - National Housing Bank Act, 1987 Companies Act, 1956
Mutual Funds	- Securities and Exchange Board of India (SEBI)	- Securities and Exchange Board of India (SEBI) Act, 1992
Insurance Companies	- Insurance Regulatory and Development Authority (IRDA)	- Insurance Regulatory and Development Authority (IRDA) Act, 1999

Commercial banks are the dominant institutions in the Indian financial landscape. According to Committee on Financial Sector Assessment, "Though public sector banks (PSBs) account for around 70 percent of commercial banking assets, competition in the banking sector has increased in recent years with the emergence of private players as also with greater private shareholding of PSBs. Listing of PSBs on stock exchanges and increased private shareholding have also added to competition. The new private banks which accounted for 2.6 percent of the commercial banking sector in March 1997 have developed rapidly and accounted for nearly 17 percent of the commercial banking assets by end-March 2008. Together with cooperative banks, the banking sector accounts for nearly 70 per cent of the total assets of Indian financial institutions". [2]

9.3 Foreign Direct Investment (FDI) in Financial Services

Government of India has put in place a policy framework on FDI, which is transparent, predictable and easily comprehensible. This framework is embodied in the Circular on Consolidated FDI Policy, which is updated from time-to-time to capture and keep pace with the regulatory changes, effected in the interregnum. Foreign investment in financial services, other than those indicated in Table 9.3, requires prior approval of the Government.

Table 9.3: FDI in Financial Services

Sector/Activity	Percent of Equity/FDI Cap	Entry Route
1. Asset Reconstruction Companies		
Asset Reconstruction Company' (ARC) means a company registered with the Reserve Bank of India under Section 3 of the Securitisation and Reconstruction of Financial Assets and Enforcement of Security Interest Act, 2002 (SARFAESI Act).	100 %	Automatic
2. Banking: Private sector	74 %	Automatic up to 49%. Government route beyond 49% and up to 74%.
3. Banking: Public Sector		
Banking-Public Sector subject to Banking Companies (Acquisition and Transfer of Undertakings) Acts, 1970/80. This ceiling (20 percent) is also applicable to the State Bank of India and its associate banks.	20 %	Government
4. Credit Information Companies (CIC)	100 %	Automatic
5. Infrastructure Companies in Securities Markets		
Infrastructure companies in securities markets, namely, stock exchanges, depositories and clearing corporations, in compliance with SEBI Regulations.	49 %	Automatic
6. Insurance.		
• Insurance company. • Insurance brokers.	49 %	Automatic

• Third party administrators. • Surveyors and loss assessors. • Other insurance intermediaries appointed under the provisions of Insurance Regulatory and Development Authority Act, 1999.		
7. Pension Sector	49 %	Automatic
8. Power Exchanges		
Power exchanges registered under the Central Electricity Regulatory Commission (Power Market) Regulations, 2010.	49 %	Automatic
9. White Label ATM Operations	100 %	Automatic
10. Non-banking Finance Companies (NBFCs)		
Foreign investment in NBFCs is allowed under the automatic route in only the following activities: • Merchant banking. • Under writing. • Portfolio management services. • Investment advisory services. • Financial consultancy. • Stock broking. • Asset management. • Venture capital. • Custodian services. • Factoring. • Credit rating agencies. • Leasing and finance. • Housing finance. • Forex broking. • Credit card business. • Money changing business. • Micro credit. • Rural credit.	100 %	Automatic

Source: Government of India, Ministry of Commerce and Industry, Department of Industrial Policy and Promotion, *Consolidated FDI Policy* (effective from June 7, 2016).

Endnotes

1. Government of India, Planning Commission, *Twelfth Five Year Plan* (2012-17), Volume I, Chapter 2, paras 2.78 and 2.79.
2. Reserve Bank of India, *Committee on Financial Sector Assessment* (Chairman: Rakesh Mohan), March 2009, Volume II, p. 64.

10

Reserve Bank of India:
Functions and Changing Role

There is only one central bank in a country whose main function is to control the operations of the rest of the banking system. Reserve Bank of India (RBI), the central bank of India, is the apex institution responsible for managing and supervising the monetary and financial system of the economy.

10.1 Establishment and Early History of RBI

The Imperial Bank of India, which emerged as a consequence of the amalgamation of three Presidency Banks of Bengal, Bombay and Madras in 1921, assumed certain central banking functions except currency management. The control of currency management continued to be with the Government of India in order to ensure that the central banking entity did not appropriate powers greater than those mandated by the political authority. The Reserve Bank of India Act was placed on the statute book on March 6, 1934. The RBI commenced operations on April 1, 1935 and was nationalised on January 1, 1949. The head office of the Bank is in Mumbai and its executive head is called the Governor.

The objective of establishing the RBI, as stated in the preamble to the RBI Act 1934, was to "regulate the issue of bank notes and the keeping of the reserves with a view to securing monetary stability in India and generally to operate the currency and credit system of the country to its advantage". The Bank's functions as laid down in the statutes were: (a) issue of currency (b) banker to Government; and (c) banker to other banks. Except in the sphere of agriculture, the Bank was not entrusted with any great promotional role and that too on a limited scale.

Central banks occupy a pivotal position in the institutional fabric of an economy. The functions of a modern central bank are vastly different from what was expected from the early central banks founded in Europe in the 17th century. The evolution of central banking in the Indian context has its own specificity. The RBI, while discharging its statutory responsibilities, has played a crucial role in the nation building process, particularly in the development of the financial sector. In fact, institution building constitutes a distinguishing feature of central banking in India.

10.2 Functions of RBI

RBI performs all the major functions of a central bank and these are discussed below.

10.2.1 Sole Currency Authority: The management of currency is one of the core functions of a central bank and one, which commands a high degree of public visibility.

This is especially so in a country like India, where people have a marked preference for cash transactions. The fact that there are a number of inaccessible pockets in the country adds to the already formidable challenges in managing currency in India.

In terms of the RBI Act, the affairs of the RBI relating to note issue and general banking business are conducted separately through Issue Department and Banking Department. The Issue Department is responsible for the aggregate value of the currency notes of the RBI in circulation from time to time and maintains the eligible assets for equivalent value. The mechanism of putting currency into circulation and its withdrawal from circulation (expansion and contraction of currency) is undertaken through the Banking Department.

Barring one-rupee notes and coins, RBI is the sole authority for the issue of currency in India. One rupee notes and coins are issued by the Central Government. However, their distribution to the public is the sole responsibility of the RBI. For the issue of notes, the RBI has a separate department, the Department of Issue. All the currency issued by the RBI is its monetary liability and is backed by assets of equal value.

Currency management by the RBI is currently passing through a modernisation phase. A number of significant steps have been taken in this sphere which includes the following.
1. Building up of the capacity of note printing presses.
2. Reforms in the operations of the Issue Department including in the note distribution network.
3. Introduction of new security features.
4. Shift towards higher denomination notes in circulation.

10.2.2 Banker to the Governments: Before the formation of the RBI, the Imperial Bank of India performed many of the functions as banker to the Government. With the establishment of the RBI, the Imperial Bank ceased to be the banker to the Government, but entered into an agreement with the RBI for providing its services as the sole agent of the RBI in places where it had a branch and there was no branch of the Banking Department of the RBI.

As the banker to the Central Government and to the State Governments by virtue of agreements entered into with them, the RBI provides a range of banking services for these Governments such as acceptance of money on government account payment/withdrawals of funds and collection and transfer of funds through different means. Sections 20, 21 and 21A of the RBI Act provide the statutory basis for these functions. The terms and conditions on which the RBI acts as banker to the Central and State Governments are set out in separate agreements, which the RBI entered into with these Governments.

Presently, RBI is the banker for all Governments in India (except Jammu and Kashmir). The RBI provides all those banking services to the Central and State Governments which a commercial bank ordinarily offers to its customers. The Governments keep their cash balances on current account deposit with the RBI and the latter carries out banking business involving receipts and payments of money on behalf of the Governments. The Governments are required, under agreement, to maintain a minimum balance with the RBI. It is the duty of the Finance Department of each Government to ensure that there are always sufficient funds in its bank account and that at no stage the cash balance falls short of the prescribed minimum.

10.2.3 Bankers' Bank and Lender-of-the-last-resort: Under the Reserve Bank of India Act, 1934 and the Banking Regulation Act, 1949, the RBI is vested with extensive powers of supervision, regulation, and control over commercial and co-operative banks. The regulatory functions of the RBI pertain to licensing, branch expansion, and amalgamation of commercial banks. The RBI calls for returns and other information from the commercial banks and periodically inspects their working.

The scheduled banks in India are required under law to deposit with the RBI a stipulated ratio (lying between 3 percent and 15 percent) of their total liabilities. These are compulsory reserves of banks with the RBI and are not available to them for meeting inter-bank clearing claims. The underlying philosophy of this statutory reserve requirement is that by varying it within limits, the RBI can use it as a weapon of monetary-credit control.

Reserves of the banks with the RBI may be used to meet the temporary cash needs of the commercial banks. Commercial banks are supposed to meet their shortfalls of cash from sources other than the RBI but in acute emergency they can approach the RBI for help and that is why the central bank is also called the lender-of-the-last-resort.

10.2.4 Controller of Money and Credit: Like other central banks, the core function of the RBI is to formulate and administer monetary policy to maintain the stability of the rupee. During Pre-Independence period, there was, however, no formal monetary policy formulation other than that of administering the supply and demand for credit in the economy. The Bank Rate [1], reserve requirements and open market operations [2] were the mechanisms for regulating the credit availability. The Bank Rate, as an instrument of control, was not used at all in this period, except once in November 1935 when the rate was reduced from 3.5 percent to 3.0 percent. The rate remained unchanged thereafter till November 1951. The RBI, however, employed the instruments of open market operations (OMOs) in a fairly substantial way. Although the RBI was vested with adequate powers to resort to the qualitative instruments, *viz.* selective credit control, no need was felt during the initial stages of its functioning due to the existence of price stability.

The RBI has multiple instruments at its command such as repo and reverse repo rates [3], cash reserve ratio (CRR), statutory liquidity ratio (SLR), open market operations, including the market stabilisation scheme (MSS) and the liquidity adjustment facility (LAF), special market operations, and sector-specific liquidity facilities. In addition, the RBI also uses prudential tools to modulate flow of credit to certain sectors consistent with financial stability. The availability of multiple instruments and flexible use of these instruments in the implementation of monetary policy has enabled the RBI to modulate the liquidity and interest rate conditions amidst uncertain global macroeconomic conditions.

An important function of RBI is to control money and credit in the country. The instruments of monetary control operated by the RBI may be classified into two categories: (a) quantitative or global or aggregative measures which affect the total amount of money supply and credit and (b) qualitative or selective measures which affect the allocation of bank credit among competing uses and users.

10.2.5 Controller of Foreign Exchange: The RBI is the custodian of the foreign exchange reserves of India. It manages exchange control and the external value of the rupee. The history of exchange control in India dates back to the outbreak of Second World War in 1939. The exchange control is operated in a manner so that the demand for foreign exchange is contained within the limits of its available supplies. In other words, the available foreign exchange is allocated among competing demands in such a way as to make its optimum use. The need for this control and planned use arises in view of the general shortage of foreign exchange reserves in most developing countries. All foreign exchange transactions made by the RBI are at the official rates of exchange.

The RBI has delegated considerable powers to the authorised dealers to release foreign exchange for a variety of purposes and has been focusing on the development of the foreign exchange market. In order to deepen the foreign exchange market, a large number of products have been introduced and the entry of newer players has been allowed. Additional hedging instruments, such as, foreign currency-rupee options have been introduced and authorised dealers have been permitted to use innovative products like cross-currency options, interest rate and currency swaps, caps/collars and forward rate agreements (FRAs) in the international forex market.

10.2.6 Source of Economic Information: The RBI provides, through its publications, useful data and information on various aspects of the economy, particularly monetary and banking activities. Three important and regular publications of the RBI are: (a) Reserve Bank of India *Bulletin* (Monthly), (b) *Report on Currency and Finance* (Annual) and (c) *Handbook of Statistics on Indian Economy.*

10.2.7 Promotional Role of RBI: Apart from performing the customary functions of a central bank, the RBI has played an important role in building, consolidating, and strengthening the financial infrastructure of India. It has also played an effective role in influencing the allocation of credit in favour of priority sectors. Commercial banking facilities have been extended to small towns and rural areas as a result of the policies of the RBI.

The RBI has paid special attention to the credit needs of the rural (agricultural) sector. Towards this end, the Agricultural Refinance and Development Corporation (ARDC) was set up as a wholly-owned subsidiary of the RBI in 1963. The National Bank for Agriculture and Rural Development (NABARD) is another example of the promotional role of the RBI in the agricultural sector. Similarly, the RBI promoted the cause of industrial finance by actively associating itself with such public sector undertakings as erstwhile Industrial Development Bank of India (IDBI). In the area of credit allocation, RBI has followed the policy of special consideration for priority sectors, like agriculture and small-scale industries, at concessional rates of interest and lenient collateral requirements.

10.3 Changing Role of RBI in the Financial Sector

Since the setting up of the Reserve Bank of India in 1935, its role in the financial sector and financial market development has undergone significant changes. Emerging primarily as a bank-based financial system, the development of financial structure in India has been to finance the planned development efforts. To this end, institutional development received considerable attention of the RBI. The broad-based development of the banking sector to meet short-term financing needs was supplemented by the setting up of specialised development finance institutions by the RBI to cater to long-term financing needs. Since the early 1990s, the introduction of financial sector reforms has provided a strong impetus to the development of financial markets. The introduction of market-based monetary policy instruments, the liberalisation of capital controls and integration of the Indian economy with global markets have exposed the country to potentially volatile capital inflows, posing new challenges and dilemmas for the RBI in monetary and exchange rate management.

The RBI has been suitably reorienting the regulatory and supervisory framework so as to meet the challenges of a new environment. It has been the endeavour of the RBI to develop a competitive, strong and dynamic banking system so that it plays an effective role in supporting the growth process of the economy. The emphasis has been on safeguarding the financial stability of the overall system through increased emphasis on prudential guidelines and effective monitoring, improving institutional soundness, strengthening the regulatory and supervisory processes by aligning with international best practices and by developing the necessary technological and legal infrastructure. While the approach towards the reforms has essentially been gradual and relevant to the context, consultative processes and appropriate timing and sequencing of measures have succeeded in aiding growth, enhancing efficiency, avoiding crises and imparting resilience to the financial system.

The role of the RBI in the financial markets assumed significance due to the following factors.

1. The primary interest of the RBI in financial markets is because of its criticality in the transmission of monetary policy. From an operational perspective, reliance on indirect instruments and money market operations for conducting monetary policy necessitated development of the money, Government securities and foreign exchange markets.

2. Financial stability has emerged as one of the increasingly important concerns for the RBI resulting in increased attention to financial market development. The money market is the focal point for RBI intervention for equilibrating short-term liquidity flows on account of its linkages with the foreign exchange market. The Government securities market has become the focal point for the entire debt market due to several considerations: (a) the fiscal deficit of the Government, both Centre and the States, continues to be fairly high, resulting in large market borrowings by the Central and State Governments. With the corporate debt market still in its nascent stage of development, the Government securities market is the largest component of the debt

market; (b) it serves as a benchmark for pricing of other debt market instruments and (c) it provides an efficient transmission channel for monetary policy.

3. Since the markets were repressed in several ways in the past by law, regulation and policies, the RBI has, therefore, been facilitating the development of markets by creating an enabling environment through legal changes, technological and institutional development and dynamic improvements in market micro-structure.

4. Technological infrastructure has become an indispensable part of the reform of the financial markets, with the gradual development of sophisticated instruments and innovations in market practices. The RBI has, therefore, taken active interest in developing appropriate technological infrastructure to facilitate market development in areas such as payment and settlement systems, delivery *versus* payment (DvP) and electronic funds transfer (EFT).

5. Modern financial markets are complex. The RBI, therefore, needs to equip and continuously update itself to perform its developmental and regulatory roles effectively. The process involves constant interaction with the global counterparts in order to identify best practices, benchmark existing practices in the Indian markets, identify gaps and take measures to move towards international standards, within the framework of India's unique country circumstances.

10.4 Financial Sector Technology Vision Document

The RBI released the draft Financial Sector Technology Vision document on May 6, 2005. It provided a broad overview of the thrust areas of the direction provided by the RBI in respect of IT for the financial sector for more than two decades and sets out a roadmap for 2005-08. The Vision document focused on the following:
- IT for regulation and supervision.
- IT for the financial sector.
- IT for Government-related functions.

The Vision Document envisaged emerging challenges in the form of implementation of standardisation across a variety of hybrid systems at different financial entities, need for decision support systems and the technology to facilitate risk based off-site supervision. It envisioned common inter-operable web-based structures for transmission of data relating to regulatory functions and the use of a single centralised database for all information, apart from hiving off the operation of non-critical functions by the RBI.

The Vision Document also visualised Institute for Development and Research in Banking Technology (IDRBT) which is to be a premier research institute, concentrating on research and development for the banking and financial sector, providing educational/training facilities and hiving off business related activities.

Recognising the requirements of IT for the financial sector, the Vision Document elucidated thrust areas of the RBI by providing generic information on various standards and approaches, IS Audit and requisite focus on business continuity plans. The Vision Document proposed that specific attention would be devoted to percolation of technology efforts to all types of banks and all sections of the customers in the banks with specific reference to the rural areas and the use of affordable technology products which can be easily used by the target clientele with inter-shareable resources.

The document also detailed the use of IT in the Government sector transactions (which has the largest potential to grow significantly in the years to come), with specific attention on the need for business process re-engineering, changes in rules and procedures for aligning them with e-governance in a manner so as to achieve implementable objectives.

Endnotes

1. Bank Rate is defined as the standard rate at which the RBI is prepared to buy or discount the bills of exchange or other commercial paper eligible for purchase under Section 49 of the RBI Act.
2. Open Market Operations refer to buying and selling of securities by the RBI, particularly from/to the scheduled commercial banks, as part of the policy to maintain orderly coordination in the securities market.
3. Repo (Repurchase Option) Operations: RBI is able to influence short-term interest rates by modulating the liquidity in the system through repo operations under the liquidity adjustment facility (LAF), reinforced by interest rate signals. RBI enforces the interest rate corridor defined by the reverse repo rate, i.e. the price at which it absorbs liquidity and the repo rate/Bank rate, i.e. the price at which it injects liquidity into the system. In other words, repo rate is the rate at which RBI repurchases government securities from banks. In return, banks get cash to meet their short-term requirements. When RBI wants to inject liquidity in the system it reduces the repo rate which also acts as the benchmark short-term lending rate. In view of the current financial turmoil, repo rate has been reduced from 9.0 to 5.0 percent since October 20, 2008. Reverse repo—which is a mirror image of repo—rate has been reduced from 6.0 to 3.5 percent since December 8, 2008.

11

Commercial Banks:
Post-Independence History and Reforms

Commercial banking in India during the pre-Independence period was largely characterised by the existence of private banks organised as joint stock companies. Most banks were small and had private shareholding of the closely-held variety. They were largely localised and many of them failed. They came under the purview of the RBI that was established as a central bank for the country in 1935. But the process of regulation and supervision was limited by the provisions of the RBI Act, 1934 and the Companies Act, 1913. The indigenous bankers and moneylenders had remained mainly isolated from the institutional part of the system. The usurious network was still rampant and exploitative. Co-operative credit was the only hope for credit in rural areas but the movement was successful only in a few regions.

11.1 Phase I: Early Years of Independence (1947-69)

As in several other developing countries, the financial system in India has traditionally been dominated by financial intermediaries, especially banking institutions. Banking in India has a long history and it has evolved over the years passing through various phases. At the time of Independence, the Indian banking system was weak. The entire banking sector was in the private sector and the credit requirements of agriculture and other needy sectors were ignored.

The period soon after Independence posed several challenges to the Indian economy including the virtual absence of institutional credit facilities in the vast rural areas of the country. Further, the non-availability of adequate assets made it difficult for people to approach banks. In 1951, India launched its First Five Year Plan (1951-56) which accorded high priority to the development of rural India, particularly agriculture. The All India Rural Credit Survey Committee recommended the creation of a State-partnered and State-sponsored bank by taking over the Imperial Bank of India and integrating with it the former State-owned or State-associated banks. Accordingly, an Act was passed in the Parliament in May 1955 and the State Bank of India was constituted on July 1, 1955. Later, the State Bank of India (Subsidiary Banks) Act was passed in 1959 enabling the State Bank of India to take over eight former State-associated banks as its subsidiaries.

During this period, the industrial sector claimed the lion's share in bank credit. Within the industry, the large-scale sector cornered the bulk of credit and the share of small-scale industries was marginal. There were many reasons for the dominance of large industrial companies in the banking sector. Firstly, many commercial banks were under the ownership/control of big industrial houses. Secondly, through common directors (called interlocking of directorship), many commercial banks were connected with industrial and business houses, facilitating the flow of credit to large industries. Thirdly, the established industrial houses could obtain industrial licenses easily and on that basis, appropriate long-term bank credit.

A disturbing feature of the banking policy during this period was the negligible share of agricultural sector in bank credit. This share hovered around 2 percent of total commercial bank credit. The privately-owned commercial banks were neither interested nor geared to meet the risky and small credit requirements of the farmers. Similarly, the share of other non-industrial sectors in bank credit was also low. Since the commercial banks were under the control of big industrialists, the lendable funds of the banks were sometimes used to finance socially undesirable activities like hoarding of essential commodities.

11.2 Phase II: From Nationalisation of Banks Till Initiation of Banking Sector Reforms (1969-91)

With a view to better aligning the banking system to the needs of planning and economic policy, the policy of social control over the banking sector began in 1967. The year 1969 was a landmark in the history of commercial banking in India. In July of that year, the government nationalised 14 major commercial banks of the country. In April 1980, government nationalised 6 more commercial banks. Leading commercial banks of the country were nationalised with the following objectives in view.

1. To break the ownership and control of banks by a few business families.
2. To prevent concentration of wealth and economic power.
3. To mobilise savings of the masses from every nook and corner of the country.
4. To pay greater attention to the credit needs of the priority sectors like agriculture and small industries.

With the nationalisation of these banks, the major segment of the banking sector came under the control of the Government. Massive expansion of the branch network that followed the nationalisation of banks resulted in large deposit mobilisation by banks, which helped in stepping up the overall savings rate of the economy. However, during this period, a major portion of resources of the banks were pre-empted at below market rates by way of directed credit and directed investments. Profitability of the banking sector was, therefore, affected. Banks were also saddled with large non-performing assets. Their capital base also became weak.

The nationalisation of banks was an attempt to use the scarce resources of the banking system for the purpose of planned development. The task of maintaining a large number of small accounts was not profitable for the banks as a result of which they had limited lending in the rural sector. The problem of lopsided distribution of banks and the lack of explicit articulation of the need to channel credit to certain priority sectors was sought to be achieved through nationalisation policy. The Lead Bank Scheme provided the blueprint of further bank branch expansion.

The course of evolution of the banking sector in India since 1969 has been dominated by the nationalisation of banks. This period was characterised by rapid branch expansion that helped to draw the channels of monetary transmission far and wide across the country. The share of unorganised credit fell sharply and the economy seemed to come out of low level equilibrium trap. However, the stipulations that made this possible and helped spread institutional credit and nurture the financial system, also led to distortions in the process. The administered interest rates and the burden of directed lending constrained the banking sector significantly. There was very little operational flexibility for the commercial banks. Profitability occupied a back seat. Banks also suffered from poor governance. Fortunately, for the Indian economy, quick action was taken to address these issues.

The biggest achievement of nationalisation was the reallocation of sectoral credit in favour of agriculture, small industries and exports which formed the core of the priority sector. Within agriculture, credit for the procurement of food grains (food credit) was a major item. Other agricultural activities preferred for credit included poultry farming, dairy, and piggeries. Certain other sectors of the economy which also received attention for credit allocation were: professionals and self-employed persons, artisans and weaker sections of society. Conversely, there was a sharp fall in bank credit to large-scale industries. However, the share of small-scale industry registered an upward trend.

Nationalisation of commercial banks was a mixed blessing. After nationalisation there was a shift of emphasis from industry to agriculture. The country witnessed rapid expansion in bank branches, even in rural areas. Branch expansion programme led to mobilisation of savings from all parts of the country. Nationalised banks were able to pay attention to the credit needs of weaker sections, artisans and self-employed. However, bank nationalisation created its own problems like excessive bureaucratisation, red-tapism and disruptive tactics of trade unions of bank employees.

11.3 Phase III: Banking Sector Reforms since 1991

The period beginning from the early 1990s witnessed the transformation of the banking sector as a result of financial sector reforms that were introduced as a part of structural reforms initiated in 1991. The reform process in the financial sector was undertaken with the prime objective of having a strong and resilient banking system. The progress achieved in the areas of strengthening the regulatory and supervisory norms has ushered in greater accountability and market discipline amongst the participants. The RBI has made sustained efforts towards adoption of international benchmarks in a gradual manner, as appropriate to the Indian conditions, in various areas such as prudential norms, risk management, supervision, corporate governance and transparency and disclosures. The reform process has helped in taking the management of the banking sector to the level, where the RBI ceased to micro-manage commercial banks and focused largely on the macro goals. The focus on deregulation and liberalisation coupled with enhanced responsibilities for banks made the banking sector resilient and capable of facing several newer global challenges.

11.4 Backdrop of Banking Sector Reforms

Until the early 1990s, the banking sector suffered from lack of competition, low capital base, low productivity and high intermediation cost. Commenting on the performance of the nationalised banks, the Reserve Bank of India observed, "After the nationalisation of large banks in 1969 and 1980, the Government-owned banks have dominated the banking sector. The role of technology was minimal and the quality of service was not given adequate importance. Banks also did not follow proper risk management systems and the prudential standards were weak. All these resulted in poor asset quality and low profitability". [1]

Prior to reforms, the Indian Government determined the quantum, allocation and the price of credit, a situation referred to as *financial repression* by some experts.

It was in this backdrop, that wide-ranging banking sector reforms in India were introduced as an integral part of the economic reforms initiated in the early 1990s. Reforms in the commercial banking sector had two distinct phases.

The first phase of reforms—implemented subsequent to the release of the Report of the Committee on Financial System (Chairman: M. Narasimham), 1992 (or Narasimham Committee I)—focussed mainly on enabling and strengthening measures. The Committee was guided by the fundamental assumption that the resources of the banks come from the general public and held by the banks in trust. These resources have to be deployed for maximum benefit of their owners, i.e. the depositors. This assumption automatically implies that even the Government has no business to endanger the solvency, health and efficiency of the nationalised banks. According to the Committee, the poor financial shape and low efficiency of public sector banks was due to: (a) extensive degree of central direction of their operations, particularly in terms of investment, credit allocation and branch expansion, and (b) excessive political interference, resulting into failure of commercial banks to operate on the basis of their commercial judgement and in the framework of internal economy. Despite opposition from trade unions and some political parties, the Government accepted all the major recommendations of the Committee some of which have already been implemented.

The second phase of reforms—implemented subsequent to the recommendations of the Committee on Banking Sector Reforms (Chairman: M. Narasimham), 1998 (or Narasimham Committee II)—placed greater emphasis on structural measures and improvement in standards of disclosure and levels of transparency in order to align the Indian standards with international best practices.

11.5 Objectives of Banking Sector Reforms

The key objective of reforms in the banking sector in India has been to enhance the stability and efficiency of banks. To achieve this objective, various reform measures were initiated that could be categorised broadly into three main groups: (a) enabling measures, (b) strengthening measures, and (c) institutional measures.

Enabling measures were designed to create an environment where banks could respond optimally to market signals on the basis of commercial considerations. Salient among these included reduction in statutory pre-emptions so as to release greater funds for commercial lending, interest rate deregulation to enable price discovery, granting of operational autonomy to banks and liberalisation of the entry norms for financial intermediaries.

The strengthening measures aimed at reducing the vulnerability of banks in the face of fluctuations in the economic environment. These included, *inter alia*, capital adequacy, income recognition, asset classification and provisioning norms, exposure norms, improved levels of transparency, and disclosure standards.

Institutional framework conducive to development of banks needs to be developed. Salient among these include reforms in the legal framework pertaining to banks and creation of new institutions.

11.6 Components of Banking Sector Reforms

With a view to overcoming several weaknesses that had crept into the system over the years and with a view to creating a strong, competitive and vibrant banking system, several measures, including the following, were initiated beginning the early 1990s. Banking sector reforms since 1991 have included, among others, the following.

1. Granting operational autonomy to banks.
2. Reduction in statutory pre-emptions so as to release greater funds for commercial lending.
3. Deregulation of interest rates.
4. Relaxation in investment norms for banks.
5. Easing of restrictions in respect of banks' foreign currency investments.
6. Withdrawal of reserve requirements on inter-bank borrowings.
7. Introduction of prudential norms in line with international best practices.
8. Allowing entry of new private sector banks and enhanced presence of foreign banks.
9. Allowing public sector banks to access the capital market and providing to them operational flexibility and functional autonomy.
10. Revamping of supervisory system for creating a sound banking system.
11. Strengthening corporate governance practices and disclosure standards of banks.

As a result of above measures, the size and structure of the banking sector has undergone a significant change. Financial repression has eased substantially with the deregulation of interest rates and substantial removal of credit allocation.

11.6.1 Deregulation of Deposit and Lending Interest Rates: Narasimham Committee-I had recommended that the level and structure of interest rates in the country should be broadly determined by market forces. All controls and regulations on interest rates should be removed.

The process of deregulation of domestic deposit rates began when banks were allowed to set interest rates for maturities between 15 days and up to 1 year subject to a ceiling of 8 percent effective April 1985. However, this freedom was withdrawn by end-May 1985 in the face of an ensuing price war. The process of deregulation was resumed in April 1992 by replacing the existing maturity-wise prescriptions by a single ceiling rate of 13 percent for all deposits above 46 days. The ceiling rate was brought down to 10 percent in November 1994, but was raised to 12 percent in April 1995. Banks were allowed to fix the interest rates on deposits with maturity of over 2 years in October 1995 which was further relaxed to maturity of over one year in July 1996.

In October 1997, the deposit rates were fully deregulated. Consequently, the RBI gave the freedom to commercial banks to fix their own interest rates on domestic term deposits of various maturities with the prior approval of their respective boards of directors/Asset Liability Management Committee. Banks were permitted to determine their own penal interest rates for premature withdrawal of domestic term deposits and the restrictions on banks that they must offer the same rate on deposits of the same maturity irrespective of the size of deposits was removed in respect of deposits of ₹ 15 lakh and above in April 1998 with the laying down of policy in this regard by the board of the bank. Presently, banks have complete freedom in fixing their domestic deposit rates, except interest rate on savings deposits which continues to be regulated and is currently fixed at 4 percent.

Prime lending rates of banks for commercial credit are now entirely within the purview of the banks and are not set by the RBI. The country has moved towards liberalised credit allocation mechanism and reduced direct control over interest rates by the monetary authorities. The purpose of deregulation is to promote healthy competition among the banks and encourage their operational efficiency.

11.6.2 Lowering of Bank Rate: In view of the importance of lower real interest rates in accelerating industrial growth and boosting India's competitiveness abroad, RBI reduced the Bank Rate [2] from 8 percent to 7 percent, effective April 2, 2000. It stood at 7 percent as in July 2016. (Trends in Bank Rate are given in Table 11.1).

11.6.3 Lowering of Cash Reserve Ratio (CRR): Scheduled banks in India are required statutorily to hold cash reserves, called cash reserve ratio (CRR), with the RBI. Increase/decrease in CRR is used by the RBI as an instrument of monetary control, particularly to mop up excess increases in the supply of money. This power was given to RBI in 1956.

Narasimham Committee I recommended that RBI should rely on open market operations increasingly and reduce its dependence on CRR. This would reduce the amount of cash balances of the banks with the RBI enabling them to increase their revenues through more investments. It proposed that CRR should be progressively reduced from the then existing level of 15 percent to 3 to 5 percent.

CRR was gradually lowered from its peak at 15 percent during July 1989 to April 1993 to 8.0 percent in April 2000. It stood at 4 percent as in June 2017. (Trends in CRR are given in Table 11.1). In this connection, the Ninth Five Year Plan (1997-2002) remarked, "the level of the cash reserve ratio (CRR) that is to be maintained by the Indian banks is considerably higher than the international levels which are specified for prudential reasons. Although in recent years there has been significant reduction in the CRR from 15 percent to 10 percent and also the interest paid on CRR deposits with the RBI has been raised from 3.5 percent to 4.5 percent, there is a view that the CRR should be reduced even further, preferably to 3 percent". [3]

11.6.4 Lowering of Statutory Liquidity Ratio (SLR): Apart from the CRR, banks in India are also subject to statutory liquidity requirement. Under this requirement, commercial banks along with other financial institutions like Life Insurance Corporation of India (LIC), the General Insurance Corporation (GIC) and the Provident Funds are required under law to invest prescribed minimum proportions of their total assets/liabilities in government securities and other approved securities. The underlying philosophy of this provision is to allocate total bank credit between the government and the rest of the economy. The assurance of a certain minimum share of bank credit to the government affects the borrowings of the government from the RBI and hence serves as a tool of quantitative monetary control.

The SLR provision has created a captive market for government securities which increases automatically with the growth in the liabilities of the banks. Moreover, it has kept the cost of the debt to the government low in view of the generally low rate of interest on government securities.

Table 11.1: Trends in Bank Rate, Cash Reserve Ratio (CRR) and Statutory Liquidity Ratio (SLR): Selected Effective Dates

Bank Rate		Cash Reserve Ratio		Statutory Liquidity Ratio	
Effective Date	Rate	Effective Date	Rate	Effective Date	Rate
28.11.1935	3.00	16.09.1962	3.00	16.03.1949	20.00
15.11.1951	3.50	29.06.1973	5.00	16.09.1964	25.00
16.05.1957	4.00	13.11.1976	6.00	05.02.1970	26.00
03.01.1963	4.50	11.06.1982	7.00	24.04.1970	27.00
02.03.1968	5.00	29.07.1983	8.00	28.08.1970	28.00
09.01.1971	6.00	04.02.1984	9.00	04.08.1972	29.00
31.05.1973	7.00	24.10.1987	10.00	17.11.1972	30.00
23.07.1974	9.00	01.07.1989	15.00	08.12.1973	32.00
12.07.1981	10.00	17.04.1993	14.50	01.07.1974	33.00
04.07.1991	11.00	11.05.1996	13.00	01.12.1978	34.00
16.04.1997	11.00	18.01.1997	10.00	30.10.1981	35.00
02.03.1999	8.00	20.11.1999	9.00	01.09.1984	36.00
17.02.2001	7.50	22.04.2000	8.00	06.07.1985	37.00
30.10.2002	6.25	02.10.2004	5.00	02.01.1988	38.00
30.04.2003	6.00	06.01.2007	5.50	25.10.1997	25.00
31.01.2007	6.00	17.01.2009	5.00	08.11.2008	24.00
15.07.2013	10.25	09.02.2013	4.00	11.08.2012	23.00
02.06.2015	8.25	27.06.2015	4.00	07.02.2015	21.50
05.04.2016	7.00	09.07.2016	4.00	09.07.2016	21.00

Sources: 1. Reserve Bank of India, *Handbook of Statistics on Indian Economy,* September 2016, Table 47 (excerpted).

Narasimham Committee I asked the Government to reduce the SLR from the then existing 38.5 percent to 25 percent over a period of five years. A reduction in the SLR levels would leave more funds with the banks which could allocate them to promote agriculture, industry and trade. The Committee further recommended that Government borrowing rates should be progressively market-related so that higher rates would help banks to increase their income from their SLR investments.

SLR was reduced from its peak of 38.5 percent during September 1990 and stood at 20.50 percent as in June 2017. (Trends in SLR are given in Table 11.1).

11.6.5 Organisation of Banking Structure: Narasimham Committee I proposed a substantial reduction in the number of public sector banks through mergers and acquisitions. The broad pattern should consist of the following.
1.   3 or 4 large banks which could become international in character.
2.   8 or 10 national banks with a network of branches throughout the country.
3.   Local banks whose operations would be generally confined to a specific region.
4.   Rural banks whose operations will be confined to rural areas.

Significantly, Narasimham Committee I recommended that RBI should permit the setting up of new banks in the private sector. It wanted a positive declaration from the Government that there would be no more nationalisation of banks. It further recommended that there should not be any difference in treatment between the public sector banks and the private sector banks.

It recommended that RBI should follow a more liberal policy in respect of allowing the foreign banks to open branches in India and they should be subjected to the same requirements as are applicable to the Indian banks.

In January 1993, RBI had issued guidelines for licensing of new banks in the private sector. It had granted licenses to 10 banks which are presently in business. Based on a review of experience gained on the functioning of new private sector banks, revised guidelines were issued in January 2000. Following are the major revised provisions.
1.   Initial minimum paid-up capital shall be ₹ 200 crore which will be raised to ₹ 300 crore within three years of commencement of business.
2.   Contribution of promoters shall be a minimum of 40 percent of the paid-up capital of the bank at any point of time. This contribution of 40 percent shall be locked in for five years from the date of licensing of the bank.
3.   While augmenting capital to ₹ 300 crore within three years, promoters shall bring in at least 40 percent of the fresh capital which will also be locked in for five years.
4.   NRI participation in the primary equity of a new bank shall be to the maximum extent of 40 percent.

11.6.6 Duality of Control: Narasimham Committee I recommended removal of duality of control over the banking system by the banking department of the Finance Ministry on the one hand, and by the RBI on the other hand. The Committee desired the RBI to assume full responsibility of overseeing the functioning of the banking system.

11.6.7 Abolition of Selective Credit Controls (SCCs): SCCs, introduced in India in 1956, pertain to regulation of credit for specific purposes. The techniques of SCCs used by the RBI include fixing minimum margins for lending against securities, ceiling on maximum advances to individual borrowers against stocks of certain commodities, and minimum discriminatory rates of interest prescribed for certain kinds of advances. SCCs have been used mainly to prevent the speculative holding of essential commodities like foodgrains to prevent price rise.

Selective credit controls have been abolished in the post-liberalisation period.

11.6.8 Managerial Autonomy for Public Sector Banks: Competition among the commercial banks has increased with the entry of private sector banks, permission to foreign banks to open up to 12 branches a year with effect from 1998-99 and relaxation of various restrictions on public sector banks which, *inter alia,* are now allowed to access the capital market to raise funds. This will dilute the shareholding of the Government.

Commenting on the emerging scenario, the RBI of India's *Report on Currency and Finance,* (1999-2000) observed, "The competition in the banking sector has so evolved in the recent years that the market structure of the banking sector has tended to be oligopolistic. While the number of banks is reasonably large, the dominance of public sector banks, and especially of a few large banks continues. Such banks accounting for large share of deposits and advances as market leaders are able to influence decisions about liquidity and rate variables in the system. But, even such banks may face challenges in the future and face tougher competition, given the gradual upgradation of skills and technologies in competing banks and the restructuring and re-engineering processes being attempted by both foreign and private sector banks". [4]

In the changed scenario, public sector banks will have to improve their efficiency. The highly regulated and directed banking system is now transforming itself into one characterised by openness, competition and prudence. This development conforms to the liberalisation and globalisation needs of the Indian economy.

The Government of India issued a managerial autonomy package for the public sector banks on February 22, 2005 with a view to providing them a level playing field with the private sector banks in India. Under the new framework, the Boards of public sector banks would enjoy more freedom to carry out their functions efficiently without any impediment. The functions, however, have to be in sync with the extant statutory requirements, government policy prescription and regulatory guidelines issued by the RBI from time to time. The revised guidelines allow the following to public sector banks.

1. Pursue new lines of business.
2. Make suitable acquisitions of companies or businesses.
3. Close/merge unviable branches.
4. Open overseas offices.
5. Set up subsidiaries.
6. Exit a line of business.

Similarly, these banks have been allowed to decide human resource issues, including staffing pattern, recruitment, placement, transfer, training, promotions and pensions as well as visits to foreign countries to interact with investors, depositors and other stakeholders. Besides, the Boards of Directors of stronger banks would have additional autonomy for framing their own human resource (HR) policies. Prescription of standards for categorisation of branches, based on volume of business and other relevant factors, have been left to the banks to decide. Public sector banks have been permitted to lay down policy of accountability and responsibility of bank officials.

The public sector banks (PSBs) continued to be a dominant part of the banking system. As on March 31, 2008, the PSBs accounted for 69.9 percent of the aggregate assets and 72.7 percent of the aggregate advances of the scheduled commercial banking system. A unique feature of the reform of the public sector banks was the process of their financial restructuring. The banks were recapitalised by the government to meet prudential norms through recapitalisation bonds. Divestment of equity and offer to private shareholders was undertaken through a public offer and not by sale to strategic investors. Thus, all the PSBs which issued shares to private shareholders, have been listed on the exchanges and are subject to the same disclosure and market discipline standards as other listed entities. To address the problem of distressed assets, a mechanism has been developed to allow sale of these assets to asset reconstruction companies which operate as independent commercial entities.

It needs to be noted that the turnaround in the financial performance of the public sector banks, pursuant to the banking sector reforms, has resulted in the market valuation of government holdings in these banks far exceeding the initial recapitalisation cost—which is something unique to the Indian banking system. Thus, the recapitalisation of banks by the government has not been merely a *holding out* operation by the majority owner of the banks. The Indian experience has shown that a strong, pragmatic and non-discriminatory regulatory framework coupled with the market discipline effected through the listing of the equity shares and operational autonomy provided to the banks, can have a significant positive impact on the functioning of the public sector banks.

11.6.9 Other Measures: Credit restrictions for purchase of consumer durables have been removed/relaxed. Similarly, coverage of priority sector has been enlarged by the inclusion of software, agro-processing industries and venture capital. These measures have given the banks the much-needed flexibility to manage their asset portfolios.

In response to reforms, the Indian banking sector has undergone radical transformation during the 1990s. Reforms have altered the organizational structure, ownership pattern and domain of operations of institutions and infused competition in the financial sector. The competition has forced the institutions to reposition themselves in order to survive and grow. The extensive progress in technology has enabled markets to graduate from outdated systems to modern market design, thus, bringing about a significant reduction in the speed of execution of trades and transaction costs.

In terms of the average capital adequacy ratio for the scheduled commercial banks, which was around 2 percent in 1997, had increased to 13.08 percent as on March 31, 2008. The improvement in the capital adequacy ratio has come about despite significant growth in the aggregate assets of the banking system. This level of capital ratio in the Indian banking system compares quite well with the banking system in many other countries.

In regard to the asset quality also, the gross NPAs of the scheduled commercial banks, which were as high as 15.7 percent at end-March 1997, declined significantly to

2.4 percent as at end-March 2008. The net NPAs of these banks during the same period declined from 8.1 percent to 1.08 percent. These figures too compare favourably with the international trends and have been driven by the improvements in loan loss provisioning by the banks, certain institutional measures, as also by the improved recovery climate enabled by the legislative environment.

The reform measures have also resulted in an improvement in the profitability of banks. The return on assets (RoA) of scheduled commercial banks increased from 0.4 percent in the year 1991-92 to 0.99 percent in 2007-08. The Indian banks would appear well placed in this regard too vis-à-vis the broad range of RoA for the international banks.

The banking sector reforms also emphasised the need to improve productivity of the banks through appropriate rationalisation measures so as to reduce the operating cost and improve the profitability. A variety of initiatives were taken by the banks, including adoption of modern technology, which has resulted in improved productivity. The business per employee (BPE), as a measure of productivity, for the public sector banks has registered considerable improvement.

The Indian experience has shown that a strong, pragmatic and non-discriminatory regulatory framework coupled with the market discipline effected through the listing of the equity shares and operational autonomy provided to the banks, can have a significant positive impact on the functioning of the public sector banks.

Commenting on the success of banking sector reforms, the Reserve Bank of India observed, "There is evidence to suggest that competition in the banking industry has intensified. Significant improvement was also discernible in the various parameters of efficiency, especially intermediation costs, which declined significantly. Profitability of commercial banks, on the whole, improved significantly despite a decline in spread and higher provisioning following the introduction and subsequent tightening of prudential norms". [5]

11.7 Credit Allocation Policies

The credit market, with commercial banks as its predominant segment, has been the major source for meeting the finance requirements in the economy, both for the private sector and the public sector enterprises. The year 1969 was a landmark in the history of commercial banking in India. In July of that year, the Government nationalised 14 major commercial banks of the country. In April 1980, Government nationalised 6 more banks. The credit policy underwent drastic changes after that historic event. For a few decades preceding the onset of banking and financial sector reforms in early 1990s, credit institutions operated in an environment that was heavily regulated and characterised by barriers to entry, which protected them against competition. The issue of allocation of bank resources among various sectors was addressed through mechanisms such as statutory liquidity ratio (SLR), Credit Authorisation Scheme (CAS), fixation of maximum permissible bank finance (MPBF) and selective credit controls. This regulated environment set in complacency in the manner in which credit institutions operated and responded to the customer needs. The interest rate played a very limited role as the equilibrating mechanism between demand and supply of resources. The resource allocation process was deficient, which manifested itself in poor asset quality. Credit institutions also lacked operational flexibility and functional autonomy.

11.7.1 Allocation of Credit between Government and the Private Sector: Commercial banks provide credit to the government in two ways. Firstly, they provide funds to the Central and the State Governments through investment in government bonds. The commercial banks (along with LIC, GIC, etc.) are part of the 'captive market' for government securities because they are statutorily required to invest a certain minimum proportion of their total assets in government securities. Commercial banks are subject not only to cash reserve requirements, but are also subject to statutory liquidity ratio.

Secondly, commercial banks also make loans and advances to public sector units. They also invest in market bonds issued by public sector enterprises. As a result of the increasing claim of government and public sector units on commercial bank credit, the share of private sector in bank credit has declined. The private sector has to rely more and more on equity and debenture capital to meet their needs.

11.7.2 Inter-sectoral Allocation of Institutional Credit: Sectoral classification refers to main sectors of the economy in terms of economic activity. These sectors are: (a) industry, (b) agriculture, (c) trade, and (d) miscellaneous services. Each such sector may be sub-divided into sub-sectors as, for example, industry into large scale industry and small-scale industry. In addition to sharing of resources between the private and the public sectors, a significant proportion of credit by commercial banks is earmarked for the priority sector. Priority sector comprises agriculture (both direct and indirect), small scale industries, small roads and water transport operators, small business, retail trade, professional and self-employed persons, state sponsored organisations for scheduled castes/scheduled tribes, education, housing (both direct and indirect), consumption loans, micro-credit, loans to software, and food and agro-processing sector.

11.7.3 Inter-regional Allocation of Credit: As regards inter-regional (i.e. State-wise) allocation of credit, there is a long-standing complaint of the poorer states that their share in total credit is meagre. Since most industrial and commercial activities are concentrated in developed states like Maharashtra, Gujarat and Karnataka therefore the flow of bank credit to these states is more, at least in terms of per capita credit allocation. In this context, it can be observed that credit policy has not been very successful in promoting regional balanced development of the country. With the new banking policy of the Government permitting private sector and foreign sector banks, the situation may worsen so far as backward states are concerned.

11.7.4 Priority Sector Lending: Directed lending through efforts such as the priority sector lending (PSL) programme of the Reserve Bank of India (RBI) have had a well-established history across many countries at different points in their development and have served a different purpose in each country. In India while priority sector focus has existed from the 1950s in some form or the other, the PSL programme in its current form was implemented by the RBI in 1974, when banks were advised to raise credit to specified priority sectors of the economy to the level of 33.3 percent by March 1979. Currently this number stands at 40 percent with the sectoral allocation specified in Table 11.2.

Table 11.2: Priority Sector Allocation of Credit

Sector	Percent of Adjusted Net Bank Credit (ANBC)	Remarks
Direct agriculture	13.5 percent	
Indirect agriculture	4.5 percent to qualify within agriculture and excess as part of the overall 40 percent target	
Small and medium enterprises (SMEs)	Within the overall 40 percent target	Sub-targets based on the size of the SMEs
Weaker sections	10 percent	Up to ₹ 50,000 for segments such as distressed farmers, scheduled castes (SCs), scheduled tribes (STs), and women

Source: Report of the Committee on Comprehensive Financial Services for Small Businesses and Low Income Households, (Chairman: Nachiket Mor), January 2014, Table 4.8.1, p. 118.

11.8 Regulation/Supervision since 1991 (Post-liberalisation Period)

The decade of the 1990s was a watershed in the history of the Indian financial system in general and the banking system in particular. Notwithstanding the remarkable progress made by the Indian banking system in achieving social goals during the 1980s, it experienced certain problems that led to decline in efficiency and productivity, and erosion of profitability. Factors such as directed investment and directed credit programmes affected the operational efficiency of the banking system. The quality of loan portfolio also deteriorated. The functional efficiency was affected due to over-staffing, inadequate progress in inducting technology and weaknesses in internal organisational structure of the banks. These factors necessitated urgent reforms in the financial system. Accordingly, a Committee on the Financial System (Chairman: M. Narasimham) was constituted in 1991 to look into various issues related to banking with a view to initiating wide ranging financial sector reforms. Following the Report of the Narasimham Committee, the RBI adopted a comprehensive approach on the reforms of the financial sector.

The Department of Supervision (DoS)—now called Department of Banking Supervision (DBS)—was set up within the RBI in 1993 to strengthen the institutional framework. A high powered Board for Financial Supervision (BFS), comprising the Governor of RBI as Chairman, one of the Deputy Governors as Vice-Chairman and four Directors of the Central Board of the RBI as members was constituted in November 1994.

Measures such as deregulation of interest rates, reduction of statutory pre-emptions such as CRR and SLR, and provision of operational autonomy to the banks were taken to strengthen the banks. Further, various prudential measures that conformed to the global best practices were also implemented. One of the major objectives of banking sector reforms has been to enhance efficiency and productivity through enhanced competition. Guidelines to facilitate entry of the private sector banks were issued in 1993 to foster greater competition with a view to achieve higher productivity and efficiency of the banking system.

11.9 Migration to Basel Norms

11.9.1 Introduction: Internationally, there were no explicit capital adequacy standards before the introduction of Basel I norms in 1988. The most common approach was to lay down minimum capital requirements for banks in the respective banking legislations and determine the relative strength of capital position of a bank by ratios such as debt-equity ratio, or its other variants for measuring the level of leverage.

In the autumn of 1974, the Bank of England began to conceptualise the formation of a G-10 group of bank supervisors leading to the formation of the Standing Committee on Banking Regulation and Supervisory Practices, or the Basel Committee, in December 1974. The initial mandate of the Committee was for sharing of and application of each others knowledge, rather than any comprehensive attempt to harmonise cross-country supervision. Nevertheless, it led to an unimaginable degree of regulatory harmonisation later.

11.9.2 Basel I Norms: In December 1987 International Convergence of Capital Measures and Capital Standards, i.e. Basel Accord (now Basel I) was achieved. In July 1988, the Basel I Capital Accord was created.

The major achievement of the Basel Capital Accord 1988 was the introduction of discipline through imposition of risk-based capital standards both as measure of the strength of banks and as a trigger device for intervention by supervisors under the scheme of prompt corrective action (PCA).

Over the years, however, several deficiencies of the design of the Basel I framework surfaced. The Basel I capital adequacy norms were criticised for the simple *one-size-fits-all* approach that did not adequately differentiate between assets that have different risk levels. Despite the amendment to the original framework in 1996, the simple risk weighting approach of Basel I did not keep pace with more advanced risk measurement approaches at large banking organisations. By the late 1990s, some large banking organisations, especially in advanced countries, had begun developing economic capital models, which used quantitative methods to estimate the amount of capital required to support various elements of risks of an organization.

The Basel Committee itself recognised the deficiencies in the Basel I framework. The rapid rate of innovation in financial markets and the growing complexity of financial transactions reduced the relevance of Basel I as a risk managing framework, especially for large and complex banking organisations. Various shortcomings also distorted the behaviour of banks and made it much more complicated to monitor them.

Given the financial innovations and growing complexity of financial transactions and also with a view to addressing the shortcomings of Basel I, the Basel Committee on Banking

Supervision (BCBS) released the New Capital Adequacy Framework for International Convergence of Capital Measurement and Capital Standards (Basel II) on June 26, 2004 to replace the 1988 Capital Accord by year-end 2007. Basel II norms aim at aligning minimum capital requirements to underlying risk profiles of banks. The framework was also designed to create incentives for better risk measurement and management.

11.9.3 Basel II Norms: While the Basel I framework was confined to the minimum capital requirements for banks, the Basel II accord expands this approach to include two additional areas, *viz.* the supervisory review process and increased disclosure requirements for banks. In terms of Basel II, the stability of the banking system rests on the following three pillars, which are designed to reinforce each other:

Pillar 1: Minimum Capital Requirements—a largely new, risk-adequate calculation of capital requirements which (for the first time) explicitly includes operational risk in addition to market and credit risk.

Pillar 2: Supervisory Review Process (SRP)—the establishment of suitable risk management systems in banks and their review by the supervisory authority.

Pillar 3: Market Discipline—increased transparency due to expanded disclosure requirements for banks.

The central focus of this framework as in Basel I, continues to be credit risk. In the revised framework, the minimum regulatory capital requirements take into account not just credit risk and market risk, but also operational risk. The measures for credit risk are more complex, for market risk they are the same, while those for operational risk are new. Besides, Basel II includes certain Pillar 2 risks such as credit concentration risks and liquidity risks.

Apart from an increase in the number of risks, banks are required to achieve a more comprehensive risk management framework. While Basel I required lenders to calculate a minimum level of capital based on a single risk weight for each of the limited number of asset classes, the capital requirements are more risk sensitive under Basel II. The credit risk weights are related directly to the credit rating of each counterparty instead of the counterparty category.

Basel II capital adequacy rules are based on a *menu* approach that allows differences in approaches in relationship to the nature of banks and the nature of markets in which they operate. The minimum requirements for the advanced approaches are technically more demanding and require extensive databases and more sophisticated risk management techniques. Basel II prescriptions have ushered in a transition from capital adequacy to capital efficiency which implies that banks adopt a more dynamic use of capital, in which capital will flow quickly to its most efficient uses. Unlike Basel I, Basel II was quite complex as it offered choices, some of which involved application of quantitative techniques.

The revised framework is designed to provide options to banks and banking systems for determining the capital requirements for credit risk, market risk and operational risk. It enables banks/supervisors to select approaches that are most appropriate for their operations and financial markets. The revised framework is expected to promote adoption of stronger risk management practices in banks. Under Basel II, capital requirements of banks will be more closely aligned with the underlying risks in the balance sheets of banks. One of the important features of the revised framework is the emphasis on operational risk.

Operational risk is defined as the risk of loss resulting from inadequate or failed internal processes, people and systems or from external events. This definition includes legal risk, but excludes strategic and reputational risks. Operational risk differs from other banking risks in that it is typically not directly taken in return for an expected reward but is implicit in the ordinary course of corporate activity and has the potential to affect the risk management process. The Basel Committee identified the following seven types of operational risk events that have the potential to result in substantial losses.

1. Internal fraud.
2. External fraud.
3. Employment practices and workplace safety.
4. Clients, products and business practices.
5. Damage to physical assets.
6. Business disruption and system failures.
7. Execution, delivery and process management.

The potential losses, in turn, vary according to the business line within the bank in which the event occurs.

Management of specific operational risks is not new. It has always been important for banks to try to prevent fraud, maintain the integrity of internal controls, reduce errors in transaction processing and so on. However, what is relatively new is the thrust on operational risk management as a comprehensive practice comparable to the management of credit risk and market risk. To manage operational risk, banks are gradually gearing to develop risk assessment techniques that are appropriate to the size and complexities of portfolios, their resources and data availability.

11.9.4 Implementation of Basel Norms in India: India has been adopting international best practices in the area of regulation and supervision with a view to strengthening the banking sector. Following the Basel Accord of 1988, the capital to risk-weighted assets ratio (CRAR)—which took into account the element of risk involved in both balance sheet as well as off-balance sheet business—emerged as a well-recognised and universally accepted measure of soundness of the banking system. Accordingly, as a part of banking sector reforms, India adopted the Basel norms in a phased manner. In fact, India went a step further and stipulated CRAR at 9 percent as against the international norm of 8 percent. Furthermore, India also prescribed the capital charge for market risk in June 2004, broadly in line with the 1996 amendment to Basel norms.

In order to ensuring migration to Basel II in a non-disruptive manner, given the complexities involved, a consultative approach was followed. The RBI released draft guidelines for implementation of Basel II in India on February 15, 2005. In terms of the draft guidelines, banks were required to adopt standardised approach for credit risk and basic indicator approach for operational risk. The standardised duration method would continue to be applied to arrive at the capital charge for market risk. Banks would need the RBI's approval for migration to advanced approaches of risk measurement.

With a view to ensuring smooth transition to the revised framework and providing opportunity to banks to streamline their systems and strategies, banks were required to commence a parallel run of the revised framework with effect from April 1, 2006. All scheduled commercial banks (except regional rural banks) were required to implement the revised capital adequacy framework with effect from March 31, 2007. However, Basel II framework in India became fully operational from end-March 2009.

Several measures were undertaken by the RBI to prepare the banking system to make a smooth migration to Basel II. Following the amendment to the Banking Companies (Acquisition and Transfer of Undertakings) Act in 1994, several public sector banks (PSBs) have raised capital both in India and abroad through global depository receipts (GDRs). Several PSBs have also raised subordinated debt through the private placement. Concurrently, a series of regulatory initiatives were taken by the RBI relevant for Basel II.

First, concerted efforts were made to ensure that the banks had suitable risk management framework oriented towards their requirements, dictated by the size and complexity of business, risk philosophy, market perceptions and the expected level of capital. Second, risk based supervision (RBS) was introduced in 23 banks on a pilot basis. Third, the RBI encouraged the banks to formalise their Internal Capital Adequacy Assessment Programme (ICAAP) in alignment with their business plans and performance budgeting system. Fourth, there has been a marked improvement in the area of disclosures, so as to have greater transparency in the financial position and risk profile of banks. Similarly, capacity building for ensuring the regulator's ability for identifying and permitting eligible banks to adopt internal ratings based/advanced measurement approaches was given due priority.

11.9.5 Migration to Advanced Approaches: Challenges: Having regard to the state of preparedness of the system, India has adopted only the simpler approaches available under the Framework. The RBI is yet to announce the timeframe for adoption of the Advanced Approaches in the Indian banking system but the migration to these Approaches is the eventual goal for which the banking system will need to start its preparations in all earnestness.

The migration to Advanced Approaches poses several significant challenges to the bankers and also to the RBI, being the banking regulator and supervisor.

First challenge is the availability of long time-series data for computing the risk parameters required under the Advanced Approaches. Good-quality, consistent and reliable data and information relating to the loan portfolios of the banks, as also sophisticated IT resources, are critical to the proper risk assessment under the Basel II framework. Data limitation is a key impediment to the design and implementation of credit risk models. This may prove to be a major challenge for the RBI and the banking sector, given the wide-spread branch network, though the increasing computerisation in the banking industry should prove to be of great help.

Second challenge is that the Advanced Approaches for credit risk and operational risk envisaged under the Basel II Framework require use of risk models by the banks. This, in turn, requires internal validation of these models by the banks themselves as also by the supervisors before the models can be permitted to be used for regulatory capital purposes. Such a validation process demands expert skills which need to be developed and nurtured.

Third challenge is that since Basel II Framework is primarily about ensuring robust risk management in the banks, its effective implementation, particularly the Advanced Approaches, will demand rapid and significant upgradation of skills, both at the level of the banking system as also within the RBI. In this context, banks are likely to face multi-faceted challenges, viz. assessing skill requirements, identifying and bridging the gaps, identifying talents, putting the available talents to optimum use, attracting fresh talents, and retention of talents. Banks would, therefore, need to pay special attention to strengthening their risk management infrastructure in all its dimensions, including the human resources.

Implementation of Basel II required closer cooperation, information sharing and co-ordination of policies among sectoral supervisors, especially in the context of financial conglomerates.

11.9.6 Basel III Norms in India: Capital Regulations: As per the circular issued by the Reserve Bank of India on March 27, 2014, it was stated that, "in view of the implementation of Basel III Capital Regulations, banks need to improve and strengthen their capital planning processes. While conducting the capital planning exercise, banks may consider the potential impact of the changing macro-economic conditions and the outcomes of periodic stress tests on the adequacy and composition of regulatory capital.

The capital requirements may be substantially lower during the initial years as compared to later years of full implementation of Basel III Guidelines. Accordingly, banks should keep this aspect in view while undertaking their capital planning exercise".

In terms of Basel III Capital Regulations issued by the Reserve Bank of India, the Capital Conservation Buffer (CCB) was scheduled to be implemented from March 31, 2015 in phases and to be fully implemented by March 31, 2018. However, it has been decided that the implementation of CCB will begin as on March 31, 2016. Consequently, Basel III Capital Regulations will be fully implemented as on March 31, 2019.

Implementation of Basel III framework will throw various challenges for Indian banks. The adoption of Basel III capital requirements by Indian banks would push down their return on equity (RoE) to an extent.

11.10 Challenges for the Banking Sector

Banking system in India has undergone significant transformation following financial sector reforms since the early 1990s. The thrust of the banking sector reforms was on increasing operational efficiency, strengthening the prudential and supervisory norms, removing external constraints, creating competitive conditions and developing the technological and institutional infrastructure. The impact of the reform measures is reflected in an improvement in profitability, financial health, soundness and overall efficiency of the banking sector. Banks have been able to maintain or increase their capital adequacy ratio, despite the sharp increase in their risk-weighted assets.

The Indian banking system is currently passing through a crucial phase. Although the banking sector has become strong, competitive, dynamic and resilient, it is faced with several newer challenges as a result of macroeconomic and financial sector developments, both domestic and global. The major issues/challenges faced by the Indian banking sector could be identified as follows:

1. Emergence of financial conglomerates, which has raised the issue of appropriate regulatory structure/arrangement.
2. Emergence of complex financial products, which pose several supervisory challenges.
3. Need to extend financial services to the large number of people who continue to remain outside the banking system.
4. Mobilising resources to sustain and even accelerate the current economic growth momentum.
5. Issues involved in allowing increased presence of foreign banks in India as the roadmap for foreign banks.
6. Progressive move towards fuller capital account convertibility, which will expose the banking system to greater risks and would require addressing certain issues in banking, including some regulatory and supervisory aspects.

In the banking industry, it is fast changing the way products are conceived, designed and delivered across channels and market segments. Today, technology enabled business models are disrupting the entire supply chain be it retail, corporate or government business. The emergence of third party aggregators for loans, personal finance management, rural banking products/services, payments etc. are making significant impact to our traditional business processes or models. With increasing adoption of technologies like mobility, cloud, social media, electronically transferable database etc., technology will continue to be critical in responding to customer expectations across identified market segments and creating the agility needed to respond to opportunities. In order to derive a competitive advantage, banks must therefore effectively leverage technology to deliver on fast-changing customer expectations, align with regulatory controls and compliances, and attract the tech-savvy Generation Y.

It is, therefore, critical for banks to increase their IT investments to align with new innovations in technology to meet their objectives. In this context, technology initiatives in the banking industry coupled with continued innovations by technology vendors will define a new growth path for the industry. In addition to IT innovations and applications, banks are also leveraging social media to reach out to the next generation.

To sum up, the process of financial development in independent India has hinged effectively on the development of banking system. Financing of emerging trade and industrial activities during the 1950s and the 1960s reflected the dominance of banking as the critical source. Functionally, banks catered to the needs of the organised industrial and trading sectors. The primary sector consisting of agriculture, forestry, and fishing had to depend largely on their own financing and on sources outside the commercial banks.

It is against this backdrop that the process of banking development was given impetus with the adoption of the policy of social control over banks in 1967, reinforced in 1969 by the nationalisation of 14 major scheduled commercial banks. Since then, the banking system has formed the core of the Indian financial system. Driven largely by public sector initiative and policy activism, commercial banks have a dominant share in total financial assets and are the main source of financing for the private corporate sector. They also channel a sizeable share of household savings to the public sector. Besides, in recent years, they have been performing most of the payment system functions. With increased diversification in recent years, banks in both public and private sectors have been providing a wide range of financial services.

Prior to reforms, the banking sector suffered from lack of competition, low capital base, inefficiency and high intermediation costs. Ever since the bank nationalisation of 1969, the banking sector had been dominated by the public sector along with a high degree of financial repression characterised by administered interest rates and allocated credit. Over the reforms period, the banking system has experienced tremendous growth in the sophistication and size of non-bank intermediation.

Banking sector reforms, introduced in the early 1990s in a gradual and sequenced manner, were directed at the removal of various deficiencies from which the system was suffering. The basic objectives of reforms were to make the system more stable and efficient so that it could contribute in accelerating the growth process. Banking sector reforms have supported the transition of the Indian economy to a higher growth path, while significantly improving the stability of the financial system. In comparison of the pre-reforms period, the Indian banking system today is more stable and efficient. However, the gains of the past decade have to be consolidated, so that these could be translated to drive the institutions, markets and practices into a mature financial system that can meet the challenges of sustaining India on a higher growth trajectory. The banks would need to reassess their core banking business to view how best they could undertake maturity transformation to step up the lendable resources in support of real economic activity.

With the entry of new private sector banks and increased presence of foreign banks, the Indian banking sector has become more competitive. Public sector banks have also been raising capital from the market and are subject to market discipline. Efficiency, productivity and soundness of the banking sector improved significantly in the post-reforms phase. Banks have increasingly diversified into non-traditional activities, as a result of which several financial conglomerates have emerged. This has posed several regulatory and supervisory challenges. Thus, while deregulation has opened up new avenues for banks to augment incomes, it has also entailed greater risks. The banking sector has witnessed the emergence of new banks, new instruments, new windows, new opportunities and, along with all this, there have been new challenges.

The focus of on-going reforms in the banking sector is on soft interest rate regime, increasing operational efficiency of banks, strengthening regulatory mechanisms and technological up-gradation. Banking sector reforms in India are grounded in the belief that competitive efficiency in the real sectors of the economy will not realise its full potential unless the banking sector was reformed as well. Thus, the principal objective of banking sector reforms was to improve the allocative efficiency of resources and accelerate the growth process of the real sector by removing structural deficiencies affecting the performance of banks.

Despite substantial improvements in the banking sector, some issues have to be addressed over time as the reform process is entrenched further. The discussion on banking developments revolves around on a wide range of issues including the following.

1. Overall redrawing of boundaries between the State ownership of financial entities and private sector ones.
2. Public sector character of the banking sector and efficiency.
3. Dilution of the government stake and its impact on the performance of the banking sector.
4. Corporate governance in banks and other segments of the financial system.
5. Transparency of policies and practices of monetary and financial agencies and accountability.
6. Prudential requirements of market participants together with comprehensive and efficient oversight of the financial system.
7. Maintenance of best practices in accounting and auditing, as also collection, processing and dissemination of symmetric and detailed information to meet the market needs.
8. Relevance of development finance institutions (DFIs).

The commonality among these concerns has given rise to a wide recognition and acceptance of having a set of international standards and best practices that every systemically important country should strive to foster and implement.

Endnotes

1. Reserve Bank of India, *Report on Currency and Finance*, 2001-2002, p. VI-1.
2. As the lender of the last resort, the RBI helps the commercial banks in temporary need of cash when other sources of raising cash are exhausted. The RBI provides credit to banks by rediscounting eligible bills of exchange and by making advances against eligible securities such as government securities. The lending rate for these advances by the RBI is called the bank rate which is a traditional weapon of control money supply. An increase in the bank rate would discourage commercial banks to borrow from the RBI and a corresponding increase in the lending rate of commercial banks to general public would decrease public borrowings from the banks.
3. Government of India, Planning Commission, *Ninth Five Year Plan* (1997-2002), Vol. I, p. 150.
4. Reserve Bank of India, *Report on Currency and Finance*, 1999-2000, p. IV-2.
5. Reserve Bank of India, *Report on Currency and Finance*, 2001-2002, p. VI-16.

12

Payment Banks

Globally, financial authorities have created room for the participation of non-bank institutions in enabling payments. In 2007, European Union (EU) adopted the Payment Services Directive (PSD) for a harmonised legal framework for retail payment services. The PSD contains both prudential requirements and civil law provisions pertaining to the various payment service providers and the payment services they provide. To promote competition, a new group of payment service providers, the so-called payment institutions, has been created. They can offer payment services without being a bank and do not have to cover the entire range of services provided by a bank. In addition, the rules pertaining to the execution of transactions have been clearly defined. In Japan, non-banks are allowed to provide funds transfers. In South Africa, non-banks can become designated clearing system participants and have full access to the clearing system provided that they meet the Central Bank's requirements.

12.1 Pre-paid Instrument Providers (PPIs)

In India, a class of companies—called pre-paid instrument (PPI) providers—has recently been introduced that are permitted to receive cash deposits from customers, store them in a digital wallet, and allow customers to pay for goods and services from their digital wallet. These companies are currently permitted to accept a maximum amount of ₹ 50,000 in their wallet from their customers and are required to maintain an escrow account with a scheduled commercial bank where these aggregate amounts received from customers are credited immediately upon receipt. PPIs are entities authorised by the Reserve Bank of India (RBI) under the Payment and Settlements Act, 2007. These players have enabled significant expansion of low-value payments services among individuals who hitherto have never used banking services.

Given all these developments, any financial inclusion strategy would not be credible if it did not envisage a clear role for independent non-bank participation in the provision of payment and deposit services.

PPIs have been provided relaxed know-your-customer (KYC) requirements for their customers in exchange for limiting the value of transacted amounts on a wallet to ₹ 50,000 and restricting cash-out on wallets to banking outlets alone. Recognising that not allowing cash-out represents a key limitation of the product, a limited pilot has recently been permitted to the PPIs for cash-out. While the restriction of transaction amounts may be justified given that the focus of PPIs is to enable payment services for unbanked individuals, these two measures do not provide adequate protection against anti-money laundering (AML)/combating financing of terrorism (CFT) risks. Given the growing spread of eKYC, it may be feasible for PPIs to benefit from this and have KYC standards at par with banks, particularly if the stipulation to obtain documentary evidence for current local address is removed for all providers, including banks.

As the PPI network is sought to be scaled up, the manner in which a customer is sought to be identified and authenticated so that repudiation and fraud risks are minimised, becomes very important. As in the case of KYC, Aadhaar is the crucial piece of infrastructure in this regard. If each of the payments points is enabled with an acquiring device with biometric capability, identification and authentication of the customer become very secure and concerns regarding AML/CFT are also addressed satisfactorily.

There is also the concern about the safety of funds being held by the PPIs that arises from contagion risk. If the sponsor bank fails for some reason then since the amounts held by the PPI with the sponsor bank are at risk, the amounts held by individuals with the PPI are also at risk and do not enjoy the benefit of deposit protection unlike the direct depositors of the sponsor bank itself. Such a nested approach creates opacity and screens the build-up of risk in the system. A PPI has to take a view on the riskiness of its sponsor bank that holds its deposit balances and the sponsor bank has to worry about the operating quality and the likelihood of a *run* on its partner PPI. All nested structures have this feature and there may be greater stability obtained from independent designs where the PPI deals directly with the RBI rather than through a sponsor bank.

Given these significant concerns with the current PPI model with respect to KYC, inability to pay interest on balances, and contagion risk; and taking into account the need to urgently provide access to payment services and deposit products to millions of individuals, experts proposed that a set of banks may be licensed under the Banking Regulation Act, which may be referred to as Payment Banks. Potential candidates for such a license could include separately capitalised subsidiaries of non-banking financial companies (NBFCs), existing corporate business correspondents (BCs), mobile phone companies, consumer goods companies, the post office system, and real sector cooperatives.

12.2 Payment Banks: Background

On September 23, 2013, Committee on Comprehensive Financial Services for Small Businesses and Low Income Households (Chairman: Nachiket Mor), was formed by the Reserve Bank of India (RBI). On January 7, 2014, the Committee submitted its final report. Among its various recommendations, it recommended the formation of a new category of banks called payments bank. On July 17, 2014, the RBI released the draft guidelines for payment banks, seeking comments for interested entities and the general public. On November 27, 2014 the RBI released the final guidelines for payment banks.

It may be recalled that in the Union Budget 2014-2015 presented on July 10, 2014, the Finance Minister had announced, "After making suitable changes to current framework, a structure will be put in place for continuous authorization of universal banks in the private sector in the current financial year. RBI will create a framework for licensing small banks and other differentiated banks. Differentiated banks serving niche interests, local area banks, payment banks etc. are contemplated to meet credit and remittance needs of small businesses, unorganized sector, low income households, farmers and migrant work force".

12.3 Guidelines for Licensing of Payment Banks

RBI released on November 27, 2014 the following guidelines for licensing of payments banks.

12.3.1 Objective: The objective of setting up of payments banks is to further financial inclusion by providing: (a) small savings accounts and (b) payments/remittance services to migrant labour workforce, low income households, small businesses, other unorganised sector entities and other users.

12.3.2 Eligible Promoters: Existing non-bank pre-paid payment instrument (PPI) issuers and other entities—such as individuals/professionals, non-banking finance companies (NBFCs), corporate business correspondents (BCs), mobile telephone companies, super-market chains, companies, real sector cooperatives—that are owned and controlled by residents; and public sector entities may apply to set up payments banks.

A promoter/promoter group can have a joint venture with an existing scheduled commercial bank to set up a payments bank. However, scheduled commercial bank can take equity stake in a payments bank to the extent permitted under Section 19 (2) of the Banking Regulation Act, 1949.

Promoter/promoter groups should be *fit and proper* with a sound track record of professional experience or running their businesses for at least a period of 5 years in order to be eligible to promote payments banks.

12.3.3 Scope of Activities: As regards acceptance of demand deposits, payment banks will initially be restricted to holding a maximum balance of ₹ 1,00,000 per individual customer. However, it may be raised by the RBI based on the performance of the bank.

Payments banks cannot issue credit cards. Payments and remittance services will be provided through various channels.

25 percent of the branches of a payment bank must be in the unbanked rural area. The bank must use the term *payments bank* to differentiate it from other types of banks. The bank will be licensed as payments bank under Section 22 of the Banking Regulation Act, 1949 and will be registered as a public limited company under the Companies Act, 2013.

12.3.4 Deployment of Funds: Payment banks cannot undertake lending activities. Apart from amounts maintained as cash reserve ratio (CRR) with the RBI on its outside demand and time liabilities, payment banks will be required to invest minimum 75 percent of their *demand deposit balances* in statutory liquidity ratio (SLR) eligible Government securities/treasury bills with maturity up to 1 year and hold maximum 25 percent in current and time/fixed deposits with other scheduled commercial banks for operational purposes and liquidity management.

12.3.5 Capital Requirement: The minimum paid-up equity capital for payment banks is ₹ 100 crore. Payments banks should have a leverage ratio of not less than 3 percent, i.e. their outside liabilities should not exceed 33.33 times their net worth (paid-up capital and reserves).

12.3.6 Promoter's Contribution: Promoter's minimum initial contribution to the paid-up equity capital of such payment banks shall, at least, be 40 percent for the first five years from the commencement of the business.

12.3.7 Foreign Shareholding: Foreign shareholding in the payment banks would be as per the foreign direct investment (FDI) policy for private sector banks as amended from time to time.

12.3.8 Voting Rights: The voting rights will be regulated by the Banking Regulation Act, 1949. The voting right of any shareholder is capped at 10 percent, which can be raised to 26 percent by RBI. Any acquisition of more than 5 percent will require approval of the RBI. The majority of the bank's board of director should consist of independent directors, appointed according to RBI guidelines.

12.3.9 Other Conditions: Operations of the bank should be fully networked and technology driven from the beginning, conforming to generally accepted standards and norms. The bank can accept utility bills. It cannot form subsidiaries to undertake non-banking activities. The bank should have a high powered Customer Grievances Cell to handle customer complaints.

12.3.10 Procedure for Application: In terms of Rule 11 of the Banking Regulation (Companies) Rules, 1949, applications shall be submitted in the prescribed form (Form III) to the Chief General Manager, Department of Banking Regulation, Reserve Bank of India, Mumbai. In addition, the applicants should furnish the business plan and other requisite information as indicated. Applications will be accepted till the close of business as on January 16, 2015. After experience gained in dealing with payments banks, applications will be received on a continuous basis. However, these guidelines are subject to periodic review and revision.

12.3.11 Procedure for RBI Decisions: An External Advisory Committee (EAC) comprising eminent professionals like bankers, chartered accountants, finance professionals etc. will evaluate the applications. The decision to issue an in-principle approval for setting up of a bank will be taken by the RBI. Decision of the RBI in this regard will be final.

The validity of the in-principle approval issued by the RBI will be 18 months. The names of applicants for bank licences will be placed on the website of RBI.

In February 2015, RBI released the list of entities which had applied for a payment bank licence. There were 41 applicants. It was also announced that an external advisory committee (EAC) headed by Nachiket Mor would evaluate the licence applications.

EAC submitted its findings on July 6, 2015. The applicant entities were examined for their financial track record and governance issues. On August 19, 2015, the RBI gave *in-principle* licences to the following 11 entities to launch payment banks:

1. Aditya Birla Nuvo.
2. Airtel M Commerce Services.
3. Cholamandalam Distribution Services.
4. Department of Posts.
5. FINO PayTech.

6.   National Securities Depository.
7.   Reliance Industries.
8.   Dilip Shanghvi, Sun Pharmaceuticals.
9.   Vijay Shekhar Sharma, Paytm.
10. Tech Mahindra.
11. Vodafone M-Pesa.

The *in-principle* license is valid for 18 months within which the entities must fulfil the requirements. They are not allowed to engage in banking activities within the period. The RBI will consider grant of full licenses under Section 22 of the Banking Regulation Act, 1949, after it is satisfied that the conditions have been fulfilled.

On February 28, 2015, during the presentation of the Union Budget it was announced that India Post [1] will use its large network to run payment banks. On June 1, 2016, Union Cabinet cleared the proposal to set up postal payment banks. There are 1,54,000 post offices in the country out of which 1,39,000 are in rural areas. 650 branches of postal payment banks will be established in the country and linked to rural post offices. By September 2017, all 650 branches of postal payment banks will become operational.

Endnote

1.   Department of Posts (India Post) is a department of the Ministry of Communications and Information Technology, Government of India. Postal services in India have touched the lives of every citizen for more than 150 years, be it through mails, banking, insurance, money transfer or retail services.

13

Foreign Banks in India

13.1 Role of Foreign Banks

It is now widely believed that for financial institutions to operate efficiently, there is a need to maintain competitive conditions. The empirical and theoretical literature in banking also suggests that a competitive banking system is more efficient. It has therefore, been the endeavour of the Government and the Reserve Bank of India (RBI) to enhance competition through entry of new private sector banks, increased presence of foreign banks and provision of operational flexibility to public sector banks. To diversify ownership, public sector banks were allowed to raise funds from the capital markets, subject to the Government shareholding being retained at 51 percent. Various other restrictions hindering the competitive process have also been, by and large, phased out. As on December 31, 2015, there were 46 foreign banks operating in India with 325 branches.

In recognition of the emergence of foreign banks as key vehicles in the international integration of the financial systems, a liberalised policy towards foreign banks' entry has become a high priority in policymakers' agenda in various countries in recent years. Liberalisation of financial services by allowing foreign financial institutions to participate in the domestic market improves competition, thereby facilitating better and cheaper financial intermediation. Apart from increasing competition and efficiency through infusion of technology and skill management, some of the other benefits of foreign banks' entry are said to include introduction of superior risk management practices and stronger capital base, which is also less sensitive to host country's business cycle.

India also liberalised the entry of foreign banks in the post-reform period. In the roadmap by the RBI released in February 2005, the opening up of the domestic banking sector to foreign banks was envisioned in two phases. The first phase envisaged that foreign banks wishing to establish presence in India for the first time could either choose to operate through branch presence or set up a 100 percent wholly owned subsidiary (WOS) following the one-mode presence criterion. In the second phase (April 2009 onwards), the policy on foreign banks is to be taken up for a review. At that stage, various issues associated with the increased presence of foreign banks such as impact on the domestic banks, supervisory and regulatory challenges in view of their sophisticated operations and their involvement in complex and sophisticated products, financial inclusion, credit to agriculture and SMEs, and public policy on credit delivery, cost and allocation would need to be weighed. The issues relating to co-ordination between home and host countries regulators would also pose a challenge.

RBI released the framework for setting up of wholly owned subsidiaries (WOS) by foreign banks in India on November 6, 2013. The policy framework is guided by the two cardinal principles of reciprocity and single mode of presence. As a locally incorporated bank, the WOSs will be given near national treatment which will enable them to open branches anywhere in the country at par with Indian banks (except in certain sensitive areas where the Reserve Bank's prior approval would be required). The policy incentivises the existing foreign bank branches to convert into WOS due to the attractiveness of near national treatment. Such conversion is also desirable from the financial stability perspective, factoring in the lessons from the global economic crisis.

13.2 Advantages and Disadvantages of Foreign Banks

The following are the commonly highlighted benefits of foreign bank entry.

First, it heightens competition and promotes efficiency leading to decline in costs or increase in productivity. When a foreign bank enters through greenfield investment and sets up a *de novo* institution, the increase in the number of banks in the host country directly enhances competition. Entry through merger and acquisition, which infuses more skilled management and upgrade governance through introducing more advanced systems and risk management, may force other banks in the host country to improve their efficiency in order to protect their market shares.

Second, entry of foreign banks improves credit allocation, as in making credit decisions, they apply formal credit standards and risk-adjusted pricing and are not influenced by other considerations.

Third, foreign banks help in the development of local financial markets since they have both the incentives and the expertise to develop certain segments of local market, such as funding, derivatives and securities markets. Foreign banks that lack a branch network to guarantee deposit financing of their activities are more likely to turn to the inter-bank market. Foreign banks can also contribute by bringing professional expertise to the local foreign currency markets. They often try to create markets or gain market share through product innovation, especially by offering a variety of new financial services to corporate clients, including structured products.

Fourth, the overall soundness of domestic financial system is enhanced by introducing the risk management practices of the foreign parent banks. Based on tighter credit review policies and practices, they adopt more aggressive measures to address asset quality deterioration and limit the build-up of non-performing assets in the financial system.

Fifth, foreign banks may exert a stabilising influence in times of financial distress, as stronger capitalisation and the possibility of an injection of additional funds by the parent, if needed, reduces the probability of failure. For the same, foreign banks are less sensitive to both home and host country business cycles, and consequently, lending to local residents in the local market is likely to be more stable in times of stress than either cross-border lending or the lending of indigenous banks in the markets. Further, when the foreign banks continue to operate in a crisis, the probability of the system as a whole remaining functional, increases.

Sixth, there could be long-term benefits from lower cost structures in the banking system. Foreign banks, in general, are found to operate with lower administrative costs as has been found in Latin America and most of other developing countries. However, in some countries such as India, operating cost of foreign banks was found to be higher than that of domestic banks.

Seventh, foreign ownership usually involves the transfer of human capital at both the managerial and the operational level. Complementary to this is the transfer of *soft* infrastructure such as back office routines or credit control systems. Such transfers have gained importance to reap economies of scale through standardisation of processes.

There could also be several costs associated with the entry of foreign banks.

First, entry of foreign banks could also lead to concentration and loss of competition. In many countries, foreign banks entered the system mainly by acquiring existing domestic banks, while in some countries domestic banks consolidation and concentration occurred in response to foreign competition.

Second, though foreign banks entry may lower interest margins and potentially foster the process of financial intermediation, the impact would depend on the form it takes and may not benefit all borrowers. The benefits would depend on whether the lower spread is the result of a more aggressive pricing strategy across the board or the banks choosing to lend only to the most transparent segments where there is more competition or at least greater market contestability.

Third, the growing presence of foreign banks can increase the complexity of the tasks facing supervisory authorities and thus lead to regulatory conflicts. This could be a particular concern in countries where foreign commercial banks expand their operations rapidly in the area of non-bank financial services such as insurance, portfolio management, and investment banking. Given the complex structure of many internationally active banks, Integral issues within foreign banks are increasingly being shown to be of potential systemic significance.

Fourth, foreign banks expose the country to some downside risks/challenges attached with their entry. More strikingly, domestic banks in emerging markets generally incur costs since they have to compete with large international banks with better reputation, particularly in developing world.

Fifth, there is a general concern that as foreign banks have historically followed home-country customers or specialised in servicing corporate customers, their entry would lead to neglect of rural customers and small and medium sized firms. Another concern is that with foreign banks using the inter-bank market for much of their funding, local banks could divert their funds from domestic loans to the inter-bank market, thereby channelling fund to large corporate at the expense of small companies.

Sixth, it is also argued that the presence of foreign banks may not necessarily yield a more stable source of credit to domestic borrowers because foreign banks can, at times, shift funds abruptly from one market to another for risk management purposes. Literature also suggests that foreign banks will be more likely to shift their funds to more attractive markets during a crisis if their parent banks are weak.

Table 13.1 provides the list of foreign banks in India.

Table 13.2 provides a list of top 10 foreign banks in India.

13.3 Road Map for Foreign Banks in India

With a view to delineate the direction and pace of reform process in this area and to operationalise the extant guidelines of March 4, 2004 in a phased manner, the RBI, on February 28, 2005, released the road map for presence of foreign banks in India. The roadmap was divided into two phases.

Table 13.1: List of Foreign Banks in India

1.	AB Bank Ltd.	16.	DBS Bank
2.	ABN-AMRO Bank	17.	HSBC
3.	Abu Dhabi Commercial Bank	18.	JP Morgan Chase Bank
4.	American Express Banking Corp	19.	JSC VTB Bank
5.	Antwerp Diamond Bank	20.	Krung Thai Bank Public Co.
6.	BNP Paribas	21.	Mashreqbank
7.	Bank of America	22.	Mizuho Corporate Bank
8.	Bank of Bahrain and Kuwait	23.	Oman International Bank
9.	Bank of Ceylon	24.	Shinhan Bank
10.	Bank of Nova Scotia	25.	Societe Generale
11.	Barclays Bank	26.	Sonali Bank
12.	Calyon Bank	27.	Standard Chartered Bank
13.	Chinatrust Commercial Bank	28.	State Bank of Mauritius
14.	Citibank	29.	The Bank of Tokyo-Mitsubishi
15.	Deutsche Bank	30.	UBS AG

Source: Website of the Department of Financial Services, Ministry of Finance, Government of India.

Table 13.2: Top 10 Foreign Banks in India and their Branches (as on December 31, 2015)

S. No.	Name of the Bank	Number of Branches in India
1.	Standard Chartered Bank	102
2.	HSBC Ltd.	50
3.	Citibank N.A.	45
4.	Deutsche Bank	18
5.	DBS Bank Ltd.	12
6.	The Royal Bank of Scotland N.V.	10
7.	BNP Paribas	8
8.	Barclays Bank PLC	7
9.	Bank of America	5
10.	The Bank of Tokyo-Mitsubishi UFJ Ltd.	5

Source: Reserve Bank of India.

13.3.1 Phase I: March 2005 to March 2009: During the first phase, foreign banks were permitted to establish presence by way of setting up a wholly owned banking subsidiary (WOS) or conversion of the existing branches into a WOS. The guidelines covered, *inter alia*, the eligibility criteria of the applicant foreign banks such as ownership pattern, financial soundness, supervisory rating and the international ranking. The WOS was required to have a minimum capital requirement of ₹ 300 crore and maintain a capital adequacy ratio of 10 percent or as was prescribed from time to time on a continuous basis, from the commencement of its operations. The WOS was treated on par with the existing branches of foreign banks for branch expansion with flexibility to go beyond the existing WTO commitments of 12 branches in a year and preference for branch expansion in under-banked areas. During this phase, permission for acquisition of share holding in Indian private sector banks by eligible foreign banks was limited to banks identified by the RBI for restructuring. The RBI—if it was satisfied that such investment by the foreign bank concerned was in the long-term interest of all the stakeholders in the investee bank—permitted such acquisition. Where such acquisition was by a foreign bank having presence in India, a maximum period of 6 months was given for conforming to the *one form of presence* concept.

13.3.2 Phase II: April 2009 onward: Phase II commenced in April 2009 after a review of the experience gained and after due consultation with all the stakeholders in the banking sector. The review examined issues concerning extension of national treatment to WOS, dilution of stake and permitting mergers/acquisitions of any private sector banks in India by a foreign bank in Phase II.

The parent foreign bank will continue to hold 100 percent equity in the Indian subsidiary for a minimum prescribed period of operation. The composition of the Board of directors should, *inter alia*, meet the following requirements: (a) not less than 50 percent of the directors should be Indian nationals resident in India, and (b) not less than 50 percent of the directors should be non-executive directors.

Foreign banks which commenced banking business in India before August 2010 shad the option to continue their banking business through the branch mode. However, they were incentivised to convert into WOS. To prevent domination by foreign banks, restrictions would be placed on further entry of new WOSs of foreign banks/capital infusion, when the capital and reserves of the WOSs and foreign bank branches in India exceed 20 percent of the capital and reserves of the banking system. The initial minimum paid-up voting equity capital for a WOS shall be ₹ 5 billion for new entrants.

14

Regional Rural Banks (RRBs)

Regional rural banks (RRBs) form an important segment of the rural financial sector. They were conceived as institutions that combine the local feel and familiarity of the co-operatives with the business capabilities of commercial banks. This sector has an exclusive role in improving financial inclusion and catering to vital sectors like agriculture and allied economic activities. Public policy, therefore, aims at keeping this sector viable and strong through various forms of active intervention.

RRBs were introduced and promoted by the Government of India with the noble objective of promoting savings habits and providing credit delivery mechanism to the rural India. The target groups were small and marginal farmers, agricultural labourers, artisans and small entrepreneurs for development of agriculture, trade, industry and other commercial activities in rural India. RRBs have wide reach in rural India and with their region-centric banking activities and closer relationship with the local authorities and population, they were expected to provide necessary banking infrastructure. They have been successful in mobilizing small savings in the rural sector.

Setting up of RRBs in the mid-1970s was a major initiative to meet credit requirements of rural people. The RRBs are specialized rural financial institutions for developing the rural economy by providing credit to small and marginal farmers, agricultural labourers, artisans and small entrepreneurs. During the 40 years of existence of RRBs, several Working Groups and Committees were set up at various points of time to deliberate on issues relating to RRBs and suggest measures to address the same. The focus has varied over time depending on the immediate concerns and the prevailing policy regime. While some of the issues relating to RRBs have lost their significance over time, others have become more relevant.

14.1 Nature and Objectives of RRBs

Agriculture and rural sectors play an important role in India's overall development strategy in terms of income and employment generation and poverty alleviation. Great significance has, therefore, been accorded to developing appropriate institutions and mechanisms for catering to the credit requirements of these sectors.

Despite the measures taken by the Government of India and the RBI—including nationalisation of 14 major commercial banks in 1969—a large proportion of the rural poor continued to be outside the banking fold. A Working Group (Chairman: M. Narasimham) was set up in 1975 to explore the possibilities of evolving an alternative rural credit agency to benefit the rural poor. The Group recommended formation of a new set of regionally-oriented rural banks which would combine the local feel and familiarity of rural problems characteristic of cooperatives and the professionalism and large resource base of commercial banks. RRBs were set up as a sequel to this recommendation.

RRBs have a special place in the multi-agency approach adopted to provide agricultural and rural credit in India. These banks were established under the Regional Rural Banks Act, 1976 "with a view to developing the rural economy by providing, for the purpose of development of agriculture, trade, commerce, industry and other productive activities in the rural areas, credit and other facilities, particularly to small and marginal farmers, agricultural labourers, artisans and small entrepreneurs, and for matters connected therewith and incidental thereto".

The capital of RRBs is contributed by the Union Government, concerned State Government and a sponsor bank in the ratio 50:15:35. RRBs have played a key role in rural institutional financing in terms of geographical coverage, clientele outreach, business volume and contribution to the development of the rural economy.

As on March 31, 2013, 11 of the 64 RRBs continued to have accumulated losses to the tune of ₹ 1,012 crore. As in June 2017, there were 56 RRBs in the country.

Besides the RRBs, commercial and co-operative banks have been catering to the credit requirements of the rural sector. While the commercial banks, with their focus on profitability had certain limitations in accelerating agricultural credit, the cooperative banks efforts were also hampered by several financial weaknesses.

Though over the years the RRBs have been able to expand their outreach and business and meet the credit requirements of the poor, several weaknesses have emerged, eroding their profitability and viability. The recent focus of the Government of India on doubling the flow of credit to the agricultural sector has warranted a re-look at the relative roles of co-operative banks, RRBs and commercial banks.

As the very objective of setting up RRBs was to extend adequate credit to the rural borrowers and particularly the economically weaker sections, owing to their rural orientation, there is a growing realization that RRBs could be used as an effective vehicle for credit delivery in the rural areas. There is, therefore, a need to devise ways and means to improve the health and viability of RRBs so as to reposition them in the credit delivery mechanism in India.

14.2 Amalgamation of RRBs

RRBs have been in sharp focus over the last few years with several measures initiated towards strengthening them and making them vibrant channels of credit delivery, particularly for the rural sector. The most prominent of these has been the process of state-wise amalgamation of RRBs sponsored by the same sponsor bank. As a result of the process of amalgamation, initiated in 2005, the number of RRBs in the country declined from 196 to 96 at the end of March 2007 and further to 56 at the end of March 2015. The Gross NPA of RRBs stood at ₹ 7,907 crore as on March 31, 2013.

The structural consolidation of RRBs has resulted in formation of new RRBs, which are financially stronger and bigger in size in terms of business volume and outreach.

They will thus be able to take advantages of the economies of scale and reduce their operational costs. With the advantages of local feel and familiarity acquired by the RRBs, they would now be in a better position to achieve the objectives of rural development and financial inclusion.

14.3 Autonomy for RRBs

Further, measures have been taken to provide greater autonomy to RRBs and enlarge their business activities. A majority of the recommendations of the Task Force on Empowering RRB Boards for Operational Efficiency (Chairman: K.G. Karmakar) have already been implemented. RRBs have also been allowed to open currency chests, conduct State government business as sub-agents of sponsor banks, take up corporate agency business without risk participation for distribution of all types of insurance products and open foreign currency non-resident (FCNR) accounts, subject to certain conditions. The branch licensing procedure for RRBs has been simplified with powers now delegated to the regional offices of Reserve Bank of India. The branch licensing policy has also been liberalised and the norms for opening new branches in hitherto uncovered districts have been relaxed. As a result, there has been a rapid increase in the number of branches of RRBs. The spread of RRBs has also increased and at the end of March 2016, they covered 525 districts of the country with a network of 14,494 branches.

14.4 RRBs as Vehicles of Financial Inclusion

RRBs have the potential to play a greater role in financial inclusion primarily because of their strategic geographical location in remote places in the country. In certain parts of the country, e.g. in the states of UP, Bihar and North-Eastern regions, the banking system mainly exists in the form of RRBs. Recognising the importance of achieving inclusive growth in the country, the RBI has permitted banks to utilise the services of non-governmental organizations (NGOs), self-help groups (SHGs), micro finance institutions (other than non-banking financial companies) and other civil society organisations as intermediaries to provide financial and banking services through the use of business facilitator and business correspondent (BC) models. The BC model allows banks to do 'cash-in-cash-out' transactions at a location much closer to the rural population, thus addressing the last mile problem. However, customers in many parts of the country have to travel long distances, spend on transportation costs besides sacrificing their daily wages to visit the banks for doing their routine banking transactions and such inaccessibility contributes to the dormancy of many accounts in RRBs as well.

The objective of financial inclusion would be fully achieved if RRBs are able to bring banking to the door step of the customers just as the commercial banks have started taking such initiatives. It is here that the large scale usage of information and communication technology (ICT) solutions lends support. RRB presence in rural areas leveraged by ICT would considerably enhance their reach, and delivery of banking services to the remote corners of the country.

The Committee on Financial Inclusion (Chairman: C. Rangarajan), also emphasised the role of IT and banking correspondents on a larger scale for achieving financial inclusion. The Committee envisaged that RRBs may extend services to unbanked areas and increase their credit to deposit ratio. The need for setting target for microfinance and financial inclusion was also envisaged. The Committee also recommended 100 percent financial inclusion of the large number of hitherto excluded farm households in order to reduce their indebtedness to the unregulated/informal sector.

The Committee estimated that 51.4 percent of the farm households do not get any credit from formal or informal sources. The North-Eastern Region, Eastern Region and Central Region taken together, account for 68 percent of the farm households having no access to credit.

The reach of RRBs particularly in regions and across population groups facing the brunt of financial exclusion is impressive. In rural areas, RRBs account for a substantial 37 percent of total offices of all scheduled commercial banks. In semi-urban areas, their share comes to 15 percent. With the process of merger strengthening, to some extent, the viability of the RRBs and also because of the local feel and familiarity they command, RRBs are in a unique position to play a very useful role in financial inclusion.

The RRBs need to be encouraged and supported in their financial inclusion initiatives for, inter alia, the following reasons:

1. Have presence in most of districts of the country.
2. Stronger presence in NER, ER and Central Regions.
3. Essential particularly for the areas where the financial exclusion rate is quite high.
4. Higher concentration of rural and semi-rural branches.
5. Have potential for intake of many more small accounts.
6. Though there are 56 RRBs with relatively reasonable performance, their net worth is not high and thus majority of RRBs are not financially very sound.

14.5 Factors Influencing the Performance of RRBs

Since their inception, the financial health of RRBs has been indifferent. A host of factors, both internal and external, have had a bearing on the performance of RRBs. Some of the major factors that had a bearing on the performance of RRBs are as follows:

14.5.1 Area of Operation and Clientele Base: The RRBs are constrained in their operations by their limited area of operation. This coupled with their narrow base of business activities and the low clientele base, has resulted in high risk exposure of RRBs. The customers of RRBs comprise small and marginal farmers, small-scale sector, small transport operators, SHGs, etc., whose credit requirements are mostly small. RRBs are unable to cross-subsidise their lending business as they do not generally provide credit to wealthy borrowers with large needs, thereby affecting their capacity to earn higher incomes.

There has been an uneven growth of RRBs due to the diffusion in the perceived objectives of RRBs over time. Despite the pressures of credit expansion, improvement in recovery performance, profit orientation and strict compliances to banking norms, the general perception has been that RRBs have got only social objectives, without any viability consideration, which has to be changed.

14.5.2 Capital Base and Organisational Structure: RRBs as a group have a low capital base, and their authorised capital of ₹ 1 crore places serious limitations on their business size. Furthermore, in the case of some of the RRBs their deposit liabilities are very large compared to their capital base. In view of their low capital base, in the event of inefficient use/misuse of funds resulting in a financial problem, the stakeholders would have to bail out the bank.

The size of financial assets, as well as linkages which are necessary for effective banking services has been limited by the small organizational structure of RRBs. This has also come in the way of growth in business volumes and garnering a larger share of the rural financial market.

14.5.3 Loan Delinquencies: RRBs loan recovery rates have declined over the years, resulting in a large over hang of NPAs which has come in their way of recycling funds and increasing the flow of credit to the rural sector. The directed lending policy for RRBs has resulted in low quality of assets. This coupled with high cost of funds and below cost interest rates on loans has led to high accumulated losses and piling up of bad assets in the case of many RRBs.

It is noteworthy that the target rural group has been one of the weaker and lowest strata of the Indian society. Smaller and marginal farmers and agricultural labourers always run short of money even for meeting their daily needs of life. Given the fact that most the villages in India still does not have clean drinking water and sanitation facilities, top it with lack of basic health facilities, makes them one of the most vulnerable groups in India. In any nature-made or man-made calamities, they are the most affected. Thus, credit facilities taken by the rural poor are mostly not utilized for specified productive objective for which it was made available. For instance, when an agricultural labourer takes a small loan from an RRB for the purpose of buying a cow and small portion of it only being utilized for the stated purpose, with the remaining amount used for household needs or for tending the sick. Such misappropriation seems very common and ultimately the labourer who took the loan would be unable to repay it. This naturally leads to substantial non-performing and lost assets in RRBs.

14.5.4 Cost Structure and Poor Financial Management Skills: RRBs are characterized by high cost of servicing numerous small accounts and high wage cost. Furthermore, RRBs get credit from sponsor banks and refinance from NABARD at rates of interest higher than the market rates. This places limitations on their ability to reduce the rates they charge to their ultimate borrowers, although they are compelled to do so on account of competition from banks.

Poor financial management skills, coupled with pressures from various quarters (like sponsor banks) appears to have resulted in inefficient allocation of resources by RRBs which in turn is reflected in the high incidence of NPAs and parking of large funds with sponsor banks.

14.5.5 Staff Structure: Limited exposure and lack of appropriate training, has resulted in RRBs staff lacking the necessary skills and capacity to cater to the changing requirements of the rural sector. Furthermore, the ban on recruitment has also resulted in ageing staff structure constraining efficiency in operations. Uniform norms and personnel policies have been applied to RRBs through out the country ignoring local touch thereby causing staff unrest, poor industrial relations, innumerable litigations and lowering of staff morale as also their involvement with the development tasks.

The chairmen of most of the RRBs are from sponsor banks, which limits the freedom and decision making capacity of the RRBs. Even for small matters RRBs have to refer to their sponsor banks, which leads to delay in decision-making and reduces efficiency. Furthermore, the board of directors of RRBs may not always function effectively as some of the members do not have necessary skills and expertise to take important financial decisions.

14.5.6 Dependence on Sponsor Banks: Another weakness observed in the case of RRBs is their failure to adequately integrate with the financial markets of the country due to their heavy dependence on sponsor banks for financial/business initiatives. RRBs are also some times perceived as potential competitors, due to the presence of the sponsor banks in the same area of operation. Despite the best intentions at the policy levels in sponsor banks, the RRBs have suffered at the ground level wherever there has been any conflict of business interests of RRBs and their sponsor banks. RRBs have therefore, not been able to establish systems and procedures required for providing efficient services to their clients, as also for efficient management of their financial resources.

Besides the above, functioning of RRBs has also been affected by certain legacy problems and policy constraints. The administered interest rate regime prevalent in the system for a considerably long time influenced the performance of RRBs. These banks were required to lend at low interest rates as they were financing the weaker sections and at the same time allowed to pay a slightly higher rate of interest on deposits.

The RRBs were required to maintain their local character or flavour with a view to identifying more with the rural populace. This was initially embedded in the wage structure designed for these banks. However, the change in the wage structure of RRBs by bringing them on par with the commercial banks led to higher wage costs, thereby affecting the performance of these banks.

14.6 Restructuring of RRBs

In order to reposition RRBs as an effective instrument of credit delivery in the Indian financial system, an Internal Working Group on RRBs (Chairman: A.V. Sardesai) was set up by the RBI in February 2005 to examine various alternatives available within the existing legal framework for strengthening the RRBs and making them viable rural financial institutions. The Group, in its final report submitted in June 2005, made several recommendations for restructuring the RRBs. The main recommendations of the Working Group related to restructuring options, change of sponsor banks, minimum capital requirements, governance and management, regulation and supervision.

The major recommendations of the Group were as follows:
1. To improve the operational viability of RRBs, the route of merger/amalgamation of

RRBs may be considered along two lines: (a) merger between RRBs of the same sponsor bank in the same State, and (b) merger of RRBs sponsored by different banks in the same State.

2. A change in sponsor banks may, in some cases, help improve competitiveness, work culture and efficiency of concerned RRBs for which new banks, both public and private sector, could be considered.

3. Merged entities and existing RRBs that have accumulated losses can be capitalised to wipe out the losses and satisfy minimum capital requirement. The CRAR may initially be kept at 5 percent.

4. For those RRBs which may not turn around within a specified time limit, say 3 to 5 years, an exit route may be considered subject to extant legal provisions.

5. Process of appointment of Chairmen of RRBs may be re-examined to explore the possibility of appointing them from the open market through a transparent process.

6. Boards of RRBs may be strengthened by making them broad-based through inclusion of professionals such as agricultural experts, bankers etc.

7. An appropriate recruitment policy, providing for greater flexibility and freedom, may be required for RRBs.

8. An appropriate incentive structure, career planning, relevant training, especially in skill upgradation and information technology, be evolved for employees of RRBs.

9. It would be appropriate if both the regulatory and supervisory functions relating to RRBs are exercised by the RBI.

10. RRBs may be encouraged to actively consider distribution of products of mutual fund/insurance companies, rationalisation of branch network, participate in consortium lending within their areas of operations.

11. RRBs may be considered for currency chest facility and empowered to collect taxes by the State Governments.

14.7 Manpower Challenges of RRBs

Measures have also been taken to address the manpower challenges in the RRBs. It is known that RRBs do not have their own training establishments so far. The existing training facilities available for RRB staff are Bankers Institute for Rural Development, Lucknow, College of Agricultural Banking, Pune, regional training colleges of NABARD at Mangalore and Bolpur, and the sponsor bank training institutes. However, all these institutions (other than sponsor bank training institutes) provide training only to officers and not to clerical or subordinate staff.

The Committee to Formulate a Comprehensive Human Resource Policy for RRBs (Chairman: Y.S.P. Thorat), had, in its report recommended that RRBs should have an exclusive training cell within the Personnel Department at Head Office and bestow more attention to the training function. It also recommended that sponsor banks can consider earmarking in any one training institute in a state, at least one channel to cater to the training requirements of all RRBs within the state and/or the adjoining states.

14.8 Computerisation in RRBs

The need for computerisation in RRBs had been felt since long and some RRBs had been taking some steps in that direction. In July 2001, Government of India and NABARD advised the RRBs to initiate immediate steps so that head office, area office and a minimum of 50 percent of the branches were computerised in a phased manner in the next 5 years. Sponsor banks were also advised to formulate RRB-wise Action Plans, keeping in view the financial position of RRBs, infrastructure facilities available in their command area and the business potential of the RRB branches. Necessary support to implement the programme was also required to come from the sponsor bank.

NABARD made a beginning by extending support to select RRBs by providing PCs, peripherals, standard software packages as also customised MIS package and training inputs under its Swiss Agency for Development and Cooperation (SDC) programme. A review made by NABARD in respect of 152 RRBs in 2005 indicated that only 9 banks had reported achieving 100 percent computerisation. Most of the RRBs were lagging behind the target of computerising 50 percent of their branches. The Task Force on Empowering RRBs for Operational Efficiency (Chairman: K.G. Karmakar) had made the following observations regarding the computerisation scenario in RRBs:

1. Level of computerisation is far behind schedule.
2. Even RRBs of same sponsor banks although following the same technology, are at different levels of computerisation due to varied financial health, environment, local conditions which has become a problem when such RRBs have been amalgamated.
3. Computerisation needs both capital and recurring expenses which are beyond the capability of some of the banks.
4. RRBs, which have progressed well, have adopted a particular technology mainly of the sponsor bank and invested sizeable amounts.
5. A few RRBs reaped the benefit of hosting their own website by way of mobilisation of deposits from non traditional segments.
6. A few of them established direct links with money market operators for investments.
7. Internet facilities have been used for faster communication with techno savvy customers and other agencies.

These observations highlighted the varying status of RRBs with regard to computerisation.

The status of computerisation at the end of March 2007 as reported by 76 of the 96 RRBs to the Committee to Formulate a Comprehensive Human Resource Policy for RRBs (Chairman: Y.S.P. Thorat) indicated that 35 of the reporting banks had achieved 100 percent computerisation while 25 banks had achieved 50 to 100 percent computerisation.

14.8.1 Working Group on Technology Upgradation of Regional Rural Banks, August 2008: In RBI's Mid-term Review of Annual Policy for 2007-08, it was stated that in order to prepare RRBs to adopt appropriate technology and migrate to core banking solutions (CBS) [1] for better customer services, it was proposed to constitute a Working Group with representatives from RBI, NABARD, sponsor banks and RRBs for preparing a road-map for migration to core banking solutions by RRBs.

Accordingly, a Working Group (Chairman: G. Srinivasan) was set up with the following terms of reference:

1. To determine the nature of core banking solutions required for RRBs having regard to the range of their business and customer service.
2. To examine various options including extending core banking solutions of the sponsor banks to their RRBs with necessary modifications and firewalls.
3. To estimate the likely costs involved and funding and training arrangements that may be necessary.
4. To draw out a time-bound road map for implementation.

The Working Group was also requested to examine the possibility of using solar power generating devices for meeting the power requirements of RRBs, especially in remote areas.

The Working Group was of the opinion that RRBs cannot afford to remain isolated from the technological developments sweeping the banking sector. With the commercial banks racing towards a higher degree of technological sophistication, the RRBs would be required to adopt technology for improving the quality of their customer service. However, given the different levels at which the different RRBs are presently placed in regard to their status of computerisation, a "one strategy fits all" approach may not be workable.

The Working Group was of the view that as a matter of policy, all RRBs should begin moving towards CBS. The CBS in RRBs should be geared towards better management control and monitoring, wider range of services offered and enhanced level of customer satisfaction. Adoption of CBS would lead to uniformity in work environment, more informed decision making, centralised processing and better MIS and reporting and improved regulatory compliance.

The Working Group also examined the use of solar power devices such as solar photovoltaic cells [2] for RRBs, particularly in respect of branches located in remote areas which are not assured of continuous power supply. In this context, the experience of one of the RRBs in Uttar Pradesh, which has made a beginning in this direction, was also studied.

To sum up, in spite of the various measures taken by the Government and the RBI through social control and the nationalisation of major commercial banks in 1969, a large proportion of the rural poor remained outside the banking fold. Therefore, the Government of India promoted regional rural banks (RRBs) through the RRBs Act of 1976 to bridge the gap in the flow of credit to the rural poor. The RRBs have a special place in the multi-agency approach adopted to provide agricultural and rural credit in India. These banks are state-sponsored, regionally based and rural-oriented.

The renewed emphasis on agricultural and rural development by the Government of India would lead to a growing demand for different types of financial services in the rural areas, as financial needs of the rural economy becomes diversified. The present structure of rural credit may not be able to cater to the same. RRBs would be called upon to play a greater role in providing such services due to their rural character and feel. RRBs have to take over a larger share of credit disbursements calling for much larger resource mobilization, as also greater efforts for their institutional strengthening.

Endnotes

1. Although there is no formal definition of CBSs, the term has been in use during the last few years. The advancement in technology, especially internet and information technology, has led to a new way of doing business in banking. The technologies have cut down time, working simultaneously on different issues and increased efficiency. The platform where information and communication technology are merged to suit core needs of banking may be referred to as CBS. In CBS, computer software performs the core operations of banking like handling and recording of transactions, maintenance of passbooks, interest calculations on deposits and loans, maintaining customer records and generating reports and statements. The software is installed at bank branches and then interconnected by means of communication lines telephone, internet and satellite communication. It allows customers to transact with the bank from any branch if it has installed CBS. This new platform has changed the way of working of banks.

    In an ideal CBS scenario, all products, processes, channels and customer relationship management tools are integrated and administered via a central database of the bank with branches and channels as delivery points. This enables data integration for various purposes including regulatory reporting and internal MIS all at considerably lower cost. The new generation private sector banks were the first to adopt CBS technologies in India followed by a few public sector banks. Gradually, the same were adopted by most of the commercial banks as part of their computerisation processes.

    As per the Report on Trend and Progress of Banking in India 2006-07, the process of computerisation in commercial banks was now reaching near completion for most of the banks. Public sector banks continued to expend large amounts on computerization and development of communication networks.

2. Solar photovoltaic cells convert the sun's energy into DC electricity using silicon cells called solar cells. When sunlight falls on the solar cells, a DC voltage is generated across the cell. The solar cell is connected to a battery through a charge controller and electrical energy is stored in the battery. From the energy stored in the battery, either a DC load or an AC load through inverter is operated.

15

Urban Co-operative Banks (UCBs)

15.1 Importance of UCBs

The co-operative banking system forms an integral part of the Indian financial system. It comprises urban cooperative banks and rural co-operative credit institutions. Urban co-operative banks (UCBs) have a single-tier structure whereas rural co-operatives have a two- or three-tier structure. As on March 31, 2016, there were 1,574 non-scheduled UCBs in India with 10,091 branches.

The single tier urban co-operative banks (UCBs)—also referred to as primary cooperative banks—play an important role in meeting the growing credit needs of urban and semi-urban areas of the country. The UCBs, which grew rapidly in the early 1990s, showed certain weaknesses arising out of lack of sound corporate governance, unethical lending, comparatively high levels of non-performing loans and their inability to operate in a liberalised environment. Accordingly, some of the weak UCBs have been either liquidated or merged with other banks.

Co-operative banks in India are more than 100 years old. These banks came into existence with the enactment of the Agricultural Credit Co-operative Societies Act in 1904. Co-operative banks form an integral part of the banking system in India. These banks operate mainly for the benefit of rural areas, particularly the agricultural sector. Co-operative banks mobilise deposits and supply agricultural and rural credit with a wider outreach. They are the main source of institutional credit to the farmers. Co-operative banks are chiefly responsible for breaking the monopoly of moneylenders in providing credit to agriculturists. They have also been an important instrument for various development schemes, particularly subsidy-based programmes for the poor. Co-operative banks operate for non-agricultural sector also but their role is small.

Though much smaller as compared to scheduled commercial banks, co-operative banks constitute an important segment of the Indian banking system. They have an extensive branch network and reach out to people in remote areas. They have traditionally played an important role in creating banking habits among the lower and middle-income groups and in strengthening the rural credit delivery system.

Urban co-operative banks play an important role in meeting the growing credit needs of urban and semi-urban areas. UCBs mobilise savings from the middle and lower income groups and purvey credit to small borrowers, including weaker sections of the society. Scheduled UCBs are under closer regulatory and supervisory framework of the RBI.

Unfortunately, financial reforms have not impacted the functioning of co-operative banks. This was brought out clearly in the following observation of the Reserve Bank of India, "Since the introduction of reforms, there has been very little perceptible improvement in either stability or efficiency of co-operative banks. In particular, the asset quality and profitability of scheduled urban co-operative banks (UCBs) showed some deterioration in the reform period. Positive impact of reforms, as has been witnessed in the case of commercial banking sector, may take longer to get manifested for co-operative banks given the late start of the reform process in this sector". [1]

The financial reforms process initiated in 1991 has tried to achieve regulatory convergence among various financial intermediaries in view of their systemic importance. Therefore, the basic objectives and instruments of reforms for co-operative banks have been the same as for state co-operative banks (SCBs). However, given the special characteristics of co-operative banks, they have been extended certain dispensations in terms of pace and sequencing of reforms.

UCBs have grown rapidly since the early 1990s. During the phase of rapid expansion, however, the sector showed certain weaknesses arising out of: (a) lack of sound corporate governance, (b) unethical lending, (c) comparatively high level of loan defaults, and (d) inability to operate in a liberalised and competitive environment. The RBI, therefore, has been striving to harness the growth of UCBs with appropriate application of prudential regulation and supervision to safeguard the interests of depositors.

Keeping in view the weak financial position of many UCBs, the RBI has undertaken a series of measures directed towards strengthening of the UCBs. Since March 31, 1993, the UCBs have been advised to adhere to the prudential norms which include, *inter alia*, the following.

1. Applying capital adequacy standards.
2. Prescribing an asset-liability management framework.
3. Enhancing the proportion of holding of Government and other approved securities for the purpose of statutory liquidity ratio (SLR) stipulation.
4. Restriction on bank finance against the security of corporate shares and debentures.
5. Limiting the exposure to capital market investment.

In view of the challenges arising from the functioning of the UCBs for the financial system, the RBI appointed a High Power Committee (Chairman: K. Madhava Rao), 1999 to review the performance of UCBs and to suggest necessary measures to strengthen this sector. Based on the recommendations of this Committee, measures have been initiated to strengthen the existing urban banking structure.

15.2 Vision Document and Medium-Term Framework (MTF) for UCBs

Various entities in the urban co-operative banking sector display a high degree of heterogeneity in terms of deposits/asset base, areas of operation and nature of business. In view of its importance, it is imperative that the sector emerges as a sound and healthy network of jointly owned, democratically controlled and professionally managed institutions. In order to achieve these objectives, the RBI has taken a series of policy initiatives in recent years. The most significant initiative in this regard was the Vision Document and Medium-Term Framework (MTF) for UCBs released in 2005. With a view to protecting depositors' interests on the one hand, and enabling UCBs to provide useful service to local communities on the other, the medium-term framework (MTF) seeks to achieve the following objectives.

1. To rationalise the existing regulatory and supervisory approach keeping in view the heterogeneous character of the entities in the sector.
2. To facilitate a focused and continuous system of supervision through enhancement of technology.
3. To enhance professionalism and improve the quality of governance in UCBs by providing training for skill upgradation and also by including large depositors in the decision making process/management of banks.
4. To put in place a mechanism that addresses the problems of dual control, given the present legal framework and the time-consuming process in bringing requisite legislative changes.
5. To put in place a consultative arrangement for identifying weak but potentially viable entities in the sector and provide a framework for nursing them back to health including, if necessary, through a process of consolidation.
6. To identify the unviable entities in the sector and provide an exit route for such entities.

The above framework is implemented through the following measures:

1. A differentiated regulatory regime as opposed to a *one-size-fits-all* approach.
2. A two-tier regulatory regime: (a) simplified regulatory regime for unit banks and single district banks with deposits less than ₹ 100 crore, and (b) regulation for all other banks on the lines of commercial banks.
3. As the strategy to deal with UCBs may need to be State-specific, a State Level Task Force for Urban Co-operative Banks (TAFCUB) is to be constituted comprising senior officials from the RBI, State Governments and local/central co-operative Federations.
4. TAFCUB would be responsible for: (i) identifying weak but viable UCBs and devise a time-bound programme for revival; and (ii) recommending: (a) the nature and extent of financial support, (b) future set up of unlicensed banks, and (c) the manner and timeframe for exit of unviable banks.
5. To address issues/difficulties relating to dual control within the existing legal framework, it has been proposed to evolve a working arrangement in the form of memorandum of understanding (MoU) between the RBI and the State Government.

15.3 Regulation and Supervision of UCBs: Strengthening Measures

The regulation and supervision of the urban co-operative banks (UCBs) was brought within the ambit of the RBI's statutory control under the Banking Laws (as Applicable to Cooperative Societies) Act, which came into force from March 1, 1966. The regulatory powers conferred on the RBI with regard to co-operative banks are limited. While the principles of supervision with regard to co-operative banks have been formulated and implemented by the RBI in respect of UCBs under the Banking Regulation Act, 1949, the Act does not apply to primary agricultural credit societies and land development banks, thus leaving them under the regulatory purview of the State.

Instances such as the Madhavapura Mercantile Co-operative Bank's failure brought to the fore the need to have stringent regulatory control over the co-operative banking system. In order to strengthen the supervisory mechanism, the RBI extended the off-site surveillance system (OSS) to all non-scheduled UCBs having deposit size of ₹ 100 crore and above. A supervisory reporting system was introduced for the scheduled UCBs from March 2001 as a first step towards setting up of OSS for all UCBs. The capital adequacy norms were introduced in a phased manner from March 2002. Better risk management through avoidance of concentration of credit risk, off-site surveillance for non-scheduled UCBs and following up of know your customer (KYC) guidelines have also been introduced to strengthen the UCBs.

A total ban has been imposed since October 2003 on grant of loans and advances to directors of UCBs, their relatives and concerns in which they have interest with a view to preventing certain irregularities. The RBI has also directed that UCBs should undertake usual due diligence in respect of investments in non-SLR securities. The RBI introduced a new system of grading of UCBs in April 2003, which is based on their CRAR, level of net NPAs, record of losses and compliance with regulatory environment. Similarly, a system of supervisory rating for UCBs under the CAMELS model has also been introduced. Initially, it was implemented for scheduled UCBs but subsequently its simplified version was extended to non-scheduled UCBs in March 2004.

Despite the structural and cultural differences between UCBs and commercial banks, the above measures suggest that the RBI has been exercising its regulatory and supervisory powers to ensure that the co-operative credit structure is strengthened on the lines similar to the regulation and supervision of commercial banks.

The RBI is entrusted with the responsibility of regulation and supervision of the banking-related activities of UCBs under the Banking Regulation Act, 1949 As Applicable to Co-operative Societies (AACS). Other aspects such as incorporation, registration, administration, management and winding-up of UCBs are supervised and regulated by the respective State Governments through Registrars of Co-operative Societies (RCS) under the Co-operative Societies Acts of the respective States. UCBs with a multi-state presence are registered under the Multi-State Co-operative Societies Act, 2002 and are regulated and supervised jointly by the Central Government through Central Registrar of Co-operative Societies and the RBI.

Thus, current legislative framework provides for dual control over UCBs. For resolving problems arising out of dual control regime, a draft legislative bill proposing certain amendments to the Banking Regulation Act, 1949 (AACS), based on the recommendations of the High Powered Committee on UCBs, was forwarded to the Government. Pending the amendment to the Act, the RBI is entering into a regulatory arrangement with the State Governments through memorandum of understanding (MoU) to facilitate proper and coordinated regulation and supervision of UCBs. MoUs have already been signed between the RBI and three States that have a large network of UCBs, viz. Andhra Pradesh, Gujarat and Karnataka. As a follow-up to the signing of

MoUs, the RBI has constituted State Level Task Force for Urban Co-operative Banks (TAFCUBs) in these States.

15.4 IT Support for Urban Co-operative Banks (UCBs)

In today's financial systems, usage of information technology is fundamental to the survival and growth of the institutions. Current regulatory and supervisory compliance demands that the institutions have a very sound usage of IT systems for their operations.

The Vision Document for Urban Cooperative Banks (UCBs), released in March 2005, proposed signing of memorandum of understanding (MoU) between RBI and Central and respective State governments for establishing a consultative approach to supervision and regulation of UCBs. The Reserve Bank has so far signed such MoUs with 16 State Governments and the Central Government.

In terms of the MoUs, the RBI is committed to facilitate IT initiatives in UCBs. In furtherance of the commitment made under the MoUs, Governor announced in the Mid-term Review of the Annual Policy 2007-08, that 'a working group comprising representatives of the Reserve Bank, State Governments and the UCBs sector' would be constituted 'to examine the various areas where IT support could be provided by the Reserve Bank'. Accordingly, the RBI constituted a Working Group on IT Support for Urban Cooperative Banks (Chairman: R. Gandhi) on December 19, 2007 with the following terms of reference:

1. To review the current level and use of IT infrastructure in UCBs.
2. To structure a model/benchmark level of IT infrastructure for UCBs in general or for identified sub-groups of UCBs.
3. To prepare a roadmap of building such an infrastructure by the UCBs.
4. To identify areas and ways in which IT support may be provided by the RBI.
5. To make recommendations on the nature, scope and delivery mechanism for IT support to UCBs by the RBI.

15.4.1 Findings of the Working Group: There exists a wide disparity with regard to the usage of information technology by the urban co-operative banks. As on March 31, 2007, 16 out of 1853 banks had implemented core banking solutions, while about 50 banks did not even have computers. The remaining banks exist somewhere along the continuum between those that had CBS on the one hand, and those without even PCs on the other.

Most banks have solutions based on total branch automation. Several banks have implemented locally developed and customised application solutions. While some big UCBs have in-house IT wings to take care of development and maintenance of systems, most banks have outsourced these services.

Anecdotal evidences are there about the problems faced by these banks because of their small size, lack of adequate IT knowledge, lack of adequate IT savvy manpower and small time vendors.

They had suffered because small vendors could not provide satisfactory AMC and adequate post-implementation support for making changes in the software on account of their inability to retain skilled staff or sometimes because of the small scale of their operations, which rendered them unviable. Moreover, such legacy systems, set up by small vendors, were not standardized and therefore made migration to new systems more cumbersome and expensive than even acquiring a new one.

The acquisition of non-standardized software developed by local/regional level vendors is fraught with the following risks:

1. **Vendor Disappearance:** Vendors who developed software for small banks are often small-time operators and are not available for support, modifications and change management subsequently. Their mortality rate is often high. Eventually, the software became obsolete and redundant.

2. **Loss of Key Personnel by Vendor:** Some times, the vendor is available but the key personnel, who were involved in the development of software, are no more with the vendor. The vendor finds it difficult to extend the required level of the support without its skilled personnel as being small it has little flexibility in the absence of backup staff. As they often also do not follow standard practice of software development and documentation, the maintenance and updation of source-codes becomes difficult for the new personnel.

3. **Lack of Regulatory Compliance Modules:** Almost all the small-vendor developed software systems do not contain important regulatory provisions such as compliance to KYC norms etc.

The Group also observed that there were several large banks which had their own data centres and were offering core banking solutions to the smaller banks and that a few successful cases of sharing of data centre facilities among banks were also known. However, as awareness of IT among UCBs was not pervasive, several banks seemed reluctant to keep their data in the data centres owned by other bank/banks.

15.5 Working Group on Umbrella Organization and Revival Fund for Urban Co-operative Banks

There are a large number of urban co-operative banks (UCBs) in the country forming a heterogeneous group in terms of size and spread. Many of these banks are very small in size and reach. They compete with larger participants in the same banking space. Over the years, a number of UCBs have become weak and non-viable thus posing systemic risk to the UCB sector. They lack avenues for raising capital funds since they cannot go in for public issue of shares nor can they issue shares to members at a premium. At the same time, there are a number of UCBs in the sector that are financially strong and viable. Some sort of cooperative bonding and mutual support system could make the sector strong and vibrant. Looking at various successful federal models internationally, especially in Europe and US, a need was felt for an umbrella organization that would be in a position to channelize their resources, aggregate their needs and also lend credibility through mutual support in the financial market.

In this backdrop, RBI constituted a Working Group (Chairman: V.S. Das) on May 28, 2008 to suggest measures including the appropriate regulatory and supervisory framework, to facilitate emergence of umbrella organization(s) for the UCB sector in the respective states.

Further, the Standing Advisory Committee for UCBs opined that the Working Group may also look into the issues concerning creation of revival fund for the sector.

15.5.1 Terms of Reference of the Working Group:

1. To study the regulatory and supervisory structure of umbrella organizations of financial co-operative institutions/banks, as prevalent in other parts of the world, especially in relation to raising of capital and intra co-operative group support system.

2. To study the existing structure and legal framework for UCBs in India and to examine the need and scope for a federated structure/umbrella organization for UCBs at the state level.

3. To suggest appropriate supervisory and regulatory framework to facilitate emergence of such umbrella organisation(s) for UCBs, taking into consideration the international experiences and systems.

4. To study and suggest modalities for setting up an appropriate mutual assistance/revival fund for urban co-operative banks and the nature of support that could be provided by such fund.

15.5.2 Recommendations:

A. Need for Umbrella Organization: Urban Cooperative Banks in India cater to the financial needs of the middle and lower middle class people in metropolitan, urban and semi-urban centres. They operate on a standalone basis, unlike rural cooperatives in India, which have a three tier structure. These banks are large in number, though of varied asset size, ranging from small to medium. Although they compete with commercial banks, their share in total deposits is barely 4 percent. There is a significant part of the UCB sector that lacks professionalism and is unable to keep pace with rapid advancements in IT, modern banking systems and financial products. The sector also has significant number of banks which are weak and need financial support. There have been occasions when, due to contagion effect, banks have encountered liquidity problems. Being in the nature of cooperative societies, the UCBs' ability to augment their capital is also restricted, thereby hindering their growth.

The organizational structure of UCBs, their small size and limited area of operation add to their vulnerability. Further, in the wake of advances in information and communication technology, payment and settlement systems and services, they need to widen their range of services to run on professional lines and match the services provided by commercial banks.

Internationally, cooperative banks, popularly called credit unions, operate in networks and have an entity which provides a wide range of services to them, such as, fund management services, lines of credit, asset management, payment and settlement system gateway, ATM networks, credit card, investment, securitisation, capital raising and other financial services. These entities act as umbrella organizations and the networks provide cooperative solidarity. International experience has shown that the presence of such an umbrella organization has contributed towards the member credit unions being stable, sound and efficient entities.

B. Umbrella Organization at the National Level: The Working Group carefully went into the important issue of whether in India we should have an umbrella organization at the national level or whether each state should have its own umbrella organization. While countries such as Canada and US have provincial umbrella organizations, Australia and European countries have preferred to consolidate and have national level organizations.

UCBs in India are not evenly spread across the country. They have predominant presence in five states, viz. Andhra Pradesh, Gujarat, Karnataka, Maharashtra and Tamil Nadu accounting for about 89 percent of the total business of the sector. Further, UCBs in Maharashtra alone had about 64 percent of the total business. In contrast, their presence was minimal in many states. Considering the regional spread and market share of UCBs, the Working Group is of the opinion that having multiple umbrella organizations for UCBs in India or state-wise umbrellas may be neither feasible nor desirable. Therefore, the Working Group recommended that there should be one Umbrella Organization at the national level for the entire UCB sector.

To sum up, the financial sector reforms have been components of the overall economic reforms undertaken in a phased manner from 1991 by the Government of India. A look has to be taken at the reform process and what it means to the co-operative credit institutions. These reforms also envisaged improving the efficiency and productivity of the co-operative credit delivery system which in turn would accelerate the requisite credit flow to the productive sectors of the economy.

The major objectives of these reforms in the cooperative sector were as under:

1. To make the institutions competitive by removing external constraints having a bearing on their operations.
2. To improve their financial health.
3. To ensure transparency in their business operations.
4. To improve their profitability.
5. Institutional building and strengthening.

It is significant to note that introduction of reforms and the consequent increase in competition has resulted in some convergence in operations of commercial banks and co-operative banks, especially scheduled UCBs. Furthermore, while most of the loss-making commercial banks are relatively small, in the case of UCBs some of the large banks are incurring losses and this has increased the vulnerability of the whole segment. Detection of irregularities in a few UCBs in the recent past has raised concerns about the conduct of the management in co-operative banks. For this purpose, the RBI has suggested the establishment of a unified supervisory authority for UCBs and the related amendment to the Banking Regulation Act, 1949.

Endnote

1. Reserve Bank of India, *Report on Currency and Finance,* 2001-2002, p. VI-18.

16

Rural Co-operative Credit Institutions

Rural indebtedness is noted as a major reason for the spurt in farmer suicides during recent times across a number of states. In most, if not all, such cases, the economic status of the suicide victim was very poor, being small and marginal farmers. After the Green Revolution, agricultural activities have become cash-based individual enterprises requiring high investment in modern inputs and wage labour. This is evident from the list of states with high incidence of farmer suicides, which are not necessarily backward or predominantly agrarian or with low income. Increased liberalization and globalisation have in fact led to a shift in cropping pattern from staple crops to cash crops like oilseeds and cotton, requiring high investment in modern inputs and wage labour, and increasing credit needs but when the prices decline farmers have no means to supplement their incomes.

The Government has taken many policy initiatives for strengthening farm credit delivery system for providing credit at affordable rates of interest to support the resource requirements of the agricultural sector. The emphasis of these initiatives has been on providing timely and adequate credit support to farmers with particular focus on small and marginal farmers and weaker sections of society to enable them to adopt modern technology and improved agricultural practices for increasing agricultural production and productivity. The policy essentially lays emphasis on augmenting credit flow at the ground level through credit planning, adoption of region specific strategies and rationalization of lending policies and procedures and bringing down the rate of interest on farm loan.

16.1 Credit Needs of the Indian Farmers

Need for agricultural credit arises because modern farm technology is costly and the personal resources of the farmers are inadequate. Provision of agricultural credit, as an input, is essential for widespread use of improved agricultural methods.

Credit requirements of the farmers may be classified: (a) on the basis of purpose, and (b) on the basis of time. They need credit for productive as well as for unproductive purposes. Productive purposes include all such activities which help in the improvement of agricultural productivity such as purchase of inputs and permanent improvements in land. Unproductive credit needs include celebration of marriages and other social and religious functions and litigation.

Finance required for productive purposes can be divided broadly into the following categories:

- Short-term (for periods up to 15 months).
- Medium-term (from 15 months up to 5 years).
- Long-term (above 5 years).

Short-term loans are required for purchasing seeds, manures and fertilizers or for meeting labour charges etc. These are expected to be repaid after the harvest.

Medium-term loans are granted for purposes such as sinking of wells, purchase of bullocks, pumping plants and other improved implements etc.

Loans repayable over a longer period (i.e. above 5 years) are classified as long-term loans. These are utilised for payment of old debts, purchase of the heavier machines, making permanent improvements and increasing the size of the holding.

16.2 Sources of Credit for the Farmers

Sources of micro credit for the poor are grouped into two categories: (a) institutional sources, and (b) non-institutional sources. Institutional sources include co-operative societies, commercial banks and other government agencies. Non-institutional sources comprise moneylenders, landlords, relatives etc.

16.2.1 Institutional (or Formal) Sources: These are as under:

A. Member-owned Organizations: These include self-help groups, credit unions, and a variety of hybrid organizations like financial service associations. Like their informal cousins, they are generally small and local, which means they have access to good knowledge about each other's financial circumstances and can offer convenience and flexibility. Since they are managed by poor people, their costs of operation are low. However, these providers may have little financial skill and can run into trouble when the economy turns down or their operations become too complex. Unless they are effectively regulated and supervised, they can be *captured* by one or two influential leaders, and the members can lose their money.

B. Non-governmental Organizations (NGOs): NGOs have spread around the developing world in the recent past. They have proven very innovative, pioneering banking techniques like solidarity lending, village banking and mobile banking that have overcome barriers to serving poor populations. However, with boards that do not necessarily represent either their capital or their customers, their governance structures can be fragile, and they can become overly dependent on external donors.

C. Formal Financial Institutions: In addition to commercial banks, these include state banks, agricultural development banks, savings banks, rural banks and non-bank financial institutions. They are regulated and supervised, offer a wider range of financial services, and control a branch network that can extend across the country. However, they have proved reluctant to adopt social missions, and due to their high costs of operation, often cannot deliver services to poor or remote populations.

In India, agricultural credit is disbursed through a multi-agency network comprising of commercial banks, regional rural banks and co-operatives. With their vast network (covering almost all the villages in the country), wider coverage and outreach extending to the remotest part of country, the co-operative credit institutions, both in short and long-term structure are the main institutional mechanism for dispensation of agricultural credit.

Agricultural growth is crucial for alleviating rural poverty. Access to institutional credit to more farmers and appropriate quantity and quality of agricultural credit are crucial for realising the full potential of agriculture as a profitable activity.

Provision of sufficient and timely credit at fair rates of interest has, therefore, to be considered as an integral part of agricultural development. Assistance rendered by way of credit has, however, to be related to specific items of productive work or of essential costs of cultivation.

16.2.2 Non-institutional (Informal) Sources: These include moneylenders, pawnbrokers, savings collectors, money-guards, input supply shops. Because they know each other well and live in the same community, they understand each other's financial circumstances and can offer very flexible, convenient and fast services. These services can also be costly and the choice of financial products limited and very short-term.

Till Independence in 1947, moneylenders and the landlords were the principal sources of rural credit. Over the years, the operations of moneylenders have declined in view of debt relief legislations, the system of licensing moneylenders and restrictions on the use and transfer of land as security. Similarly, the abolition of all privileged tenures, both in zamindari and ryotwari areas, has discouraged investment by the landlords and larger cultivators.

Historically, moneylenders have played a significant role in meeting the credit needs of the rural producers. With stringent laws against money lending and the phenomenal growth of the formal credit delivery system, it was thought that money lenders would soon be out of business. Instead they have been in the business of lending in several disguises.

There are two types of moneylenders in rural areas: (a) agriculturist moneylenders who carry on the business of money lending along with farming, and (b) professional moneylenders whose only occupation is money lending. Although the relative importance of moneylenders has declined over the years, they are still an important source of credit for the rural people, particularly the small farmers and the artisans.

Moneylenders usually charge higher rates from poorer borrowers than from less poor ones. While moneylenders are often demonized and accused of usury, their services are convenient and fast, and they can be very flexible when borrowers run into problems. Moneylenders are popular because, unlike government agencies, they give credit for every purpose. They are easily approachable by the credit seekers and there are not many formalities in transacting a loan. However, the malpractices adopted by the moneylenders to exploit the needy farmers cannot be overlooked. These malpractices pertain to charging of high rate of interest and adopting unfair means in the maintenance of accounts.

Perhaps influenced by traditional Western views about usury, the role of the traditional moneylender has been subject to much criticism, especially in the early stages of modern micro finance. As more poor people gained access to loans from micro credit institutions, it became apparent that the services of moneylenders continued to be valued. Borrowers were prepared to pay very high interest rates for services like quick loan disbursement, confidentiality and flexible repayment schedules. They do not always see lower interest rates as adequate compensation for the costs of attending meetings, attending training courses to qualify for disbursements or making monthly collateral contributions. They also find it distasteful to be forced to pretend they were borrowing to start a business, when they were often borrowing for other reasons (such as paying for school fees, dealing with health costs or securing the family food supply). The more recent focus on inclusive financial systems affords moneylenders more legitimacy, arguing in favour of regulation and efforts to increase competition between them to expand the options available to poor people.

It is true that the institutional sources of credit have weakened the hold of moneylenders on the rural masses. However, the benefits of institutional credit have not percolated to all sections of rural population. Landless workers and marginal farmers have not benefited adequately due to their ignorance of new sources of credit and also on account of their weak repaying capacity. These underprivileged rural sections still depend on the moneylenders and suffer their exploitative practices.

16.3 Co-operative Credit Societies

These societies form an integral part of the rural credit system in India. They are the main source of institutional credit to the farmers. These societies are chiefly responsible for breaking the monopoly of moneylenders in providing credit to the agriculturists. There are around 92,789 such societies in the country at present. In spite of their suitability and useful role in building up a just socio-economic rural life, co-operative societies suffer from various weaknesses. The heavy overdues of co-operative societies are a cause for concern. The rising overdues have reduced the borrowing and lending activities of these societies. Moreover, these societies have paid inadequate attention to the needs of landless workers and rural artisans. Influential people in the villages have been the main beneficiaries of co-operative credit. Of late, there has been a tendency on the part of political leadership to write-off loans of the farmers. The RBI has repeatedly expressed concern in this regard because non-repayment of loans by the existing borrowers can adversely affect recycling of funds and the credit chances of the prospective borrowers.

16.4 Co-operative Banks

Co-operative banks in India are more than 100 years old. These banks came into existence with the enactment of the Agricultural Credit Co-operative Societies Act in 1904. Co-operative banks form an integral part of the banking system in India. These banks operate mainly for the benefit of rural areas, particularly the agricultural sector. Co-operative banks mobilise deposits and supply agricultural and rural credit with a wider outreach. They are the main source of institutional credit to the farmers. Co-operative banks are chiefly responsible for breaking the monopoly of moneylenders in providing credit to agriculturists. They have also been an important instrument for various development schemes, particularly subsidy-based programmes for the poor. Co-operative banks operate for non-agricultural sector also but their role is small.

Though much smaller as compared to scheduled commercial banks, co-operative banks constitute an important segment of the Indian banking system. They have an extensive branch network and reach out to people in remote areas. They have traditionally played an important role in creating banking habits among the lower and middle-income groups and in strengthening the rural credit delivery system.

Unfortunately, financial reforms have not impacted the functioning of co-operative banks. This was brought out clearly in the following observation of the Reserve Bank of India, "Since the introduction of reforms, there has been very little perceptible improvement in either stability or efficiency of co-operative banks. In particular, the asset quality and profitability of scheduled urban co-operative banks (UCBs) showed some deterioration in the reform period. Positive impact of reforms, as has been witnessed in the case of commercial banking sector, may take longer to get manifested for co-operative banks given the late start of the reform process in this sector". [1]

The financial reforms process initiated in 1991 has tried to achieve regulatory convergence among various financial intermediaries in view of their systemic importance. Therefore, the basic objectives and instruments of reforms for co-operative banks have been the same as for state co-operative banks (SCBs). However, given the special characteristics of co-operative banks, they have been extended certain dispensations in terms of pace and sequencing of reforms.

16.4.1 Classification of Co-operative Banks: The co-operative banking structure in India comprises urban co-operative banks and rural co-operative credit institutions.

A. Urban Co-operative Banks (UCBs): UCBs consist of a single tier, *viz.* primary co-operative banks, commonly referred to as urban co-operative banks.

B. Rural Co-operatives: Based on the nature of their lending operations, rural credit co-operatives have traditionally been bifurcated into two parallel wings: short-term and long-term.

16.5 Rural Co-operatives

16.5.1 Short-term Rural Co-operatives: The short-term provide crop and other working capital loans to farmers and rural artisans primarily for short-term purposes. These credit institutions have a three-tier federal structure: (a) at the apex of the system is a state co-operative bank (SCB) in each State, (b) at the middle (or district) level, there are central co-operative banks (CCBs) also known as district co-operative banks, and (c) at the lowest (or village) level are the primary agricultural credit societies (PACS). The smaller States and Union Territories (UTs) have a two-tier structure with SCBs directly meeting the credit requirements of PACS.

A. State Co-operative Bank (SCB): SCB is the highest agency of the three-tier co-operative credit structure in a state. It serves as a link between RBI and the CCBs and PACS. The RBI provides credit to lower level co-operatives through the SCB. This function of the RBI has now been taken over by NABARD. The SCB also acts as a *balancing centre* for CCBs in the sense that surplus funds of some CCBs are made available to other needy CCBs. The SCB exercises general control and supervision over CCBs and PACS.

B. Central Co-operative Banks (CCBs): These banks act as a link between the SCB and the PACS. The main task of CCBs is to lend money to affiliated village primary societies. The CCBs are expected to attract deposits from the general public.

C. Primary Agricultural Credit Societies (PACS): These societies form the basic unit of the co-operative credit system in India. These voluntary societies based on the principle of one man one vote have posed challenge to the exploitative practices of the village moneylenders.

The farmers and other small-time borrowers come in direct contact with these societies. The success of the co-operative credit movement depends largely on the strength of these village level societies. There are around 92,789 such societies in the country at present.

As a result of the expansion of the activities of PACS, the role of moneylenders in providing credit to agriculturists has decreased over the years. A major objective of PACS is to serve the needs of weaker sections of the society. For this purpose, the people with limited means, particularly scheduled castes and scheduled tribes, are encouraged to become members of these societies. Government has promoted multi-purpose societies in tribal areas for the benefit of people living there.

16.5.2 Long-term Rural Co-operatives: The long-term provide typically medium and long-term loans for making investments in agriculture, rural industries and, in the recent period, housing. Generally, these co-operatives have two tiers, viz.:

A. State Co-operative Agriculture and Rural Development Banks (SCARDBs): These banks operate at the State level.

B. Primary Co-operative Agriculture and Rural Development Banks (PCARDBs): These banks operate at the *taluka/tehsil* level.

16.6 Rural Co-operatives: History and Recent Policy Measures

Rural credit co-operatives in India were originally envisaged as a mechanism for pooling the resources of people with small means and providing them with access to different financial services. Democratic in features, the movement was also an effective instrument for development of degraded waste lands, increasing productivity, providing food security, generating employment opportunities in rural areas and ensuring social and economic justice to the poor and vulnerable.

The history of the co-operative credit movement in India can be traced back to 1904 when the Co-operative Societies Act was passed. In 1919, *co-operation* became a provincial subject. The Co-operative Planning Committee, 1945 found that a large number of co-operatives were "saddled with the problem of frozen assets because of heavy overdues in repayment".

The co-operative banks in India play an important role in catering to the banking needs of the rural population. Soon after Independence in 1947, the inadequacy of rural credit engaged the attention of the Government of India and the RBI. The agricultural credit system as it has emerged over the years is the result of both evolution and intervention, and symbolises the nation's response to the dissatisfaction with the discredited colonial credit delivery system.

The Reserve Bank of India Act, 1934 has specific provisions relating to agricultural credit. Section 54 of the RBI Act specifically authorised the creation of an Agricultural Credit Department within the RBI to deal not only with the rural credit but also with the long-term finance including refinance. Section 17 of the Act empowered it to provide agricultural credit through state co-operative banks or any other banks engaged in the business of agricultural credit.

The foundation for building a broader credit infrastructure for rural credit was laid down by the All India Rural Credit Survey (1954). The Committee of Direction that conducted the survey recommended the creation of National Agricultural Credit Fund, which was subsequently created by the RBI. The Agricultural Refinance Corporation (ARC) set up by the RBI in 1963 provided funds by way of refinance, but credit co-operatives still did not function too well. Decentralised credit planning through the Lead Bank Scheme was also introduced to spearhead the credit allocation for, *inter alia*, agricultural lending. In order to emphasise the developmental and promotional role assigned to the ARC in addition to refinancing, the ARC was renamed as the Agricultural Refinance and Development Corporation (ARDC) in 1975.

Despite all these efforts, the flow of credit to the agricultural sector failed to exhibit any appreciable improvement as the co-operatives lacked resources to meet the expected demand. To solve these problems, the regional rural banks (RRBs) were set up in 1975. In order to strengthen the institutional credit for agriculture and rural development, National Bank for Agriculture and Rural Development (NABARD) was set up on July 12, 1982. On its establishment, NABARD took over the entire functions of the ARDC, the refinancing functions of the RBI in relation to co-operatives and regional rural banks (RRBs).

The rural credit co-operative system has served as an important instrument of credit delivery in rural and agricultural areas. The separate structure of rural co-operative sector for long-term and short-term loans has enabled these institutions to develop as specialised institutions for rural credit delivery. At the same time, their federal structure has helped in providing support structure for the guidance and critical financing for the lower structure. These institutions have wide outreach with as many as 92,789 primary agricultural co-operative societies (PACS), the grass root organisation of the rural co-operative banking structure, operating in the country at end-March 2015.

The rural co-operative credit institutions, however, are beset with many problems which include the following.

1. Low resource base.
2. High dependence on refinancing agencies.
3. Lack of diversification.
4. Huge accumulated losses.
5. Persistent NPAs.
6. Low recovery levels.
7. Various other types of organisational weaknesses.

NABARD and the RBI, therefore, have been taking several supervisory and developmental measures in consultation with the Government of India for the revival of weak institutions and orderly growth of this important segment of the financial sector.

16.7 Primary Agricultural Credit Societies (PACS)

Primary agricultural credit societies (PACS) are the foundation of the co-operative credit system on which the superstructure of the short-term co-operative credit system rests. It is the PACS which directly interface with individual farmers, provide short-term and medium-term credit, supply agricultural inputs, distribute consumer articles and arrange for marketing of produce of its members through a co-operative marketing society.

PACS continue to rely heavily on external support and have not yet been able to become self-reliant in respect of resources through deposit mobilisation and internal accruals, affecting their growth and expansion of business activities.

PACS need to function as viable units responsive to the needs, aspirations and convenience of its members, particularly those belonging to the more vulnerable sections of the society. They must function effectively as well-managed and multi-purpose institutions mobilising the savings of the rural people and providing a package of services including credit, supply of agricultural inputs and implements, consumer goods, marketing services and technical guidance with focus on weaker sections.

Some of the critical challenges facing primary level co-operative credit institutions, apart from improving resource mobilisation, are the following.
1. Increasing diversification in business portfolio.
2. Improving volume of business.
3. Arresting decline in membership by the borrowers.
4. Reducing cost of management.
5. Correcting imbalances in loans outstanding.
6. Improving skills of the staff and imparting professionalisation.
7. Strengthening the management information system (MIS).
8. Reducing involvement in non/less profitable business.

16.8 Problems of Rural Co-operatives

Rural co-operatives form an integral part of the rural credit system in India. They are the main source of institutional credit to the farmers. These societies are chiefly responsible for breaking the monopoly of moneylenders in providing credit to the agriculturists. There are around 92,789 such societies in the country at present.

Despite the phenomenal outreach and volume of operations, the financial health of a very large proportion of rural credit co-operatives has deteriorated significantly. The institutions are beset with problems like low resource base, high dependence on external sources of funding, excessive governmental control, dual control, huge accumulated losses, imbalances, poor business diversification, low recovery etc. These institutions do not, therefore, inspire confidence among their existing and potential members, depositors, borrowers and lenders. Thus, there is a need to find ways for strengthening the co-operative movement and making it a well-managed and vibrant medium to serve the credit needs of rural India, especially the small and marginal farmers.

Moreover, these societies have paid inadequate attention to the needs of landless workers and rural artisans. Influential people in the villages have been the main beneficiaries of co-operative credit. Of late, there has been a tendency on the part of political leadership to write-off loans of the farmers. The RBI has repeatedly expressed concern in this regard because non-repayment of loans by the existing borrowers can adversely affect recycling of funds and the credit chances of the prospective borrowers. A national approach on this issue is required so that co-operative credit system may fulfil the task assigned to it.

It is part of a historic policy infirmity which allowed co-operatives to be treated as *refinance windows* instead of incentivising them into becoming genuine thrift and credit institutions.

The rural co-operative credit institutions are beset with many problems which include the following:

1. Low resource base.
2. High dependence on refinancing agencies.
3. Lack of diversification.
4. Huge accumulated losses.
5. Persistent non-performing assets (NPAs).
6. Low recovery levels.
7. Various other types of organisational weaknesses.

NABARD and the RBI, therefore, have been taking several supervisory and developmental measures in consultation with the Government of India for the revival of weak institutions and orderly growth of this important segment of the financial sector.

16.9 Task Force on Revival of Rural Co-operative Credit Institutions

The Government of India had constituted this Task Force (Chairman: A. Vaidyanathan), 2005 to propose an action plan for reviving the rural co-operative banking institutions and suggest an appropriate regulatory framework for these institutions. The Task Force in its Report submitted to the Central Government on February 15, 2005 made several recommendations to strengthen the rural co-operative credit structure in the country.

The major recommendations of the Task Force were as under:

1. Co-operative credit structure (CCS) is impaired in governance, managerial and financial fronts and hence needs to be revived and restructured.
2. Financial restructuring should be contingent on commitment to and implementation of legal and institutional reforms by the State Governments.
3. Financial assistance should be made available for: (a) wiping out accumulated losses, (b) covering invoked but unpaid guarantees given by the State Governments, (c) increasing the capital to a specified minimum level, (d) retiring Government share capital, and (e) technical assistance.
4. Availability of financial assistance from the Government of India should be strictly subject to legal and institutional reforms in the co-operative sector to ensure that the co-operatives become truly democratic and member-driven. These reforms should

include: (a) ensuring full voting membership rights on all users of financial services including depositors, (b) removing state intervention in administrative and financial matters in co-operatives, (c) removing provision for Government equity and participation in the Boards of Co-operatives, (d) withdrawing restrictive orders on financial matters, and (e) permitting co-operatives the freedom to take loans from any financial institution and not necessarily from only the upper tier and similarly place their deposits with any financial institution of their choice.

5. The Task Force also recommended certain major amendments to the provisions of the Banking Regulation Act, 1949 enabling removal of dual control and bringing the co-operatives under the regulatory control of the RBI. These included: (a) all co-operative banks should be on par with the commercial banks as far as regulatory norms are concerned (b) RBI should prescribe *fit and proper* criteria for election to the Boards of Co-operative Banks, (c) RBI should prescribe certain criteria for professionals to be on the Boards of Co-operative Banks, (d) CEOs of the co-operative banks should be appointed by the respective banks themselves, and (e) co-operatives, other than co-operative banks as approved by the RBI, should not accept non-voting member deposits. Such co-operatives should also not use words such as *bank, banking, banker* or any other derivative of the word *bank* in their registered name.

6. Total financial assistance was estimated tentatively at ₹ 14,839 crore. The Task Force, however, recommended a special audit to ascertain the exact requirement of assistance. The financial assistance should be shared by the Government of India, State Governments and the CCS, based on the origin of losses within a flexible matrix.

7. NABARD should be designated as the nodal *implementing and pass through agency* to co-ordinate and monitor the progress of the programme representing the Government of India. NABARD should prepare model MoUs, model balance sheet proforma for PACS and CCBs.

16.10 NABARD and the Co-operative Sector

National Bank for Agriculture and Rural Development (NABARD) provides refinance to state co-operative agriculture and rural development banks (SCARDBs), state co-operative banks (SCBs), regional rural banks (RRBs) and other financial institutions approved by the RBI. The ultimate beneficiaries of refinance from NABARD could be individuals, partnership concerns, companies, State-owned corporations or co-operative societies.

16.10.1 Credit Extended by NABARD: NABARD provides short-term credit facilities to SCBs in respect of eligible CCBs for the following purposes:

1. Financing seasonal agricultural operations.
2. Marketing of crops.
3. Pisciculture activities.
4. Production and marketing activities of primary weavers and other industrial co-operative societies.
5. Labour contract/forest labour co-operative societies.

6. Individual rural artisans through PCS.
7. Procurement, stocking and distribution of chemical fertilisers.

Besides short-term credit limits are also sanctioned to SCBs on behalf of apex/regional weavers/other industrial societies for financing procurement and marketing and trading-in-yarn.

Short-term limits are also provided to RRBs for financing seasonal agricultural operations, marketing of crops and pisciculture activities.

Medium-term facilities are also provided to SCBs and RRBs for converting short-term into medium-term loans and for approved agricultural investments.

Long-term loans are provided to the State Governments for contributing to the share capital of co-operative credit institutions.

In pursuance of the announcement made by the Finance Minister in June 2004 for enhancing the credit flow to the agriculture sector, NABARD advised SCBs, CCBs and RRBs on the measures to be taken under various schemes to give relief to farmers. It was apprehended that the implementation of these measures coupled with providing conversion/rescheduled loans to farmers may result in a liquidity problem for co-operative banks and RRBs, impairing their ability to provide fresh loans and achieve the desired growth rate during the year. In order to mitigate this, NABARD introduced a liquidity support scheme during 2004-05 for these institutions. SCBs were sanctioned a liquidity support of ₹ 1,770 crore during 2004-05. NABARD also sanctioned long-term loans to 9 State Governments amounting to ₹ 39 crore as contribution to the share capital of co-operative credit institutions.

To sum up, historically, rural co-operative credit institutions (or simply rural co-operatives) have played an important role in providing institutional credit to the agricultural and rural sectors. The structure of rural co-operative banks is not uniform across all the States of the country. Some States have a unitary structure with the State level banks operating through their own branches, while others have a mixed structure incorporating both unitary and federal systems.

India is a country with a population of 121 crore (2011 Census) of which around 70 percent resides in around 6 lakh villages. On grounds of outreach, co-operatives cannot be ignored. The outreach is significant not merely in absolute numbers but also in terms of location of outlets. The number of PACS located in hilly terrains, deserts and other areas with poor access far exceed the number of rural branches of commercial banks and RRBs. Though the network of commercial banks and RRBs has spread rapidly, their reach in the countryside both in terms of the number of clients and accessibility to the small and marginal farmers and other poorer segments is far less than that of co-operatives.

Endnote

1. Reserve Bank of India, *Report on Currency and Finance,* 2001-2002, p. VI-18.

17

Development Finance Institutions (DFIs)

DFIs were set up with the specific objective of meeting the medium to long-term requirement of funds. However, DFIs in the present form are finding it difficult to sustain their operations. Their business has slowed down and their operations have become less profitable. This has raised issues relating to the viability of DFIs.

17.1 Categorization and Sub-categorization of DFIs

Development finance institutions (DFIs) or simply financial institutions were set up in India at various points of time starting from the late 1940s to cater to the medium to long-term financing requirements of industry as the capital market in India had not developed sufficiently. After Independence in 1947, the national government adopted the path of planned economic development and launched the First Five Year Plan in 1951. This strategy of development provided the critical inducement for establishment of DFIs at both all-India and state-levels. In order to perform their role, DFIs were extended funds of the RBI and government guaranteed bonds, which constituted major sources of their funds. Funds from these sources were not only available at concessional rates, but also on a long-term basis with their maturity period ranging from 10-15 years. On the asset side, their operations were marked by near absence of competition.

A large variety of financial institutions have come into existence over the years to perform various types of financial activities. While some of them operate at all-India level, others are state level institutions. Besides providing direct loans (including rupee loans, foreign currency loans), financial institutions also extend financial assistance by way of underwriting and direct subscription and by issuing guarantees. Recently, some DFIs have started extending short-term/working capital finance, although term-lending continues to be their primary activity. DFIs in India can be categorised and sub-categorised in the following manner:
1. All-India Financial Institutions (AIFIs) which include:
- All-India Development Banks.
- Specialised Institutions.
- Investment Institutions.
- Refinance Institutions.
2. State-level Institutions which include:
- State Financial Corporations (SFCs).
- State Industrial Development Corporations (SIDCs).

17.2 All-India Financial Institutions (AIFIs)

17.2.1 All-India Development Banks: These banks are the main source of medium

and long-term project financing. These banks promote economic development of India by: (a) providing medium and long-term finance to industry. It is provided in the form of term loans and advances and subscription to shares and debentures, (b) providing guarantees for term loans and underwriting new equity. Guarantees and underwriting by development banks create confidence among investors and thus facilitate the raising of funds by companies, and (c) performing various types of promotional roles for the private entrepreneurs as, for example, identification of investment projects, and arrangement for managerial and technical advice.

Development banks are different from commercial banks in several respects. Firstly, development banks do not accept deposits from the public as commercial banks do. For example, financial resources of development banks in India come from Government of India, Reserve Bank of India and from international agencies like World Bank and its affiliate International Development Association (IDA). Secondly, they specialise in providing medium-term and long-term finance while commercial banks generally provide short-term credit. Thirdly, development banks perform promotional role for industrial development of the country whereas commercial banks provide utility and other services to their customers.

Some important institutions of this category are the following:

A. Industrial Finance Corporation of India (IFCI): It was set up in 1948 by an Act of Parliament with the objective of meeting the medium and long-term credit needs of industrial concerns in the country. Its establishment marked the begging of the era of development banking in India. Being the first such institutions in the post-Independence period, it has undertaken a wide range of promotional activities.

B. Industrial Development Bank of India (IDBI): It is the principal financial institution for providing credit and other facilities for the development of industry. Set up under the Industrial Development Bank of India Act, 1964, it co-ordinates the working of institutions engaged in financing, promoting industries and for assisting the development of such institutions. [1] It provides direct financial assistance to large and medium industrial concerns and helps small industries through State level financial institutions. It is the apex organisation in the field of development banking. It may be noted that IDBI was established as a subsidiary of the RBI. However, it was delinked from the RBI in 1976 and was converted into a holding company.

Taking into account the changing operating environment following the initiation of economic reforms in the early 1990s, the Government decided to transform IDBI into a commercial bank without eschewing its traditional development finance obligations. It was thought that migration to the new business model of commercial banking, with its access to low cost current/saving bank deposits, would enable it to overcome most of the limitations of the current model of development finance. In fulfilment of these objectives, the IDBI (Transfer of Undertaking and Repeal) Act, 2003 was enacted in December, 2003, which came into effect from July 2, 2004. The Act provides for repeal of the IDBI Act, corporatisation of IDBI, and its transformation into a commercial bank. IDBI was transformed into IDBI Limited on October 1, 2004, a company under the Companies Act,

1956 and a scheduled bank (on October 11, 2004) under the RBI Act, 1934.

In a parallel move, the Government approved IDBI's proposal to set up a Stressed Assets Stabilisation Fund (SASF), which provides for stressed assets of IDBI amounting to ₹ 9,000 crore to be transferred to SASF against an equivalent amount of 20 years bond issued by the Government of India in favour of SASF on cash/budget neutral basis.

C. Industrial Credit and Investment Corporation of India Ltd. (ICICI): It was established as a public limited company in 1955 to encourage and assist individual industrial enterprises in the country. Unlike the IDBI and IFCI which are public sector development banks, the ICICI is a private sector institution which provides term loans in rupees and foreign currencies, underwrites issues of shares and debentures, and makes direct subscriptions to these issues. It is noteworthy that ICICI was merged with ICICI Bank on March 30, 2002.

D. Industrial Investment Bank of India (IIBI): In 1971, Industrial Reconstruction Corporation of India (IRCI) Ltd. was jointly set up by the IDBI, LIC and banks to look after the rehabilitation of sick units. It was renamed as the Industrial Reconstruction Bank of India (IRBI) in 1984. It was converted into a full-fledged public financial institution in 1997 and was renamed as the Industrial Investment Bank of India (IIBI).

E. Small Industries Development Bank of India (SIDBI): It was established in April 1990 as the apex refinance bank and the principal development financial institution for the promotion, financing and development of the small industries sector and to coordinate the functions of other institutions engaged in similar activities. It has 5 regional offices and 33 branch offices for the channelling of direct and indirect credit. As regards indirect assistance, SIDBI provides refinance to and discounts bills of primary lending institutions with the provision of the following assistance:

1. Marketing of SSI products.
2. Setting up of new ventures.
3. Availability of working capital.
4. Expansion, modernization, human resource development.
5. Diversification of existing units for all activities.

The direct assistance comprises of loans for new ventures, diversification, technology upgradation, industrialization, expansion of well-run SMEs. Foreign currency loans are provided for import of equipment to export-oriented SMEs. Venture capital assistance is provided to innovative entrepreneurs.

17.2.2 Specialised Financial Institutions: Some of the important institutions in this category are the following.

A. Export-Import Bank (EXIM Bank): Established in 1982, it operates as a co-ordinating agency in the field of international finance and for the development of merchant banking activities in export-oriented industries.

B. Infrastructure Development Finance Company (IDFC): Set up in 1997, it operates in the area of infrastructure.

C. Tourism Finance Corporation of India (TFCI): Established in 1989, it caters to the financial requirements of the tourism industry.

17.2.3 Investment Institutions: These have played significant roles in the mobilisation of household sector savings and their deployment in the credit and the capital markets. Major institutions in this category are the following.

A. Unit Trust of India (UTI): Set up in 1964, it reflected the efforts of the Government of India to popularise unit trusts and mutual funds in the country to encourage indirect holding of securities by the public. The UTI was established to mobilise the savings of the small investors who constitute the bulk of India's population. Government has extended, from time to time, various types of concessions including tax benefits to UTI and its unit holders. The UTI with a large investor base, has been running various schemes including the flagship, US-64, various assured returns schemes, and other NAV-based schemes. Recently, important decisions have been taken to tide over the financial problems faced by the UTI. On October 28, 2002, an ordinance was promulgated which repealed the UTI Act, and created two entities, UTI-1 and UTI-2. UTI-2 is an unencumbered mutual fund, with only NAV-based schemes. UTI-1 has US-64 and the assured returns schemes. On 15 January 2003, the handover of UTI-2 to a new set of owners (State Bank of India, Bank of Baroda, Punjab National Bank and Life Insurance Corporation of India) took place.

B. Life Insurance Corporation of India (LIC): It was established in 1956 when the life insurance business was nationalised in India.

C. General Insurance Corporation of India (GIC): It was established when the general insurance business was nationalised in India with effect from January 1, 1973.

17.2.4 Refinance Institutions: Two institutions in this category are noteworthy. Both of them are also vested with certain supervisory functions.

A. National Bank for Agriculture and Rural Development (NABARD): Set up in 1982, NABARD is the apex institution accredited with all matters concerning policy, planning and operations in the field of credit for agriculture and other economic activities in rural areas in India. NABARD serves as an apex refinancing agency for the institutions providing investment and production credit in rural areas.

(a) Establishment: The Committee to Review Arrangements for Institutional Credit for Agriculture and Rural Development (CRAFICARD) [Chairman: B. Sivaraman] set up by the RBI in its report submitted in 1979 recommended the establishment of NABARD. The Parliament through the Act 61 of 1981, approved its setting up.

The Committee after reviewing the arrangements came to the conclusion that a new arrangement would be necessary at the national level for achieving the desired focus and thrust towards integration of credit activities in the context of the strategy for Integrated Rural Development. Against the backdrop of the massive credit needs of rural development and the need to uplift the weaker sections in the rural areas within a given time horizon the arrangement called for a separate institutional set up. Similarly, The Reserve Bank had onerous responsibilities to discharge in respect of its many basic functions of central banking in monetary and credit regulations and was not therefore in a position to devote undivided attention to the operational details of the emerging complex credit problems. This paved the way for the establishment of NABARD.

CRAFICARD also found it prudent to integrate short term, medium term and long-term credit structure for the agriculture sector by establishing a new bank. NABARD is the result of this recommendation. It was set up with an initial capital of ₹ 100 crore, which was enhanced to ₹ 2,000 crore, fully subscribed by the Government of India and the RBI.

(b) Objectives: NABARD was established in terms of the Preamble to the Act, "for providing credit for the promotion of agriculture, small scale industries, cottage and village industries, handicrafts and other rural crafts and other allied economic activities in rural areas with a view to promoting IRDP and securing prosperity of rural areas and for matters connected therewith in incidental thereto".

The main objectives of the NABARD as stated in the statement of objectives while placing the bill before the Lok Sabha were categorized as under:

1. The National Bank will be an apex organisation in respect of all matters relating to policy, planning operational aspects in the field of credit for promotion of agriculture, small-scale industries, cottage and village industries, handicrafts and other rural crafts and other allied economic activities in rural areas.
2. The Bank will serve as a refinancing institution for institutional credit such as long-term, short-term for the promotion of activities in the rural areas.
3. The Bank will also provide direct lending to any institution as may approved by the Central Government.
4. The Bank will have organic links with the Reserve Bank and maintain a close link with in.

(c) Major Activities: These are as under:

1. Preparing of potential linked credit plans for identification of exploitable potentials under agriculture and other activities available for development through bank credit.
2. Refinancing banks for extending loans for investment and production purpose in rural areas.
3. Providing loans to State Governments/non-governmental organizations (NGOs)/panchayati raj institutions (PRIs) for developing rural infrastructure.
4. Supporting credit innovations of non-governmental organizations (NGOs) and other non-formal agencies.
5. Extending formal banking services to the unreached rural poor by evolving a supplementary credit delivery strategy in a cost effective manner by promoting self-help groups (SHGs).
6. Promoting participatory watershed development for enhancing productivity and profitability of rainfed agriculture in a sustainable manner.
7. On-site inspection of cooperative banks and regional rural banks (RRBs) and off-site surveillance over health of co-operatives and RRBs.

(d) Role and Functions:

1. NABARD is an apex institution accredited with all matters concerning policy, planning and operations in the field of credit for agriculture and other economic activities in rural areas.

2. It is an apex refinancing agency for the institutions providing investment and production credit for promoting the various developmental activities in rural areas.

3. It takes measures towards institution building for improving absorptive capacity of the credit delivery system, including monitoring, formulation of rehabilitation schemes, restructuring of credit institutions, training of personnel, etc.

4. It co-ordinates the rural financing activities of all the institutions engaged in developmental work at the field level and maintains liaison with Government of India, State Governments, Reserve Bank of India and other national level institutions concerned with policy formulation.

5. It prepares, on annual basis, rural credit plans for all districts in the country; these plans form the base for annual credit plans of all rural financial institutions.

6. It undertakes monitoring and evaluation of projects refinanced by it.

7. It promotes research in the fields of rural banking, agriculture and rural development.

(e) Mission: It has the mission of promoting sustainable and equitable agriculture and rural development through effective credit support, related services, institution building and other innovative initiatives.

In pursuing this mission, NABARD focuses its activities on:

- **Credit Functions**, involving preparation of potential-linked credit plans annually for all districts of the country for identification of credit potential, monitoring the flow of ground level rural credit, issuing policy and operational guidelines to rural financing institutions and providing credit facilities to eligible institutions under various programmes.

- **Development Functions**, concerning reinforcement of the credit functions and making credit more productive.

- **Supervisory Functions**, ensuring the proper functioning of cooperative banks and regional rural banks.

(f) NABARD and its Role in Training: Section 38 of the NABARD Act provides that the Bank shall:

1. Maintain expert staff to study all problems relating to agriculture and rural development and be available for consultation to the Central Government, the Reserve Bank, the State Governments and the other institutions engaged in the field of rural development.

2. Provide facilities for training, for dissemination of information and the promotion of research including the undertaking of studies, researches, techno-economic and other surveys in the field of rural banking, agriculture and rural development.

3. Provide technical, legal, financial, marketing and administrative assistance to any person engaged in agriculture and rural development activities.

4. Provide consultancy services in the field of agriculture and rural development and other related matters in or outside India, on such terms and against such remuneration, as may be agreed upon.

In this context, the role played by NABARD for capacity building in client institutions, partner agencies and other developmental agencies is important.

In pursuance of the Bank's mandate as stated in the Act, the Bank provides training facilities for the RFIs and agencies involved in rural development through BIRD and the two RTCs. With a view to broad-base the training and capacity building efforts, the Bank encourages the RFIs to set up their own training systems and provides these training institutes the necessary support to conduct meaningful and quality training. Options and avenues for strengthening the training interventions at the client level are continuously examined so that the human resources in these institutions are developed to take on the challenges, reckon with the competition, improve customer service, expand outreach, develop suitable products and thereby contribute to rural development.

(g) **Nabcons:** NABARD Consultancy Services (Nabcons) is a wholly owned subsidiary promoted by NABARD and is engaged in providing consultancy in all spheres of agriculture, rural development and allied areas. Nabcons leverages on the core competence of the NABARD in the areas of agricultural and rural development, especially multidisciplinary projects, banking, institutional development, infrastructure, training, etc., internalized for more than two decades.

In tune with NABARD's mission to bring about rural prosperity, Nabcons has more than just commercial interest in the assignments it undertakes.

(h) **Bankers Institute of Rural Development (BIRD):** Established in 1983, at Lucknow, is an autonomous institute promoted and funded by NABARD. BIRD was established primarily to cater to the training needs of RRB personnel. The Institute, has, since 1st April 1992, been catering to the training and information needs of rural bankers through its topical training programs/seminars. The Institute's mandate also includes research and consultancy in the related areas.

B. National Housing Bank (NHB): Against the milieu of rapid urbanisation and a changing socio-economic scenario, the demand for housing in the country has been expanding at a fast pace. In India, investment in housing till recently was mainly financed by own sources or from informal credit market. Since the 1990s, efforts have been directed at the development of housing finance institutions to meet the large resource gap that exists for housing finance in the country. The emergence of organised housing finance has been a relatively late development in India. When the NHB was set up in 1988, nearly 80 percent of the housing stock in the country was financed from informal sources. The organised sources of housing finance included, *inter alia*, the housing finance companies (HFCs) which then numbered about 400 and were essentially non-banking financial companies (NBFCs) that were regulated by the RBI. These included small companies with operations restricted to localised areas and companies engaged in construction/development, which also offered housing credit. Several of the companies relied on public deposits for their resources. A notable exception was the Housing Development Finance Corporation (HDFC).

In recognition of the need for developing a network of specialised housing finance institutions in the country, NHB was set up in July 1988 as a wholly owned subsidiary of the RBI under the National Housing Bank Act, 1987, to function as an apex bank for the housing finance. NHB was established with a mandate 'to operate as a principal agency to promote housing finance institutions both at local and regional levels and to provide financial and other support to such institutions and for matters connected therewith or incidental thereto'.

As chief refinance institution in the housing sector, NHB regulates housing finance companies (HFCs), refinances their operations and expands the spread of housing finance to different income groups all over the country, while functioning within the overall framework of the housing policy. It has also helped in diverting increasing proportions of annual provident fund accumulations for housing finance through housing linked savings schemes for provident fund subscribers.

Since then the sector has grown with many new HFCs being set up, including several sponsored by banks and financial institutions. The important among these are the following: LIC Housing Finance Ltd., GIC Housing Finance Ltd., BOB Housing Ltd. (since merged with its parent bank, viz. Bank of Baroda), PNB Housing Finance Ltd., HDFC Ltd. and ICICI Home Finance Ltd. Some of these were set up with equity support from the NHB as part of their developmental mandate. These HFCs have provided aspiring home owners with access to housing finance and facilitated home ownership in a big way.

The State Governments are responsible for implementing social housing schemes. Almost all the States have set up Housing Boards in order to facilitate the implementation of the social housing schemes. Community-operative banks have been financing housing schemes. Community-operative banks cater to economically weaker sections, low and middle income groups as well as community-operative or group housing societies.

It is noteworthy in the present context that Housing and Urban Development Corporation (HUDCO) was set up in April 1970 as an apex techno-finance organization in order to provide loans and technical support to state and city level organizations. Among the HFCs, HUDCO has dominated in terms of profits and total disbursements. Government also recognised the need to strengthen HUDCO through augmenting its resources for meeting the requirements for shelter provisions for lower income groups in a large measure in rural and urban areas including the shelters and the slum dwellers and for expanding infrastructure facilities in the urban areas.

17.3 State Level Institutions

Operations of the state-level institutions are generally confined to their respective States. The two important institutions in this category are the following.

17.3.1 State Financial Corporations (SFCs): They are set up under the State Financial Corporations Act, 1951. At present, there are 18 SFCs in the country, assisting small and medium enterprises.

The mandate of the SFCs is to promote regional growth in the country through the development of SMEs by grants or loans and participation in their equity. The 18 SFCs across the country provide financial assistance by way of term loans. The lending is in the format of loans and debentures and they also operate schemes of IDBI/SIDBI in addition to extending working capital loans under the composite loan scheme. Many of the SFCs have failed to achieve these objectives and some of them are now almost defunct. Much of the failure could be attributed to the absence of managerial autonomy, professional management and a host of other problems related to the functioning of state-level public sector institutions.

17.3.2 State Industrial Development Corporations (SIDCs): These institutions provide funds for promoting industrial development in their respective states.

17.4 Regulation and Supervision of DFIs

Over the years, the RBI has been involved in setting up of financial institutions such as the erstwhile Industrial Development Bank of India (IDBI), Unit Trust of India (UTI), National Bank for Agriculture and Rural Development (NABARD), National Housing Bank (NHB) and Infrastructure Development Finance Company (IDFC) Ltd. Interestingly, although the RBI helped to create and foster these institutions, it did not regulate them until the early 1990s. However, the RBI had the statutory powers to call for information and give directions to them.

DFIs expanded rapidly, especially in the 1980s. Therefore, in the early 1990s, DFIs were brought under the monitoring arrangement of the RBI as an adjunct to monetary and credit policy. In 1994, major term lending institutions [IDBI, ICICI, IFCI, SIDBI, IIBI and Exim Bank] were subjected to prudential guidelines relating to income recognition, asset classification, provisioning and capital adequacy. These norms were subsequently extended to Tourism Finance Corporation of India (TFCI) and IDFC.

In April 1995, select all-India financial institutions were brought under the supervisory purview of the Board of Financial Supervision (BFS). Subsequently, the regulatory and supervisory framework of financial institutions changed significantly along with the accelerated pace of commercial development of banks in the globalised environment.

In 1996, refinancing institutions such as SIDBI, NABARD and NHB were also brought under the purview of the prudential regulations. Credit exposure norms relating to single borrower/group of borrowers have also been prescribed for all-India term-lending and refinancing institutions.

In view of the dichotomy among the DFIs that gave rise to large variations in the interest rates offered and maturity pattern etc. which could eventually result in disorderliness of the market, the resource mobilization by DFIs was brought under the purview of regulations in 1998. After reviews on an ongoing basis, the regulations were liberalised and made flexible in line with developments in the debt market. Faced with rising resource cost, increased competition and decline in asset quality, DFIs have diversified their operations into para-banking activities. This necessitated a review of the regulatory mechanism for the DFIs.

In June, 2002, the RBI introduced the supervisory rating system based on CAMELS model for financial institutions on lines similar to commercial banks. The RBI had evolved a time frame for completion of projects to ensure that loan assets relating to projects under implementation are appropriately classified and asset quality correctly reflected. The new guidelines issued by RBI effective from March 31, 2002 stipulated that in case of time overruns longer than two years, the asset is to be classified as sub-standard regardless of the record of recovery. For projects to be financed by financial institutions in future, the date of completion should be indicated at the time of financial closure. If the date of commencement of commercial production extends beyond 6 months after the originally envisaged date of project completion, the account should be treated sub-standard.

Other policy initiatives relate to audit, connected lending, loans against guarantees extended by banks, and prudential norms. Financial institutions have been advised to rotate the partners of the audit firms, if the same firm has contributed for more than four years. The RBI in consultation with the Government of India issued detailed guidelines in regard to connected lending in December 2002. Pursuant to the directions of the Audit Sub-Committee of the BFS, a Committee on Computer Audit was constituted. This Committee classified the possible areas of audit interest in the information system (IS) environment into 15 broad categories and prepared standardised checklists under each category to facilitate the conduct of computer audit in banks and financial institutions and to ensure that the requisite controls are applied by their computerised branches.

Banks have been permitted to extend guarantees in respect of infrastructure projects, in favour of other lending institutions, provided the bank issuing the guarantee takes a funded share in the infrastructure project at least to the extent of 5 percent of the project cost and undertakes normal credit appraisal, monitoring and follow up of the project. The loan extended by a financial institution against such a guarantee of a bank would attract a risk weight of 20 percent in the computation of CRAR. The risk weight of 20 percent would apply only to that part of the loan which is covered by bank's guarantee and the remaining amount of loan, if any, would attract 100 percent risk weight. For the purpose of exposure norms, however, the entire loan transaction is reckoned as an exposure on the borrowing entity and not on the bank guaranteeing the loan, so as to correctly reflect the degree of credit concentration.

Prudential norms were liberalised in August 2002. Housing loans extended by financial institutions against the mortgage of residential housing property attracts a risk weight of 50 percent (as against 100 percent earlier), investment by financial institutions in mortgage backed securities (MBS) attracts a risk weight of 50 percent in addition to 2.5 percent weightage for market risk, subject to certain terms and conditions issued by the RBI.

In September 2002, RBI issued guidelines in respect of consolidated supervision of financial institutions. These institutions were advised that the provisions held by them in respect of accounts related to projects with project cost of ₹ 100 crore or more should not be reversed even in cases where the deemed date of completion of such project, certain amounts might become eligible for upgradation to the standard category.

17.5 DFIs in the Changed Scenario

Prior to financial sector reforms initiated in 1991, DFIs operated in an over-protected environment with most of the funding coming from assured sources at concessional terms. In the wake of financial sector reforms, the RBI started monitoring the functioning of DFIs with a view to impart market orientation to their operations. In tune with the emerging scenario, their access to low cost funds of the RBI was discontinued.

In spite of the withdrawal of concessional funds, operations of DFIs were not adversely affected during the early years of the reform, as there were several factors that worked to their advantage. Lending interest rates both for banks and DFIs were deregulated in the early 1990s. However, this was the period when the inflation rate was very high. As a result, interest rates ruled very high. While the marginal cost of funds for DFIs increased sharply, they had the advantage of recycling some of the past concessional borrowings at high rate of interest. Taking advantage of flexibility provided to them in the matter of raising and deploying external commercial borrowings, DFIs also raised significant funds from the international market. In view of the booming conditions in the domestic capital market, some of the DFIs could also raise resources successfully both by way of debt and equity at handsome premia. On the asset side, there was a good demand for funds due to acceleration of economic activity in general and industrial sector in particular.

On their part, DFIs took several steps to reposition themselves and reorient their operations in the new competitive environment. They have diversified their activities into new areas of business such as investment banking, stock broking and other fee and commission based business. Nevertheless, their business has slowed down and their operations have become less profitable. The Committee on Banking Sector Reforms (Chairman: M. Narasimham), 1998 recommended that DFIs should, over a period of time, convert themselves into banks or non-banking financial companies (NBFCs). It is noteworthy that ICICI, one of the leading DFIs, has merged with the ICICI Bank.

Financial institutions, which constitute an important source of funds for the commercial sector, have been losing ground fast. The situation has come about as a result of the distinction between development and commercial banking getting blurred, high cost of funds and asset-liability mismatches. With reforms in the financial sector, the facility of low cost funds under long-term operations funds, funds from bilateral and multilateral agencies and bond issues under statutory liquidity ratio is no more available. Now the financial institutions are raising funds at market-related rates of interest. The RBI had advised financial institutions to chart a path for their evolution into universal banks. The merger of ICICI with the ICICI Bank was approved by the RBI in April 2002. The merger was approved subject to ICICI fulfilling conditions relating to reserve requirements and prudential norms after the merger.

Lately, DFIs have taken several steps to reposition themselves and reorient their operations in the competitive environment by offering innovative products and diversifying their activities into new areas of business (such as investment banking, stock broking, custodial services, etc.) so as to harness the synergies and to reduce the risk arising out of narrow specialisation.

As a result of liberalisation of trade and industrial sectors, competition in the commodity market increased. While some companies were able to cope with the increased competition effectively, some others were not. This also had an adverse effect on the asset quality of DFIs. In a declining interest rate scenario, high cost of funds raised by DFIs in the past became a cause of concern. As a result, some of the DFIs by exercising call option redeemed the long-term bonds long before their final maturity. Competition on the asset side also increased with some banks stepping up their project finance activity. All these factors have significantly impinged on the profitability of DFIs. As DFIs have high NPAs, they would be required to provide for them, which is likely to put a further pressure on their profitability.

To sum up, DFIs in India have had a long and successful history and were visualised in a role complementary to commercial banks and other private financial agents, primarily to fill the gaps in lending activities of long gestation that were not catered to by the commercial banks. DFIs owed their origin to the objective of state-driven planned economic development after Independence in 1947, when the capital markets were relatively underdeveloped and judged to be incapable of meeting adequately the long-term requirements of the economy. Over the years, a wide range of DFIs, mostly Government-owned, came into existence to cater to the medium to long-term financing requirements of different sectors of the economy.

The setting up of specialised financial institutions and refinance institutions provided depth to financial intermediation outside the banking sector. Of late a number of financial institutions have diversified into several new activities, such as investment banking, infrastructure financing, and providing guarantees for domestic and offshore lending for infrastructure projects. Coupled with increased financial market liberalization, these developments have enhanced competition in the Indian financial system.

With the progressive blurring of functions between banks and financial institutions, the AIFIs are fast losing ground and adopting the business model of a bank to remain viable in the long run. The merger of ICICI with ICICI bank on March 30, 2002 was the beginning of conversion of AIFIs into universal banks.

Endnote

1. It may be recalled that the Government of India had set up Refinance Corporation of India (RFI) Ltd. in 1958 to provide refinance to the banks against term loans granted by them to medium and small enterprises. The RCI was merged with the IDBI in 1964.

18

Non-banking Financial Companies (NBFCs)

In the multi-tier financial system of India, NBFCs stand apart for more than one reason. Though these companies essentially do the job of financial intermediation, they are still not fully comparable with the other segments of the financial system. This is so in view of the wide variations in the profile of the players in this sector in terms of their nature of activity—lending, investment, lease, hire purchase, chit fund, pure deposit mobilisation, fee based activity etc.—the volume of activity, the sources of funding they rely on (public deposits and non-public deposits), method of raising resources, deployment pattern etc. This has naturally resulted in the creation of multifarious categories of NBFCs and therefore, diverse regulatory dispensation by RBI.

18.1 Classification of NBFCs

NBFCs comprise a heterogeneous lot of privately-owned, small-sized financial intermediaries which provide a variety of services including equipment leasing, hire purchase, loans, investments and chit fund activities. These companies play an important role in providing credit to the unorganised sector and to the small borrowers at the local level. Hire purchase finance is by far the largest activity of NBFCs.

Though heterogeneous, NBFCs can be broadly classified into three categories: (a) asset finance companies (such as equipment leasing and hire purchase), (b) loan companies and (c) investment companies.

A separate category of NBFCs, called the residuary non-banking companies (RNBCs), also exists as it has not been categorised into any one of the above referred three categories.

Besides, there are miscellaneous non-banking companies (chit funds), mutual benefit financial companies (*Nidhis* and unnotified *Nidhis*) and housing finance companies.

In terms of regulation and supervision, there are two broad categories of non-banking financial companies (NBFCs), viz. Non-banking Financial Companies–Deposit Taking (NBFCs-D) and Non-banking Financial Companies–Non-deposit Taking (NBFCs-ND). While NBFCs-D have been regulated by the RBI from 1963, an amendment to the RBI Act in 1997 empowered the RBI to regulate and supervise all categories of NBFCs more comprehensively. NBFCs-ND, until recently, were subject to minimal regulation as they were non-deposit taking. Recognising, however, the growing importance of this segment and their linkages to banks and other financial institutions, capital adequacy and exposure norms were made applicable to NBFCs-ND with assets above ₹ 100 crore from April 1, 2007.

18.2 Regulatory Responsibility of NBFCs

The heterogeneous nature of the non-banking financial companies sector is widely recognised. They perform diverse activities and are currently categorised under various sectors. Depending on their primary sphere of specialisation, the regulatory responsibility of these entities is distributed across regulators (Table 18.1).

Table 18.1: Regulators of Non-banking Financial Companies (NBFCs)

Type of Non-banking Finance Company	Regulator
Asset finance companies	Reserve Bank of India (RBI)
Loan companies	RBI
Investment companies	RBI
Infrastructure finance	RBI
Mortgage guarantee companies	RBI
Residuary non-banking companies (RNBCs)	RBI
Potential *nidhi* companies	RBI
Mutual benefit financial companies (*Nidhi* companies)	Central Government (Ministry of Company Affairs)
Miscellaneous non-banking companies (chit fund companies)	Registrar of Chit Funds
Housing finance companies (HFCs)	National Housing Bank (NHB)
Merchant banking companies	Securities and Exchange Board of India (SEBI)
Venture capital fund companies	SEBI
Stock exchange/stock broker/sub-broker	SEBI
Insurance companies	Insurance Regulatory and Development Authority (IRDA)
Micro finance companies	No regulatory body

Source: Reserve Bank of India, *Financial Stability Report*, March 2010, p. 56.

A company is considered as an NBFC and is within the regulatory jurisdiction of the Reserve Bank if it carries on as its business or part of its business, any of the activities listed in Section 45 I (c) of the RBI Act, 1934. In other words, to be an NBFC, an institution has to be: (a) a company under Companies Act, (b) it should be engaged in financial activity, and (c) its principal business should not be agricultural, industrial or trading activity or real estate business.

18.3 Importance of NBFCs

Although NBFCs in India have existed for a long time, they shot into prominence in the second half of the 1980s and in the first-half of the 1990s, as deposits raised by them grew rapidly. NBFCs were historically subjected to a relatively lower degree of regulation vis-à-vis banks. Prior to reforms in this sector, operations of NBFCs were characterized by several distinctive features viz., no entry barriers, limited fixed assets and no holding of inventories-all of which led to a proliferation of NBFCs.

Primarily engaged in the area of retail banking, they face competition from banks and financial institutions. With the increasing services sector activity in India, the NBFCs have been playing a critical role in providing credit. NBFCs have extensive networks with some of them accepting public deposits.

The role of NBFCs in transferring the funds from lenders to borrowers has been well-recognized. The main advantages of these companies are as under:

1. Customer orientation and prompt provision of services.
2. Concentration in the main financial centres.
3. Attractive rates of return offered.
4. Lower transactions costs of operations.
5. Quick decision-making ability.
6. Simplified sanction procedures.
7. Flexibility and timeliness in meeting the credit needs of specified sectors (like equipment leasing and hire purchase).

On account of these advantages, NBFCs have in recent years grown sizeably both in terms of their numbers as well as the volume of business transactions.

NBFCs have been the subject of focussed attention since the early 1990s. The rapid growth of NBFCs has led to a gradual blurring of dividing lines between banks and NBFCs, with the exception of the exclusive privilege that commercial banks exercise in the issuance of cheques.

NBFCs are widely dispersed across the country and their management exhibits varied degrees of professionalism. Furthermore, the depositors have varied degrees of perceptions regarding safety of their deposits while making an investment decision.

18.4 Supervisory Framework for NBFCs

Coupled with the process of regulatory tightening, the RBI has instituted a comprehensive supervisory mechanism over NBFCs.

18.4.1 On-site Inspection: The process of on-site inspection aims at ascertaining the level and quality of adherence by the inspected entities to the regulatory norms prescribed by the RBI in relation to their deposit taking, asset quality, capital adequacy etc.

A. Extent and Periodicity of Inspections: The on-site inspection procedure is tailored to be need-based. Accordingly, on-site inspection is sought to be carried out on a random basis, taking into account the various factors such as the track record of compliance of the NBFCs with the Directions, adherence to the prescribed norms, incidence of complaints etc. The primary focus of on-site inspection is directed towards large (with public deposits of ₹ 50 crore and above) NBFCs, the remaining companies being monitored mainly through off-site surveillance involving scrutiny of statutory returns, balance sheets, profit and loss account, auditors reports etc. All NBFCs holding public deposits, irrespective of the size of their NOF, are subjected to at least one round of on-site inspection on an annual basis to ensure that they function within the regulatory framework.

18.4.2 Off-site Surveillance System: The RBI has also devised comprehensive formats for conducting off-site surveillance of NBFCs with asset size of ₹ 100 crore and above. The returns so prescribed are designed to provide the comparative position of their operational data for 3 years in regard to various items of their balance sheet, profit and loss account and certain key ratios. Further, in terms of the off-site system, it is mandatory on the part of all NBFCs to submit various returns at quarterly/half-yearly/annual intervals, irrespective of the size of their NOF or their acceptance or otherwise of public deposits. Errors/discrepancies in such analyses, if any, trigger on-site inspections to ensure supervisory comfort. Steps have also been initiated by the RBI to computerize the off-site surveillance mechanism in its entirety. Besides, the market intelligence system is also being strengthened in major regional offices, under the overall guidance of a market intelligence officer. Steps have also been initiated for closer co-ordination with other regulatory bodies like SEBI and credit rating agencies.

18.4.3 External Auditing: The responsibilities of ensuring compliance of the directions issued by the RBI as well as adherence to the provisions of the RBI Act has been entrusted with the statutory auditors of the NBFCs. The statutory auditors of the NBFCs are required to report to the RBI any irregularity or violation of the RBI's regulations concerning acceptance of public deposits, credit rating, prudential norms and exposure limits, capital adequacy, maintenance of liquid assets and regularisation of excess deposits held by the companies.

18.5 Regulations over NBFCs Accepting Public Deposits

Companies which accept public deposits are required to comply with all the prudential norms on income recognition, asset classification, accounting standards, provisioning for bad and doubtful debts, capital adequacy, credit/investment concentration norms etc. The RBI has been vigorously disseminating through the news media information about the NBFCs seeking deposits. Prospective depositors are cautioned, through advertisements and otherwise, that they should be careful in understanding the actual financial position of the company concerned and the statements or representations made by the management in their advertisement while placing their deposits with the NBFCs. Instant publicity is also provided for companies whose certificate of registration have been rejected or against whom prohibitory orders have been issued.

18.5.1 Regulations over NBFCs not Accepting Public Deposits: The NBFCs not accepting public deposits are regulated in a limited manner. Such companies have been exempted from the regulations on interest rates, period as well as the ceiling on quantum of borrowings. The ceiling on the aforesaid factors for NBFCs accepting public deposits is expected to act as a benchmark for NBFCs not accepting public deposits. However, prudential norms having a bearing on the disclosure of true and fair picture of their financial health have been made applicable to ensure transparency in the financial statements to these companies, excepting those relating to capital adequacy and credit concentration norms.

18.5.2 Regulations over Core Investment Companies: The core investment companies, not accepting public deposits and are holding investments to the extent of 90 percent or more of their assets as securities issued by their group/subsidiary companies and are not trading in these securities have been exempted from all the provisions of directions except the statutory provisions of: (a) registration, and (b) creation of reserve fund.

18.6 Residual Non-banking Companies (RNBCs)

RNBCs are a class of NBFCs which cannot be classified as equipment leasing, hire purchase, loan, investment, *nidhi* or *chit fund* companies, but which tap public savings by operating various deposit schemes, akin to recurring deposit schemes of banks.

Prior to the regulatory framework of Chapter III of the RBI Act, 1997, the operations of RNBCs were characterized by a host of dubious features including the following:
1. Systematic understatement of their deposit liability.
2. Payment of high rates of commission.
3. Forfeiture of deposits.
4. Low or negligible rate of return on deposits.
5. Appropriation of capital receipt to revenue account and consequent non-disclosure of the entire deposit liability in their books of accounts/balance sheets.
6. Levy of service charges on the depositors etc.
7. Non-compliance with the core provisions of the RBI directions.
8. Diversion of the depositors' money to associate concerns and/or investment in illiquid assets.
9. Violations of investment requirements/pattern etc.

The track record of regulatory compliance for RNBCs has been significantly lower vis-à-vis other NBFC groups. Monitoring and inspection of these companies, from time to time, revealed continuance of many unsatisfactory features. These features were impinging upon the interests of the depositors.

The RBI adopted several measures to remove these unsatisfactory features but the results were limited. The RBI could only prohibit the errant companies from accepting deposits any further. However, keeping in view both the depositors' interests as well as the interest of the employees of the companies, imposing prohibitory orders in all cases was not a solution to the problem, particularly in the case of large RNBCs with substantial public deposits.

Accordingly, persistent efforts were made by the RBI to spruce up their operations and ensure compliance with its Directions. In cases where adherence to Directions was found unavoidable, the RBI had to resort to issue of prohibitory orders on a case-by-case basis. However, in many cases, the actions initiated by the RBI were constrained when some of these companies approached the courts of law and obtained stay orders and at the same time continued to mobilise deposits. Some of the ingenious promoters floated new companies and started accepting deposits through new entities or shifted their areas of operations to other states.

Equipped with the new regulatory framework of Chapter III-B of the RBI Act, 1997, the RBI has extended prudential norms to the RNBCs. The requirement for compulsory registration for RNBCs before commencing business coupled with other concerted action against such companies has curbed the unhealthy tendency of mushrooming growth of these companies. The inspections and monitoring of the activities of the RNBCs have been stepped up to ensure that the erring companies should rectify the irregularities and fall in line with the regulatory framework.

18.7 Mutual Benefit Financial Companies

A *Nidhi* company notified under Section 620A of the Companies Act, 1956 is classified as mutual benefit financial company (MBFC) by the RBI and is regulated by the RBI for its deposit taking activities and by the Department of Company Affairs (DCA) for its operational matters as also the deployment of funds. The companies incorporated after January 9, 1997 have been considered as mutual benefit companies only if they have minimum NOF of ₹ 25 lakh and have obtained a Certificate of Registration from the RBI under the provisions of the RBI Act. These companies have been exempted from substantial provisions of the RBI Act, namely requirement of registration, maintenance of liquid assets and creation of reserve fund. They have also been exempted from almost all the provisions of RBI Directions except those relating to: (a) interest rate on deposits, (b) prohibition from paying brokerage on deposits, (c) ban on advertisement, and (d) requirements of submission of certain returns. However, they are allowed to deal only with their shareholders both for the purpose of accepting deposits and making loans.

On the other hand, the companies which are purportedly working like *nidhis* without their names being notified under Section 620A of the Companies Act, 1956, were adversely affected by the RBI's directions to classify such companies as loan companies, as they could not obtain the special dispensation available to notified *nidhi* companies. As a result, the Government decided to give a special dispensation to these companies working on the lines of *nidhi* companies. Accordingly, a separate class of such companies termed as mutual benefit companies (MBCs) or un-notified *nidhi* companies was created subject to certain norms, till they are notified as *nidhi* companies.

18.7.1 Expert Committee on Nidhis: The Government of India constituted an Expert Committee in March 2000 (Chairman: P. Sabanayagam) to examine various aspects of the functioning of the *nidhi* companies and suggest an appropriate policy framework for overall improvement of these companies. This was done with a view to facilitate their healthy functioning and restore the confidence of the investing public.

The Expert Committee submitted its Report to the Government on September 28, 2000. The Committee observed that although *nidhis* essentially operate on the principle of mutual benefit (i.e. they accept deposits only from members and lend only to members), given the large number of failures in this sector, the regulatory framework governing such companies should be on the same lines as that applicable to NBFCs, without stifling the basic principle on which they are formed or disturbing their local character. Accordingly, the regulatory framework for such companies recommended by the Expert Committee encompassed entry point barriers, minimum capital funds, debt-equity ratio, liquid asset requirements, restrictions on dividend, ceiling on interest rates on deposits and loans, regulations of various managerial aspects, disclosure norms, prudential norms, adequate supervisory framework, role of auditors and other measures for protection of depositors' interests.

The statutory regulatory framework for *nidhis* suggested by the Expert Committee encompassed the following stipulations:

Entry Point Norms:

1. Entry point barriers of minimum members of 500 and minimum capital fund of ₹ 10 lakh.
2. Use of *Nidhi* as part of the name of the company to distinguish between a NBFC and a *nidhi* company, restrictions on opening branches by *nidhi* companies.
3. Regulation over issue of equity and preference share capital.

Prudential Norms:

1. Prudential norms on income recognition, asset classification, credit concentration, provisioning for bad and doubtful debts.
2. Restrictions over voting rights and other managerial aspects including remuneration and loans to directors, norms for conduct of affairs of the board of directors, prohibition of grant of loans to directors etc.
3. Sectoral exposure ceilings for aggregate loans against each type of collateral security.

Regulatory Stipulations:

1. Ceiling on interest rates on deposits and loans.
2. Minimum and maximum period of deposits.
3. Advertisement and disclosure norms for deposit acceptance.
4. Net owned fund to deposit ratio of 1:20.
5. Liquid asset requirements of not less than 10 percent of deposits.
6. Adequate reporting system and supervisory framework, submission of quarterly and other periodical returns by the *nidhis* to the regulatory authority after certification by the auditor.

Other Measures:

1. Dividend not to exceed 25 percent per annum, subject to transfer of equivalent amount to the Reserve Fund.
2. Penal provisions for various violations.
3. Other depositors' protection measures like contingency fund, insurance cover, if possible.

*Nidhi*s are governed under the provisions of the Companies Act in force. However, the RBI is also empowered to issue directions in matters relating to deposit acceptance activities. The Expert Committee, therefore, suggested that the dual regulatory control over *nidhis* should be done away with and that the sole responsibility for regulating and supervising of *nidhis* could be under the Department of Company Affairs, Government of India and the RBI could tender advice from time to time.

18.8 NBFCs in Insurance Business

In June 2000, NBFCs registered with the RBI were permitted, with prior approval of the RBI, to set up insurance joint ventures for undertaking insurance business with risk participation. Similarly, NBFCs registered with the RBI that have net owned funds of ₹ 5 crore and more are permitted to undertake insurance business as agent of insurance companies on a fee basis, without any risk participation. A minimum 12 percent capital adequacy for NBFCs which want to enter into insurance joint ventures has been prescribed. If the company holds public deposits, the minimum capital adequacy has been proposed at 15 percent. Further, minimum net worth requirement of ₹ 500 crore, three years of continuous net profit, and maximum non-performing assets of 5 percent of the total outstanding leased/hire purchase assets and advances have been prescribed for NBFCs.

In February 2004, it was decided to allow NBFCs registered with the RBI to take up insurance agency business on a fee basis and without risk participation, without the approval of the RBI subject to certain conditions.

To sum up, prior to the Reserve Bank (Amendment) Act, 1997, there was lack of adequate regulation and supervision mechanism for most types of NBFCs. It is true that NBFCs were regulated by the RBI but the focus of the latter was mainly on the liability side. Keeping in view various systemic issues, the need was felt for further strengthening the regulatory and supervisory framework for NBFCs. Accordingly, the Reserve Bank of India (Amendment) Act was enacted in 1997. It conferred extensive powers on the RBI for regulation and supervision of NBFCs. Given the immense diversity among NBFCs, norms were strengthened particularly for public deposits.

Following this Amendment, a comprehensive regulatory framework for NBFCs sector was put in place. The regulatory framework was tightened further. Non-submission of periodic returns to RBI by NBFCs is a common feature. To address this problem, RBI decided to impose penalties besides considering cancellation of certificate of registration of NBFCs having deposits of ₹ 50 crore and above.

The Amended Act also prescribed the revised entry point norms, compulsory registration with the RBI, maintenance of certain percentage of liquid assets in the form of unencumbered approved securities, formulating a reserve policy and transferring certain proportion of profits every year.

In order to ensure that the depositors are served appropriately and systemic risks are avoided, the current focus of the RBI is on improving their functioning, including transparency of operations, corporate governance, know your customer (KYC) rules etc.

There are indications that the reform process has not as yet resulted in any noticeable improvement in the operational efficiency of NBFCs. In fact profitability position has showed some signs of deterioration in recent years. Similarly, operations of NBFCs have witnessed significant changes especially on the liability side. With the tightening of regulations, many of the NBFCs with insufficient capital base have been weeded out. This combined with the tightening of regulations for raising deposits has resulted in reduction in size of this sector.

As NBFCs provide important services in certain niche areas of the financial sector, improvement in the efficiency of these entities is of crucial importance. The RBI has continued to pursue with various State Governments the case for enacting legislation for protection of interest of depositors in financial establishments. Creating public awareness about activities and risk-profile of NBFCs is yet another important area, which needs to be focussed upon. Improvement in corporate governance practices and financial disclosures by NBFCs also need to be focused upon in future.

In addition to banks, existing and new, there is also a continuing role for NBFCs. The bulk of the NBFC sector in India remains very small, does not have the ability to garner public deposits, and in aggregate has performed at a very high level of quality. The sector as a whole, therefore, does not constitute a source of systemic instability. It has instead been playing the role of extending the reach of the banking system to the more difficult parts of the economy.

19

Mutual Funds

Mutual fund is a financial intermediary established in the form of a trust to utilize savings from public at large (mostly household savings) and invest the pooled fund in various instruments of capital and money market. Mutual funds are very popular all over the world and they play an important role in the financial system of many countries. Mutual funds are an ideal medium for investment by small investors in the stock market. Mutual funds pool together the investments of small investors for participation in the stock market. Being institutional investors, mutual funds can afford market analysis generally not available to individual investors. Furthermore, mutual funds can diversify the portfolio in a better way as compared with individual investors due to the expertise and availability of funds. A diversified portfolio always has a lower risk profile than a concentrated portfolio.

19.1 Types of Mutual Funds

Mutual funds can be of various types.

- **Open-ended Funds:** They are the most liquid funds. Units can be bought from and sold to the fund itself throughout the year (except book closure period), There is no fixed maturity period. Sale and purchase is at NAV-related prices which are disclosed on daily basis
- **Closed-ended Funds:** They are open for subscription only during a specific period. They are listed on stock exchange after specified period. They have a fixed maturity period (say 3 to 15 years).
- **Growth Funds:** The objective is to generate long-term capital appreciation from a portfolio.
- **Income Funds:** The objective is to generate regular income with safety of investment.
- **Balanced Funds:** The objective is to generate capital appreciation along with current income from a balanced portfolio of equity and debt
- **Gilt Funds:** The objective is to generate risk-free returns by investments in sovereign securities issued by Central and State Governments.

19.2 Legal and Regulatory Framework

In general, the mutual fund regulatory framework in India is much more extensive and developed than in many other countries. Indian mutual funds are unit trusts, formed under the Indian Trusts Act of 1882. Their operation is governed by mutual fund regulations, totalling 78, promulgated by SEBI in exercise of the powers conferred by

Section 30, read with clause (c) of sub-section (2) of Section 11 of the Securities and Exchange Board of India, Act 1992. The first set of mutual fund regulations was originally promulgated in 1996, and has since been amended from time to time. In order to remove any difficulties in the application or interpretation of these regulations, Regulation 77 of the mutual funds regulations additionally authorises SEBI to issue "clarifications and guidelines in the form of notes or circulars which shall be binding upon the sponsor, mutual funds, trustees, asset management companies and custodians".

19.3 History of Mutual Funds

Mutual funds in India were first created in 1963 when the Unit Trust of India (UTI), a state-sponsored entity, came into being. Until 1987, UTI was the only mutual fund in the country. Between 1987 and 1993 other entities belonging to the public sector were permitted to offer mutual funds—basically state-controlled banks and insurers. As part of financial sector reforms, the mutual fund industry was opened to the private sector in 1993. Thus, from 1993 onwards, private sector organisations were permitted to enter the market and the first mutual fund regulations were promulgated, which were subsequently replaced by the SEBI (Mutual Fund) Regulations of 1996. These private sector organisations comprised both Indian and foreign joint ventures as well as purely Indian firms.

Since then, the expansion of mutual fund business has intensified competition and led to product innovation. Mutual funds presently offer a variety of options to investors such as income funds, balanced funds, liquid funds, gift funds, index funds, exchange traded funds, sectoral funds etc. The deceleration in the growth of mutual funds in the 1990s could be attributed partly to the relatively poor performance of the stock markets and partly due to withdrawal of tax benefits under Section 80M of the Indian Income Tax Act, 1961. Some of the mutual funds had offered assured return schemes enabling them to mobilise large resources. A number of mutual funds faced difficulties in meeting their redemption obligations relating to such schemes. In several cases, the sponsors of mutual funds had to infuse additional funds to meet the shortfall. As a result, mutual funds, by and large, discontinued the floatation of assured return schemes, which had some dampening effect on the resource mobilisation by mutual funds.

19.3.1 Bifurcation of UTI: While most of the mutual funds were somehow able to meet their commitments on account of assured return schemes, UTI faced a somewhat different problem on two different occasions between October 1998 and July 2001. US-64, which was the flagship scheme of UTI and enjoyed the investors' faith, first faced problem in December 1998 when the reserves under the scheme were reported negative. In order to restore investors' confidence, several measures were initiated by the Government/UTI. While these measures helped the US-64 to make a turnaround, the problem resurfaced again in July 2001 when UTI slashed down the dividend rates for the year 2000-01 and suspended sales and repurchases of US-64 for a period of 6 months from July 2001 to December 2001. This created a crisis of confidence and to restore investors' confidence various measures were initiated again, which culminated in splitting the UTI into two parts.

On October 28, 2002, an ordinance was promulgated which repealed the UTI Act, and bifurcated UTI into two separate entities. One is the Specified Undertaking of the Unit Trust of India. The Specified Undertaking of Unit Trust of India, functioning under an administrator and under the rules framed by Government of India and does not come under the purview of the mutual fund regulations. It has US-64 and the assured returns schemes. The second is the UTI Mutual Fund Ltd, sponsored by State Bank of India (SBI), Bank of Baroda (BoB), Punjab National Bank (PNB) and Life Insurance Corporation of India (LIC). It is registered with SEBI and functions under the mutual fund regulations. It is an unencumbered mutual fund, with only NAV-based schemes.

The problem with US-64 scheme of UTI adversely affected the resource mobilisation by mutual funds in general and UTI in particular. On both the occasions, when UTI faced difficulties and while resource mobilisation by UTI declined sharply, private sector mutual funds were able to fill the gap created by UTI only partially as overall mobilisation by all mutual funds on both the occasions declined sharply after the occurrence of the problem.

In March 2002, guidelines were issued to enable mutual funds to invest in rated securities in countries with fully convertible currencies. This marked an important milestone, through which mutual funds will be able to deliver better risk/return tradeoffs through international diversification.

19.4 Features of Mutual Fund Industry in India
These are as under:
1. Mutual funds are popular mainly with the middle and high-income groups.
2. Investors are largely based in the urban centres, particularly the metropolitan cities.
3. Penetration of mutual funds in the rural areas remains small.
4. UTI and other state-owned asset management companies have lost market share, while private sector funds have grown rapidly.
5. Asset management companies are divided into those that are predominantly owned by the state (UTI, bank sponsored and institutions) and those that are in the private sector.
6. Mutual fund industry has to compete with attractive assured returns from Government schemes and this is possibly the single most important impediment to the growth of the industry.

Thus, if mutual funds have to grow fast, they would need to devise appropriate schemes to attract the saving of low-income groups, especially in rural areas. This is the only way to ensure participation of all categories of investors into the capital market, which is so crucial for its long-term development.

19.5 Problems of Mutual Funds
India has a high household savings ratio. Indians, like most people anywhere, are conservative in their habits, and it would take many years to change this behaviour, particularly when it comes to the use of their savings. As in most countries, investment in

physical assets (mainly housing and gold) accounts for the most important percentage of household assets. Owning a home is usually a first priority once a family has any disposable income at all.

19.5.1 Competition with Government Schemes: Mutual funds compete against a host of high yielding government-backed savings schemes such as public provident fund (PPF), national savings scheme (NSS), RBI bonds, and so on, as well as against life insurance products and, in the future, against the new pension schemes for the unorganised sector. [1] The political and social reasons for keeping yields higher than the market for small savers, particularly retired savers, is understandable. The market is distorted by such a policy. Government should have the strategic aim of discontinuing over time or at least reducing the availability of the unrealistically high yielding avenues for small savings. The objective of widening and deepening ownership of mutual funds is unlikely to be met until this happens.

Fixed income and balanced mutual funds have offered a reasonably competitive rate of return but they are not guaranteed, a key attraction to Indian investors. The net result is that mutual funds fail to attract much money from retail investors, who prefer to invest in a no-risk, high return product, i.e. government saving schemes or provident funds or keep their money safely in the bank.

Government-sponsored instruments *crowd out* mutual funds since for the majority of Indians buying mutual funds, before they have their full complement of government-backed savings instruments, would be both wrong and foolish.

In most countries government guaranteed financial instruments offer returns that are likely to be significantly lower than private sector investments available from mutual funds or insurance companies. This is the penalty that investors are prepared to pay for little or no risk. However, Indian retail investors are not being asked to sacrifice any substantial amount of return in exchange for a government guarantee. Conversely, returns on government assured investments are often better than those available elsewhere. While conventional government bonds do give lower returns than equivalent private sector corporate bonds, the retail government assured products give higher returns for almost no risk. It is thus hardly surprising that an investor of modest means would choose to invest in, for instance, national savings certificates, since he can thus obtain a better return for a much lower risk. Any investor would be well advised to invest the maximum permitted in the various government assured schemes before considering other forms of investment.

The reasons why the government is prepared to pay above market rates of interest on certain financial products is understandable. At a time when interest rates have fallen substantially from their previous levels, savers who had counted on the interest on their savings to provide an income, particularly in retirement, are being subsidised. Given that pension arrangements, particularly in the unorganised sector, are not widespread, such an approach is reasonable and indeed most small savers are acting rationally when they choose the low risk option. However, this approach conflicts with a desire to widen and deepen participation in capital markets through mutual funds or other non-governmental savings products by the less well-off sectors of the population.

19.5.2 Competition from Insurance: The take up life assurance is growing rapidly and may be pre-empting some of the market that mutual funds could aim at. Life assurance is an easier product to sell, since in the mind of the investor the payment of a premium is often linked to a specific outcome, a lump sum payment on death or a guaranteed minimum sum on maturity. It also pays higher commissions to sales agents (typically the amount of the first 5 to 6 months premium). Thus, a sales agent will usually prefer to sell a life policy since it will reward him better.

19.5.3 Volatility of Mutual Fund Performance: There is a perception that mutual funds have somehow let down their investors and given them poor returns. In July 2001 when UTI slashed down the dividend rates for the year 2000-01 and suspended sales and repurchases of US-64 for a period of 6 months from July 2001 to December 2001, it created a crisis of confidence among the investors with long-term effects.

19.5.4 Tax System Encourages Short-term Objectives: Mutual funds are regarded in most countries as a diversified, professionally managed and well-regulated vehicle for mobilising household savings and are often accorded tax privileges specifically in pursuit of a government policy goal to encourage long-term savings, notably for retirement. [2] It is unusual for such tax privileges to impel mutual funds towards short-term goals, which is what seems to be the case in India. True, Indian unit trusts are diversified, professionally managed and well-regulated, but they are certainly not serving long-term objectives.

19.6 Mutual Funds and the Stock Market

Mutual funds in India, because of their small size and slower growth in the recent past, have tended to play only a limited role in the stock market. In view of small size of their operations, mutual funds in normal times hardly exert any influence on the stock market. Mutual funds with large funds at their disposal are expected by the government to act as a counterweight to foreign institutional investors (FIIs), which generally exert a significant influence on the stock market. Some leading asset management companies in India are listed in Table 19.1.

Table 19.1: Leading Asset Management Companies in India
(as in March 2017)

S. No.	Name of the Company
Bank Sponsored	
1.	BOI AXA Investment Managers Pvt. Ltd.
2.	Canara Robeco Asset Management Co. Ltd.
3.	SBI Funds Management Pvt. Ltd.
4.	Union Asset Management Co. Pvt. Ltd.
5.	Baroda Pioneer Asset Management Co. Ltd.
6.	IDBI Asset Management Ltd.
7.	UTI Asset Management Co. Ltd.

Institutions	
1.	IIFCL Asset Management Co. Ltd.
2.	LIC Mutual Fund Asset Management Ltd.
Private Sector (Indian and Foreign)	
1.	Edelweiss Asset Management Ltd.
2.	Escorts Asset Management Ltd.
3.	IIFL Asset Management Ltd.
4.	IL&FS Infra Asset Management Ltd.
5.	Indiabulls Asset Management Co. Ltd.
6.	JM Financial Asset Management Ltd.
7.	Kotak Mahindra Asset Management Co. Ltd.
8.	L&T Investment Management Ltd.
9.	Mahindra Asset Management Co. Pvt. Ltd.
10.	Motilal Oswal Asset Management Co. Ltd.
11.	Peerless Funds Management Co. Ltd.
12.	PPFAS Asset Management Pvt. Ltd.
13.	Quantum Asset Management Co. Pvt. Ltd.
14.	Sahara Asset Management Co. Pvt. Ltd.
15.	Shriram Asset Management Co. Ltd.
16.	Sundaram Asset Management Co. Ltd.
17.	Tata Asset Management Ltd.
18.	Taurus Asset Management Co. Ltd.
19.	BNP Paribas Asset Management (India) Pvt. Ltd.
20.	Franklin Templeton Asset Management (India) Pvt. Ltd.
21.	Invesco Asset Management (India) Pvt. Ltd.
22.	Mirae Asset Global Investments (India) Pvt. Ltd.
Joint Ventures (Indian and Foreign)	
1.	Axis Asset Management Co. Ltd.
2.	Birla Sun Life Asset Management Co. Ltd.
3.	DSP BlackRock Investment Managers Pvt. Ltd.
4.	HDFC Asset Management Co. Ltd.
5.	ICICI Prudential Asset Management Co. Ltd.
6.	IDFC Asset Management Co. Ltd.
7.	Reliance Nippon Life Asset Management Ltd.
8.	HSBC Asset Management (India) Pvt. Ltd.
9.	Principal PNB Asset Management Co. Pvt. Ltd.
10.	DHFL Pramerica Asset Managers Pvt. Ltd.

Table 19.2 presents the value of assets under management of mutual funds in India.

Table 19.2: Assets under Management of Mutual Funds: 2000-2017

S. No.	Year (ending March 31)	Amount (₹ crore)
1.	2000	1,07,946
2.	2001	90,587
3.	2002	1,00,954
4.	2003	1,09,229
5.	2004	1,39,616
6.	2005	1,49,600
7.	2006	2,31,862
8.	2007	3,26,292
9.	2008	5,05,152
10.	2009	4,17,300
11.	2010	6,13,979
12.	2011	5,92,250
13.	2012	5,87,217
14.	2013	7,01,443
15.	2014	8,25,240
16.	2015	10,82,757
17.	2016	12,32,824
18.	2017	17,54,619
19.	**As on May 31, 2017**	**19,03,975**

Sources: www.rbi.org and www.amfiindia.com

To sum up, the mutual fund industry in India is quite sophisticated and successful. It is dominated by good and reputable institutions, both Indian and international. Nevertheless improvements are always possible and desirable in order to enhance the ability of the mutual fund industry to mobilise savings on a wider scale and to contribute to the further development of capital market.

Endnotes

1. Many of the government assured schemes are probably not fulfilling their original purpose. For example the Public Provident Fund (PPP) was set up in 1968-69 with the objective of providing unorganised sector workers with a facility to accumulate savings for old age income security. As a result of premature withdrawal facilities and tax breaks, individuals largely misuse this scheme for legitimised tax evasion and it does not serve the intended purpose of old age income security.
2. There is no perfect system for taxing the income and gains of mutual funds and their investors. The main principle that almost all regimes follow is that there should be broadly equality of treatment between all mutual fund investors and between mutual fund investors and direct investors in securities. In other words, an investor purchasing assets indirectly through a mutual fund should be no worse off tax-wise than if that same investor bought those assets directly on their own behalf. This is the principle of *fiscal neutrality*.

The taxation of funds is a key issue for funds and their management companies. Taxation affects both the attractiveness of funds compared with other investments, and also the systems that may have to be designed and implemented in order for funds to operate efficiently and cost effectively. Fund managers in virtually every market in the world lobby governments hard either to remove tax disadvantages or to achieve favourable treatment, so that their product can become more competitive in the market and more attractive to potential buyers.

20

Pension Funds

Noting that only about 12-13 percent of the total workforce was covered by any formal social security system, pension sector reforms were initiated in India to establish a robust and sustainable social security arrangement in the country.

20.1 National Pension System (NPS)

NPS (earlier New Pension System) reflects Government's effort to find sustainable solutions to the problem of providing adequate retirement income. As a first step towards instituting pensionary reforms, Government of India moved from a defined benefit pension to a defined contribution-based pension system by making it mandatory for its new recruits (except armed forces) with effect from January 1, 2004.

Since April 1, 2008, the pension contributions of Central Government employees covered by NPS are being invested by professional pension fund managers (PFMs) in line with investment guidelines of Government applicable to non-Government provident funds.

NPS has been made available to every citizen from April 1, 2009 on a voluntary basis. With the extension of NPS to all citizens, every citizen in the country now has the opportunity to participate in a regulated pension market. This will contribute significantly to old age income security in the country.

Features of the NPS design are self-sustainability, portability and scalability. Based on individual choice, it is envisaged as a low-cost and efficient pension system backed by sound regulation. As a pure *defined contribution* product with no defined benefit element, returns are totally market-related. NPS provides various investment options and choices to individuals to switch over from one option to another or from one fund manager to another, subject to certain regulatory restrictions.

NPS architecture is transparent and web-enabled. It allows a subscriber to monitor his/her investments and returns under NPS, the choice of PFM and the investment option also rest with the subscriber. The design allows the subscriber to switch his/her investment options as well as pension funds. The facility for seamless portability and switch between PFMs is designed to enable subscribers to maintain a single pension account throughout their saving period.

Full NPS architecture—comprising a central recordkeeping agency (CRA), pension fund managers (PFMs), trustee banks, custodians and NPS Trust—has been put in place and is fully operational. National Securities Depository Limited (NSDL) has been selected as the CRA.

NPS has been designed to enable the subscriber to make optimum decisions regarding his/her future and provide for his/her old-age through systemic savings from the day he/she starts his/her employment. It seeks to inculcate the habit of saving for retirement amongst the citizens.

Efforts are under way to extend the reach of the NPS to new segments like Central and State autonomous bodies and the organized sector and introduce micro-pension initiatives focusing on a low cost model of the NPS to be implemented through self-help groups (SHGs) and similar bodies.

20.1.1 Swavalamban Scheme: The Government is extremely concerned about the old age income security of the working poor and is focused on encouraging and enabling them to join the NPS. To encourage workers in the unorganized sector to save voluntarily for their old age, an initiative called the Swavalamban Scheme was launched on September 26, 2010. It is a co-contributory pension scheme whereby the Central Government would contribute a sum of ₹ 1,000 per annum in each NPS account opened having a saving of ₹ 1,000 to ₹ 12,000 per annum. The Swavalamban Scheme was initially announced for 3 years for beneficiaries who enrolled themselves in 2010-11. It was extended to 5 years for beneficiaries enrolled in 2010-11 and 2011-12. For the Swavalamban accounts opened during 2013-2014 to 2016-2017, the benefits will extend till 2016-2017.

Although the NPS is perhaps one of the cheapest financial products available in the country, Swavalamban Scheme enables groups of people to join the NPS at a substantially reduced cost. As per existing scheme under NPS, Swavalamban can be availed either in unorganized sector or in NPS Lite. NPS Lite is a model specifically designed to bring NPS within easy reach of the economically disadvantaged sections of the society. NPS Lite is extremely affordable and viable due to its optimized functionalities available at reduced charges.

20.1.2 NPS Corporate Sector Model: A customized version of the core NPS model, known as the NPS Corporate Sector Model was also introduced from December 2011 to enable organized-sector entities to move their existing and prospective employees to the NPS under its Corporate Model. All the public sector banks have been asked to provide a link on their website to enable individual subscribers to open online NPS Accounts. Several State Governments, autonomous bodies, and undertakings are in dialogue with PFRDA for extending the NPS to their employees. In the non-government NPS segment, clearly NPSLite/Swavalamban has emerged as the vehicle of choice.

20.2 Pension Fund Regulatory and Development Authority (PFRDA)

PFRDA was established by Government of India on August 23, 2003. The Government has, through an executive order dated October 10, 2003, mandated PFRDA to act as a regulator for the pension sector. The mandate of PFRDA is development and regulation of pension sector in India.

PFRDA, set up as a regulatory body for the pension sector, is engaged in consolidating the initiatives taken so far regarding the full NPS architecture and expanding the reach of the NPS distribution network.

Presently, PFRDA has appointed the following 8 pension fund managers (PFMs) for

government and private sector NPS:
1. LIC Pension Fund.
2. SBI Pension Funds.
3. UTI Retirement Solutions.
4. HDFC Pension Management Company.
5. ICICI Prudential Pension Fund Management Company.
6. Reliance Capital Pension Fund.
7. Kotak Mahindra Pension Fund.
8. Birla Sun Life Pension Management.

PFMs manage three separate schemes consisting of three asset classes, namely: (i) equity, (ii) Government securities, and (iii) credit risk-bearing fixed income instruments, with the investment in equity subject to a cap of 50 percent. The fund managers will invest only in index funds that replicate either the BSE sensitive index or NSE Nifty 50 index. The subscriber will have the option to decide the investment mix of his pension wealth. In case the subscriber is unable/unwilling to exercise any choice regarding asset allocation, his contribution will be invested in accordance with the *auto choice* option with a predefined portfolio.

PFRDA has set up a Trust under the Indian Trusts Act, 1882 to oversee the functions of the PFMs. The NPS Trust is composed of members representing diverse fields and brings wide range of talent to the regulatory framework. PFRDA also intends to intensify its effort towards financial education and awareness as a part of its strategy to protect the interest of the subscribers. PFRDA's efforts are an important milestone in the development of a sustainable and efficient voluntary defined contribution based pension system in India.

PFRDA has also enhanced the maximum entry age into NPS from 55 years to 60 years. These initiatives are expected to help realize the full potential of the NPS in terms of economies of scale and benefit the subscribers in terms of lower fees and charges and higher returns.

For all citizens including workers in the unorganized sector, NPS is currently available through over 1,000 service provider (SP) branches of 57 Points of Presence (PoP). PFRDA has also recently appointed the Department of Posts as PoP in addition to other financial institutions which will expand the PoP-SP network by more than five times.

While Tier I, the non-withdrawable pension account under the NPS has been in operation since May 1, 2009, Tier II, the withdrawable account was made operational from December 1, 2009.

NPS implementation in the Central Government has stabilized with more than 5.64 lakh employees already covered. NPS has also been well received by the State Governments and 23 State Governments/Union Territories have notified similar schemes for their new recruits under the ambit of the NPS. PFRDA has been working with all the States to enable them to log on to the NPS architecture with ease.

NPS represents a major reform of Indian pension arrangements, and lays the foundation for a sustainable solution to ageing in India by shifting to an individual account, defined-contribution system.

21

Insurance Organisations

Insurance has been an important part of the Indian financial system. Until recently, insurance services were provided by the public sector i.e. life insurance by the Life Insurance Corporation of India (LIC) since the mid-1950s, and general insurance by the General Insurance Corporation (GIC) and its four subsidiaries since the 1970s. The insurance industry was opened up to the private sector in August 2000. The primary objective of liberalisation in the insurance sector was to deepen insurance penetration by enlarging consumer choices through product innovation. The increased competition has led to rapid product innovations for catering to the diverse requirements of the various segments of the population. Besides statutory commitments in respect of weaker sections of society, competitive pressures are pushing life insurers to adopt innovative marketing strategies to extend insurance penetration, especially targeting lower income groups. Insurance industry in India is broadly classified into: (a) life insurance, and (b) non-life insurance business.

21.1 Nationalisation of Insurance Business in India after Independence

After Independence, the Government came to the conclusion that a strong public sector under its direct control is necessary to meet national objectives of growth, equity, and employment generation. The financial sector was construed as one of the strategic sectors capable of mobilising resources and placing it at the disposal of the Government for being developed as per the national priorities. In pursuance of the above objectives, life insurance was nationalised in 1956, major commercial banks in 1969 and 1980, and general insurance business in 1973.

21.1.1 Nationalisation of Life Insurance (1956): By the Life Insurance (Emergency Provisions) Ordinance, 1956, promulgated by the President of India on January 19, 1956, the management and control of life insurance business in India, including the foreign business of Indian insurers, and the Indian business of foreign insurers, vested with immediate effect in the Central Government. With this the life insurance business passed from the private sector to the public sector. This was the first step towards complete nationalisation of life insurance business in India, a step never before attempted anywhere in the world on such a large scale.

Though the Ordinance was promulgated in January 1956, the Life Insurance Corporation Act was passed in the next session of parliament. Thus, the Life Insurance Corporation of India (LIC) came into existence on September 1, 1956.

In 1968, the Insurance Act, 1938 was amended which empowered the Controller of Insurance to regulate deployment of assets, provide for maximum solvency margin, issue licenses to surveyors, investigate, search and seize their books of accounts etc. The amendment also facilitated setting up of Tariff Advisory Committee to be chaired by the Controller of Insurance. Its functions comprised of controlling and regulating rates, terms and advantages of general insurance business in India.

21.1.2 Nationalisation of General Insurance Business: The general insurance business was nationalised with effect from January 1, 1973, through the General Insurance Business (Nationalisation) Act, 1972. However, as a prelude to the above Act, the Government took over the management of all the operating companies in 1971 through General Insurance (Emergency Provision) Act, 1971. The emergency Act provided for the appointment of custodians who were empowered to exercise control over these companies subject to the directions of the Central Government. At the time of nationalisation, there were a total of 107 companies underwriting general insurance business in India. All these companies were amalgamated and grouped into four, namely the National Insurance Company Limited, the New India Assurance Company Limited, the Oriental Insurance Company Limited, and the United India Insurance Company Limited with head offices at Kolkata, Mumbai, Delhi and Chennai respectively. The General Insurance Company (GIC) was formed as a holding company in November 1972. The GIC was constituted for the purpose of superintending, controlling and carrying out the business of general insurance. The entire capital of GIC was subscribed by the Government and that of four companies by the GIC on behalf of the Government of India.

21.1.3 Reinsurance Business: At the time of Independence in 1947, a good volume of the general insurance business underwritten by Indian insurers was reinsured with foreign concerns, with the result that Indian insurers were not able to retain with them a significant part of the premium that they had collected. This outflow of a good part of insurance income from India was on account of the fact that there was no Indian reinsuring concern. In order to stop the net drain arising out of reinsurances out of India, the Reinsurance Corporation of India Ltd. was registered under the Companies Act on October 29, 1956 and commenced business from January 1, 1957.

All the insurance companies voluntarily decided to cede 10 percent of their gross direct premium to the above Corporation. In 1961, the Government constituted Indian Guarantee and General Insurance Company Ltd., as a Government-owned reinsurance company, which coexisted with Indian Reinsurance Corporation. The insurance companies were required to cede 10 percent of their premium to each of these two companies. In addition, insurers established two other organisations, namely fire insurance pool and the marine insurance pool and a percentage of fire and hull insurance business of the companies was ceded to these pools respectively. The business ceded to these pools was retroceded to the ceding companies thereby ensuring the spread of risks amongst the members of pools.

21.2 Weaknesses of Insurance Industry Prior to Reforms of Late 1990s

People in general have all along been grumbling against LIC's monopolistic exploitation, poor service and high premium rates. Same was the case with general insurance business which was also monopolised by the Government. Articulating the inefficiency of the Government-controlled insurance sector and the need to allow private participation in it, the Ninth Five Year Plan (1997-2002) observed, "...the average premium charged by the insurance companies in India tends to be relatively high due to obsolete and rigid actuarial practices and inefficient operations. There is a pressing need to reorient the insurance sector in India in a manner that it fulfils its principal mandate of providing risk cover. It is unlikely that this sector would attain the requisite degree of efficiency and professionalism unless it is exposed to a certain degree of competition". [1]

21.2.1 Low Productivity: Being a monopoly of the Government, the insurance industry in India could not develop on modern and competitive lines after Independence. It suffered from various infirmities. There can be several parameters to measure the productivity in the insurance sector. These can be in terms of collection of premium per development officer, issuance of documents per employee, claim settlement per employee, underwriting results, yield on investment income etc. Productivity of the Indian insurance industry in terms of these indicators was quite low prior to the reforms of late 1990s.

21.2.2 Lack of Information Technology: The adoption of information technology in the industry was not to the desired extent. There was lack of computerisation and hence database for being utilised by the insurance companies, agents and consumers. Technology infrastructure, such as electronic fund transfer, internet, automatic teller machines, interactive voice response, electronic data inter change, was almost non-existent. The use of internet and e-commerce for selling the insurance products had not yet commenced in the industry.

21.2.3 Limited Availability of Insurance Products: Insurance policies in the segments of health and household risks were not properly marketed and publicised. The entire thrust on health insurance was on products after the occurrence of illness while the preventive aspects were ignored. The products covering environmental and financial risks were non-existent. Another area, which remained untapped, was the development of saving-linked non-life insurance policies.

21.2.4 Poor Quality of Insurance Services: By and large, the quality of insurance services provided was low. The quality of insurance services is evaluated, inter alia, in terms of expeditious settlement of claims, delivery of policy documents and after sales services. The delivery of insurance documents took long times. There was neither proper control on management expenses nor optimal utilisation of investible resources.

21.3 Committee on Reforms in Insurance Sector, 1994

In an effort to change India from being a controlled economy to a market-driven one, inviting participation of private investors, both foreign and Indian, the Government of India initiated a programme of economic reforms in 1991. India, being a member of World Trade Organization (WTO), is also committed to integrate the Indian economy with that of the other member nations in a phased manner.

In this background, the Government set up in April 1993, a high-powered committee headed by R.N. Malhotra, former Governor, Reserve Bank of India to examine the structure of the insurance industry and recommend changes to make it more efficient and competitive, keeping in view the structural changes in other parts of the financial system of the economy. The Committee interacted with the insurance companies, their staff unions, various chambers of commerce, trade bodies and a cross section of the country's public and analysed the present Indian insurance industry. The Committee, which submitted its report on January 7, 1994, felt that the insurance regulatory apparatus should be activated even in the nationalised insurance sector, and recommended, inter alia, the establishment of a strong and effective Insurance Regulatory Authority (IRA), in the form of a statutory autonomous board on the lines of Securities and Exchange Board of India (SEBI). The Committee observed:

1. Indian insurance industry lacks depth, diversity and reach, both geographically as well as in terms of insurable population, as there was immensely vast potential yet to be tapped.
2. It provides poor customer service in terms of pricing, adequacy and appropriateness of covers and the much needed and timely claims settlement.
3. It lacks the global dimensions having remained in isolation too long.

The year 1999 will go down in the insurance history of India as a landmark year when, after prolonged hesitation, Government of India pushed through the Insurance Bill opening up the insurance sector to private players, almost 6 years after the submission of the Report of the Committee.

21.4 Indian Insurance Business: From State Monopoly to Competition

The public sector monopoly of insurance business was ended with the enactment of the Insurance Regulatory and Development Act, 1999. The insurance business was thrown open for private participation (including foreign equity participation up to 26 percent of the paid-up capital). Further, the Insurance Regulatory and Development Authority (IRDA) Act, was enacted in 1999 and a separate Insurance Regulatory and Development Authority was set up. In order to ensure solvency of insurers and protection of policyholders' interests, the IRDA Act stipulates prudential norms for investments and service obligations in the less-lucrative rural sector. Following this, the Insurance Regulatory and Development Authority (IRDA) was set up on April 19, 2000. Its major functions include: (a) regulation of investment funds by insurance companies, (b) adjudication of disputes between insurers and intermediaries, and (c) supervision of Tariff Advisory Committee. The IRDA has been notifying regulations, from time to time, which, *inter alia,* pertain to registration of Indian insurance companies, insurance advertisements and disclosures, licensing of insurance agents and intermediaries, reinsurance, and obligation of insurers to rural and social sectors.

The insurance industry was opened up to the private sector in August 2000. The primary objective of liberalisation in the insurance sector was to deepen insurance penetration by enlarging consumer choices through product innovation. The increased competition in the insurance sector has led to product innovations for catering to the diverse requirements of various segments of the population.

Commercial banks and non-banking financial companies satisfying the prescribed criteria have also been permitted to enter the insurance business with prior approval of the Reserve Bank of India.

The avowed objective of IRDA Act is to provide for an authority to protect the interests of policyholders, to regulate, to promote and to ensure orderly growth of the insurance business in India.

The opening of the life insurance industry has benefited consumers in a number of ways: There has been an explosion in the choice of products, service levels have improved and price wars have brought down term insurance rates and administration charges in unit-linked policies.

Indian insurance industry remained a state-owned monopoly for more than 40 years in the case of life and not less than 25 years in the case of non-life. It remained in a cloistered world of its own The reasons then prevailing which prompted the state ownership are no longer valid in view of the rapidly changing global as well as local milieu.

21.5 Insurance Regulatory and Development Authority (IRDA)

The supervisory control of insurance companies is exercised by Insurance Regulatory and Development Authority (IRDA) and these powers flow from Insurance Act, 1938 as well as from IRDA Act, 1999. IRDA Act 1999 states: "Subject to the provisions of this Act and any other law for the time being in force, the Authority shall have the duty to regulate, promote and ensure orderly growth of insurance business and reinsurance business".

21.5.1 Mission Statement of IRDA:

1. To protect the interest of and secure fair treatment to policyholders.
2. To bring about speedy and orderly growth of the insurance industry (including annuity and superannuation payments), for the benefit of the common man, and to provide long term funds for accelerating growth of the economy.
3. To set, promote, monitor and enforce high standards of integrity, financial soundness, fair dealing and competence of those it regulates.
4. To ensure speedy settlement of genuine claims, to prevent insurance frauds and other malpractices and put in place effective grievance redressal machinery.
5. To promote fairness, transparency and orderly conduct in financial markets dealing with insurance and build a reliable management information system to enforce high standards of financial soundness amongst market players.
6. To take action where such standards are inadequate or ineffectively enforced.
7. To bring about optimum amount of self-regulation in day-to-day working of the industry consistent with the requirements of prudential regulation.

21.5.2 Regulatory and Supervisory Powers of IRDA: These are wide and pervasive. These can be summarised as under.

1. **Registration/Licensing:** Any company proposing to enter in the insurance business has to apply to the authority for registration certificate. The authority has the powers to issue the licence subject to its satisfaction that the proposed company is financially sound and has the managerial expertise to run the business. The authority

has also got the powers to renew it, modify it or even suspend and cancel such registration.

2. **Product and its Pricing:** The authority shall be satisfied about the nature of the product and its pricing before it is placed for marketing amongst the consumers. The powers to control the price of the product is in addition to the premium rates which are fixed by the Tariff Advisory Committee (TAC) constituted under Section 64U of Insurance Act, 1938. Chairman of the authority is also ex-officio Chairman of TAC. The authority should also be satisfied with the terms and conditions mentioned in the policy documents.

3. **Investment of Funds:** The investment policy of the insurance companies is governed by the broad guidelines framed by the authority. It may direct the insurer to invest certain proportion of their funds in specified securities. For instance, the present directives are that general insurance companies have to invest minimum of 30 percent of their funds in government securities and 15 percent in housing projects including purchase of fire fighting equipments by state governments. Only 55 percent of the funds may be invested in market securities and amongst market securities only in approved securities.

4. **Solvency Margin:** The authority has to ensure that insurers maintain the solvency margin as laid down in the Act. In case companies fail to comply to solvency margin requirements, the authority can initiate disciplinary action against the defaulting companies.

5. **Appointment of Actuary:** As per the directives of the authority, it is mandatory for insurer to appoint an actuary. The qualifications of actuary have been laid down. The functions and duties of actuary have been prescribed by the authority.

6. **Appointment to Chief Executive/Managing Director:** It is obligatory on the part of insurance companies to take prior approval of the authority before appointing chief executive, managing director or whole time director in the company. The authority has also been vested with the power to remove any managerial person and also appoint any additional director in the company.

7. **Power of Investigation and Inspection:** The authority can institute any inquiry against the insurer to investigate the affairs of the company and for this purpose can appoint any person as investigator. Based on the report, authority can take disciplinary action against the insurer including suspension of its registration.

8. **Accounts and Balance Sheets:** The insurers are required to prepare a balance sheet, a profit and loss account, a separate account of receipts and payments and a revenue account in respect of each class of business. These are to be audited by a qualified auditor.

9. **Intermediaries:** The authority shall also monitor the activities of intermediaries who are being engaged by the insurers to market their products. The licence to the agents will be issued by the authority. As and when brokers are allowed to operate, they will also have to obtain the licence from the authority.

10. **Surveyors and Loss Assessors:** The qualifications for surveyors to be eligible to

obtain a licence are prescribed by the authority. Their licences are also being issued by the authority.

11. **Reinsurance:** Reinsurance programmes of insurance companies are being monitored by the authority on a continuous basis. As per the directives of the authority, insurance companies are required to cede a part of their premium income to designated Indian reinsurer. Insurers are supposed to keep the authorities apprised of their insurance programme, both outward and inward, and seek authority's approval.

21.6 Post-liberalisation Developments in Insurance Business

The Indian insurance industry has witnessed a sea-change since opening up to private players in 1999. The liberalisation has transformed the industry's outlook towards the vast Indian market. The spurt in the number of players has led to innovation in product development and distribution channels, thus treating the Indian customer to a whole new range of insurance products, each suited to match unique requirements of different societal segments.

The ultimate objective of reforms is to increase insurance-density and insurance penetration levels by designing more tailor-made products for customers, both individuals and institutions.

21.6.1 Changes in the Nature and Structure of Products: The driving force behind the record growth of the industry is the increasing demand for specialised covers by customers. With increasing buying capacity, asset procurement has been on the rise. This is turn has set the trend for increasing demand to protect assets against eventualities, including natural calamities. Competition has become an essential ingredient in this scenario with guaranteed benefits to the customer and the society at large. It is evident that the customer has a wider menu to choose from and customer service benchmarks have begun to improve as a result of competitive pressures.

Numerous new initiatives have been taken by the private players, and even by the LIC. Some insurers such as ICICI Pru-Life have fulfilled their mission to be a scale player in the mass market by introducing a complete range of products to meet the individual needs of customers. Others have taken a more focused approach, introducing select products that they believe hold potential and fill market gaps. Service standards are being set and implemented and a series of distribution channels have thrown open new opportunities.

With heightened awareness and consumer education there are more customer-friendly products and a willingness to view life insurance as an integral part of one's financial portfolio. Insurance is no longer a poorly-understood product pushed onto the people or a product only to be bought hurriedly at the time of the closing of the financial year to avail tax benefits.

New private players have pioneered many significant trends as, for example, the introduction of products which do not have long-term guarantees. In an environment where interest rates are volatile, the days of long-term, high-guaranteed return products are over. Products are now priced flexibly, realistically and sustainably. With greater education, consumers are in a better position to understand the risks and the benefits.

The introduction of unit-linked products has brought about a new level of transparency and flexibility to what was always considered a black box product. Policyholders now have the choice of deciding how much premium they want to pay, the level of their sum assured and fund in which they would like to invest their money. Charges are disclosed upfront, and NAVs and portfolio allocations of the various funds are available on a regular basis. Though such products are more complex than their traditional counterparts, the opportunities they offer to the policyholder make them appealing to a wider range of investors.

Apart from protection, life insurers are being recognised for their ability to manage long-term retirement savings and pension funds. In fact, insurers such as ICICI Prudential were among the first to recognise the need for structured retirement planning among the Indian populace and to invest the necessary resources to build this segment.

Some of the innovative products, which have been introduced by the life insurers, include unit linked products, health insurance products and micro insurance products. The initiatives taken by the general industry include weather insurance, index-based crop insurance, mutual fund package policy, pollution liability package policy and export credit (short-term) policy, coverage for pre-existing diseases based on the recommendations of the health subcommittee set up by the IRDA, health insurance plans such as hospital cash, and critical illness insurance policies.

The general insurance industry is also examining the feasibilities of introducing savings linked insurance products. The general and health insurance companies are providing state-wide cover for citizens under group policies in collaboration with the respective State Governments, towards health, accident, death, etc.

21.6.2 Broad-based Marketing of Insurance Products: Prior to reforms in the insurance sector, direct branch network of LIC and GIC and their subsidiaries together with their agents were instrumental in marketing of insurance products in India. In the post-reforms period, there has been not only a change in the structure and nature of products, but also in the way they are sold. From being a purely advisor-driven business, the insurance sector has seen the emergence of a number of channels, including commercial banks, non-banking financial companies, co-operative credit institutions, corporate agents and direct marketing.

A. Commercial Banks in Insurance Business: In developing countries, one important character of insurance business and of long-term life insurance in particular, is that insurance policies are generally a combination of risk coverage and savings. The savings component in the insurance policies is seen as a possible source of competition for the banking industry, as the insurance industry develops on a competitive basis. There are, however, other considerations that point to the possible complementarities and synergies between the insurance and banking business.

The most important source of complementarity arises due to the critical role that banks play in distributing and marketing of insurance products. With further simplification of insurance products, the vast branch network and the depositor base of commercial banks are expected to play an important role in marketing insurance products over the counter. The eagerness on the part of several banks to enter into insurance business following the opening up of the industry to private participation reflects this emerging process.

In line with the regulations on registration of Indian insurance companies as issued by the IRDA and subsequent Government Notification specifying *insurance* as a permissible form of business that could be undertaken by banks under Section 6(1)(o) of the Banking Regulation Act, 1949, commercial banks were permitted in August 2000 to set up insurance joint ventures on a risk participation basis and also to undertake insurance business as agents of insurance companies on a fee basis, without any risk participation by banks and their subsidiaries.

The RBI, in recognition of the symbolic relationship between banking and the insurance industries, has identified three routes for participation of banks in the insurance business, viz.: (a) providing fee-based insurance services without risk participation, (b) investing in an insurance company for providing infrastructure and services support, and (c) setting up of a separate joint venture insurance company with risk participation.

The third route, due to its risk aspects, involves compliance to stringent entry norms. Further, the bank has to maintain an arms length relationship between its banking business and its insurance outfit. For banks entering into insurance business with risk participation, the prescribed entity also enables to avoid possible regulatory overlaps between the Reserve Bank and the Government/ IRDA. The joint venture insurance company would be subjected entirely to the IRDA/government regulations.

With effect from October 2002, commercial banks were allowed to undertake referral business through their network of branches with the prior approval of the IRDA and the RBI. The requirement of such approval from the RBI was dispensed with in September 2003.

Presently, almost all leading banks have tied up with insurance companies, both general and life, to distribute their products. The fact that some have an insurance joint venture simply aids the process. The selling of insurance products by banks gives a seal of credibility in the minds of the individual. Bancassurance has emerged as a key distribution channel for both life and non-life insurance. It is a win-win deal for all the parties involved. The customer gets yet another product from an institution he already trusts, banks have the opportunity to expand their product offerings and receive fee-income, and the insurers get the benefits of a larger footprint, without the related investment. Judging from the progress made thus far, it seems that bancassurance is here to stay.

B. Non-banking Financial Companies (NBFCs) in Insurance Business: In June 2000, NBFCs registered with the RBI were permitted, with prior approval of the Reserve Bank, to set up insurance joint ventures for undertaking insurance business with risk participation and also to undertake insurance business as agents of insurance companies on a fee basis, without any risk participation subject to satisfaction of some eligibility criteria. This facility was later extended to financial institutions in November 2001.

In February 2004, it was decided to allow NBFCs registered with the RBI to take up insurance agency business on a fee basis and without risk participation, without the approval of the Reserve Bank subject to certain conditions.

C. Co-operative Credit Institutions in Insurance Business: Besides commercial banks, rural community-operative credit institutions are also envisaged as an important vehicle for distributing insurance products in under-served rural areas. The Task Force to Study the Community-operative Credit System and Suggest Measures for its Strengthening (Chairman: J. Capoor) noted that this could have an attendant benefit of portfolio diversification for these institutions.

In August 2003, a decision was taken to allow financially strong scheduled primary (urban) co-operative banks having a minimum net worth of ₹ 100 crore and complying with certain other norms to undertake insurance business as corporate agents without risk participation.

In October 2004, regional rural banks (RRBs) were allowed to undertake, with prior permission of the RBI, insurance business as corporate agents without risk participation, subject to fulfilling certain terms and conditions such as positive net worth, compliance with prudential norms, NPAs not exceeding 10 percent, continuous profits in the last 3 years and no accumulated losses. Besides, subject to certain conditions, they have also been allowed to undertake insurance business on a referral basis, without any risk participation, through their network of branches.

D. Other Intermediaries: Agents and brokers are increasingly become an important part of the Indian insurance scene. With agents working on behalf of insurers and brokers on behalf of the insured, they both will enable the client receive the best advice on the most suitable insurance products. Also they allow the insurer reach parts of the country where the companies—geographically and otherwise—may find it impractical to expand their corporate presence.

Third-party administrators (TPAs) have helped in the popularisation and spread of health insurance through customisation of products and promotion of cashless hospitalisation. Modifications in the mode of payment of insurance premium by allowing credit cards have facilitated easier distribution of insurance through the internet and also via telemarketing.

In recent years, there has been significant growth in the number of agents, corporate agents, brokers, surveyors, third party administrators and increase in the number of agents training institutes. Opportunities in the information technology sector are on a rise on account of insurance sector relying heavily on IT both for its internal processing and for the customer servicing requirements.

21.6.3 Rising Service Levels: Another area of vast improvement is in service attitude and delivery. From a system that left policyholders running from pillar-to-post to get claims, service levels are steadily rising to make the customer the focus of every initiative. In fact, customers need not rely solely on their advisor, but have the option to reach the life insurer directly. For customers, there are multiple touch points—contact centres, e-mail, facsimile, websites—which enable the customer to get in touch with insurance companies quickly, easily and directly.

In some companies, advisors too have been given access to information that they need to have. They can get onto the insurer's website or they can access computers from the insurer's offices and download information on their customers, read industry news and view their commission statements. In all cases, the advisor or customer is in control of the process—response time has come down dramatically and information availability has become immediate.

As with privatisation in any industry, the benefits are not restricted to the customer, but extend to the society at large, by generating employment opportunities for thousands.

21.6.4 Increased Penetration in the Rural and Social Sectors: Recognising the potential of the rural and semi-urban markets—particularly in the context of these markets having exhibited the purchasing power to take insurance cover as also the need for insurance in these areas—the new players are also making an effort to tap these markets. Coverage of lives in the social sectors has also shown a positive trend. Not only have the insurance companies complied with the obligations as stipulated under the Regulations framed by the IRDA in this regard, but are also developing it as a business opportunity. Globally, insurance is sold rather than bought. Recognising the tremendous opportunity waiting to be tapped in the semi-urban and rural areas, branch and satellites offices have been opened.

21.6.5 Investment in Infrastructure and Social Sectors: Investment in infrastructure and social sectors has been mandated for insurance companies. In fact, given the liability profile of insurance companies, more particularly the life insurers, they are the ideal source of long-term debt and equity for infrastructure projects. Simultaneously, long-term infrastructure projects are ideal avenues for parking the resources available for investment with the insurers. In addition, these avenues offer market-related returns on investments made. It is expected that as the premiums in the insurance sector grow, additional funds will be channelised to finance infrastructure and social sector projects. The investment regulations prescribe that not less than 15 percent of the controlled fund and 10 percent of the total assets of the life and general insurance companies must be kept invested in infrastructure and social sector investments. In addition, funds are also directed towards these sectors through the various investments in government securities under the Pension and General Annuity business.

21.6.6 Health Insurance: One of the benefits of opening up of the insurance sector has been the extension of health cover. The industry has recognised both the huge potential and the need for providing health insurance cover to the populace. While a number of initiatives have been taken to promote health insurance in the country, some of the innovative features proposed to be offered through health insurance products include: (a) inclusion of cervical cancer and hysterectomy in the critical illness cover specially designed for women, and (b) offering of telemedicine consultations as a rider to the stand-alone health insurance policy. In addition, some initiatives have already been taken in the context of offering cover for pre-existing diseases. The definition of *pre-existing disease* has been rationalised in some of the products by bringing in a cooling-off or a waiting period. Also, rather than excluding pre-existing conditions such as hypertension and diabetes per se, certain specific complications arising out of such conditions have been excluded.

The health segment has also witnessed the entry of third party administrators (TPAs), post-opening of the sector to facilitate extension of cashless hospitalisation services and to enable insurance companies to utilise their services for customer servicing and claims processing.

21.6.7 Micro Insurance: By helping the rural poor in managing financial risks to their livelihoods and lives, micro insurance offers innovative ways to combat poverty in India. Micro insurance should provide greater economic and psychological security to the poor as it reduces exposure to multiple risks and cushions the impact of a disaster. Micro insurance in conjunction with micro savings and micro credit could go a long way in keeping this segment away from the poverty trap and ensuring its financial inclusion. In 2003, Government of India constituted a Consultative Group on Micro Insurance to examine existing insurance schemes for rural and urban poor. The report of the Consultative Group brought out the following key issues:

1. Micro insurance is not viable as a stand-alone insurance product.
2. Micro insurance has not penetrated rural markets. Traditional insurers have not made much headway in bringing micro insurance products to the rural poor. In addition, micro insurance has not penetrated even among the urban poor).
3. Partnership between an insurers and social organisations, NGOs would be desirable to promote micro insurance by drawing on their mutual strengths.
4. Design of micro insurance products must have the features of simplicity, availability, affordability, accessibility and flexibility.

The Consultative Group studied four different models for delivering micro insurance services to the targeted clientele, viz. partner-agent model, full service model, community-based model and provider model.

To sum up, after a long period of a monopolistic environment, the insurance sector was opened to private participation with the enactment of the Insurance Regulatory and Development Authority Act in 1999. Since then, the number of participants operating in life, general and reinsurance, in both the public and private sectors, has increased. The opening up has augured well for the sector which has been witness to introduction of new products. Presently, a wider choice is available to the customer, with products being tailor-made to the needs of the insured. Availability of riders, particularly health riders, has been a positive development. Insurers are putting in much more research into development of products both in the life and general segments. The customer perspective has also undergone a change in recent times with a significant component of the first year premium accruing to pension products.

Endnote

1. Government of India, Planning Commission, *Ninth Five Year Plan* (1997-2002), Volume I, p. 146.

22

Digital Technology in Banking Sector

Information technology (IT) has transformed the functioning of businesses, the world over. It has: (a) bridged the gaps in terms of the reach and the coverage of systems (b) enabled better decision-making based on latest and accurate information, (c) reduced costs and (d) improved overall improvement in efficiency. In the Indian context, the financial sector, especially the banking sector, has been a major beneficiary from the inroads made by IT. Many new processes, products and services offered by banks and other financial intermediaries are now IT-centred. Banks have traditionally been in the forefront of harnessing technology to improve their products, services and efficiency. They have, over a long time, been using electronic and telecommunication networks for delivering a wide range of value added products and services. The delivery channels include, inter alia, direct dial-up connections, private networks, public networks and the devices including telephone, personal computers (PCs), automated teller machines (ATMs), networking of ATMs in the form of shared payment networks, and core banking solutions.

With the popularity of PCs, easy access to internet and world wide web (www), internet is increasingly used by banks as a channel for receiving instructions and delivering their products and services to their customers. This form of banking is generally referred to as internet banking, although the range of products and services offered by different banks vary widely both in their content and sophistication.

22.1 Internet Banking

22.1.1 Internet Banking and Electronic Banking: Electronic banking (e-banking) is a generic term encompassing internet banking, telephone banking, mobile banking etc. In other words, it is a process of delivery of banking services and products through electronic channels such as satellite, telephone, internet, cell phone etc. The concept and scope of e-banking is still evolving. Internet banking is a major component of e-banking.

Internet banking offers different online services like balance enquiry, requests for cheque books, recording stop-payment instructions, balance transfer instructions, account opening and other forms of traditional banking services. These are mostly traditional services offered through internet as a new delivery channel. Banks are also offering payment services on behalf of their customers who shop in different e-shops, e-malls etc.

22.1.2 Levels of Banking Services Offered through Internet: Internet banking applications run on diverse platforms and operating systems and use different architectures. The product may support centralized (bank-wide) operations or branch level automation. It may have a distributed, client server or three-tier architecture based on a file system. Moreover, the product may run on computer systems of various types ranging from PCs, open (Unix based) systems, to proprietary main frames. These products allow different levels of access to the customers and different range of facilities. The products accessible through Internet can be classified into three types based on the levels of access granted.

A. Basic Level Services (or Information Only Systems): These refer to websites of banks which disseminate information on different products and services offered to customers and members of public in general. A bank may receive and reply to queries of customers through e-mail. General purpose information like interest rates, branch locations, product features, loan and deposit calculators are provided on the web (www) site of a bank. The sites also allow downloading of application forms. Interactivity is limited to a simple form of e-mail. No identification or authentication of customers is done and there is no interaction between the bank's production system (where current data of accounts are kept and transactions are processed) and the customer.

B. Simple Transactional Systems: These allow customers to submit their instructions, applications for different services, queries on their account balances etc., but do not permit any fund-based transactions on their accounts. These systems provide customer-specific information in the form of account balances, transaction details, statement of account etc. The information is still largely *read only*. Identification and authentication of customer takes place using relatively simple techniques (like passwords). Information is fetched from the production system of the bank in either the batch mode or offline. Thus, the main application system of the bank is not directly accessed.

C. Fully Transactional Websites: These allow the customers to operate on their accounts for transfer of funds, payment of different bills, subscribing to other products of the bank and to transact purchase and sale of securities etc. These systems provide bi-directional transaction capabilities. The bank allows customers to submit transactions on its systems and these directly update customers' accounts. Therefore, security and control system need to be strongest here.

The above forms of internet banking services are offered by traditional banks as an additional method of serving the customer or by new banks who deliver banking services primarily through internet or other electronic delivery channels as the value added services. Some of these banks are known as *virtual banks* or *internet-only-banks* (IOBs) and may not have any physical presence in a country despite offering different banking services. Thus, internet banking is nothing more than traditional banking services delivered through an electronic communication backbone, viz. internet. However, in the process it has thrown open issues which have ramifications beyond what a new delivery channel would normally envisage. Hence, it has compelled regulators world over to take note of this emerging channel.

22.1.3 Internet Banking in India: Internet banking—both as a medium of delivery of banking services and as a strategic tool for business development—has gained wide acceptance internationally and is fast catching up in India with more and more banks entering the fray. India can be said to be on the threshold of a major banking revolution with net banking having already been unveiled.

The growth potential of internet banking in India is immense. Further incentives provided by banks would dissuade customers from visiting physical branches, and thus get 'hooked' to the convenience of arm-chair banking. The facility of accessing their accounts from anywhere in the world by using a home computer with Internet connection, is particularly fascinating to non-resident Indians and high net worth individuals having multiple bank accounts.

Costs of banking service through the internet form a fraction of costs through conventional methods. The cost conscious banks in the country have therefore actively considered use of internet as a channel for providing services. Fully computerized banks, with better management of their customer base are in a stronger position to cross-sell their products through this channel.

A. Products and Services Offered: Banks in India are at different stages of the web-enabled banking cycle. Initially, a bank, which is not having a web site, allows its customer to communicate with it through an e-mail address; communication is limited to a small number of branches and offices which have access to this e-mail account. As yet, many scheduled commercial banks in India are still in the first stage of Internet banking operations.

With gradual adoption of information technology, the bank puts up a website that provides general information on the banks, its location, services available e.g. loan and deposits products, application forms for downloading and e-mail option for enquiries and feedback. It is largely a marketing or advertising tool. Customers are required to fill in applications on the internet and can later receive loans or other products requested for at their local branch. A few banks provide the customer to enquire into his demat account (securities/shares) holding details, transaction details and status of instructions given by him.

Some of the banks permit customers to interact with them and transact electronically with them. Such services include request for opening of accounts, requisition for cheque books, stop payment of cheques, viewing and printing statements of accounts, movement of funds between accounts within the same bank, querying on status of requests, instructions for opening of letters of credit and bank guarantees etc.

Banks are thus looking to position themselves as one-stop financial shops. Some banks have tied up with computer training companies, computer manufacturers, internet services providers and portals for expanding their internet banking services, and widening their customer base. Setting up of Internet kiosks and permeation through the cable television route to widen customer base are other priority areas in the agendas of the more aggressive players.

Banks providing internet banking services have been entering into agreements with their customers setting out the terms and conditions of the services. The terms and conditions include information on the access through user-id and secret password, minimum balance and charges, authority to the bank for carrying out transactions performed through the service, liability of the user and the bank, disclosure of personal information for statistical analysis and credit scoring also, non-transferability of the facility, notices and termination etc.

The race for market supremacy is compelling banks in India to adopt the latest technology on the internet in a bid to capture new markets and customers. Under mobile banking services, customers can scan their accounts to seek balance and payments status or instruct banks to issue cheques, pay bills or deliver statements of accounts.

Compared to banks abroad, Indian banks offering online services still have a long way to go. For online banking to reach a critical mass, there has to be sufficient number of users and the sufficient infrastructure in place. Though various security options like line encryption, branch connection encryption, firewalls, digital certificates, automatic sign-offs, random pop-ups and disaster recovery sites are in place or are being looked at, there is as yet no certification authority in India offering public key infrastructure which is absolutely necessary for online banking. The customer can only be assured of a secured conduit for its online activities if an authority certifying digital signatures is in place. The communication bandwidth presently available in India is also not enough to meet the needs of high priority services like online banking and trading. Banks offering online facilities need to have an effective disaster recovery plan along with comprehensive risk management measures. Banks offering online facilities also need to calculate their downtime losses, because even a few minutes of downtime in a week could mean substantial losses.

Some banks even today do not have uninterrupted power supply unit or systems to take care of prolonged power breakdown. Proper encryption of data and effective use of passwords are also matters that leave a lot to be desired. Systems and processes have to be put in place to ensure that errors do not take place.

Users of internet banking services are required to fill up the application forms online and send a copy of the same by mail or fax to the bank. A contractual agreement is entered into by the customer with the bank for using the internet banking services. In this way, personal data in the applications forms is being held by the bank providing the service. The contract details are often one-sided, with the bank having the absolute discretion to amend or supplement any of the terms at any time. For these reasons domestic customers for whom other access points such as ATMs, telebanking, personal contact etc. are available, are often hesitant to use the internet banking services offered by Indian banks. Internet banking, as an additional delivery channel, may, therefore, be attractive/appealing as a value added service to domestic customers. Non-resident Indians for whom it is expensive and time consuming to access their bank accounts maintained in India find net banking very convenient and useful.

B. Role of the Reserve Bank of India: The RBI has played a proactive role in the implementation of IT in the banking sector. IT-based initiatives are focused on meeting the three-pronged objective of better house keeping, improved customer service and overall efficiency. The RBI has come out with a Financial Sector Technology Vision Document outlining the approach to be followed for IT implementation for the medium-term period of about three years.

Several initiatives taken by the Government of India as well as the Reserve Bank of India (RBI) have facilitated the development of internet banking in India. As a regulator and supervisor, the RBI has made considerable progress in consolidating the existing payment and settlement systems, and in upgrading technology with a view to establishing an efficient, integrated and secure system functioning in a real time environment, which has further helped the development of internet banking in India. The Government of India enacted the Information Technology Act, 2000 with effect from October 17, 2000, which provides legal recognition to electronic transactions and other means of electronic commerce.

The RBI has been gearing up to upgrading itself as a regulator and supervisor of the technologically dominated financial system. It issued guidelines on Risks and Control in Computer and Telecommunication System in February 1998 to all the banks advising them to evaluate the risks inherent in the systems and put in place adequate control mechanisms to address these risks, which can be broadly put under three heads, *viz.*, IT environment risks, IT operations risks and product risks.

The existing regulatory framework over banks has also been extended to internet banking. These guidelines cover various issues that would fall within the framework of technology, security standards and legal and regulatory issues. Virtual banks, which have no offices and function only online are not permitted to offer electronic banking services in India and that only banks licensed under the Banking Regulation Act and having a physical presence in India are allowed to offer such services. Further, banks are required to report to the RBI every breach or failure of security systems and procedures in internet banking, while the RBI at its discretion may decide to commission special audit/inspection of such banks.

As per guidelines, banks no longer need any prior approval of the Reserve Bank for offering the internet banking services. Nevertheless, banks must have their internet policy and they need to ensure that it is in line with parameters as set by it.

RBI has taken the initiative for facilitating real time funds transfer through the real time gross settlement (RTGS) System. Under the RTGS system, transmission, processing and settlements of the instructions will be done on a continuous basis. Gross settlement in a real time mode eliminates credit and liquidity risks. Any member of the system will be able to access it through only one specified gateway in order to ensure rigorous access control measures at the user level. Further, generic architecture, both domestic and cross border, aimed at providing inter-connectivity across banks has been accepted for implementation by RBI.

C. Challenges: Innovations are mixed blessings. They bring benefits as well as pose challenges. Innovations in information technology (IT) are no exception to this rule. The most prominent challenge arising from these innovations relates to the concept of security. Considering the scope for fraud in the electronic banking area and the possibility of contagion, the Reserve Bank of India—as a regulator and supervisor—has been proactive in addressing the risks associated with electronic banking. The RBI has been promptly addressing issues related to fraud with the use of electronic banking facility. Even after issuing guidelines for a secured electronic banking, the RBI advises the banks, from time to time, on control mechanisms to combat such frauds.

In India, the legal infrastructure for promoting internet banking has not yet been put in place in a comprehensive manner. India does not have a licensed certifying authority appointed by the Controller of Certifying Authorities to issue digital signature certificates. Also, India is not yet a signatory to the International Cyber Crime Treaty, which seeks to intensify co-operation among different signatory nations for exchanging information concerning crime and cyber criminals. Further, there are unresolved legislative issues related to cyber crime laws, clarification relating to regulatory authority over e-money products, consumer protection and privacy laws. To make the electronic banking operations in India more widespread, secure and efficient, these issues need to be addressed by relevant authorities.

As the banking practices and legislations concerning electronic banking are still in the process of evolution in India and abroad because of technological innovations, there is a need for a constant review of various legislations and regulatory framework relating to banking and commerce. The RBI is monitoring and reviewing the legal and other requirements of electronic banking on a continuous basis to ensure that the e-banking would develop on sound lines and the e-banking related challenges would not pose a threat to financial stability.

22.2 Mobile Banking

22.2.1 Introduction: Developments in mobile telephony, as also the mobile phone density in the India, present a unique opportunity to leverage the mobile platform to meet the objectives and challenges of financial inclusion. By harnessing the potential of mobile technology, large sections of the un-banked and under-banked society can be empowered to become inclusive through the use of electronic banking services.

The Payment and Settlement Systems (PSS) Act, 2007 empowers the Reserve Bank of India to authorize and regulate entities operating payment systems in the country. RBI has, over a period of time, placed importance on the move towards electronic payments and thereby a *less-cash* society. Towards this end, the RBI has been promoting and nurturing the growth of various modes of electronic payments including the pre-paid payment instruments, card payments, mobile banking etc.

The Payment Systems Vision Document 2012-15 of RBI, reflects the commitment towards provision of safe, efficient, accessible, inclusive, interoperable and authorised payment and settlement systems in the country. Recent experience shows that the share of paper-based instruments in the volume of total non-cash transactions has been declining in favour of electronic payments. In addition to the growth in volume as well as value processed by RTGS, the retail electronic segment too has registered a significant growth. Though overall volume of transactions in mobile banking is low, there has been significant growth in the volume recently.

22.2.2 Mobile Banking: Regulatory Framework: Recognising the potential of mobile as a channel for offering financial services in the country, RBI issued the first set of guidelines on mobile banking in October 2008. The mandate was that all transactions should originate from one bank account and terminate in another bank account. At this time, a few banks had already started offering information-based services like balance enquiry, stop payment instruction of cheques, transactions enquiry, location of the nearest ATM/branch etc. through this medium.

The guidelines issued by RBI in October 2008, permitted banks to facilitate funds transfer from one bank account to another bank account, both for personal remittances and purchase of goods and services. Banks were directed on the regulatory/supervisory issues, registration of customers for mobile banking, to ensure technology standards, interoperability, inter-bank clearing and settlement arrangements for fund transfers, customer grievance and redressal mechanism and transaction limits in an attempt to ensure safe, secure transfer of funds.

Under extant regulatory prescriptions, there is no monetary restriction on fund transfer effected through mobile banking as it is left to the risk perception of each bank and policies approved by their respective Boards. However, end-to-end encryption for transactions in excess of ₹ 5,000 has been mandated by RBI. Similarly, mobile as a channel for funds transfer from a bank account for cash payout to a beneficiary who does not have a bank account at ATMs/BCs—₹ 10,000 per transaction with a cap of ₹ 25,000 per beneficiary has also been permitted by RBI (under the Domestic Money Transfer Guidelines).

In line with these guidelines, banks have been offering mobile banking services to their customers through various channels such as SMS, USSD channel, mobile banking application etc. However, real time inter-bank mobile banking payments have been facilitated through the setting up of the inter-bank mobile payment services (IMPS), now termed as immediate payment service, and operated by the NPCI with the approval of RBI. The IMPS has enhanced the efficiency of mobile banking by enabling real time transfer of funds between bank accounts and providing a centralised inter-bank settlement service for mobile banking transactions. The IMPS has also been enhanced to support merchant payments using mobile phones to promote less cash society.

Under the PSS Act, RBI has given approval for mobile banking services to 80 banks, of which 64 have commenced operations. The customer base of banks who had subscribed to mobile banking services stood at nearly 30 million as of October 2013.

22.2.3 Various Channels for Mobile Banking:

A. Mobile Banking: SMS-based Channel: SMS is a popular and widely used channel in mobile phones. It is ubiquitously available in all handsets irrespective of make and model and also GSM and CDMA enabled handsets. Most customers are very conversant with the SMS channel and use the same for various services including the short messaging. Many popular mobile VAS services such as cricket, jokes, horoscopes, etc. are based on SMS and used widely by customers.

Given the advantages offered by SMS channel, many banks have offered mobile banking services through the SMS channel. This includes non-financial services such as balance enquiry, mini statement, cheque book request, transaction alerts etc., and financial services such as funds transfer, mobile/DTH recharge, bill payments etc.

B. Mobile Banking: USSD-based Channel: Unstructured supplementary service data (USSD) is a protocol used by GSM cellular telephones to communicate with the telecom service provider's systems. USSD can be used for WAP browsing, pre-paid callback service, mobile-money services, location-based content services, menu-based information services, and as part of configuring the phone on the network.

USSD messages are up to 182 alphanumeric characters in length. Unlike short message service (SMS) messages, USSD messages create a real-time connection during a USSD session. The connection remains open, allowing a two-way exchange of a sequence of data. This makes USSD more interactive and advantageous than services that use SMS.

USSD platform which is MNO dependent can be efficiently used by the mobile banking platforms. Realizing the benefits and potential of USSD-based mobile banking, some of the banks have launched USSD-based mobile banking services, e.g. State Bank of India, Canara Bank, ICICI Bank, with the help of telecom aggregators who in turn have tied up with few MNOs. For instance, ICICI Bank has tied up with Idea, Aircel, Tata Docomo, Reliance and MTNL for offering USSD platform to its customers on their GSM network.

C. Mobile Banking: Application-based: All banks who have received the approval from RBI for mobile banking are offering the application-based mobile banking channel to their customers. Customers can download the mobile banking application and perform variety of services including the following: (a) Non-financial transactions such as balance enquiry, mini statement, cheque book request, (b) financial transactions such as funds transfer, mobile/DTH recharge, bill payments etc

The mobile application is offered on various platforms such as Java, Symbian, Blackberry OS, Windows, Android, Apple iOS etc. Many Banks have made the mobile application available in the app stores such as Google, Apple, Blackberry, etc. for easy search and download by the customers.

Following are the advantages of the application-based mobile banking:

- Applications once downloaded are easy to use for the customers who are proficient in using the smart phone based applications.
- Banks have made these applications compliant with most of the latest operating systems covering the large range of smart phones in use.
- It has been experienced by the banks that once customer has used the application-based mobile banking, he continues to use the same unless there is a change of the handset and/or mobile number.
- The application-based mobile banking can also communicate using SMS and GPRS (data) channels with the mobile banking system of the bank.

22.2.4 Challenges Faced by Banks in Providing Mobile Banking Services: Despite the potential for mobile banking and the regulatory provisions enabling greater use of mobiles as a channel for financial services in general, and for financial inclusion in particular, banks are facing some challenges in taking mobile banking to the desired level. These challenges are essentially in two fronts:

1. Customer enrolment related issues.
2. Technical issues.

A. Customer Enrolment Related Issues: These are as under:
1. Mobile number registration.
2. M-PIN generation process.
3. Concerns relating to security are a factor affecting on-boarding of customers.
4. Bank staff education.
5. Customer education.

(a) Mobile Number Registration: For a customer, in order to conduct a mobile payment transaction, his/her mobile number needs to be registered with the bank. The process for mobile number registration is implemented differently across banks. Currently, the process for mobile number registration involves the following:

- Customer mandatorily needs to go to the bank branch for most of the banks to register his number and fill in the application form (paper-based). After verification, his number gets registered in the CBS and in the bank's mobile banking system.
- Some leading banks have provided the facility for customer to register mobile number at their bank's ATMs using 2FA authentication of ATM card + ATM PIN.

In both the above cases, the customer needs to physically go to the branch/ATM in order to register their mobile number, which acts as a barrier in many cases, besides delaying the entire process. Further, even where the above process of registration through ATMs is provided, it is restricted to the use of own-bank ATMs and the same is not possible at present by going to any other bank ATMs. The process for mobile number registration needs to be simpler for customer to get on-boarded.

(b) M-PIN Generation: M-PIN is the second factor of authentication that customer needs to use in order to conduct mobile banking transaction. Customer needs M-PIN from his respective bank in order to get started with mobile payments. Currently, the process for M-PIN generation is implemented differently across banks, and involves the following:

- For most banks, after the mobile number registration at branch/any bank ATM, customer receives M-PIN via SMS on their registered mobile number. In certain cases, customer receives the M-PIN through postal mail.
- Some leading banks have provided the facility for generating and changing M-PIN from the handset itself using the mobile banking application and providing the authentication parameters as required by the bank (e.g. debit card details such as debit card number, ATM PIN, expiry date). These inputs are captured and sent through registered mobile number, for the purpose of M-PIN generation.
- Some leading banks have also provided the facility to generate and change M-PIN through alternate channels such as IVR, ATM, and Internet Banking. Customer may be able to make merchant payment using just his mobile number and M-PIN/OTP on the merchant interface. The M-pin can be only interfaced on acquiring bank's interface such as USSD, Application etc. for security reasons. The merchant based interfaces can accept OTP (one-time password) for authentication.

(c) Concerns Related to Security: One of the major factors affecting customer on-boarding and usage of mobile banking services is the concern relating to security of transactions effected using the mobile phone. While mobile banking application is an end-to-end encrypted channel, the other access channels viz. SMS, USSD, IVR, are not end-to-end encrypted. However, in order to enjoy the higher level of security available in the application-based mobile banking, the customer's handset has to be GPRS-enabled.

Since SMS facility is available on all handsets, the issue of security can be addressed if the SMS can be encrypted end-to-end, thus allaying any concerns relating to lack of security in this channel.

In addition to this, another important aspect adding to the concerns on the part of customers relate to how their complaints and grievances will be addressed for transacting on this channel—whether through their bank or through their mobile service provider.

(d) Bank Staff Training: For effective and efficient implementation of providing mobile banking facilities to the customers it is imperative that the banks staff is well versed and thoroughly trained in various aspects of the mobile banking.

(e) Customer Education: Banks must continue to invest in handholding and educating customers to increase the awareness of various aspects of mobile banking. Banks collectively may invest in marketing and advertising for widespread promotion of mobile banking.

B. Technical Issues: Technical aspects which are posing a challenge relate to the following:

1. Access channels for transactions.
2. Cumbersome transaction process.
3. Co-ordination with MNOs in mobile banking eco-system.

(a) Access Channels for Transaction: Once the customer mobile number is registered and M-PIN is generated, customer may use any of the access channels provided by the bank for conducting mobile banking transactions. Currently, while most banks have provided mobile banking application and SMS facility as access channels, a few banks have also provided other access channels such as USSD, WAP, IVR, etc. Some banks also provide a combination of a few of these channels (application + SMS, application + USSD) for offering better security.

(b) Cumbersome Transaction Process: In the present scenario, with various banks offering various channels for their customers to undertake mobile banking transactions, the user experience is certainly not uniform across banks/channels. The customer is required to provide different set of inputs (authentication parameters) for each type of access channel, thus making the entire transaction process cumbersome.

(c) Co-ordination with MNOs in Mobile Banking Eco-system: In order to offer a more secure and better user experience to their customers through their mobile banking channels, banks need a greater level of coordination with the telecom service providers.

22.2.5 RBI's Technical Committee on Mobile Banking, 2014: Reserve Bank of India constituted a Technical Committee (Chairman: B. Sambamurthy), to study in depth, the present challenges faced in mobile banking, the adoption of particular technologies to meet the requirements of banks as well as vast numbers of mobile users and draw up a road-map for implementation of the solutions. [1]

Major recommendations of the Committee were as under:

1. Banks need to explore other means of facilitating customer/user registration process for mobile banking which does not require a visit to the bank branch. The potential of inter-operable ATM networks and business correspondent arrangements has to be effectively harnessed towards meeting this objective. Standardization is required in: (a) user registration for mobile banking, (b) user authentication process and (c) user interfaces. Recognising the crucial role that customer/user awareness plays in adoption of any technology for financial transactions, as well as the need for optimal utilization of resources, the joint customer education programmes by banks will go a long way in facilitating usage of mobile banking.

2. Mobile network operators (MNOs) need to see a business model in it for themselves and play out their role in ensuring mobile banking reaches its full potential by co-operating with banks in their endeavour to provide the appropriate technology/channel to the targeted users. Mobile banking can result in customer stickiness and reduce churn for MNOs. Mobile banking can increase revenue to MNOs and reduce costs to banks. The current solutions already provided by banks and various technological alternatives available can be put in place through a concerted effort between banks and telecom service providers.

3. Common mobile banking applications and common technological platforms need to be built for reaping the benefits of *network effects*. While bank-specific applications and individual platforms have a major role in building brand loyalty, an alternate uniform/common platform, interoperability and similar seamless transactional experience to the users/customers of all banks would encourage mobile banking.

4. The Government of India can explore the options of offering fiscal incentives/economic subventions to the stakeholders in order to ensure participation of various players to offer the solutions recommended here in this Report. The committee would like to draw attention to similar law *Lei Do Bem* (Law of the Goods) enacted by Brazil in October 2013 which mandates that smart phones give visibility to Brazilian made apps by either pre-loading phones with these home-grown apps or providing a dedicated marketplace on smart phones to display them. Similar intervention in India can support and incentivise the relevant stakeholders to either *pre-burn* common mobile banking application on mobile handsets/SIM cards or send *over-the-air* using dynamic STK to facilitate financial transactions. This is a *build-it-they-will-come* approach.

Endnote

1. Reserve Bank of India, *Report of the Technical Committee on Mobile Banking*, January 2014.

Part III

Financial Market Reforms

23

Financial Markets: An Overview

23.1 Importance of Financial Markets

A well-functioning financial market enables efficient use of market-based instruments of monetary policy by improving interest rate signals in the economy. Apart from enhancing the efficiency of monetary policy, deep and well-functioning financial markets promote mobilisation of domestic savings and improve the allocative efficiency of financial intermediation, and foster the necessary conditions to emerge as an international or a regional financial centre. Strong domestic financial markets also act as a buffer against external disturbances and help in absorbing shocks to the domestic banking system during crises. Further, they provide incentives for development of hedging instruments, and lower macroeconomic volatility and financial instability. Efficient financial markets also have several indirect benefits such as rapid accumulation of physical and human capital, more stable investment financing, and faster technological progress.

Developed and well-integrated financial markets are critical for sustaining high growth, for the effective conduct of monetary policy, for developing a diversified financial system, financial integration and ensuring financial stability. The question therefore is not whether developed financial markets are needed, but how to go about in developing them fully. Financial markets presently deal with complex and sophisticated products. Introduction of such products would require clear regulatory frameworks, appropriate institutions and development of human resource skills. The speed for further changes in the financial markets would thus depend on how quickly are we able to meet these requirements.

The need for developed financial markets also arises in the context of increasing integration of domestic financial markets with international financial markets. The concept of globalisation is no longer restricted to its traditional sense—variety of cross-border transactions in goods and services—but also extends to international capital flows, driven by rapid and widespread diffusion of technology. In fact, most of the literature in recent years on globalisation has centred around financial integration due to the emergence of worldwide financial markets and the possibility of better access to external financing for a variety of domestic entities.

Financial market development is a complex and time-consuming process. There are no short cuts for developing well-functioning markets with depth and liquidity. Some of the preconditions for financial market reform are the following.

1. Macroeconomic stability.
2. Sound and efficient financial institutions and structure.

3. Prudential regulation and supervision.
4. Strong creditor rights.
5. Contract enforcement.

23.2 Types of Financial Markets

The financial markets can broadly be divided into money and capital market.

23.2.1 Money Market: Money market is a market for debt securities that pay off in the short term usually less than one year, for example the market for 90-days treasury bills. This market encompasses the trading and issuance of short term non equity debt instruments including treasury bills, commercial papers, bankers acceptance, certificates of deposits etc.

23.2.2 Capital Market: Capital market is a market for long-term debt and equity shares. In this market, the capital funds comprising of both equity and debt are issued and traded. This also includes private placement sources of debt and equity as well as organized markets like stock exchanges. Capital market can be further divided into primary and secondary markets.

In the primary market securities are offered to public for subscription for the purpose of raising capital or fund. Secondary market is an equity trading venue in which already existing/pre-issued securities are traded among investors.

Secondary market refers to a market where securities are traded after being initially offered to the public in the primary market and/or listed on the stock exchange. Majority of the trading is done in the secondary market. Secondary market comprises of equity markets and the debt markets.

For the general investor, the secondary market provides an efficient platform for trading of his securities. For the management of the company, secondary equity markets serve as a monitoring and control conduit by facilitating value-enhancing control activities, enabling implementation of incentive-based management contracts, and aggregating information (via price discovery) that guides management decisions.

23.3 Regulation and Supervision of Financial Markets in India

Financial markets in India have evidenced significant development since the financial sector reforms initiated in the 1990s. The development of these markets has been done in a calibrated, sequenced manner and in step with those in other markets in the real economy. The emphasis has been on strengthening price discovery, easing restrictions on flows or transactions, lowering transaction costs, and enhancing liquidity. Benefiting from a series of policy initiatives over time, greater domestic market integration has also been witnessed.

The equity, government securities, foreign exchange and money markets along with their corresponding derivatives segments have developed into reasonably deep and liquid markets and there has been significant increase in domestic market integration over the years. However, the credit derivative market is yet to take off in any significant manner. As regards corporate bonds, though the primary market has seen an increase in issuance, the secondary market has not developed commensurately.

Financial markets in India are regulated and supervised by the Reserve Bank of India (RBI) and the Securities and Exchange Board of India (SEBI). Financial markets under the purview of the RBI include the following:

1. Money market and derivatives.
2. Foreign exchange market and derivatives.
3. Government securities market and interest rate derivatives.
4. Credit markets and derivatives.
   Financial markets under the control and supervision of SEBI are as under:
1. Equity market and derivatives.
2. Corporate bond market.

23.4 Financial Markets and Monetary Policy of the RBI

From the point of view of RBI, developed financial markets are critical for effective transmission of monetary policy impulses to the rest of the economy. Monetary transmission cannot take place without efficient price discovery, particularly with respect to interest rates and exchange rates. The transmission process for policy actions by RBI involves two stages. In the first stage, policy actions are transmitted to financial markets. The second stage of the transmission mechanism involves the propagation of monetary policy impulses from the financial system to the real economy and aggregate prices. A successful implementation of policy requires a reasonably accurate assessment of how rapidly the effects of policy actions are transmitted through the financial system to the real economy, affecting aggregate spending decisions of households and firms, and from there to aggregate demand and inflation.

As a debt manager to the Government, the development of a deep and liquid market for government securities is of critical importance to the RBI as it results in better price discovery and cost effective Government borrowing. The government securities market also provides an effective transmission mechanism for monetary policy, facilitates the introduction and pricing of hedging products and serves as a benchmark for pricing other debt instruments. Although the government securities market has developed considerably over the years, more needs to be done for it to become fully developed.

23.5 Reforms in the Financial Markets

Financial markets in India have existed for a long time. However, they remained relatively underdeveloped for a variety of reasons. India introduced financial sector reforms as a part of structural reforms in the early 1990s. Several measures have been taken by regulatory authorities to develop and strengthen India's financial system in order to make it compatible with best international practices.

Reforms in the financial markets encompassed all segments—money market, credit market, government securities market, foreign exchange market, equity market and corporate debt market. The development of financial markets in India has been pursued to bring about a transformation in the structure, efficiency and stability of markets as also to facilitate integration of markets. The emphasis has been on strengthening price discovery, easing of restrictions on flows or transactions, lowering of transaction costs, and enhancing liquidity. Development of these markets has been done in a calibrated, sequenced and careful manner in step with those in other markets in the real economy. The sequencing has also been informed by the need to develop market infrastructure, technology and capabilities of market participants and financial institutions in a consistent manner. In a low income economy like India, the cost of downside risk is very high, so the objective of maintaining financial stability has to be constantly kept in view while developing financial markets.

The objectives of developing financial markets are as under:

1. To encourage competitive forces.
2. To facilitate the use of a variety of instruments.
3. To promote the growth of different kinds of institutions offering a wide range of financial instruments and services to potential savers and investors.
4. To protect the interests of savers by reducing their risks.
5. To promote the development of instruments that help in risk management.

For regulating financial markets, regulators are guided by various considerations in the larger interest of society. Broadly, the objective of regulation is to protect the interests of depositors and investors (safety and conduct of business), promote financial inclusion, ensure monetary and financial stability and achieve sustained economic progress.

During the post-reforms period, the structure of financial markets has witnessed a remarkable change in terms of financial instruments traded in various segments of the financial market and market participants.

Reforms in the financial markets have encompassed all segments. The development of financial markets in India has been pursued to bring about a transformation in the structure, efficiency and stability of the markets as also to facilitate their integration. The emphasis has been on strengthening price discovery, easing restrictions on flows or transactions, lowering transaction costs, and enhancing liquidity. During the post-reform period, the structure of financial markets has witnessed a significant change in terms of financial instruments traded in various segments of the financial market and market participants. The development of these markets has been done in a calibrated, sequenced and careful manner in step with those in other markets in the real economy. Sequencing has also been informed by the need to develop market infrastructure, technology and the capabilities of market participants and financial institutions in a consistent manner.

The gradual removal of structural bottlenecks in the Indian financial markets and a shift away from the erstwhile administered rates has led to greater domestic market integration. This has also benefited from a series of other policy initiatives over time which included enabling market-determined price discovery through interest rate deregulation; expansion and diversification of the investor base; introduction of a variety of instruments of varying features and tenor; and improvement in market infrastructure. Some of the markets which show strong co-movement are money and government securities markets, exchange rate and stock markets, and foreign exchange forward and money markets.

The need to further develop financial markets has also been underlined by the two high-powered committees, *viz.* Committee on Fuller Capital Account Convertibility (FCAC) [1] and the High Powered Expert Committee on Making Mumbai an International Financial Centre. [2] The Committee on Fuller Capital Account Convertibility in its Report submitted in July 2006 indicated that in order to make a move towards fuller capital account convertibility, it needs to be ensured that different financial market segments are not only well-developed but also that they are well-integrated. Otherwise, shocks to one or more market segments would not get transmitted to other segments efficiently so that the entire financial system is able to absorb the shocks with minimal damage.

To sum up, financial markets in India have seen considerable development since financial sector reforms were initiated in the 1990s. Given the imperatives of the prevailing context, the initial nudge had to be provided through specific policy instruments and actions, but over a period of time these markets have acquired a dynamic of their own. The process of transition in respect of all financial market segments has been largely disruption-free, accommodating the unique features of the existing system while trying to align with the best international practices.

Indian financial markets can be broadly categorised into the money market, government securities market, equity market, corporate bond market, credit market and foreign exchange market. While equity, government securities, foreign exchange and money markets along with their corresponding derivatives segments have developed into reasonably deep and liquid markets, credit derivatives markets are yet to take off in any significant manner. As regards corporate bonds, while primary issuances have been significant, though concentrated in terms of issuers to public sector financial institutions, these have largely been on a private placement basis and the secondary market has not developed commensurately.

In an emerging market like India, where the cost of downside risk is very high, the objective of maintaining financial stability has always been kept in view while developing financial markets. Financial intermediaries like banks have also gained from better determination of interest rates in financial markets by pricing their own products better. Moreover, their own risk management has also improved through the availability of different varieties of financial instruments. The access of real sector entities to finance has also been assisted by the appropriate development of the financial market and the availability of transparent information on benchmark interest rates and prevailing exchange rates. Though several reform measures have recently been initiated to develop the financial markets in India, resulting in various segments of the financial market being better developed and integrated, the financial markets need to develop further in line with the evolving financial and economic scenario.

These developments have facilitated the growth of deeper and more efficient domestic markets, facilitating a more effective channel for transmission of monetary and financial policy impulses.

India's experience once again demonstrates that the development of financial markets is an arduous and time-consuming task that requires conscious policy actions and effective implementation. Financial markets have to be created, nurtured and monitored on a continuous basis, as they attain maturation.

Endnotes

1. Reserve Bank of India, *Report of the Committee on Fuller Capital Account Convertibility* (Chairman: S.S. Tarapore), 2006.
2. Government of India, *High Powered Expert Committee Report on Making Mumbai an International Financial Centre*, April 2007.

24

Money Market

24.1 Meaning and Functions of Money Market

Money market is the most important segment of the financial system as it provides the fulcrum for equilibrating short-term demand for and supply of funds, thereby facilitating the conduct of monetary policy. It is a market for short-term funds with a maturity of up to one year and includes financial instruments that are close substitutes for money. [1] The main instruments comprising the money market are: (a) call money/notice money, (b) certificates of deposit (CDs), (c) treasury bills (abolished with effect from April 1997), (d) repurchase agreements (repos), (e) commercial bills, (f) commercial paper (CPs), and (g) inter-corporate funds.

While inter-bank money markets and central bank lending via repo operations or discounting, provide liquidity for banks, private non-bank money market instruments, such as commercial bills and commercial paper provide liquidity to the commercial sector. Unlike in developed economies where money markets are promoted by financial intermediaries out of efficiency considerations, in India, as in many other developing countries, the evolution of the money market and its structure has been integrated into the overall deregulation process of the financial sector.

The money market is generally expected to perform three broad functions.

1. It provides an equilibrating mechanism to even out demand for and supply of short-term funds.
2. It also presents a focal point for central bank intervention for influencing liquidity and general level of interest rates in the economy.
3. It provides reasonable access to providers and users of short-term funds to fulfil their borrowing and investment requirements at an efficient market clearing price.

24.2 Reserve Bank of India (RBI) and the Money Market

The RBI is the most important constituent of the money market. Owing to its implications for conducting monetary policy, the money market falls under the direct purview of regulation of the RBI. The primary objective of the RBI's operations in the money market has been to ensure that short-term interest rates and liquidity are maintained at levels which are consistent with the overall monetary policy objectives, viz. maintaining price stability, ensuring adequate flow of credit to the productive sectors of the economy and maintaining orderly conditions in the financial markets. Liquidity and interest rates in the system are influenced by the RBI through the use of various instruments at its disposal which, *inter alia*, include the following.

1. Variations in cash reserve ratio.
2. Standing facilities/refinance schemes.

3. Repo and reverse repo transactions.
4. Changes in the Bank Rate.
5. Open market operations.
6. Foreign exchange swap operations.

Recognising the important role of the market in the monetary policy process, the RBI has taken active interest in continuously refining the money market instruments in order to have greater control over the liquidity in the system and for creating an efficient mechanism to impart interest rate signals.

24.3 Evolution of Money Market in India

24.3.1 Pre-Independence Period: Money market prior to Independence was characterised by paucity of instruments, lack of depth and dichotomy in the market structure. The inter-bank call money market was the core of the Indian money market. Before the establishment of the RBI in 1935, the money market consisted of two fairly distinct sectors, *viz.* the organised and unorganised sectors. While the organised sector consisted of the Imperial Bank of India—a quasi-central bank till 1935, [2] the Indian joint-stock banks and the exchange banks, the indigenous bankers such as the shroffs, money lenders, chit funds etc. formed the unorganised part. Co-operative credit institutions occupied an intermediate position between the two sectors.

The Imperial Bank, the foremost commercial bank of the country and a few of the leading Indian joint-stock banks discounted *hundis* (internal bills of exchange). This was the main credit instrument of the unorganised sector which provided the only link between the two sectors. Owing to the absence of a proper central bank, the money market was characterised by sharp imbalances between the supply and demand for funds, wide fluctuations in interest rates during the busy and slack seasons and marked regional variations in interest rates. The Imperial Bank could not, however, lend stability to the money market as it had to borrow from the Government at high rates of interest. Nevertheless, the bank rendered assistance to the money market by using the large Government balances at its disposal, which constituted its major investible resources.

The Bank Rate was the prime lending rate at which the Imperial Bank generally advanced money against Government securities. This rate was determined by the Committee of the Central Board of the Imperial Bank and depended on the demand for money which in turn was determined almost entirely by the requirements of trade, particularly foreign trade, in staple commodities such as foodgrains, raw cotton, raw jute and jute manufactures. The rates of interest on loans, including the Bank Rate, fluctuated according to the ebb and flow of this trade. The Imperial Bank would usually not reduce the Bank Rate when its cash to liabilities ratio (an indication of liquidity) was found to be low. Apart from the Bank Rate, the Imperial Bank also periodically announced a *hundi* rate, which was generally equal to or slightly higher than the Bank Rate. Through the rates which the Imperial Bank charged on its advances and the discount of *hundis,* and by its willingness or refusal to extend financial assistance, it could profoundly influence the provision of credit as well as money market rates.

After the formation of the RBI in 1935, the organised market comprised the RBI, the Imperial Bank, foreign banks and the Indian joint stock banks. [3] *Quasi*-Government bodies and large-sized joint stock companies also participated in the money market as lenders, the money lent by them being usually termed as *house money*. Financial intermediaries such as call loan brokers, general finance and stock brokers also functioned in the market. Although the magnitude of funds dealt within the call market was not large in relation to the deposit resources of banks, it was the most sensitive segment of the money market. The Imperial Bank did not participate in the call money market, but other banks obtained loans and advances from it. Subsequently, however, banks increasingly shifted their demand for accommodation to the RBI. Besides the call money market, there was no other significant segment in the market.

With the establishment of the RBI in April 1935, the task of determining the Bank Rate was taken over by it from the Imperial Bank. It was on July 4, 1935, i.e. the day before the scheduled banks were to lodge their statutory deposits with the RBI, that the Bank Rate of 3.5 percent was officially announced for the first time by the RBI. It was the standard rate at which the RBI was prepared to buy or re-discount bills of exchange or other eligible commercial papers. Subsequently, the official rate of the Imperial Bank was re-designated as the Imperial Bank advance rate (as distinct from the Imperial Bank *hundi* rate), which was to be the rate for advances against Government securities and the benchmark for the calculation of interest on other advances on which a fluctuating rate of interest was charged.

24.3.2 Post-Independence Period: At the time of Independence in 1947, money market structure in India was loose though not entirely uncoordinated. The indigenous bankers enjoyed rediscount facilities from the Imperial Bank and other commercial banks which, in turn, had access to the RBI. Recourse on the part of the indigenous money market to the resources of the organised market took place usually during the busy season when the crops were being harvested and moved from the producer to the wholesaler.

Though the RBI was empowered, under the statute, to use the usual instruments of monetary policy, the choice of the instruments of monetary control that could be used was limited by the structural characteristics of the money market. An important aspect of the money market in India was the seasonality in the demand for money and credit which broadly followed the course of the agricultural season. The incidence of closing of accounts of the Government at the end of the financial year in March also added to the element of seasonality in the money market.

The introduction of Bill Market Scheme by the RBI on January 16, 1952 was a landmark in the growth of money market in India. [4] Under the scheme, the RBI made advances to scheduled banks in the form of demand loans against their promissory notes supported by 90 days usance bills or promissory notes of their constituents. It was primarily a scheme for providing accommodation to banks. The scheme, however, did not succeed in developing a market in genuine bills.

In order to serve the economy in general and the rural sector in particular, the All-

India Rural Credit Survey Committee recommended the creation of the state-partnered and state-sponsored bank by taking over the Imperial Bank of India, and integrating with it, the former state-owned or state-associate banks. An Act was, accordingly, passed in the Parliament in May 1955 and the State Bank of India was constituted on July 1, 1955.

A new scheme called the Bills Rediscounting Scheme was introduced with several new features in November 1970 under which the RBI rediscounted genuine trade bills at the Bank Rate or at a rate specified by it, at its discretion. Over the years the rediscounting facility was made restrictive and made available on a discretionary basis. The other instrument in the money market was participation certificates (introduced in 1970). Both of these were, however, not significant.

Prior to financial sector reforms initiated in early 1990s, money market in India was characterised by poor liquidity, the paucity of instruments and limited number of participants. The major features of the Indian money market were the following.

1. Restricted market with a narrow base and limited number of participants— banks and two all India financial institutions. The entry into the market was tightly regulated. Moreover, the market was lopsided with a few large lenders and a large number of borrowers. The market lacked participants who could make for an active market by alternating between lending and borrowing.

2. The overall size of the market was also very small relative to the size of the economy—overall transactions barely formed 3 to 4 percent of the bank deposits.

3. The market was also characterised by paucity of instruments and dealings were generally confined to overnight call and short notice (up to 14 days), inter-bank deposits/loans, Repo market and bills rediscounting.

4. The interest rates in the market were also tightly regulated and controlled (by a voluntary agreement between the participants through the Indian Banks' Association (IBA) intermediation). However, during periods of tight liquidity, the prescribed rates were not strictly adhered to, and more often breached.

Owing to the above features, the unorganised money market used to meet the sectoral financing gaps (i.e. the requirements of unsatisfied borrowers in the organised financial system). Interest rates in the unorganised sector were higher than those in the organised sector and were more market-related.

The Committee to Review the Working of the Monetary System in India (Chairman: Sukhamoy Chakravarty), 1985 first underlined the need to develop money market instruments in India, while the Working Group on the Money Market (Chairman: N. Vaghul), 1987 laid the blueprint for the institution of money markets. Based on the recommendations of the Chakravarty Committee and the Vaghul Working Group, the RBI has gradually developed money market in India through the following measures.

First, interest rate ceilings on inter-bank call/notice money (10 percent), inter-bank term money (10.5-11.5 percent), rediscounting of commercial bills (12.5 percent) and inter-bank participation without risk (12.5 percent) were withdrawn effective May 1, 1989.

Secondly, several financial innovations in terms of money market instruments, such as auctions of Treasury Bills (beginning with the introduction of 182-day Treasury Bills effective November 1986), certificates of deposit (June, 1989), commercial paper (January 1990) and RBI repo (December 1992) were introduced.

Thirdly, barriers to entry were gradually eased by: (a) increasing the number of players (beginning with the Discount and Finance House of India (DFHI) in April 1988 followed by primary and satellite dealers and money market mutual funds), (b) relaxing both issuance restrictions and subscription norms in respect of money market instruments and allowing determination of yields based on demand and supply of such paper, and (c) enabling market evaluation of associated risks, by withdrawing regulatory restrictions such as bank guarantees in respect of CPs.

Fourthly, the development of markets for short-term funds at market determined interest rates has been fostered by a gradual switch from a cash credit system to a loan-based system, shifting the onus of cash management from banks to borrowers and phasing out the 4.6 percent 91-day tap Treasury bills, which in the past provided an avenue for investing short-term funds.

Finally, institutional development has been carried out to facilitate inter-linkages between the money market and the foreign exchange market, especially after a market-based exchange rate system was put in place in March 1993.

24.4 Developments in the Money Market since 1991

The money market in India witnessed significant progress particularly from the mid-1990s, in terms of refinements in money market instruments, introduction of new instruments and supplementary measures to add depth and liquidity to the market.

During the 1990s, the participation in the call money market was widened to cover primary and satellite dealers and corporates (through primary dealers) besides other participants. While banks and primary dealers are permitted to lend and borrow in the market, other entities can participate only as lenders. Following the recommendations of the Committee on Banking Sector Reforms (Chairman: M. Narasimham), 1998 and the RBI's Internal Working Group to Examine the Development of Call Money Market (1997), steps were initiated to reform the call money market and make it a pure inter-bank market, in a phased manner starting in 1999. With the development of the repo market since the late 1990s, the call money market has gradually been transformed into a pure inter-bank market including primary dealers. This process, which was initiated in 1999, was completed in August 2005.

A significant development in the Indian money market has been the introduction of Rupee derivatives, i.e. interest rate swaps (IRS)/forward rate agreements (FRA) in 1999 to further deepen the money market and enable market participants to hedge their risks. In addition to several other measures taken since its introduction, with effect from May 20, 2005, market participants were advised to use only domestic Rupee benchmarks for interest rate derivatives. Market participants were, however, given a transition period of six months for using Mumbai inter-bank forward offered rate (MIFOR) as a benchmark, subject to review. However, on request from the Fixed Income Money Market and Derivatives Association (FIMMDA), market participants have been allowed to use

MIFOR swaps in respect of transactions having underlying permissible forex exposures, for market making purpose, subject to appropriate limit as may be approved by the RBI.

Following the recommendations of the Technical Group on Money Market (May 2005), the focus and policy thrust of the RBI in the money market has been towards encouraging the growth of collateralised market, ensuring transparency and better price discovery, providing avenues for better risk management and strengthening monetary operations.

Trading in money market instruments can take place on a trading platform or in the OTC market. Electronic platforms are available for deals in the call, notice and term money market transactions, market repo and collateralised borrowing and lending obligation (CBLO). OTC deals are done for commercial paper (CP) and certificate of deposit (CD), as well as for call/notice/term money markets. Settlement is done over the real time gross settlement system—either as a gross settlement or as a multilateral netted batch. CP and CD deals, which are mostly in the form of private placements, are done OTC.

The RBI's regulatory powers over money market securities was strengthened under Clause 45 (W) of the RBI Amendment Act, 2006, wherein the RBI was given specific powers to 'regulate the financial system of the country to its advantage, determine the policy relating to interest rates or interest rate products, and give directions on that behalf to all agencies or any of them, dealing in securities, money market instruments, foreign exchange, derivatives, or other instruments of like nature as the Bank may specify from time to time'.

To sum up, the money market is an important channel for monetary policy transmission and has generally conformed to being a liquid market. The gradual shift towards a collateralised inter-bank market, policy directions towards reductions in statutory reserve requirements, the introduction of new instruments such as CBLO, implementation of RTGS, significant transformation of monetary operations framework towards market-based arrangements and facilitating trading through NDS-CALL are some of the factors that have contributed to the development of a relatively vibrant and liquid money market. However, the inability of market participants to take a medium-to long-term perspective on interest rates and liquidity, coupled with the absence of a credible long-term benchmark, is a major hurdle for further market development and needs to be addressed.

Money market in India, which traditionally consisted largely of call/notice money market, now comprises many other instruments such as CPs, CDs, repos and FRAs/IRS. Various reform measures have helped in improving the depth and efficiency of money market operations. The operationalisation of the LAF has provided an informal corridor for overnight call money borrowing rate, which has further imparted stability and flexibility in the interest rate structure and to the market. The other money market instruments such as CPs and CDs have also been developed through alignment in maturity (with deposit instruments like term deposits) and easing of issuance norms. With proper development of other money market segments, non-banks have been able to smoothly switch over from the call/notice money market to other segments.

Historically, the call money market has constituted the core of the money market in

India. However, the collateralized segments, viz., market repo and CBLO, have come into prominence recently. The market structure is broad-based with the participation of banks, primary dealers, insurance companies, mutual funds, provident funds, and corporates. Such a broad participation has contributed to an active interest across market segments.

Endnotes

1. There is no demarcated distinction between the short-term money market and the long-term capital market, and in fact there are integral links between the two markets as the array of instruments in the two markets invariably forms a continuum.
2. The Imperial Bank acted as the bankers' bank, though not statutorily, till 1935 and held the balances of other banks (both Indian and exchange) and also granted accommodation to them when in difficulty or during periods of tight money conditions. (This position remained unchanged even after 1935 in regions where the RBI had not set up offices). Advances were generally granted by way of demand loans against the Government or other gilt edged securities, though at times these were also in the nature of overdrafts.
3. As early as in 1931, the Indian Central Banking Enquiry Committee (1931) had underscored the need for integration of the two sectors of the Indian money market. It had recommended linking of indigenous bankers satisfying certain conditions such as minimum capital and reserves, nature of business, having audited accounts *etc.*, with the RBI. Subsequently, the RBI drew up a scheme in August 1937 for inclusion of indigenous bankers doing banking business under the Second Schedule of the Reserve Bank of India Act, 1934.
   At around the time the RBI was established, the unorganised money market was the most important segment accounting for as much as 90 percent of the transactions. Since then, its importance in overall terms fell considerably. But for certain sectors such as agriculture, retail trade, various classes of small borrowers and also to an extent small scale industry, this market continued to remain an important source of finance, its chief advantages being flexibility in operations and ease of access to the borrowers. But these advantages were more than offset by the highly onerous terms on which resources were made available to the borrowers. One of the most important objectives of policy at that time was, therefore, to devise methods to facilitate the flow of credit to these sectors from the organised sector and to provide it on reasonable terms.
4. Rediscounting bills were among the most important instruments of credit control and the Indian Central Banking Enquiry Committee (1931) had recommended early establishment of a market in commercial bills. No steps could, however, be taken by the RBI in this direction until the beginning of 1952 because of the War and the difficulties arising out of the partition of the country.

25

Government Securities Market

Markets for government securities have gained importance in many countries in the overall financial system in recent years. Initiatives have been taken to make them more vibrant and active by: (a) improving liquidity and depth, (b) enhancing transparency of primary issuances, (c) widening investor base, (d) fine-tuning auction procedures, (e) developing new instruments, and (f) putting in place appropriate safeguards and sound trading and settlement infrastructure. Furthermore, managers of public debt across countries are paying greater attention to minimising the cost of borrowings in the medium to long-term, while striking a balance between the costs and the risks in the short-run.

In India, the government securities market has witnessed significant transformation in its various dimensions, viz. market-based price discovery, widening of the investor base, introduction of new instruments, establishment of primary dealers and electronic trading and settlement infrastructure. This is the outcome of persistent and high-quality reforms in developing the government securities market. There are still areas where further development needs to be undertaken. Increased transparency and disclosures, gradual scaling down of mandated instruments and development of newer instruments are some major areas which could be considered. Regulatory incentives to increase the size of the trading book could be considered as a measure to further develop the government securities market.

Presently, investor base includes not only banks and insurance companies, but also private companies, private mutual funds, finance companies and individuals. Keeping this in view, a number of reform measures were initiated in this segment, which had a positive impact on both the primary and the secondary markets. Reforms in the government securities market have been introduced to impart liquidity and depth to the market by widening the investor base and by ensuring market-clearing interest rate mechanisms.

25.1 Meaning of Securities and Government Securities

Under Section 2 of the Securities Contracts (Regulation) Act, 1956, securities include the following:
1. Shares, scrips, stocks, bonds, debentures, debenture stocks, or other marketable securities of a like nature in or of any incorporated company or other body corporate.
2. Government securities.
3. Such other instruments as may be declared by the Central Govt. to be securities.
4. Rights or interests in securities.

Government Securities mean securities created and issued—whether before or after the commencement of the Securities Contracts (Regulations) Act, 1956—by the Central

Government or a State Government for the purpose of raising a public loan and having one of the forms specified in Section 2(2) of the Public Debt Act, 1944 (since replaced by the Government Securities Act, 2006).

25.2 Importance of Government Securities Market

The government securities market deals with tradable debt instruments issued by the Government for meeting its financing requirements. It is an important segment of the financial market in most countries. The development of the primary segment of this market enables the managers of public debt to raise resources from the market in a cost effective manner with due recognition to associated risks. A vibrant secondary segment of the government securities market helps in the effective operation of monetary policy through application of indirect instruments such as open market operations, for which government securities act as collateral.

Existence of a well-developed government securities market is essential for the pursuit of a market-based monetary policy. The Government securities market in India forms an overwhelming part of the overall debt market. Interest rates in this market provide benchmarks for other segments of the financial market. Historically, the impetus for development of the Government securities market in India has come from the large Government borrowing requirements while an additional reason during the 1990s was the increased capital flows and the need for sterilisation.

As a debt manager to the Government, the development of a deep and liquid market for government securities is of critical importance to the RBI as it results in better price discovery and cost effective Government borrowing. The government securities market also provides an effective transmission mechanism for monetary policy, facilitates the introduction and pricing of hedging products and serves as a benchmark for pricing other debt instruments. Although the government securities market has developed considerably over the years, more needs to be done for it to become fully developed.

The government securities market is also regarded as the backbone of fixed income securities markets as it provides the benchmark yield and imparts liquidity to other financial markets. The existence of an efficient government securities market is seen as an essential precursor, in particular, for development of the corporate debt market. Furthermore, the government securities market acts as a channel for integration of various segments of the domestic financial market and helps in establishing inter-linkages between the domestic and external financial markets.

From the perspective of the issuer, i.e. the Government, a deep and liquid government securities market facilitates its borrowings from the market at reasonable cost. A greater ability of the Government to raise resources from the market at market determined rates of interest allows it to refrain from monetisation of the deficit through central bank funding. It also obviates the need for a captive market for its borrowings. Instead, investor participation is voluntary and based on risk and return perception.

A series of institutional and structural reform measures undertaken in the government securities market since the early 1990s with the objective of creating a deep and liquid market have brought about significant improvements. With the aligning of coupons on government securities with market interest rates, markets gradually widened with the participation of several non-bank players. Presently, investor base includes—apart from banks and insurance companies—private corporate sectors, private sector mutual funds, finance companies as also individuals. Recent steps to allow retailing of government securities and introduction of trading in government securities at stock exchanges are expected to give a further impetus to this trend. As a result, the market has become deeper and more liquid and the Government is able to mobilise adequate funds from the market. The RBI's absorption of primary issues has come down drastically. Even the limited primary purchases, taken as private placement/development, are off-loaded in the market. This, in turn, has enabled the elimination of automatic monetisation by the RBI and reduction in statutory pre-emption of banks. These arrangements have provided functional autonomy to the RBI in the conduct of monetary policy.

As a result of a series of structural and institutional reforms, a deep, wide and vibrant gilt market has emerged. The secondary market turnover of government securities in India has been rising steadily, reflecting increased liquidity in the market and increased trading activity by market participants. This sharp increase in turnover was due to a sustained rally in the government securities market.

The RBI earlier held Government securities predominantly for supporting the Government borrowing programme as also for conducting open market operations. Banks have been the dominant investors in the Government securities primarily on account of SLR requirements. The investor-base in the Government securities market has widened since the early 1990s, which now comprises commercial banks, cooperative banks, insurance companies, provident funds, financial institutions (including term-lending institutions), mutual funds, gilt funds, primary dealers, non-bank finance companies and corporate entities.

In recent years, it has been found that banks have invested in the Government securities well beyond the statutory requirements partly because of relatively attractive rates of return and zero risk-weight assigned to such investments under capital adequacy norms and partly because of relatively sluggish demand for commercial credit.

25.3 Government Securities Market: Legal Framework and Role of the RBI

The RBI, as a monetary authority, has a special interest in developing the government securities market given its criticality in acting as the transmission channel of monetary policy. Moreover, it is important for the RBI, as a manager of public debt, to have a well-developed government securities market as it provides flexibility to exercise various options for optimising maturity as well as interest cost to the Government. It also helps in minimising the market impact of large or lumpy government debt operations and ensuring better coordination between monetary policy and debt management policy. A comprehensive legal framework exists, which defines the role of the RBI in the government securities market.

The legal basis for RBI's operations in the Government securities market is provided by Sections 20, 21 and 21A of the Reserve Bank of India Act, 1934, according to which the RBI is entrusted with the function of management of public debt and issue of new loans of the Union Government and State Governments. The provisions of the Public Debt Act, 1944 (since replaced by the Government Securities Act, 2006) also enjoin upon the RBI the responsibility of administration of the public debt. The functions include issuance of new loans, payment of interest every half year, retirement of rupee loans and all matters pertaining to debt certificates and registration of debt holdings.

The RBI actively operates in the gilt-edged market in order to create orderly conditions in the market by influencing the prices and yields of securities. Under Section 17(8) of the Reserve Bank of India Act, 1934, the RBI is authorised to purchase and sell securities of the Union Government or a State Government of any maturity and the security of a local authority specified by the Central Government on the recommendations of the Central Board of the RBI. In fact, this section provides the legal setting for the conduct of open market operations and liquidity adjustment facility (LAF). Effective April 3, 2007, the State Development Loans were also permitted as eligible securities for LAF operations. The new Chapter III-D of the Reserve Bank of India (Amendment) Act, 2006 has empowered the RBI to determine policy relating to interest rate products and regulate the agencies dealing, *inter alia,* in securities.

However, at present the RBI deals only in the securities issued by the Central Government and not in those of State Governments and local authorities.

The RBI derives its regulatory power over the government securities market from Section 16 of the Securities Contract (Regulation) Act (SCRA), 1956, amended in March 2000, under which the Government has delegated the powers exercisable by it to the RBI. The RBI is, thus, authorised to regulate dealings in government securities, money market securities, gold related securities and securities derived from these securities as also ready forward contracts in debt securities.

The Government Securities Act, which replaced the Public Debt Act, 1944, was passed in August 2006. This Act envisages the consolidation and amendment of the law relating to issue and management of government securities by the RBI. The Act includes the provisions of the erstwhile Public Debt Act relating to issuance of new loans, payment of half-yearly interest, retirement of rupee loans and all matters pertaining to debt certificates and registration of debt holdings. Besides, the new Act gives flexibility for holding government securities in depositories, while at the same time specifically excluding government securities from the purview of the Depositories Act, 1996. The Act enables lien marking and pledging of securities for raising loans against government securities, recognises electronic form of record maintenance, enlarges dematerialisation facility through Bond Ledger Account and liberalises norms relating to nomination and legal representation. The Act also provides the RBI with substantive powers to design and introduce an instrument of transfer suited to the computer environment. It also allows the RBI to issue duplicate securities, new securities on conversion, consolidate with other like government securities, strip (separately for interest and principal) or reconstitute the securities.

Apart from the comprehensive legal framework which defines the role of the RBI in the government securities market, there are other agencies which come into the picture. As government securities are listed on the stock exchanges and could be traded through stock exchange brokers, they also come under the regulatory ambit of Securities and Exchange Board of India (SEBI) to that extent. An element of self-regulation is in place through the Fixed Income Money Market and Derivatives Association of India (FIMMDA) and the Primary Dealers Association of India (PDAI), though they are not formally recognised as Self-regulatory Organizations (SROs).

25.4 Mandated Investments in Government Securities: Categories of Investors

Banks are the largest investors in government securities. In terms of the SLR provisions of the Banking Regulation Act, 1949, banks are required to maintain a minimum of 25 percent of their net demand and time liabilities (NDTL) in liquid assets such as cash, gold and unencumbered government securities or other approved securities as statutory liquidity ratio (SLR).

The minimum SLR stipulation for scheduled urban co-operative banks (UCBs) is the same as for scheduled commercial banks (SCBs) from April 1, 2003. However, for non-scheduled UCBs, the minimum SLR requirement is 15 percent for banks with NDTL of over ₹ 25 crore and 10 percent for the remaining non-scheduled UCBs.

The minimum SLR stipulation for regional rural banks (RRBs) is the same as for SCBs. From April 1, 2003, the coverage under the SLR has also been made akin to SCBs. All deposits with sponsor banks, which were earlier considered as part of the SLR, were to be converted into approved securities on maturity in order to be reckoned for the SLR purpose.

The Banking Regulation Amendment Act, 2007 has removed the floor limit of 25 percent for SLR for scheduled banks. SLR was reduced to 24 percent in November 2008 in view of the global financial crisis and the consequent need to pump additional liquidity in the market.

The second largest category of investors in the government securities market is the insurance companies. According to the stipulations of the Insurance Regulation and Development Authority of India (IRDA), all companies carrying out the business of life insurance should invest a minimum of 25 percent of their controlled funds in government securities. Similarly, companies carrying on general insurance business are required to invest 30 percent of their total assets in government securities and other guaranteed securities, of which not less than 20 per cent should be in Central Government securities. For pension and general annuity business, the IRDA stipulates that 20 percent of their assets should be invested in government securities.

The non-Government provident funds, superannuation funds and gratuity funds are required by the Central Government from January 24, 2005 to invest 40 percent of their incremental accretions in Central and State government securities and/or units of gilt funds regulated by the Securities and Exchange Board of India (SEBI) and any other negotiable securities fully and unconditionally guaranteed by the Central/State Governments.

Non-banking financial companies (NBFCs) accepting public deposits are required to maintain 15 percent of such outstanding deposits in liquid assets, of which not less than 10 percent should be maintained in approved securities, including government securities and government guaranteed bonds. Investment in government securities should be in dematerialised form, which can be maintained in Constituents' Subsidiary General Ledger (CSGL) Account of a SCB/Stock Holding Corporation of India Limited (SHCIL). In order to increase the security and liquidity of their deposits, residuary non-banking companies (RNBCs), are required to invest not less than 95 percent of their aggregate liability to depositors (ALD) as outstanding on December 31, 2005 and entire incremental deposits over this level in directed investments, which include government securities, rated and listed securities and debt oriented mutual funds. From April 1, 2007, the entire ALD is required to be invested in directed investments only.

25.5 Evolution of Government Securities Market

At the time of Independence in 1947, Government securities market was not significant due mainly to the artificially low coupon rates on Government securities. Financing of the budget deficit of the Central Government by the RBI took place through an arrangement of automatic monetisation through *ad hoc* Treasury Bills. To ensure absorption of the large supply of Government bonds in the face of administered rates, the RBI mandated maintenance of a minimum statutory liquidity ratio (SLR) whereby the commercial banks had to set aside substantial portions of their liabilities for investment in Government securities at below market interest rates. The market was also characterised by several peculiarities such as voucher trading, switch quotas, cash purchase and separate purchase and sale lists. Investors in the gilt-edged securities included individuals as well as financial institutions. Over a period, the gilt-edged market had assumed the nature of captive market with the financial institutions as the major subscribers.

Effective from March 16, 1949, banks had to maintain liquid assets in cash, gold or unencumbered approved securities amounting to not less than 20 percent of their total demand and time liabilities (DTL) under Section 24 of the Banking Regulation Act, 1949. The SLR was the outcome of the action taken to prevent banks from offsetting the impact of variable reserve requirements by liquidating their Government security holdings.

From 1970, the SLR was gradually increased with the objective of restricting the expansionary trend in bank credit as also for augmenting investments of banks in Government securities particularly in the context of financing of the Five Year Plans. The regional rural banks (RRBs) and cooperative banks were permitted to maintain the SLR at the minimum of 25 percent. The SLR was frequently increased in the 1970s touching 34 percent in December 1978, 35 percent in October 1981, and further to 38.5 percent in September 1990. Following the recommendations of the Committee on Financial Sector Reforms (Chairman: M. Narasimham), 1991, SLR was gradually reduced to stand at 25 percent in October 1997. To deal with the global financial crisis—and the consequent need to pump more liquidity in the market—SLR was reduced from

25 percent to 24 percent in November 2008.

25.5.1 Pre-reforms Period: One aspect of the financial market structure in India during the pre-1991 period was the narrowness of the market for Government and semi-Government securities. This meant that there was little scope for using open market operations in Government securities for controlling liquidity. The RBI's operations in this sphere were, therefore, directed mainly at ensuring orderly conditions in the Government securities market so that there was a reasonable allocation of the available resources between the Government sector and the rest of the economy.

The development of the government securities market in India in the pre-reform period was mainly constrained, like in most developing countries, by almost unlimited automatic monetisation of the Central Government budget deficits, captive investors (predominantly banks and insurance companies) and administered coupon rates on government securities at artificially low levels. As a result, the secondary market for government securities was almost non-existent. This impinged on the price discovery process, which is crucial for the development of any market. Since interest rates were kept low in order to ensure low cost of Government borrowing, real rates of return remained negative for several years. Artificially low yields on government securities affected the interest rate structure in the system. In order to compensate for low yield on government securities, banks charged higher interest rates to the commercial sector.

Higher interest rates for the private commercial sector not only adversely impacted investment activity and economic growth, but also affected the financial health of the banking system as bad debts mounted over time. Low economic growth resulted in lower revenues for the Government, both tax and non-tax, necessitating higher borrowing. This was largely met through the mechanism of *ad hoc* Treasury Bills issued by the Government to the RBI and the progressive increase in SLR, as a result of which the government securities market remained dormant. Driven by the compulsions of automatic monetisation, which resulted in expansion of monetary base, the RBI had to progressively raise the cash reserve ratio (CRR) of banks for monetary management. In the face of large government borrowings and the need to restore the health of the financial system, the RBI, in consultation with the Government, initiated reforms in the government securities market as a part of financial sector reforms in the early 1990s. These reforms were broadly aimed at removing the imperfections in the market and creating enabling conditions for its development.

Prior to introduction of reforms, the investor base for government securities consisted of institutions such as banks, financial institutions, provident funds, insurance companies and pension funds, which are statutorily mandated to invest in these securities. To meet the growing financing needs of the Government, the SLR for banks was raised over a period of time to reach the peak rate of 38.5 percent of NDTL in February 1992.

25.6 Post-1991 Measures to Promote Government Securities Market

As the debt manager to the Government, the development of a deep and liquid market for Government securities is of critical importance to the RBI for facilitating the process of price discovery and reducing the cost of Government debt. The RBI has taken several structural and development measures for deepening and widening the Government securities market. In recent years, the approach to the development of Government securities market has focused on greater transparency, risk free settlement, liquidity, and broad-based participation.

Recognising the importance of the government securities market, the RBI, in consultation with the Government, undertook wide-ranging reforms to develop this market. The major objectives of reforms were as follows:

1. To grant operational autonomy to the RBI.
2. To improve institutional infrastructure.
3. To impart liquidity and increase the depth of the market.
4. To improve market microstructure.
5. To create an enabling sound legal and regulatory framework.
6. To increase transparency.

Keeping these objectives in view, reforms were undertaken to strengthen the primary and the secondary segments of the government securities market. In the primary segment, measures were taken to raise resources from the market in a cost effective manner, particularly in the light of the transition to market-related interest rate structure from the administered interest rate regime. In the secondary segment, measures were initiated to improve liquidity in the market. Measures were also undertaken to improve the trading systems, clearing and settlement infrastructure and the risk management framework.

The 1990s marked a watershed in the development of the Government securities market with wide ranging reforms in terms of instruments, institutions and procedures. A major development in the market was the introduction of an auction system for dated securities in June 1992, which marked a move towards market-related rates on the Government securities. Key instruments were also introduced at the longer end of the maturity spectrum with special features to hedge various risks and suit investor preferences during the 1990s. Innovations were also introduced with respect to long-term bonds, such as zero coupon bonds (January 1994), floating rate bonds (1995-96) and capital-indexed bonds (December 1997). Bonds with call and put options were also issued.

Significant steps taken by the RBI in the recent period have included the following.

1. Elongation of maturity.
2. Development of new benchmark Government securities by consolidating new issuances in key maturities.
3. Enhancing fungibility and liquidity by re-issuances of the existing loans.
4. Promoting retailing of Government securities.
5. Introduction of floating rate bonds.
6. Announcement of a calendar for conducting auctions.
7. Enhanced transparency of the Central Government's borrowing programme.

Consequently, the government securities market has witnessed significant transformation in various dimensions, viz. market-based price discovery, widening of investor base, introduction of new instruments, establishment of primary dealers, and electronic trading and settlement infrastructure. This, in turn, has enabled the RBI to perform its functions in tandem with the evolving economic and financial conditions.

Wide-ranging reforms in the government securities market were largely undertaken in response to the changing economic environment. Increased borrowing requirements of the Government, stemming from high fiscal deficits, had to be met in a cost-effective manner without distorting the financial system. The underlying perspective of the reform process was, therefore, to raise government debt at market related rates through an appropriate management of market borrowing. There was also a need to develop a benchmark for other fixed income instruments for purposes of their pricing and valuation. An active secondary market for government securities was also needed for operating monetary policy through indirect instruments such as open market operations and repos. Reforms, therefore, focussed on the development of appropriate market infrastructure, elongation of maturity profile, increasing the width and depth of the market, improving risk management practices and increasing transparency.

As stipulated under the Fiscal Responsibility and Budget Management Act, 2003, the Reserve Bank has withdrawn from participating in the primary market for government securities from April 1, 2006. The increasing move towards fuller capital account convertibility as recommended by the Committee on Fuller Capital Account Convertibility (Chairman: S.S. Tarapore), 2006 would necessitate measures that promote greater integration of the domestic financial markets with global markets. The deepening of the government securities market is, therefore, essential not only for transmission of policy signals but also for developing the derivatives market which would meet future challenges thrown up by further liberalisation of the capital account.

Moreover, an environment of freer capital flows will also necessitate widening of the government securities market with further diversification of the investor base. The RBI is continuing its efforts to further deepen and broaden the Government securities market. A number of initiatives have been taken to modernise the operations relating to Government securities.

To sum up, development of the Government securities market is critical for facilitating active public debt management policy, development and integration of financial markets and operation of indirect instruments of monetary policy. The development of the government securities market has been pursued since the early 1990s with the objectives of ensuring smooth conduct of the government's market borrowings, enlarging the investor base and facilitating the emergence of a risk-free rupee yield curve.

26

Capital Market

26.1 Meaning and Importance of Capital Market

Capital market is a market for long-term funds. The distinction between capital market and money market is not watertight. Broadly speaking, capital market focuses on financing of fixed investment (machinery and equipment) while money market provides working capital finance (raw material etc.).

Capital market channelises household savings to the corporate sector and allocates funds to firms. In this process, it allows both firms and households to share risks associated with business. Moreover, capital market enables the valuation of firms on an almost continuous basis and plays an important role in the governance of the corporate sector.

An efficient capital market is an important constituent of a sound financial system. In India, efforts have been made in recent years to set up an effective regulatory framework covering major participants in the capital market. Similarly, the technology of trading and settlements in the stock exchanges has been upgraded. Internet-based trading in securities has been permitted. Foreign institutional investors (FIIs) and pension funds were allowed to enter the Indian stock market from 1993 onwards. The market has undergone a major transformation in terms of its structure, products, practices, spread, institutional framework and other important aspects like transparency, integrity and efficiency since then. The size of the market has also grown manifold.

The capital market fosters economic growth in following ways:

1. It augments the quantum of savings and capital formation in the economy.
2. It allocates capital efficiently thereby raising the productivity of investment.
3. It enhances the efficiency of a financial system as diverse competitors vie with each other for financial resources.
4. It adds to the financial deepening of the economy by enlarging the financial sector and promoting the use of innovative, sophisticated and cost-effective financial instruments, which ultimately reduce the cost of capital.
5. Well-functioning capital markets also impose discipline on firms to perform.
6. Equity and debt markets stress on the banking sector by diversifying credit risk across the economy.

26.2 Capital Market in the Pre-reforms (i.e. Pre-1991) Period

Historically, different kinds of financial intermediaries have existed in the Indian financial system. At the time of Independence in 1947, working capital requirements of corporates were financed mainly by commercial banks. As the capital market was underdeveloped, a number of development finance institutions (DFIs) were set up at the all-India and the State levels to meet the long-term fund requirements of companies.

Prior to the onset of financial sector reforms in 1991, the capital market structure in India was subject to several controls and opaque procedures. The objective of control over capital issues was to channel the limited capital resources available for investment in the country into desired areas. Apart from this main objective, capital issues control was put to several other uses, these being the following:

1. Regulation of bonus issues.
2. Regulation of terms and conditions of foreign capital participation in Indian companies and the regulation of the terms and conditions of dilution or repatriation of foreign equity.
3. Regulation of capital re-organisation plans of companies, including mergers and amalgamations.
4. Regulation of the capital structure of companies, as well as the terms and conditions of additional issues.
5. Regulation of the volume and timing of the private issue of capital.

Moreover, the trading and settlement system was outdated and not in tune with international practices. Raising of capital from the market was regulated by the Capital Issues (Control) Act, 1947 which was administered by the Controller of Capital Issues (CCIs) in the Ministry of Finance, Government of India. The scheme of controls under the Act required all the companies to obtain prior consent for issues of capital to the public. Pricing as well as the features of the capital structure (such as debt-equity ratios), were controlled by the Government. Similarly, the Securities Contracts (Regulation) Act, 1956 was administered by the Directorate of Stock Exchanges also in the Ministry of Finance. It empowered the Government to recognise/derecognise stock exchanges, stipulate rules and by-laws for their functioning, compel listing of securities by public companies etc. Such a system of regulation and control was fragmented and inadequate in the context of liberalisation wave sweeping across the world. Urgent measures were needed to relax controls and modernise the functioning of capital market.

26.3 Establishment of Securities and Exchange Board of India (SEBI)

In 1992, the Capital Issues (Control) Act, 1947 was repealed and the office of the Controller of Capital Issues (CCIs) was abolished.

The Securities and Exchange Board of India (SEBI) was constituted on April 12, 1988 as a non-statutory body through an Administrative Resolution of the Government for dealing with all matters relating to development and regulation of the securities market and investor protection and to advise the government on all these matters. SEBI was given statutory status and powers through an Ordinance promulgated on January 30, 1992. SEBI was established as a statutory body on February 21, 1992. The Ordinance was replaced by Securities and Exchange Board of India Act 1992 on April 4, 1992.

With this ended all controls related to raising of funds from the market. The move was aimed at enhancing the efficiency, safety, integrity and transparency of the market. Presently, issuers of capital are required to meet the guidelines of SEBI on disclosures and protection of investors.

SEBI has emerged as an autonomous and independent statutory body. Its legally mandated objectives are the following:

1. Protection of the interests of investors in securities.
2. Development of the securities market.
3. Regulation of the securities market.
4. Matters connected therewith and incidental thereto.

The SEBI prohibits fraudulent and unfair trade practices, including insider trading. It also regulates substantial acquisition of shares and takeovers. In order to ensure protection of investors and to safeguard the integrity of the markets, there is a comprehensive surveillance system. Stock exchanges are the primary targets for detection of market manipulation, price rigging and other regulatory breaches regarding capital market functioning.

The SEBI regulates and supervises the securities market through its various regulations, guidelines and schemes issued from time to time.

The powers and functions of SEBI—as the securities market regulator—have been laid down in the SEBI Act, 1992. SEBI also exercises powers under the Securities Contracts (Regulation) Act, 1956, the Depositories Act, 1996 and certain provisions of the Companies Act, 1956. It regulates the securities markets, securities market institutions and market intermediaries, such as the stock exchanges, depositories, mutual funds and other asset management companies, securities dealers and brokers, merchant bankers, credit rating agencies and venture capital funds.

The statutory powers and functions of SEBI were strengthened through the promulgation of the Securities Laws (Amendment) Ordinance on January 25, 1995, which was subsequently replaced by an Act of Parliament.

The SEBI is equipped with the following powers:

1. Powers to register and regulate, inspect, enquire and investigate and undertake audits, and to cancel registration (though in this last case this applies to the mutual fund rather than the AMC); also to prohibit issue of an offer document including prospectus or advertisement.
2. Powers to summon and enforce attendance and examine on oath, inspect registers and documents, discover and enforce disclosure of books of account and other documents.
3. Powers to restrain from business, suspend, search, impound and retain proceeds, access bank data and attach bank accounts, prevent alienation of assets and issue cease and desist orders.
4. Powers to require compensation to be paid to investors.

Those who appeal against SEBI judgements are heard by the Securities Appellate Tribunal (SAT) and can also go to the Supreme Court if they do not accept the Tribunal's judgement. The SAT has three members, one of whom is required to be the presiding officer who is a sitting or retired judge of the Supreme Court or High Court. The two other members must be of ability, integrity and standing with experience of corporate law, securities law, finance, economics or accountancy.

SEBI has around 650+ staff and regional offices in five cities, viz. Mumbai, New Delhi, Chennai, Kolkata and Ahmedabad.

The experience of SEBI during episodes of market misconduct revealed many limitations in the legal provisions of the SEBI Act. In addition, the growing importance of the securities markets in the economy has placed new demands upon SEBI. On October 28, 2002, an ordinance was promulgated which sought to strengthen SEBI. This ordinance involved organisational strengthening of SEBI, giving SEBI more powers for investigations and penalties, and making clearer concepts like insider trading and market manipulations.

The regulatory ambit has been widened in tune with the emerging needs and developments in the equity markets. Apart from stock exchanges, various intermediaries such as mutual funds, stock brokers and sub-brokers, merchant bankers, portfolio managers, registrars to an issue, share transfer agents, underwriters, debentures trustees, bankers to an issue, custodian of securities, venture capital funds and issuers have been brought under the SEBI's regulatory purview.

26.4 Capital Market Reforms since 1991

The Indian equity market has witnessed a series of reforms since the early 1990s. The reforms have been implemented in a gradual and sequential manner, based on international best practices and modified to suit the needs of the country. The reform measures were aimed at the following:

1. Creating growth-enabling institutions.
2. Boosting competitive conditions in the equity market through improved price discovery mechanism.
3. Putting in place an appropriate regulatory framework.
4. Reducing the transaction costs.
5. Reducing information asymmetry, thereby boosting the investor confidence.

These measures were expected to increase the role of the equity market in resource mobilisation by enhancing the access of corporate sector to large resources through a variety of marketable securities. Institutional development was at the core of the reform process.

Reforms in the capital market have had a multi-dimensional impact. The significance of the capital market has improved in providing a mechanism for allocation of resources as is reflected in increase in its share in the sources of finance for the corporates. Various indicators such as reduced volatility are pointers in the direction of increase in the safety of the market. The safety of the market has also been considerably enhanced by adoption of risk management practices and the setting up of settlement guarantee funds and investor protection funds. The integrity and transparency of the market has also gone up with the wider availability of information regarding the performance of corporates. The trading and settlement framework in the Indian stock exchanges now compares favourably with the best international practices. Liquidity in the market has improved considerably.

26.5 Modernisation of Stock Exchanges

26.5.1 Stock Market: A stock (or share) market deals mainly in corporate securities. The securities are chiefly in the form of equity shares and debentures. The purpose of these securities is to raise long-term funds for companies engaged in production. The function of the stock market is two-fold: (a) to arrange for the raising of new capital (primary market function), and (b) to provide liquidity to existing securities (secondary market function).

The new capital is raised by the issue of shares and debentures. The corporate enterprises raising new capital may be new companies or existing companies planning expansion of their operations. Sometimes, existing private firms go public, i.e. become public limited companies.

The stock market helps the floatation of new issues by providing a variety of services like underwriting, distribution, and listing of the issue. Underwriting means guaranteeing the purchase of a fixed amount of new issues by the underwriter. The new issues of capital may be a public issue or a rights issue or both in certain proportions. It may be in the form of equity shares or debentures. Debentures, in turn, may be fully convertible, partly convertible, or non-convertible into shares. A public issue implies that the general public is invited to subscribe to the new issue. A rights issue is restricted for subscription by existing shareholders.

Stock market provides facilities for secondary market, i.e. transaction in existing securities. People desirous of converting their cash into securities can go to the stock exchange and buy securities with the help of brokers there. Similarly, securities can be converted into cash by selling them in the market. Transactions in the secondary market reflect the investment climate in the economy. A well-developed stock market helps to access external capital which allows financially constrained domestic firms to expand. It is argued that countries with developed stock markets tend to grow faster.

A list of important stock exchanges in India is given in Table 26.1.

Table 26.1: List of Important Stock Exchanges in India

S. No.	Name of the Stock Exchange	S. No.	Name of the Stock Exchange
1.	Ahmedabad Stock Exchange	11.	Hyderabad Stock Exchange*
2.	Bombay Stock Exchange (BSE)	12.	Inter-connected Stock Exchange*
3.	Calcutta Stock Exchange	13.	Jaipur Stock Exchange*
4.	Magadh Stock Exchange	14.	Ludhiana Stock Exchange*
5.	Metropolitan Stock Exchange of India	15.	Madhya Pradesh Stock Exchange*
6.	National Stock Exchange (NSE)	16.	Madras Stock Exchange*
7.	Bangalore Stock Exchange*	17.	OTC Exchange of India*
8.	Coimbatore Stock Exchange *	18.	Pune Stock Exchange*
9.	Delhi Stock Exchange*	19.	Uttar Pradesh Stock Exchange*
10.	Gauhati Stock Exchange*	20.	Vadodra Stock Exchange*

* These stock exchanges have been granted exit by SEBI vide different orders.

A. Limitations of Stock Market: It is argued that stock market expansion is not a necessary indication of a country's financial development and stock market development may not help in achieving quicker industrialisation and faster long-term economic growth because of following reasons:

1. Due to inherent volatility and arbitrariness of the stock market, the resulting pricing process is a poor guide to efficient investment allocation.
2. In the wake of unfavourable economic shocks, the interactions between the stock and currency markets may exacerbate macroeconomic instability and reduce long-term economic growth.
3. Stock market development is likely to undermine the financial inclusion role of existing banking systems in developing countries like India.

26.5.2 Trading Infrastructure in Stock Exchanges: There are 6 permanent stock exchanges in India, including the old established Bombay Stock Exchange (BSE) and the National Stock Exchange (NSE) that was set up as a model exchange to provide nation-wide services to investors. The Bombay Stock Exchange (BSE) was set up in 1875 as 'The Native Share and Stock Brokers Association'.

Equity trading is most active in the two major competing stock exchanges, viz. NSE and the BSE. Trading infrastructure in the stock exchanges is anonymous and order-driven, with all orders from market participants being matched based on strike price/time priority.

The Indian capital market is significant in terms of its degree of development, its volume of trading and of the quality of its automated trading and settlement.

The capital markets—though they have suffered from periodic scandals and problems in the past—look much closer in quality to those of developed markets than those in the majority of emerging markets. The range and quality of available securities is evidenced by the substantial flows of foreign institutional investors.

26.5.3 Bombay Stock Exchange (BSE): BSE is a stock exchange located on Dalal Street, Mumbai. It was the 11th largest stock exchange in the world by market capitalisation as of March 2017.

Established in 1875, BSE Ltd. (formerly known as Bombay Stock Exchange Ltd.), is India's second oldest stock exchange (Oldest being the Calcutta Stock Exchange located at Lyons Range, Kolkata) and one of India's leading exchange groups.

In August 31, 1957, the BSE became the first stock exchange to be recognized by the Indian Government under the Securities Contracts Regulation Act. In 1980 the exchange moved to the Phiroze Jeejeebhoy Towers at Dalal Street, Fort area. In 1986 it developed the BSE SENSEX index, giving the BSE a means to measure overall performance of the exchange. In 2000, the BSE used this index to open its derivatives market, trading SENSEX futures contracts. The development of SENSEX options along with equity derivatives followed in 2001 and 2002, expanding the BSE's trading platform.

BSE has facilitated the growth of the Indian corporate sector by providing it an efficient capital-raising platform. BSE is a corporatized and demutualised entity, with a broad chorholder-base which includes two leading global exchanges, Deutsche Bourse, Fuse and Singapore Exchange as strategic partners. BSE provides an efficient and transparent market for trading in equity, debt instruments, derivatives, mutual funds. It also has a platform for trading in equities of small-and-medium enterprises (SME). More than 5,500 companies are listed on BSE making it world's top most exchange in terms of listed members.

BSE is world's fifth most active exchange in terms of number of transactions handled through its electronic trading system. It is also one of the world's leading exchanges (5th largest in December 2013) for Index options trading (Source: World Federation of Exchanges).

BSE also provides a host of other services to capital market participants including risk management, clearing, settlement, market data services and education. It has a global reach with customers around the world and a nation-wide presence.

BSE systems and processes are designed to safeguard market integrity, drive the growth of the Indian capital market and stimulate innovation and competition across all market segments. BSE is the first exchange in India and second in the world to obtain an ISO 9001:2000 certification. It is also the first exchange in the country and second in the world to receive Information Security Management System Standard BS 7799-2-2002 certification for its On-Line Trading System (BOLT).

It operates one of the most respected capital market educational institutes in the country (the BSE Institute Ltd.). BSE also provides depository services through its Central Depository Services Ltd. (CDSL) arm.

BSE's popular equity index—the S&P BSE SENSEX (formerly SENSEX)—is India's most widely tracked stock market benchmark index. It is traded internationally on the EUREX as well as leading exchanges of the BRCS nations (Brazil, Russia, China and South Africa). On February 19, 2013, BSE entered into Strategic Partnership with S&P DOW JONES INDICES and the SENSEX was renamed as S&P BSE SENSEX.

Historically an open outcry floor trading exchange, the BSE switched to an electronic trading system in 1995. This automated, screen-based trading platform is called BSE on-line trading (BOLT). The BSE has also introduced the world's first centralized exchange-based internet trading system, BSEWEBx.co.in to enable investors anywhere in the world to trade on the BSE platform.

26.5.4 National Stock Exchange of India Limited (NSE): It is located in Mumbai, India. NSE was established in the mid-1990s as a demutualised electronic exchange. NSE provides a modern, fully automated screen-based trading system, with over two lakh trading terminals, through which investors in every nook and corner of India can trade. NSE has played a critical role in reforming the Indian securities market and in bringing unparalleled transparency, efficiency and market integrity.

Though a number of other exchanges exist, NSE and the Bombay Stock Exchange (BSE) are the two most significant stock exchanges in India, and between them are responsible for the vast majority of share transactions. NSE's flagship index, the CNX NIFTY 50, is used extensively by investors in India and around the world to take exposure to the Indian equities market.

NSE was started by a clutch of leading Indian financial institutions. It offers trading, clearing and settlement services in equity, debt and equity derivatives. It is India's largest exchange, globally in cash market trades, in currency trading and index options. NSE has diversified shareholding. There are many domestic and global institutions and companies that hold stake in the exchange.

NSC was incorporated in 1992 and recognised as a stock exchange in 1993, at a time when P.V. Narasimha Rao was the Prime Minister of India and Dr. Manmohan Singh was the Finance Minister. It was set up to bring in transparency in the markets. Promoted by leading financial institutions, essentially led by IDBI at the behest of the Government of India, it was incorporated in November 1992 as a tax-paying company. In April 1993, it was recognised as a stock exchange under the Securities Contracts (Regulation) Act, 1956. NSE commenced operations in the Wholesale Debt Market (WDM) segment in June 1994. The capital market (equities) segment of the NSE commenced operations in November 1994, while operations in the derivatives segment commenced in June 2000.

NSE changed the way the Indian markets functioned, in the early 1990s, by replacing floor-based trading with nationwide screen-based electronic trading, which took trading to the doorstep of the investor. The exchange was mainly set up to bring in transparency in the markets. Instead of trading membership being confined to a group of brokers, the NSE ensured that anyone who was qualified, experienced and met minimum financial requirements was allowed to trade.

In this context, the NSE was ahead of its times, when it separated ownership and management in the exchange under SEBI's supervision. The price information which could earlier be accessed only by a handful of people can now be seen by a client in a remote location with the same ease. The paper-based settlement has been replaced by electronic depository-based accounts and settlement of trades. A robust risk management system is in place, so that settlement guarantees could protect investors against broker defaults.

NSE was also instrumental in creating the National Securities Depository Limited (NSDL) which allows investors to securely hold and transfer their shares and bonds electronically. It also allows investors to hold and trade in as few as one share or bond. This not only makes holding financial instruments convenient, but more importantly eliminates the need for paper certificates and greatly reduces the incidents of forged or fake certificates and fraudulent transactions that had plagued the Indian stock market. NSDL's security, combined with the transparency, lower transaction prices and efficiency that the NSE offers, has greatly increased the attractiveness of the Indian stock market to domestic and international investors.

Currently, NSE has the following major segments of the capital market:

- **Equities:** Equities, indices, mutual funds, exchange traded funds, initial public offerings, and security lending and borrowing scheme.
- **Derivatives:** Equity derivatives (including Global Indices like S&P 500, Dow Jones and FTSE), currency derivatives, and interest rate futures.
- **Debt:** Corporate bonds.

A. Equity Derivatives: NSE commenced trading in derivatives with the launch of index futures on June 12, 2000. The futures and options segment of NSE has made a mark for itself globally. In the futures and options segment, trading in CNX Nifty Index, CNX IT Index, Bank Nifty Index, Nifty Midcap 50 index and single stock futures are available. Trading in Mini Nifty Futures and Options and Long-term Options on CNX Nifty are also available.

On August 29, 2011, NSE launched derivative contracts on the world's most followed equity indices, the S&P 500 and the Dow Jones Industrial Average. NSE is the first Indian exchange to launch global indices. This is also the first time in the world that futures contracts on the S&P 500 index were introduced and listed on an exchange outside of their home country, USA. The new contracts include futures on both the DJIA and the S&P 500, and options on the S&P 500.

On May 3, 2012, NSE launched derivative contracts (futures and options) on FTSE 100, the widely tracked index of the UK equity stock market. This was the first of its kind of an index of the UK equity stock market launched in India. FTSE 100 includes 100 largest UK listed blue chip companies.

On January 10, 2013, NSE signed a letter of intent with the Japan Exchange Group, Inc. (JPX) on preparing for the launch of CNX Nifty Index futures, a representative stock price index of India, on the Osaka Securities Exchange Co., Ltd. (OSE), a subsidiary of JPX. Moving forward, both parties will make preparations for the listing of yen-denominated CNX Nifty Index futures by March 2014. Retail and institutional investors in Japan will be able to take a view on the Indian markets in their own currency and in their own time zone. Investors will therefore not face any currency risk, because they will not have to invest in dollar denominated or rupee denominated contracts.

B. Currency Derivatives: In August 2008, currency derivatives were introduced in India by NSE with the launch of currency futures in US$ and INR. It also added currency futures in Euros, Pounds and Yen.

C. Interest Rate Futures: Interest rate futures were introduced for the first time in India by NSE on August 31, 2009, exactly one year after the launch of currency futures. NSE became the first stock exchange to get an approval for interest rate futures, as recommended by the SEBI-RBI committee.

D. Debt Market: On May 13, 2013, NSE launched India's first dedicated debt platform to provide a liquid and transparent trading platform for debt related products. The debt segment provides an opportunity to retail investors to invest in corporate bonds on a liquid and transparent exchange platform. It also helps institutions who are holders of corporate bonds. It is an ideal platform to buy and sell at optimum prices and help corporates to get adequate demand, when they are issuing the bonds.

E. Financial Literacy: NSE is keen to ensure that the people of India are empowered to take sound financial decisions and invest wisely. It has collaborated, among others, with several universities like Gokhale Institute of Politics and Economics, Pune; Bharati Vidyapeeth Deemed University, Pune; Guru Gobind Singh Indraprastha University, Delhi; Ravenshaw University of Cuttack and Punjabi University, Patiala, to offer MBA and BBA courses. NSE has also provided mock market simulation software called NSE Learn to Trade (NLT) to develop investment, trading and portfolio management skills among the students. The simulation software is very similar to the software currently being used by the market professionals and helps students to learn how to trade in the markets.

The exchange has also worked with a missionary zeal to educate investors about the opportunities in the market, the precautions they should take and their rights and obligations. In order to educate investors and help them invest wisely, NSE conducts nearly 1,500 seminars every year in the metros as well as the smallest towns of India.

NSE also conducts online examination and awards certification, under its Certification in Financial Markets (NCFM) programmes. At present, certifications are available in 46 modules, covering different sectors of financial and capital markets, both at the beginner and advanced levels. The list of various modules can be found at the official site of NSE India. In addition, since August 2009, it offers a short-term course called NSE certified capital market professional (NCCMP). The NCCMP is a 100 hour programme for over 3-4 months, conducted at the colleges, and covers theoretical and practical training in subjects related to the capital markets. NCCMP covers subjects like equity markets, debt markets, derivatives, macroeconomics, technical analysis and fundamental analysis. Successful candidates are awarded joint certification from NSE and the concerned college.

The competition between NSE and BSE is a unique one by international standards, where both exchanges are in the same city and have the same trading hours. All major stocks trade on both exchanges, so the exchanges compete for order flow, and not just listings. The rise of NSE has proved to be a powerful spur to reforms at the BSE. Months after NSE started operations, the BSE also launched electronic trading, and improved rules governing admission of corporate and foreign brokerage firms. Presently, the BSE also uses an open electronic limit order book market, using satellite communications to reach locations outside Bombay.

Associated with the NSE are the National Securities Depositary Ltd. (NSDL) and the National Securities Clearing Corporation Ltd. (NSCCL). The NSDL acts as the registrar for what are now predominantly dematerialized securities and the NSCCL as a clearing house.

The setting up of the NSE as an electronic trading platform set a benchmark of operating efficiency for other stock exchanges in the country. The establishment of NSDL in 1996 and Central Depository Services (India) Ltd. (CSDL) in 1999 has enabled paperless trading in the exchanges. This has also facilitated instantaneous electronic transfer of securities and eliminated the risks to the investors arising from bad deliveries in the market, delays in share transfer, fake and forged shares and loss of scrips. The electronic funds transfer (EFT) facility combined with dematerialisation of shares has created a conducive environment for reducing the settlement cycle in stock markets.

26.5.5 Demutualisation and Corporatisation of Stock Exchanges: Stock exchanges all over the world were traditionally formed as *mutual* organisations. The trading members not only provided broking services, but also owned, controlled and managed such exchanges for their mutual benefit. Demutualisation refers to the transition process of an exchange from a *mutually-owned* association to a company *owned by shareholders.* In other words, transforming the legal structure of an exchange from a mutual form to a business corporation form is referred to as demutualisation. The above, in effect means that after demutualisation, the ownership, the management and the trading rights at the exchange are segregated from one another.

In a mutual exchange, the three functions of ownership, management and trading are intervened into a single group. Here, the broker members of the exchange are both the owners and the traders on the exchange and they further manage the exchange as well. A demutualised exchange, on the other hand, has all these three functions clearly segregated, i.e. the ownership, management and trading are in separate hands.

In India, NSE was set up as a demutualised corporate body, where ownership, management and trading rights are in the hands of three different sets of groups from its inception. The Stock Exchange, Mumbai—one of the two premier exchanges in the country—has since been corporatised and demutualised and renamed as the Bombay Stock Exchange Ltd. (BSE).

Corporate governance has emerged as an important tool for protection of shareholders. The corporate governance framework in India has evolved over a period of time since the setting up of the Kumar Mangalam Birla Committee by SEBI. India has a reasonably well-designed regulatory framework for the issuance and trading of securities, and disclosures by the issuers with strong focus on corporate governance standards.

To enhance the level of continuous disclosure by the listed companies, SEBI amended the listing agreement to incorporate segment reporting, related party disclosures, consolidated financial results and consolidated financial statements. The listing agreement between the stock exchanges and the companies has been strengthened from time to time to enhance corporate governance standards.

26.6 Depository System, Dematerialisation (Demat) and Rematerialisation

26.6.1 Depository System: Shares are traditionally held in physical (paper) form. This method has weaknesses like loss/theft of certificates, forged/fake certificates, cumbersome and time consuming procedure for transfer of shares etc. To eliminate these weaknesses, a new system called depository system has been established. A depository is a system which holds shares of an investor in the form of electronic accounts in the same way a bank holds money of a depositor in a savings account.

A depository holds securities in dematerialised form. It maintains ownership records of securities in a book entry form and also effects transfer of ownership through book entry.

Depository system provides the following advantages to an investor:

1. Shares cannot be lost, stolen or mutilated.
2. An investor never needs to doubt the genuineness of his shares i.e. whether they are forged or fake.
3. Share transactions like transfer, transmission etc. can be effected immediately.
4. Transaction costs are usually lower than on the physical segment.
5. There is no risk of bad delivery.

6. Bonus/rights shares allotted to an investor will be immediately credited to his account.
7. An investor receives the statement of accounts of his transactions/holdings periodically.

SEBI has introduced some degree of compulsion in trading and settlement of securities in demat form while the investors have a right to hold securities in either physical or demat form, SEBI has mandated compulsory trading and settlement of securities in select securities in dematerialised form. This was initially introduced for institutional investors and was later extended to all investors.

26.6.2 Dematerialisation (Demat): The concept of demat was introduced in Indian capital market in 1996 with the setting up of NSDL. Demat is the process by which the physical certificates of an investor are converted to an equivalent number of securities in electronic form and credited in the investor's account with his depository participant (DP).

When an investor decides to have his shares in electronic form, he should approach a depository participant (DP)—who is an agent of the depository—and open an account. He should then request for the dematerialisation of certificates by filling up a dematerialisation request form (DRF), which is available with the DP and submitting the same along with the physical certificates.

The investor has to ensure that before the certificates are handed over to the DP for demat, they are defaced by marking *Surrendered for Dematerialisation* on the face of the certificates. Before defacing the share certificate, the investor must ensure that it is available for dematerialisation. The investor must therefore check with his depository participant (DP) whether the ISIN (code number for the security in a depository system) has been activated and made available for dematerialisation by the depository. If yes, then the investor may deface the share certificate. Only those certificates can be dematerialised that are already registered in the investor's name and are in the list of securities admitted for dematerialization by National Securities Depository Limited (NSDL).

His DP will arrange to get them sent to and verified by the company, and on confirmation credit his account with an equivalent number of shares. This process is known as dematerialisation (demat). An investor can always reverse this process if he so desires and get his shares reconverted into paper format. This process is known as rematerialisation.

A. Benefits of Demat: These are the following:
1. Elimination of bad deliveries.
2. Elimination of all risks associated with physical certification.
3. No stamp duty.
4. Immediate transfer and registration of securities.
5. Faster settlement cycle.
6. Faster disbursement of rights, bonus etc.
7. Reduction in brokerage by many brokers for trading in dematerialised securities.
8. Reduction in handling of huge volumes of paper and postal delays.
9. Periodic status report.
10. Elimination of problems relating to change of address of investor, transmission etc.
11. Elimination of problems related to selling securities on behalf of a minor.

12. Ease in portfolio monitoring.

26.6.3 Rematerialisation: If the investor wishes to get back his securities in physical form, all he has to do is to request his DP for rematerialisation of the same. Rematerialisation is the term used for converting electronic holdings back into certificates. An investor's DP will forward his request to NSDL, after verifying that he has the necessary balance. NSDL in turn will intimate the registrar who will print the certificates and dispatch the same to the investor.

26.7 National Securities Depository Limited (NSDL)

It was created in 1995. Based in Mumbai, it was the first central securities depository in India. Promoted by institutions of national stature responsible for the economic development of India, it has established a national infrastructure of international standards that handles most of the securities held and settled in dematerialised form in the Indian capital market.

Although India had a vibrant capital market which is more than a century old, the paper-based settlement of trades caused substantial problems such as bad delivery and delayed transfer of title. The enactment of Depositories Act in August 1996 paved the way for establishment of NSDL, the first depository in India. It went on to establish infrastructure based on international standards.

NSDL has the objective of ensuring the safety and soundness of Indian marketplaces by developing settlement solutions that increase efficiency, minimise risk and reduce costs. NSDL plays a quiet but central role in developing products and services that will continue to nurture the growing needs of the financial services industry.

In the depository system, securities are held in depository accounts, which are similar to holding funds in bank accounts. Transfer of ownership of securities is done through simple account transfers. This method does away with all the risks and hassles normally associated with paperwork. Consequently, the cost of transacting in a depository environment is considerably lower as compared to transacting in certificates.

NSDL is promoted by Industrial Development Bank of India Limited (IDBI)—the largest development bank of India, Unit Trust of India (UTI)—the largest mutual fund in India and National Stock Exchange of India Limited (NSE)—the largest stock exchange in India. Some of the prominent banks in the country have taken a stake in NSDL.

26.8 National Securities Clearing Corporation Ltd (NSCCL)

NSCCL, a wholly-owned subsidiary of NSE, was incorporated in August 1995 and commenced operating as a clearing corporation in April 1996. Clearing and settlement operations of the NSE are managed by NSCCL. It was the first clearing corporation to provide novation/settlement guarantee that revolutionised the entire concept of settlement system in India. It was set up to: (a) bring and sustain confidence in clearing and settlement of securities, (b) promote and maintain short and consistent settlement cycles, (c) provide counterparty risk guarantee, and (d) operate a tight risk containment system.

The settlements of trade in the equities market (both cash and derivative segments) are settled in the BSE by clearing house called BOISL which is a company jointly promoted by BSE (49 percent) and Bank of India (51 percent). BOISL, *inter alia*, handles some of the settlement-related activities of BSE as per instructions and directions of BSE. Responsibility of the clearing house is to handle such settlement activities including co-ordination with the market participants, viz. depositories, clearing banks etc.

However, the overall responsibility of settlement and risk management functions, viz. collection of margins, collateral management etc. pertaining to transactions done on BSE Online Trading (BOLT) System lies with the BSE.

NSCCL undertakes clearing of transactions executed on the National Stock Exchange for Automated Trading (NEAT) system of NSE. It carries out clearing and settlement functions as per the settlement cycles of different sub-segments in the equities segment. The reforms in the securities settlement systems have resulted in following benefits:

1. Reduction and mitigation of systemic, structural and operational risks.
2. Increase speed of transaction, execution and settlement of trade and quicker settlement of transactions with finality.
3. Safety of the settlement process.
4. Reduction of transaction costs and, thereby, making market more efficient and transparent for investors and participants.

26.9 Introduction of Free Pricing

Raising of capital from the securities market before 1992 was regulated under the Capital Issues (Control) Act, 1947. Firms were required to obtain approval from the Controller of Capital Issues (CCI) for raising resources in the market. New companies were allowed to issue shares only at par. Only the existing companies with substantial reserves could issue shares at a premium, which was based on some prescribed formula. In 1992, the Capital Issues (Control) Act, 1947 was repealed and with this ended all controls related to raising of resources from the market. Since then the issuers of securities can raise capital from the market without requiring any consent from any authority, either for making the issue or for pricing it. Restrictions on rights and bonus issues have also been removed. New as well as established companies are now able to price their issues according to their assessment of market conditions.

However, issuers of capital are required to meet the guidelines of SEBI on disclosure and investor protection. Companies issuing capital are required to make sufficient disclosures, including justification of the issue price and also material disclosure about the risk factors in their offer prospectus. These guidelines have served as an important measure for protecting the interest of investors and promoting the development of primary market along sound lines.

It may be recalled that in the early 1990s, the liberalisation of the industrial sector and free pricing of capital issues led to an increased number of companies tapping the primary capital market to mobilise resources. Several corporates charged a high premium not justified by their fundamentals. Also, several companies vanished after raising resources from the capital market. SEBI, therefore, strengthened the norms for public issues while retaining the freedom of the issuers to enter the new issues market and to freely price their issues. The disclosure standards were also strengthened for companies coming out with public issues for improving the levels of investor protection. Strict disclosure norms and entry point restrictions prescribed by SEBI made it difficult for most new companies without an established track record to access the public issues market. Whereas this helped to improve the quality of paper coming into the market, it contributed to a decline in the number of issues and the amount mobilised from the market.

26.10 Strengthening of Disclosure Norms

The central goal of securities markets is to obtain a widely-dispersed ownership and trading in securities. There is conflict of interest between the management team, which controls the firm, and the shareholders, who run the firm. Many policy efforts in recent years have been devoted, towards improving incentives to managers to maximise the interests of shareholders.

Improvements in disclosure are a central tool for containing the conflicts of interest between the managers and shareholders. In order to foster improvements in disclosure, SEBI set up a system named electronic data information filing and retrieval (EDIFAR) in July 2002. This system offers a mechanism through which firms would electronically file mandatory disclosures to SEBI, and these documents would be available to individuals over the internet, with a near-zero delay. It is envisaged that in the future, disclosure would take place through company websites, exchange websites, and EDIFAR.

For strengthening the process of information flow from the listed companies, several measures have been introduced: (a) while sufficient disclosures are mandatory for the companies at the stage of public issues, the listed companies are also required under the listing agreement to make disclosures on a continued basis, (b) for ensuring quick flow of information to the public, the decision pertaining to dividend, bonus and right announcements or any material event are now required to be disclosed to the public within 15 minutes of the conclusion of the board meeting in which the disclosures are taken, and (c) accounting practices were streamlined with norms introduced for segment reporting, related to party transactions and consolidated balance sheets.

There is a substantial scale of securities issuance taking place through the private placement route. The private placement route has become a mechanism where securities can be placed with a few wholesale buyers of securities, without incurring the overheads of the public issue. SEBI is working on devising clear institutional mechanisms through which some public disclosure is made about these issues, while preserving the rights of issuers to not use the public issue route if it is considered to involve excessive overhead costs.

Without seeking to control the freedom of the issuers to enter the market and freely price their issues, the norms for public issues were made stringent in April 1996 to prevent fraudulent companies from accessing the market. Issuers of capital are now required to disclose information on various aspects such as track record of profitability, risk factors etc. As a result, there has been an improvement in the standards of disclosure in the offer documents for the public and rights issues and easier accessibility of information to the investors. The improvement in disclosure standards has enhanced transparency, thereby improving the level of investor protection.

26.11 Transparency and Efficiency

The National Stock Exchange (NSE) introduced screen-based trading at its inception in 1992 which was followed by other stock exchanges. Screen-based trading makes online, electronic, anonymous and order-driven transactions possible. It is a transparent system which provides equal access to all investors, irrespective of their geographical locations.

The move to an electronic trading system has resulted in transparency in trades, better price discovery and lower transaction costs. The efficiency of the market has improved through faster execution of trades. The operational efficiency of the stock market has also been strengthened through improvements in the clearing and settlement practices and the risk management process. Almost the entire delivery of securities now takes place in dematerialised form. Over the past few years or so, there has been no instance of postponement or clubbing of settlements at two main stock exchanges (BSE and NSE) despite defaults by brokers. The cases of bad deliveries are close to nil. Insider trading has been made a criminal offence. Non-transparent products like *badla* have been banned.

The setting up of trade/settlement guarantee funds in most of the exchanges has considerably reduced settlement risks for investors. Corporate governance practices and disclosure norms have led to transparency in information flows, which in turn have improved the price discovery process.

In order to bring greater transparency to the debt market, and to move away from bilateral negotiation towards anonymous order-matching, trading in government bonds began on stock exchanges on January 16, 2003. This has involved exploiting the identical process flow used for trading in equities. Trade takes place by anonymous order matching for all orders across the country, risk management is done by the clearing corporation, and settlement takes place at the depository. Under this system, government bonds appear in the depository statement of an investor alongside corporate equities and bonds. This system has several strengths.

1. Anonymous trading avoids the supervisory and regulatory difficulties of the telephone market, where counterparties are aware of identities and can engage in trades at off-market prices.

2. This market design offers symmetric market access from locations all over India and over the internet, as opposed to the telephone market, which favours entities in south Bombay.

3. It exploits information technology to guarantees that orders are matched against the best price available in the country. This is in contrast with the telephone market, where traders can search for counterparties, but are not sure of having found the best counterparty.

4. It is fully transparent in that orders and trades are visible in real time. This is in contrast with the telephone market, where orders are not visible, and the

transparency of trades is limited and delayed.

5. It exploits the information technology of the depositories of the equity market (NSDL and CDSL), which have the full range of functionality required for investors such as a wide network of IT-enabled depository participants, internet access, strong computer security, access to data about the beneficial owner down to the end-investor.

Issuers also have the option of raising resources through fixed price mechanism or the book building process. [1] Book building was introduced to improve the transparency in pricing of the scrips and determine proper market price for shares.

26.12 Shortening of Settlement Cycle

Capital, unlike labour, is perpetually recycled, and the shorter the cycle, the more efficient is the use of such capital.

Following the enactment of the Depository Act, 1996, two depositories were set up: Central Depository Services Ltd. (CDSL) and National Securities Depository Limited (NSDL). The CDSL and NSDL have been successful in the dematerialisation of securities almost to the full extent. Presently, the transfer of ownership is mostly done through book-entry form. This has greatly improved the speed, accuracy and security of the settlement system. Prior to these arrangements, the settlement cycle was as high as 14 days for specified scrips and 30 days for others. The settlement risk was very high because of unforeseen happenings between the transaction and the settlement. To begin with, the settlement cycle was reduced to a week. Thereafter, rolling settlement was introduced on a T+5 basis in July 2001. From December 2001, all scrips which had established connectivity with the above-mentioned Depositories were moved to rolling settlement. The settlement cycle was further reduced to T+3 in April 2002 and to T+2 in April 2003.

26.13 Growth of Service Providers

Besides strengthening the institutional design of the markets, the reforms have also brought about an increase in the number of service providers who add value to the market. The most significant development in this respect has been the setting up of credit rating agencies. By assigning ratings to debt instruments and by continuous monitoring and dissemination of the ratings, they help in improving the quality of information. At present, six credit rating agencies are operating in India. Besides, two other service providers, *viz.* registrars to issue and share transfer agents, have also grown in number, which help in spreading the services easily and at competitive prices.

26.14 Protection of Investors

The stock exchanges have put in place a system for redressal of investor grievances for matters relating to trading members and companies. They ensure that critical and price-sensitive information reaching the exchange is made available to all classes of investor at the same point of time. Further, to protect the interests of investors, the Investor Protection Fund (IPF) has also been set up by the stock exchanges. The exchanges maintain an IPF to take care of investor claims, which may arise out of non-settlement of obligations by the trading member, who has been declared a defaulter, in respect of trades executed on the exchange. Measures of investor protection that have been put in place over the reform period have led to increased confidence among investors. [2] To improve the availability of information to investors, all listed companies are required to publish unaudited financial results on a quarterly basis.

A continuing increase in the savings rate of households suggests that there is no supply constraint in terms of financial resources that could be channelled into the equity market. After the exuberance of the stock market in the mid-1990s and its decline thereafter, a large number of individual investors took flight to safety in bank deposits, safe retirement instruments and insurance. Households in India have increasingly tended to prefer savings in the form of safe and contractual instruments as opposed to capital market based instruments. Although retail investors have started showing some increased interest in the equity market in recent years, there is a need to increase their participation further.

26.15 Cross Border Portfolio Investment Flows

Since early 1990s there has been enhanced flow of cross border portfolio investments, especially by foreign institutional investors (FIIs), from developed countries to the developing countries. Portfolio investors provide institutional character to the capital markets, flavoured by highly intensive research and diversified investments. FII investments inject global liquidity into the markets, raise the price-earning ratio and thus reduce the cost of capital.

FIIs make investments in various countries to provide a measure of portfolio diversification and hedging to their assets. The forces driving the recent change in the investment portfolio of FIIs—as reflected in the growing emphasis on equities of emerging market economies—have included, *inter alia*: (a) increased accessibility of these markets after liberalisation, (b) improved marketability, (c) fewer problems relating to thin trading, and (d) improved macroeconomic fundamentals of these countries.

Merits of FII flows apart, the Mexican crisis and more recently the East Asian crisis highlighted the downside risks of such flows. The downside risks include political risk, currency risk, problems associated with low liquidity and volatility on returns. Reversal of portfolio flows can be disorderly and result in substantial economic hardship for developing countries.

The main problem in managing portfolio flows towards developing countries emanates from the larger volatility associated with such flows as compared to FDI. It has been argued that under the process of globalisation, highly diversified investors participate in cross-border movement of capital. Such investors pay little attention to economic fundamentals and in the presence of asymmetric information they resort to herd behaviour, which results in volatility of international capital flows. Such a view has, however, been challenged and it has been argued that there is high level of substitutability between various forms of foreign capital.

Economies with modest growth potentials and semi-developed financial market infrastructure are most vulnerable to reversal of portfolio investment flows. Existence of large asymmetry of information among the domestic companies and foreign investors in such countries can lead to sharp changes in portfolio and private debt flows in the face of even a slight change in investor perception about the health of the recipient economy or its financial system. This type of volatility is, however, not limited to portfolio flows. Even external commercial borrowings, in the form of bank borrowing or bond financing, show similar pattern.

FII investments first started flowing to India in 1993. Portfolio investment inflows have since then been substantial. ADR/GDR issues by Indian companies are another important source of cross-border portfolio investment in India. Volatility of cross-border portfolio investment flows into India has been less than what has been experienced by other emerging market economies (EMEs). The stability in portfolio flows to India has been attributed to factors such as robust economic performance since early 1990s and relatively low level of co-movements between Indian and global stock prices.

Prior to 1992, only non-resident Indians (NRIs) and overseas corporate bodies (OCBs) were allowed to undertake portfolio investment in India. In line with the recommendations of the High Level Committee on Balance of Payments (Chairman: C. Rangarajan), 1993, FIIs were allowed to invest in the Indian debt and equity market. Ceilings on FII investments have been progressively relaxed, and at present aggregate investment by FIIs in a company is allowed within the sectoral cap prescribed for FDI. Apart from equity, FIIs registered under the 100 percent debt route can invest in debt instruments—both Government as well as corporate, the current aggregate ceiling being US$ 1 billion.

Indian corporates are also allowed to access equity capital from foreign sources in the form of ADR/GDR and Euro issues. Policies on international offerings on ADRs/GDRs have been liberalised substantially and corporates are allowed to raise funds by way of ADRs/GDRs under an automatic route, subject to specified guidelines.

Two-way fungibility in ADR/GDR issues of Indian companies has been introduced under which investors in India can purchase shares and deposit them with an Indian custodian for issue of ADRs/GDRs by the overseas depository to the extent of the ADRs/GDRs converted into underlying shares.

With a view to increase access to Indian capital markets, qualified foreign investors (QFIs) were allowed to directly invest in the Indian equity market in January 2012. This was done to widen the class of investors, attract more foreign funds, reduce market volatility, and deepen the Indian capital market.

The QFIs include individuals, groups, or associations, resident in a foreign country which are compliant with the Financial Action Task Force (FATF) and which are signatory to International Organisation of Securities Commissions' multilateral memorandum of understanding (MoU). QFIs do not include FIIs/sub-accounts. Earlier, only FIIs/sub-accounts and non-resident Indians (NRIs) were allowed to directly invest in the Indian equity market. Thus, a large number of QFIs, particularly individual foreign nationals who were desirous of investing in the Indian equity market, did not have direct access to it. The RBI and SEBI issued the relevant circulars on January 13, 2012 to operationalize this scheme.

In order to further liberalize the portfolio investment route, the Budget for 2011-12 permitted SEBI-registered MFs to accept subscriptions for equity schemes from foreign investors who meet the know your customer (KYC) requirements.

The scope of the Budget announcement has now been expanded to allow SEBI-registered MFs to accept subscriptions from QFIs for debt schemes in the infrastructure sector. The QFI scheme was operationalized on August 9, 2011. Furthermore, the Union Finance Minister in his 2012-13 Budget allowed QFIs to access Indian corporate bond market.

To sum up, capital market structure has evolved over time with the market practices and conditions generally reflecting the policies put in place. Till the onset of reforms in the early 1990s, raising of resources in the primary segment of the market was subject to several controls, disallowing pricing to be determined by market conditions. Trading in the secondary market was subject to opaque practices. The trading and settlement system was outdated and out of tune with internationally followed practices. The volumes, however, increased and securities continued to exist in physical form. Physical securities also created uncertainties for investors and increased the transaction costs. Besides, long and uncertain settlement cycles created serious problems for clearing houses. Informational flows to the market participants were also deficient. It was considered necessary to orient the SEBI to undertake the tasks of regulation and supervision. The SEBI was, for this purpose, given statutory powers through a separate legislation in 1992.

Although the capital market in India has a long history, during the most part, it remained on the periphery of the financial system. Various reforms undertaken since the early 1990s by the Securities and Exchange Board of India (SEBI) and the Government have brought about a significant structural transformation in the Indian capital market. As a result, the Indian equity market has become modern and transparent.

The improvement in clearing and settlement system has brought a substantial reduction in transaction costs. Several measures were also undertaken to enhance the safety and integrity of the market. These include capital requirements, trading and exposure limits, daily margins comprising mark-to-market margins and VaR based margins. Trade/settlement guarantee fund has also been set up to ensure smooth settlement of transactions in case of default by any member. Another important development of the reform process was the opening up of mutual funds industry to the private sector in 1992, which earlier was the monopoly of the Unit Trust of India (UTI) and mutual funds set up by public sector financial institutions.

Since 1992, foreign institutional investors (FIIs) are permitted to invest in all types of securities, including corporate debt and government securities in stages and subject to limits. Further, the Indian corporate sector was allowed to access international capital markets through American depository receipts (ADRs), global depository receipts (GDRs), foreign currency convertible bonds (FCCBs) and external commercial borrowings (ECBs). Eligible foreign companies have been permitted to raise money from domestic capital markets through issue of Indian depository receipts (IDRs).

Regulations governing substantial acquisition of shares and takeovers of companies have also been put in place. These are aimed at making the takeover process more transparent and to protect the interests of minority shareholders.

To sustain confidence in clearing and settlement of securities, NSE set up the National Securities Clearing Corporation Ltd. (NSCCL) in August, 1995 which carries out the clearing and settlement of the trades executed in the equities and derivatives segments and operates the subsidiary general ledger (SGL) for settlement of trades in government securities. Similarly, the BSE has its own clearing house.

The equity market has witnessed widespread development in infrastructure and its functioning is comparable to international standards. It has seen significant increase in growth and diversity in composition since early 1990s.

Trading infrastructure in the stock exchanges has been modernised by replacing the open outcry system with on-line screen-based electronic trading. This has improved the liquidity in the Indian capital market and led to better price discovery. The trading and settlement cycles were initially shortened from 14 days to 7 days. Subsequently, to enhance the efficiency of the secondary market, rolling settlement was introduced on a T+5 basis. With effect from April 1, 2002, the settlement cycle for all listed securities was shortened to T+3 and further to T+2 from April 1, 2003. Shortening of settlement cycles helped in reducing risks associated with unsettled trades due to market fluctuations.

As a result of these initiatives, there has been a significant rise in the volume of transactions and the emergence of new and innovative instruments. In addition to the two national stock exchanges, viz., the NSE and BSE, there are 17 regional stock exchanges. The importance of regional stock exchanges, however, has been on the decline in recent times.

However, the role of equity market in capital formation continues to be limited. The private corporate debt market is active mainly in the form of private placements, while the public issue market for corporate debt is yet to pick up. It is the primary equity and debt markets that link the issuers of securities and investors and provide resources for capital formation. A growing economy requires risk capital and long-term resources in the form of debt for enabling the corporates to choose an appropriate mix of debt and equity. Long-term resources are also important for financing infrastructure projects. Therefore, in order to sustain India's high growth path, the capital market needs to play a major role. The significance of a well-functioning domestic capital market has also increased as banks need to raise necessary capital from the market to sustain their growing operations.

A major issue which will influence India's securities markets in the future is the challenge of globalisation. RBI has increasingly moved in the direction of giving access to international diversification to institutional investors and individual investors in India. Financial intermediaries and exchanges in India will also experience global competition. There is a need for fully integrating a global perspective into the plans of firms, exchanges, regulators and policy makers.

To sum up, the Indian capital market has become modern in terms of market infrastructure and trading and settlement practices. The capital market has also become a much safer place than it was before the reform process began. The secondary capital market in India has also become deep and liquid. There has also been a reduction in transaction costs and significant improvement in efficiency and transparency. However, the role of the domestic capital market in capital formation in the country, both directly and indirectly through mutual funds, continues to be less significant.

According to Twelfth Five Year Plan (2012-17), "The capital market has been an important source of funding for larger companies and the opening of the economy to portfolio flows from Foreign Institutional Investors (FIIs). In recent years, it has produced a buoyant capital market where companies have raised significant funds through new issues. However, this mechanism has been used mainly by the larger companies to raise funds. We do not have effective institutions that can channel equity funding to smaller companies and start-ups. In a knowledge economy, we need to do much more to encourage the growth of venture capital funds and angel investors". [3]

Post-liberalization, the Indian stock market witnessed a number of scams due to which small investors are reluctant to enter the market. History has witnessed how regulators remained mute spectators, allowing brokers to trap investors. If the government wants investors back in the capital market, it needs to strengthen the regulators, make them efficient, accountable and investor-friendly. In the current scenario of volatile stock market, which is now a fact of life in the globalised economy, investors have to be on their toes and take proactive decisions. They cannot be docile investors, either be active or be out of business. They should not take the market as a place for speculators and punters.

In civilized societies, the law and legal system are supposed to protect the interests of those who lend and not those who fail to repay.

Endnotes

1. Book-building is a process by which demand for the securities proposed to be issued is built-up and the price for securities is assessed for determination of the quantum of such securities to be issued.

2. The World Bank in its survey of *Doing Business* has worked out an investor protection index, which measures the strength of minority shareholders against directors' misuse of corporate assets for his/ her personal gain. The index is the average of the disclosure index, director liability index, and shareholder suits index. The index ranges from 1 to 10, with higher values indicating better investor protection. Based on this index, India fares better than a large number of economies, including even some of the developed ones such as France and Germany.

3. Government of India, Planning Commission, *Twelfth Five Year Plan (2012-17)*, Volume I, Chapter 1, para 1.9⁵.

27

Corporate Debt Market

Sound development of various segments of the capital market is a pre-requisite for a well-functioning financial system. The equity market in India has been modernised over the years and is now comparable with the international markets. There has been a visible improvement in trading and settlement infrastructure, risk management systems and levels of transparency. These improvements have brought about a reduction in the transaction costs and led to improvement in liquidity. However, the size of the public issue segment has remained small as corporates have tended to prefer the international capital market and the private placement market. This has affected the growth of the public issues market and led to under-participation by the investors in the capital market. The corporate bond market, in particular, has remained underdeveloped, possibly due to the absence of a reliable and liquid yield curve, long time taken for floating an issue, high cost of issuance and lack of liquidity in the secondary market. The promotion of a vibrant corporate bond market is essential for meeting the demand for long-term funds, especially for infrastructure requirements.

27.1 Significance of the Corporate Debt Market

There are many reasons why bond markets are important for an emerging economy. Prominent among these is the fact that they lead to more efficient entrepreneurship and greater value creation. When an entrepreneur takes a loan or issues bonds, all additional profit over and above the pre-fixed repayment amount accrues to the entrepreneur. So he or she is better incentivized to take sharper decisions. By having a weak bond market, this efficiency is lost. Further, this efficiency gap may well mean that there is less lending and hence less investment and entrepreneurship in the economy than is feasible.

In any country, companies face different types of financing choices at different stages of development. Reflecting the varied supplies of different types of capital and their costs, regulatory policies and financial innovations, the financing patterns of firms vary geographically and temporally. While developed countries rely more on market-based sources of finance, the developing countries rely more on bank-based sources. The development of a corporate bond market, for direct financing of the capital requirements of corporates by investors assumes paramount importance, particularly in a liberalised financial system.

Corporate debt market provides an alternative means of long-term resources to corporates—alternative to financing by banks and financial institutions. The size and growth of private corporate debt market depends upon several factors, including financing patterns of companies. Among market-based sources of financing, while the equity markets have been largely developed, the corporate bond markets in most developing countries have remained relatively underdeveloped. This has been the result of dominance of the banking system combined with the weaknesses in market infrastructure and inherent complexities. However, credit squeeze following the Asian financial crisis in the mid-1990s drew attention of policy makers to the importance of multiple financing channels in an economy. Alternative sources of finance, apart from banks, need to be actively developed to support higher levels of investment and economic growth. The development of corporate debt market has, therefore, become the prime concern of regulators in developing countries.

From the perspective of developing countries, a liquid corporate bond market can play a critical role in supporting economic development in the following ways:

1. It supplements the banking system to meet the requirements of the corporate sector for long-term capital investment and asset creation.
2. It provides a stable source of finance when the equity market is volatile.
3. With the decline in the role of specialised financial institutions, there is an increasing realisation of the need for a well-developed corporate debt market as an alternative source of finance.
4. Corporate bond markets can also help firms reduce their overall cost of capital by allowing them to tailor their asset and liability profiles to reduce the risk of maturity and currency mismatches.
5. Corporate bond market is important for nurturing a credit culture and market discipline.
6. The existence of a well-functioning bond market can lead to the efficient pricing of credit risk as expectations of all bond market participants are incorporated into bond prices.

Apart from providing a channel for financing investments, the corporate bond markets also contribute towards portfolio diversification for holders of long-term funds. Effective asset management requires a balance of asset alternatives. In view of the underdeveloped state of the corporate bond markets, there would be an overweight position in government securities and even equities. The existence of a well-functioning corporate bond market widens the array of asset choices for long-term investors such as pension funds and insurance companies and allows them to better manage the maturity structure of their balance sheets.

27.2 Lessons from East Asian Crisis

In many Asian economies, banks have traditionally been performing the role of financial intermediation. The East Asian crisis of 1997 underscored the limitations of weak banking systems. The primary role of a banking system is to create and maintain liquidity that is needed to finance production within a short-term horizon. The crisis showed that over-reliance on bank lending for debt financing exposes an economy to the risk of a failure of the banking system. Banking systems, therefore, cannot be the sole source of long-term investment capital without making an economy vulnerable to external shocks. In times of financial distress, when banking sector becomes vulnerable, the corporate bond markets act as a buffer and reduce macroeconomic vulnerability to shocks and systemic risk through diversification of credit and investment risks. By contributing to a more diverse financial system, a bond market can promote financial stability. A bond market may also help the banking system in difficult conditions by allowing banks to recapitalise their balance sheets through securitisation.

Presently, when India is endeavouring to sustain its high growth rate, it is necessary that financing constraints in any form are removed and alternative financing channels are developed in a systematic manner for supplementing traditional bank credit. The problem of *missing* corporate bond market, however, is not unique to India alone. Predominantly bank-dominated financial systems in most Asian economies faced this situation. Many Asian economies woke up to meet this challenge in the wake of the Asian financial crisis. During less than a decade, the domestic bond markets of many Asian economies have undergone significant transformation. In the case of India, however, the small size of the private corporate debt market has shrunk further. This trend needs to be reversed soon. India could learn from the experiences of countries that have undertaken the process of reforming their domestic corporate bond markets.

27.3 Corporate Debt Market in India

India is now one of the fastest growing economies in the world and is endeavouring to step up the growth rate. Limited availability of adequate long-term resources could adversely affect India's infrastructure development. Infrastructure financing requirements are large and could not be expected to be met by the banking sector alone. Banks already appear to have significant exposure to long-term funds. They may, therefore, not be in a position to fund long-term projects in future to the extent they have been able to do in recent years. Inadequate long-term resources could, therefore, act as a constraint on India's future growth prospects. In the absence of a well-functioning debt market, even large corporates fund their requirements from the banking system, limiting the availability of bank funds for small and medium enterprises and other sectors. This also raises the cost of borrowings for them. Thus, development of the capital market, in general, and the debt market, in particular, is crucial from the point of view of reducing corporate sector's reliance on the banking system so as to enable it to focus more on lending to small and medium enterprises, and agriculture and allied activities.

Corporates in India have traditionally relied heavily on borrowings from banks and financial institutions (FIs) to finance their investments. Equity financing has also been used, but largely during periods of surging equity prices. However, bond issuances by companies have remained limited in size and scope. Given the huge funding requirements, especially for long-term infrastructure projects, the corporate debt market has a crucial role to play and needs to be nurtured.

In India, banks and FIs have traditionally been the most important external sources of finance for the corporate sector. The second half of the 1980s saw some activity in primary bond issuances, but these were largely by the public sector undertakings (PSUs). The corporates relied more on banks for meeting short-term working capital requirements and DFIs for financing long-term investment. However, in view of the declining role of DFIs in recent years, a gap has appeared for long-term finance. Commercial banks have managed to fill this gap, but only to an extent as there are asset-liability mismatch issues for banks in providing longer-maturity credit.

In the 1990s, the equity market in India witnessed a series of reforms, which helped in bringing it on par with international standards. However, the corporate debt market has not been able to develop due to lack of market infrastructure and a comprehensive regulatory framework. For a variety of reasons, the issuers resorted to private placement of bonds as opposed to public issues of bonds.

27.3.1 Emergence of Private Placement Market: In private placement, resources are raised privately through arrangers (merchant banking intermediaries) who place securities with a limited number of investors such as financial institutions, corporates and high net worth individuals. Under Section 81 of the Companies Act, 1956, a private placement is defined as 'an issue of shares or of convertible securities by a company to a select group of persons'. An offer of securities to more than 50 persons is deemed to be a public issue under the Act. Corporates access the private placement market because of its following advantages:

1. It is a cost and time-effective method of raising funds.
2. It can be structured to meet the needs of the entrepreneurs.

Private placement does not require detailed compliance of formalities as required in public or rights issues.

The emergence of private placement market has provided an easier alternative to the corporates to raise funds. Although the private placement market provides a cost-effective and time-saving mechanism for raising resources, the unbridled growth of this market has raised some concerns. The quality of issues and extent of transparency in the private placement deals remain areas of concern even though privately placed issues by listed companies are now required to be listed and also subject to necessary disclosures. In the case of public issues, all the issues coming to the market are screened for their quality and the investors rely on ratings and other public information for evaluation of risk. Such a screening mechanism is missing in the case of private placements. This increases the risk associated with privately placed securities. Further, the private placement market appears to be growing at the expense of the public issues market, which has some distinct advantages in the form of wider participation by the investors and, thus, diversification of the risk.

The private placement market was not regulated until May 2004. In view of the mushrooming growth of the market and the risk posed by it, SEBI prescribed that the listing of all debt securities, irrespective of the mode of issuance, i.e. whether issued on a private placement basis or through public/rights issue, shall be done through a separate listing agreement. The RBI also issued guidelines to the financial intermediaries under its purview on investments in non-SLR securities, including private placement. In June 2001, boards of banks were advised to lay down policy and prudential limits on investments in bonds and debentures, including cap on unrated issues and on a private placement basis. The policy laid down by banks should prescribe stringent appraisal of issues, especially by non-borrower customers, provide for an internal system of rating, stipulate entry-level minimum ratings/quality standards and put in place proper risk management systems.

27.3.2 Credit Default Swaps (CDS) for Corporate Bonds: The objective of introducing CDS for corporate bonds is to provide market participants a tool to transfer and manage credit risk in an effective manner through redistribution of risk. CDS, as a risk management product, offers the participants the opportunity to hive off credit risk and also to assume credit risk which otherwise may not be possible. Since CDS have benefits like enhancing investment and borrowing opportunities and reducing transaction costs while allowing risk transfers, such a product would increase investors' interest in corporate bonds and would be beneficial to the development of the corporate bond market in India.

Guidelines on CDS for corporate bonds were issued by the RBI on May 23, 2011, outlining broad norms including the eligible participants and other requirements. It was also indicated that market participants would have to follow the capital adequacy guidelines for CDS issued by their respective regulators. Subsequently, guidelines were issued stating that NBFCs shall participate in CDS market only as users. As users, they are permitted to buy credit protection only to hedge their credit risk on the corporate bonds they hold. They are not permitted to sell protection and hence not permitted to enter into short positions in the CDS contracts. However, they are permitted to exit their bought CDS positions by unwinding them with the original counterparty or by assigning them in favour of the buyer of the underlying bond.

27.4 Reasons for Slow Growth of Corporate Debt Market

Development of the domestic corporate debt market in India is constrained by a number of factors as listed below:

1. Low issuance leading to illiquidity in the secondary market.
2. Narrow investor base.
3. Inadequate credit assessment skills.
4. High costs of issuance.
5. Lack of transparency in trades.
6. Non-standardised instruments.
7. Comprehensive regulatory framework.
8. Underdevelopment of securitisation products.

The market suffers from deficiencies in products, participants and institutional framework. This is despite the fact that India is fairly well-placed insofar as pre-requisites for the development of the corporate bond market are concerned.

There is a reasonably well-developed government securities market, which generally precedes the development of the market for corporate debt securities. The major stock exchanges have trading platforms for the transactions in debt securities. The infrastructure also exists for clearing and settlement. The Clearing Corporation of India Limited (CCIL) has been successfully settling trades in government bonds, foreign exchange and other money market instruments. The experience with the depository system has been satisfactory. The presence of multiple rating agencies meets the requirement of an assessment framework for bond quality.

27.5 High Level Expert Committee on Corporate Debt and Securitisation

With the intent of the development of the corporate bond market along sound lines, some initiatives have been taken by the SEBI in the past few years. These measures have largely aimed at improving disclosures in respect of privately placed debt issues. In view of the immediate need to design a suitable framework for the corporate debt market, the Union Budget 2005-06 announced the setting up of a High Level Expert Committee on Corporate Bonds and Securitisation to look into the legal, regulatory, tax and mortgage design issues for the development of the corporate bond market. The High Level Committee (Chairman: R.H. Patil), which submitted its report in December 2005, looked into the factors inhibiting the development of an active corporate debt market in India and made several suggestions for developing the market infrastructure for development of primary as well as secondary corporate bond market.

The key recommendations of the Committee are summed up below.

27.5.1 Corporate Debt Market:

A. Primary Market

1. The stamp duty on debt instruments be made uniform across all the States and linked to the tenor of securities.
2. To increase the issuer base, the time and cost for public issuance and the disclosure and listing requirements for private placements be reduced and made simpler. Banks be allowed to issue bonds of maturities of 5 year and above for ALM purpose, in addition to infrastructure sector bonds.
3. A suitable framework for market making be put in place.
4. Disclosure requirements be substantially abridged for listed companies. For unlisted companies, rating rationale should form the basis of listing. Companies that wish to make a public issue should be subjected to stringent disclosure requirements. The privately placed bonds should be listed within 7 days from the date of allotment, as in the case of public issues.
5. Role of debenture trustees should be strengthened. SEBI should encourage development of professional debenture trustee companies.
6. To reduce the relative cost of participation in the corporate bond market, the tax deduction at source (TDS) rule for corporate bonds should be brought at par with the government securities. Companies should pay interest and redemption amounts to the depository, which would then pass them on to the investors through ECS/warrants.
7. For widening investor base, the scope of investment by provident/pension/gratuity funds and insurance companies in corporate bonds should be enhanced. Retail investors should be encouraged to participate in the market through stock exchanges and mutual funds.

8. To create large floating stocks, the number of fresh issuances by a given corporate in a given time period should be limited. Any new issue should preferably be a reissue so that there are large stocks in any given issue and issuers should be encouraged to consolidate various existing issues into a few large issues, which can then serve as benchmarks.

9. A centralised database of all bonds issued by corporates be created. Enabling regulations for setting up platforms for non-competitive bidding and electronic bidding process for primary issuance of bonds should be created.

B. Secondary Market

1. Regulatory framework for a transparent and efficient secondary market for corporate bonds should be put in place by SEBI in a phased manner. To begin with, a trade reporting system for capturing information related to trading in corporate bonds and disseminating on a real time basis should be created. The market participants should report details of each transaction within a specified time period to the trade reporting system.

2. Clearing and settlement of trades should meet the standards set by IOSCO and global best practices. The clearing and settlement system should migrate within a reasonable timeframe from gross settlement to net settlement. The clearing and settlement agencies should be given access to the RTGS system. For improving secondary market trading, repos in corporate bonds be allowed.

3. An online order matching platform for corporate bonds should be set up by the stock exchanges or jointly by regulated institutions such as banks, financial institutions, mutual funds, insurance companies etc. In the final stage of development, the trade reporting system could migrate to STP-enabled order matching system and net settlement.

4. The Committee also recommended: (a) reduction in shut period for corporate bonds; (b) application of uniform coupon conventions such as, 30/360 day count convention as followed for government securities; (c) reduction in minimum market lot from ₹ 10 lakh to ₹ 1 lakh, and (d) introduction of exchange traded interest rate derivative products.

27.5.2 Securitised Debt Market:

1. A consensus should evolve on the affordable rates and levels of stamp duty on debt assignment, pass-through certificates (PTCs) and security receipts (SRs) across States.

2. An explicit tax pass-through treatment to securitisation SPVs/Trust SPVs should be provided. Wholesale investors should be permitted to invest in and hold units of a close-ended passively managed mutual fund whose sole objective is to invest its funds in securitised paper. There should be no withholding tax on interest paid by the borrowers to the securitisation trust and on distributions made by the securitisation trust to its PTCs and/or SR holders.

3. PTCs and other securities issued by securitisation SPVs/Trust SPVs should be notified as securities under SCRA.

4. Large-sized NBFCs and non-NBFCs corporate bodies established in India may be permitted to invest in SRs as QIBs. Private equity funds registered with SEBI as venture capital funds (VCFs) may also be permitted to invest in SRs within the limits

that are applied for investment by VCFs into corporate bonds.

5. The Committee also recommended: (a) introduction of credit enhancement mechanism for corporate bonds, (b) creation of specialised debt funds to cater to the needs of the infrastructure sector, and (c) fiscal support, like tax benefits, bond insurance and credit enhancement, for municipal bonds and infrastructure SPVs.

Learning from the experience of developing the government securities market, the development of the corporate debt market needs to proceed in a measured manner with well thought out sequencing. Such development also requires cooperation of and coordination with the key players. The initial steps towards developing the corporate bond market based on the recommendations of the High Level Expert Committee on Corporate Bonds and Securitisation have already been initiated. The Union Budget for 2006-07 had proposed to create a single unified exchange-traded market for corporate bonds. As a first step towards creation of a Unified Exchange Traded Bond Market, the SEBI has initiated steps to establish a system to capture all information related to trading in corporate bonds as accurately and as close to execution as possible through an authorised reporting platform. The market development process for bonds in India is likely to be a gradual process as has been experienced in other countries. For step by step development of the corporate bond market, it is necessary to lay down the broad objectives, which may include: (a) building a liquid government securities benchmark yield curve for appropriate pricing of debt instruments, (b) promoting the growth of an active secondary market for spot and derivative transactions, and (c) providing encouragement to issuers and investors to participate in the bond market. All these objectives are mutually reinforcing.

27.6 Development of Corporate Bond Market in Select Countries

27.6.1 South Korea: South Korea had an underdeveloped local government bond market till 1997 as the Government was running a surplus, but a developed market for corporate bonds, which had come up in the early 1970s. However, a majority of Korean corporate bond issues had guarantees from commercial banks. The experience of South Korea shows that too much Government intervention (either in exchange rate or implicit or explicit guarantees) results in serious distortion of markets. Since the currency crisis, the corporate bond market in South Korea grew remarkably fast as the companies had to substitute bank lending by bond issues and large quantities of asset-backed securities (ABSs) had to be issued in the process of financial restructuring.

Although the bond market in South Korea grew fast, it followed boom-bust cycle due to collapse of one of its leading corporate houses. The authorities, therefore, had to intervene from time to time to stabilise the market. The Korean experience is important in that corporates were able to replace bonds guaranteed by banks with bonds without bank guarantees. As a result, corporate bonds in South Korea increasingly reflected corporate credit risk rather than credit risk of banks. South Korea introduced mark-to-market accounting on bond funds as it promotes transparency and enhances market liquidity.

27.6.2 Malaysia: Malaysia succeeded in giving a boost to its corporate bond market by reducing impediments and enhancing coordination. The National Bond Market Committee, which consolidated regulatory responsibility under one umbrella, brought about a reduction in approval process for corporate issuance from 9-12 months to 14 days. In order to enhance cost-effectiveness and efficiency, the Malaysian authorities also computerised several processes and made some others online, to speed up securities tendering, reduce settlement risk, promote transparency of information and more efficient trading. Securities lending and borrowing programme was introduced *via* real-time gross settlement system.

The Malaysian bond market also benefited from regional cooperation in East Asia. The growth of Malaysia's corporate bond market was spurred by the increasing presence of institutional investors, such as pension funds, unit trust funds and insurance companies on the one hand and increasing demand from the private sector for innovative forms of finance, on the other. Malaysia promoted its indigenous Islamic bond market through the Malaysia International Islamic Financial Centre initiative, which abolished withholding taxes on interest income earned on multilateral-issued bonds. It is significant to note that the corporate and government bond markets in Malaysia share the same infrastructure, dealers, reporting system and RTGS system, thus, taking advantage of the economies of scale in infrastructure like dealer networks, reporting and settlement.

27.6.3 Singapore: Singapore has a developed debt market. Despite the small size of the economy, the authorities made attempts to attract non-resident issuers in both local and foreign currencies to enhance the size and depth of the corporate bond market. Singapore took various steps to encourage foreign investors and issuers, which included removal of restrictions on Singapore-based financial institutions trading with non-financial institutions, and on trading of interest rate swaps (IRS), asset swaps, cross-currency swaps and options. Issue of bonds was also encouraged by streamlining of prospectus requirements.

Under a debenture issuance programme, an issuer in Singapore can make multiple offers of separate tranches of debentures, by issuing a base prospectus that is applicable for the entire programme and by lodging a brief pricing statement for subsequent offers under the programme. The validity of the base prospectus has been extended from six months from the date of initial registration to 24 months. Financial institutions offering continuously issued structured notes have been exempted from the requirement to lodge and register a pricing statement as there were practical difficulties for the issuer of these notes in lodging a pricing statement before such an offer. These streamlined disclosure requirements have ensured that proper risk and product disclosures are made available to investors. There has been a sharp surge in foreign entities issuing Singapore dollar-denominated bonds. Local institutions, particularly quasi-government entities, were also encouraged to issue bonds.

In Singapore, key issues that were designated as benchmarks were augmented by re-opening these issues and buying back others. This was done based on market feedback about minimum issue size that is needed for active trading. Therefore, issues that were smaller in size were bought back to concentrate liquidity in the larger issues. For faster processing of applications, an internet based facility was created for primary dealers to submit bids. An electronic trading platform, which publishes details of transactions on a real time basis, also helped in improving the transparency of the yield curve. Singapore introduced investor tax exemptions on interest income derived from infrastructure bonds to diversify the range of attractive debt products.

27.6.4 Australia: A well-functioning corporate bond market has emerged in Australia over the years due to a combination of factors such as strong economic growth leading to demand for funds, reduction in government's borrowing requirements, thereby easing competition for investible funds and introduction of a compulsory retirement savings system in the early 1990s that expanded the pool of funds. The growth of corporate bond market in Australia is also attributable to its openness to foreign issuers and investors. To enable these investors and issuers to hedge against currency risk, Australia developed liquid markets in currency swaps. Australia also removed interest withholding tax on foreign investment.

27.6.5 Thailand: The regulatory authorities in Thailand have been actively promoting their local bond market. Thailand implemented a no tax policy on special purpose vehicle (SPV) transfers for marketable securities to promote investor liquidity and lower financing costs. The Bond Electronic Exchange of Thailand recently set up an electronic trading platform to facilitate trade and reduce transaction costs.

To sum up, the stock markets in India have become modern and are comparable to the best in the world in terms of market infrastructure, trading and settlement practices and risk management systems. However, given the size of the Indian economy, the capital raised from the securities market has remained quite small. Corporates, by and large, tend to finance their investment activities through alternative sources, which have inhibited the growth of the market. Large and well-known corporates in India have tended to prefer international capital markets. Huge resources have also been raised by way of debt issues from the private placement market, which is less cumbersome, fast and economical. However, this segment lacks transparency and appears to be growing at the expense of the public issues segment. Lack of sufficient capital market activity has hindered the process of diversification of investment from fixed income instruments to equity-based instruments by the households.

The development of any market requires removal of bottlenecks on supply as well as demand side, while putting in place alongside sound institutional and legal framework. In India, high economic growth has created ample demand for funds from the corporate sector which is reflected in sharp growth in bank credit and increased resource mobilisation from the international equity market and the private placement market. Encouraging business outlook and congenial investment climate have created stimulus for companies to undertake capacity expansion. On the supply side too, rising income levels and savings would require alternative investment options, including equity and corporate debt. The need, therefore, is to ensure that the capital market is well positioned to take advantage of these favourable factors.

There is a need to ensure that the corporates are able to raise resources from the capital market in a timely and cost-effective manner. The need is also felt to develop strong domestic institutional investors, which would serve many purposes. As the market evolution is an ongoing process, the Indian equity market would have to continuously strive to keep up to the international standards. In particular, corporate governance practices need to be strengthened further to raise the confidence level of a common investor. This would also enhance flow of institutional money to equities.

The development of financial markets, especially the government securities market, is important for the entire debt market as it serves as a benchmark for pricing other debt market instruments, thereby aiding the monetary transmission process across the yield curve. Therefore, efforts have been made in India to broaden and deepen the government securities market so as to enable the process of efficient price discovery in respect of interest rates. While developing the private corporate debt market, the experience gained from developing the government securities market should prove useful.

The corporate debt market is not yet large enough to have a significant impact on systemic stability. The Indian financial system is dominated by bank intermediation. Corporates in India have traditionally relied on borrowings from banks and financial institutions. Equity financing has also been used during periods of surging equity prices. The corporate bond market, which was reasonably vibrant in the mid-1980s, has however shrunk with respect to its alternate sources of funding. The lack of buying interest, low transparency and absence of pricing of spreads against the benchmark are some of the other reasons. The opening up of the capital account could, however, see the growth of the corporate bond market as there may be demand from foreign investors seeking exposure to high-quality corporate debt.

Even on the supply side, the need for the corporate bond market by the corporates is inadequate. This is due to their increased access to the off-shore market and improving off-shore spreads/risk perception resulting in greater liquidity off-shore rather than on-shore. Further, a sizable market is captured by the large issuance of credit risk-free government securities and issuance of low-risk subordinated debts at attractive interest rates by banks as part of their Tier II capital. While SEBI has initiated steps to simplify issuance procedures and reduce the costs of public issuance, the relative ease in raising corporate debt through private placements has resulted in the large share of private placement issuance of corporate bonds. This has rendered the corporate bond market relatively less transparent which has, in turn, impacted the liquidity of such bonds.

The secondary market in corporate bonds is limited to highly rated securities (AA and above). The wholesale debt segments of the stock exchanges have not picked up and the OTC market in corporate bonds lacks an automated order matching system and centralised settlement. The absence of DVP is another obstacle in market development. The tax deducted at source (TDS) system for corporate bonds acts as an impediment to the development of secondary market activities, especially since government securities are not subject to TDS. The delay in contract enforcement also hampers market development.

The development of the corporate bond market currently suffers from a lack of buying interest, absence of pricing of spreads against the benchmark and a flat yield curve. It requires regulatory and legislative reforms for its development.

28

Foreign Exchange Market

28.1 Pre-Independence Period

Prior to Independence in 1947, India's forex market lacked depth and liquidity. Exchange control and the fixed exchange rate regime came in the way of forex market development. Exchange control was introduced in India on September 3, 1939 following the outbreak of the Second World War, mainly to conserve the non-sterling area currencies and utilise them for essential purposes. The objective of exchange control was primarily to regulate the demand for foreign exchange for various purposes, within the limits set by the available supply. It, thus, involved rationing of foreign exchange among various competing demands for it. In the closing stages of the War, it became clear that control over foreign exchange transactions would have to continue in the post-War period in the interest of making the most prudent use of the foreign exchange resources. It was, therefore, decided to place the control on a statutory basis and the Foreign Exchange Regulation Act of 1947 was accordingly enacted. The Act came into force on March 25, 1947.

28.2 Pre-reforms Period (1947-90)

Foreign exchange market was highly regulated prior to 1991. In view of the scarcity of foreign exchange reserves, banks, exporters and individuals had to surrender the foreign exchange earned/received by them to the RBI.

In the early 1990s, the foreign exchange market in India was in the initial stages of development and suffered from several shortcomings. The spot as well as forward markets lacked depth and liquidity. The market was skewed with a handful of public sector banks accounting for bulk of the merchant business and the foreign banks a greater share of inter-bank business. The forward rates reflected demand and supply, rather than interest rate differentials due to absence of integration between the money and forex markets and the restrictions placed on borrowing/lending in the international market. On account of ceilings on open positions and gaps, there was a virtual absence of market making. The cross-currency market had not developed on account of prohibition on initiating transactions in the overseas market. Besides forward contracts and cross currency options, there was no free access to other hedging products. It was, therefore, felt that any attempt at vitalising the foreign exchange market should necessarily start with relaxation of regulations governing these issues.

28.3 Post-reforms Period (1991 onward)

Post-reforms period has been marked by wide-ranging measures to widen and deepen the market, besides exchange rate liberalisation. The impetus for forex market reform was provided by recommendations of the: (a) High Level Committee on Balance of Payments (Chairman: C. Rangarajan), 1993; (b) Expert Group on Foreign Exchange Markets in India (Chairman: O.P. Sodhani), 1995, and (c) Committee on Capital Account Convertibility (Chairman: S.S. Tarapore), 1997.

28.3.1 Expert Group on Foreign Exchange Markets: The reform phase began with the Sodhani Committee (1994) which in its report submitted in 1995 made several recommendations to relax the regulations with a view to vitalising the foreign exchange market. Most of the recommendations of the Sodhani Committee relating to the development of the foreign exchange market were implemented during the latter half of the 1990s.

The Expert Group on Foreign Exchange Markets in India (Chairman: O.P. Sodhani), which submitted its Report in 1995, identified various regulations inhibiting the growth of the market. The Group's main recommendations were as follows:

1. Corporates may be permitted to take a hedge upon declaring the existence of an exposure.
2. Banks should be permitted to fix their own exchange position limits such as intra-day and overnight limits, subject to ensuring that the capital is provided/earmarked to the extent of 5 percent of this limit based on internationally accepted guidelines.
3. Fixation of Aggregate Gap Limit (AGL)—which would also include rupee transactions—by the managements of the banks based on capital, risk taking capacity etc.
4. Banks be allowed to initiate cross currency positions abroad and to lend or borrow short-term funds up to 6 months, subject to a specified ceiling.
5. Allowing exporters to retain 100 percent of their export earnings in any foreign currency with an authorised dealer (AD) in India, subject to liquidation of outstanding advances against export bills.
6. Permitting ADs to determine the interest rates and maturity period in respect of FCNR (B) deposits.
7. Selective intervention by the RBI in the market so as to ensure greater orderliness in the market.

In pursuance of the recommendations of the Sodhani Committee, the RBI had set up the Clearing Corporation of India Ltd. (CCIL) in 2001 to mitigate risks in the Indian financial markets. The CCIL commenced settlement of foreign exchange operations for inter-bank USD-INR spot and forward trades from November 8, 2002 and for inter-bank USD-INR cash and tom trades from February 5, 2004. The CCIL undertakes settlement of foreign exchange trades on a multilateral net basis through a process of novation and all spot, cash and tom transactions are guaranteed for settlement from the trade date. Every eligible foreign exchange contract entered between members gets novated or replaced by two new contracts—between the CCIL and each of the two parties, respectively. Following the multilateral netting procedure, the net amount payable to, or receivable from, the CCIL in each currency is arrived at, member-wise. The Rupee leg is settled through the members' current accounts with the RBI and the USD leg through CCIL's account with the settlement bank at New York. The CCIL sets limits for each member bank on the basis of certain parameters such as member's credit rating, net worth, asset value and management quality. The CCIL has consistently endeavoured to add value to the services and has gradually brought the entire gamut of foreign exchange transactions under its purview. Intermediation, by the CCIL thus, provides its members the benefits of risk mitigation, improved efficiency, lower operational cost and easier reconciliation of accounts with correspondents.

28.3.2 Technical Group on Foreign Exchange Market, 2005: In order to review comprehensively the initiatives taken by the RBI from time to time in the foreign exchange market and to identify areas for further improvement, the RBI constituted an internal Technical Group. The Group, which submitted its Report in June 2005, reviewed foreign market liberalisation in select emerging markets and examined the current regulatory regime in the light of liberalisation in related sections to identify areas for further liberalisation. The Group noted that although the external sector is fundamentally stronger and more resilient than ever before, some of the pre-conditions for further liberalisation laid down by the Tarapore Committee on Capital Account Convertibility were yet to be achieved. In order to embark upon further deregulation of the foreign exchange market, including relaxation of the remaining capital controls, an enabling environment was needed for the reforms to proceed on a sustainable basis. In this context, liberalisation of various sectors of the economy had to proceed in tandem to derive synergies of the reform process. The Group also took into account the risks associated with internationalisation of the rupee and concluded that a gradual and need-based approach would be more suited to the prevailing conditions.

The Group proposed a number of measures for implementation in the short-term for resident entities, banks and non-residents. Some of the important recommendations made by the Group are as under.

A. Resident Entities:

1. In order to provide greater flexibility to resident entities for dynamically managing their exposures, to further the development of the forward segment of the market and to bring about uniformity with respect to booking of such contracts, all forward contracts booked by residents, regardless of tenor, may be allowed to be cancelled and rebooked freely.

2. Foreign currency-rupee swaps booked to hedge genuine foreign currency exposures may also be permitted to be rebooked/reinstated on cancellation.

3. Corporates with derived foreign exchange exposures arising out of rupee-foreign currency swaps may be permitted to hedge the interest rate risk and cross currency exposures (not involving the rupee).

4. Corporates may be permitted to sell/write covered call and put options subject to adequate accounting standards and risk management systems being in place.

B. Commercial Banks:

1. Banks would be required to put in place a customer suitability and appropriateness policy.

2. Banks may be permitted to provide capital on the actual overnight open exchange

position maintained by them, rather than on their open position limits.

3. Banks may be given the freedom to decide on the period of crystallisation of unpaid export bills; the exchange gain and loss on crystallisation may be passed on to exporters symmetrically.

4. Banks having expertise in managing commodity price risk and hence specifically authorised by the RBI in this regard may be allowed to approve commodity hedging proposals from their corporate customers.

5. The closing time for inter-bank foreign exchange market in India may be extended by one hour from 4.00 p.m. to 5.00 p.m.

6. Forex data, including traded volumes for derivatives such as foreign currency-rupee options may be made available to the market on a regular basis.

C. Non-Resident Entities:

1. The Group was of the view that as at present apart from US dollar (US$), Pound sterling (GBP), Euro and Japanese yen (JPY), Foreign Currency Non-Resident (FCNR) (B) deposits may also be accepted in Canadian dollar (CAD), Australian dollar (AUD) and New Zealand dollar (NZD).

Based on the recommendations of the Technical Group, the Annual Policy Statement of the RBI for the year 2005-06 initiated several measures.

First, cancellation and rebooking of all eligible forward contracts booked by residents, irrespective of tenor, were permitted.

Second, in order to guard against international price fluctuations in tradables, banks were allowed to approve proposals for commodity hedging in international exchanges from their corporate customers.

Third, the closing time for inter-bank foreign exchange market in India was extended by one hour up to 5.00 p.m.

Fourth, it was proposed to disseminate additional information, including traded volumes for derivatives such as foreign currency-rupee options to the market.

With a view to further liberalising the norms for raising resources abroad as also ensuring better effective use of foreign exchange reserves, it was decided to raise the ceiling of overseas investment by Indian entities in overseas joint ventures and/or wholly-owned subsidiaries from 100 percent to 200 percent of their net worth under the automatic route. Concurrently, in order to further liberalise the procedure, the authorised dealers (ADs) were accorded general permission to open foreign currency accounts of the project offices set up in India by foreign companies and operate the accounts flexibly. Earlier, ADs were required to obtain approval of the RBI.

28.4 Measures Undertaken to Develop Foreign Exchange Market

The Indian foreign exchange market has come a long way since the period prior to 1978 when banks were required to maintain square position at all points of time. The important measures undertaken to broaden and deepen the foreign exchange market are as follows:

28.4.1 General Measures:

- **March 1992:** The exchange rate of rupees was partially floated in March 1992 with

the introduction of LERMS.
- **March 1993:** Unified exchange rate was introduced.
- **August 1993:** Direct quotation system was introduced
- **July 1995:** In order to ensure that the exchange rate of the rupee reflected fully the demand supply situation and in furtherance of the move towards eliminating transactions through reserves, it was decided to route government debt service payment (civil) through the market.
- **October 1995:** With a view to minimising the influence on the process of rate formation, the Reserve Bank discontinued quoting its buying and selling rate.

28.4.2 Relaxation for Banks:
- **September 1995:** As against overnight limit of ₹ 15 crore, banks were given freedom to fix their own open exchange position limit and apply to the Reserve Bank for approval. The revised limits became operative from January 1996.
- **April 1996:** Depending upon the asset liability profile, dealing expertise and such other relevant factors, the ADs were accorded freedom to fix their own gap limits for more efficient management of their assets and liabilities subject to the Reserve Bank approval. The banks which are permitted higher limits should be in a position to mark to market their gaps on a daily basis using value at risk models.
- **April 1996:** The banks which had put in place adequate risk management systems were permitted to freely trade in the overseas markets, subject to the overall position/gap discipline.
- **October 1996:** Banks were permitted to provide foreign currency denominated loans to their customers out of the pool of FCNR (B) deposits.
- **April 1997:** Cash reserve requirements on inter-bank borrowings were removed.
- **April 1997:** The Reserve Bank permitted banks to borrow and invest in the overseas markets. At present, banks are permitted to borrow up to 25 percent of Tier I capital and invest up to any amount.

28.4.3 Relaxation for Corporates:
- **April 1992:** EEFC scheme was introduced. Currently, exchange earners in select categories are permitted to retain 100 percent of foreign exchange receipts in foreign currency accounts, while all others are permitted to retain 50 percent.
- **September 1996:** Corporates were accorded greater freedom to undertake active hedging. They were given freedom to choose the currency of hedge irrespective of the currency of the exposure.
- **September 1996:** Corporates were given complete freedom to book and cancel cross currency options.

Besides, several measures have been undertaken to develop the forward market. The participants in the forward market have increased considerably. Several instruments have been introduced to hedge exposures.

28.5 Hedging for Foreign Currency Exposure
28.5.1 Hedging Facilities for Residents:

- **March 1992:** Residents in India were permitted to enter into a forward contract with an authorised dealer (AD) to hedge an exposure to exchange risk in respect of a transaction for which sale and/or purchase of foreign exchange is permitted subject to certain terms and conditions. Currently, forward contracts booked in respect of foreign currency exposures of residents falling due within one year may be freely cancelled and rebooked, among other stipulations.

- **September 1996:** Residents in India were permitted to enter into a foreign currency option contract with an AD in India to hedge foreign exchange exposure arising out of his trade, provided that in respect of cost effective risk reduction strategies like range forwards and ratio-range forwards, there is no net inflow of premium. Cross currency options should be written on a fully covered back-to-back basis. At present, the cover transaction may be undertaken with a bank outside India, an off-shore banking unit situated in a special economic zone or an internationally recognised option exchange or another AD in India.

- **April 1997:** Residents who owe a foreign exchange or rupee liability, may enter into a contract for foreign currency-rupee swap with an AD in India to hedge long term exposure under certain terms and conditions.

- **October 1997:** Residents who have borrowed foreign exchange were permitted to enter into an interest rate swap or currency swap or coupon swap or foreign currency option or interest rate cap or collar (purchases) or forward rate agreement (FRA) contract with an AD in India or with a branch outside India of an AD for hedging loan exposure and unwinding from such hedges. The contract, however, should not involve the rupee and maturity of the hedge should not exceed the unexpired maturity of the underlying loan besides other conditions.

- **September 1998:** Residents in India, engaged in import and export trade, may hedge the price risk of all commodities except crude oil and petroleum products. Hedging of price risk on these products was also permitted with effect from September 2000 in the international commodity exchanges/markets.

- **April 2003:** ADs were permitted to enter into forward contracts with residents in respect of transactions denominated in foreign currency but settled in Indian rupees. These contracts shall be held till maturity and cash settlement would be made on the maturity date by cancellation of the contracts.

- **July 2003:** Foreign currency-rupee options were introduced. ADs were permitted to offer the product on back to back basis or run an option book as per the specified terms and conditions.

- **December 2003:** Residents having overseas direct investments were permitted to hedge the exposure under certain terms and conditions.

28.5.2 Hedging Facilities for Authorised Dealers (ADs):

- **January 1997:** ADs were permitted to use certain instruments like interest rate swaps, currency swaps, and forward rate agreements to hedge their assets-liability portfolio based on appropriate policy as approved by their top management.

- **April 1997:** A beginning for rupee based derivatives was made in India and banks were permitted to offer dollar-rupee swaps to corporates to actively manage their foreign exchange exposures. Currently no limits are placed on the ADs for undertaking swaps to facilitate corporates to hedge their foreign exchange exposures; a limit of US $ 50 million per AD is, however, fixed for net supply in the market on account of swaps enabling corporates to move from rupee to foreign currency liability.

- **October 1999:** ADs may also purchase call or put options to hedge their cross currency proprietary trading positions. The value and maturity of the hedge should not exceed that of the underlying instrument.

- **October 2002:** Authorised banks were permitted to enter into forward contracts with their constituents (exporters of gold products, jewellery manufacturers, trading houses, *etc.*) in respect of the underlying sale, purchase and loan transactions in gold.

- **November 2002:** Banks, which are allowed to enter into forward gold contracts in India were allowed to cover their price risk by hedging abroad in a similar manner.

- **November 2002:** Foreign banks were allowed to hedge the entire Tier I capital held by them in Indian books. The capital funds should be available in India to meet local regulatory and CRAR requirements. The forward contract should be for tenor of one year or more and may be rolled over on maturity. Foreign banks were permitted to hedge their Tier II capital in the form of head office borrowing as subordinated debt, by keeping it swapped into Indian rupees at all times.

28.5.3 Hedging Facilities for Non-Residents:

- **October 1997:** ADs were allowed to enter into forward/option contracts with NRIs to hedge (i) the amount of dividend due on shares held in an Indian company; (ii) the amount of investment made under portfolio scheme in accordance with the relevant provisions for the purpose; and (iii) the balances held in the Foreign Currency Non-Resident (FCNR) account or the Non-Resident External Rupee (NRE) account.

- **November 2002:** Earlier, designated branches of ADs maintaining accounts of FIIs could provide forward cover under certain terms and conditions and limits. Currently, ADs can provide forward/option contracts to FIIs with rupee as one of the currencies to such customers on the basis of their declaration of the market value of their entire investment in equity and/or debt in India as on a particular date. The cost of hedge is to be met out of repatriable funds and/or inward remittance through normal banking channel. If the hedge becomes naked, the hedge may be allowed to continue to the original maturity.

- **October 2003:** Earlier, entities with foreign direct investment in India had to approach the Reserve Bank for case by case approval to hedge their investment. This has now been delegated to ADs who may enter into forward/option contracts with residents outside India to hedge the foreign direct investments made in India subject to verification of the exposure in India. All foreign exchange derivative contracts permissible for a person resident outside India once cancelled, are not eligible to be rebooked.

28.6 Foreign Exchange Exposure Norms of Commercial Banks

With the objective of providing greater operational flexibility, banks were given freedom to fix their own open exchange position limit.

Depending upon the asset liability profile, dealing expertise and other relevant factors, authorised dealers (ADs) in foreign exchange were accorded freedom to fix their own gap limits for more efficient management of their assets and liabilities.

The foreign exchange exposure norms for banks authorised to deal in foreign exchange, i.e. authorised dealers (ADs) are set out below:

28.6.1 Positions and Gaps:

1. RBI has stipulated foreign exchange exposure limits in the form of net overnight open position limit (including gold) (OPL) and aggregate gap limit (AGL) for banks. The OPL and AGL are required to be approved by the RBI.

2. Boards of directors of ADs are required to frame an appropriate policy and fix suitable limits for various treasury functions.

28.6.2 Investments in Overseas Markets:

1. ADs can undertake investments in overseas money market instruments (including any debt instrument whose life to maturity does not exceed one year as on the date of purchase) and/or debt instruments issued by a foreign state with a residual maturity of less than one year, up to the limits approved by their board of directors. The instruments, however, are to be rated at least as AA (-) by Standard & Poor's or Aa3 by, Moody's. For the purpose of investments in debt instruments other than the money market instruments of any foreign state, the Boards of banks may lay down country ratings and country-wise limits separately, wherever necessary.

2. ADs may also invest the undeployed FCNR(B) funds in overseas markets in long-term fixed income securities provided the maturity of the securities invested in does not exceed the maturity of the underlying FCNR(B) deposits.

3. ADs can also invest surplus in *Nostro* accounts through overnight placement and investments with their overseas branches/correspondents subject to adherence to the gap limits approved by the RBI.

28.6.3 Overseas Foreign Currency Borrowings:

1. The aggregate limit for almost all categories of overseas foreign currency borrowings of ADs is placed at 25 percent of their unimpaired Tier-I capital or USD 10 million (or its equivalent), whichever is higher. Funds so raised may be used for purposes other than lending in foreign currency to constituents in India and repaid without reference to the RBI. As an exception to this rule, ADs are permitted to use borrowed funds as also foreign currency funds received through swaps for granting foreign currency loans for export credit subject to certain stipulations. Besides this, subordinated debt placed by head offices of foreign banks with their branches in India as Tier-II capital is also treated outside the above limit.

28.6.4 Gold Transactions:

1. Only banks authorised by the RBI can deal in gold. Such banks can enter into forward contracts in India for buying and selling gold with those banks which are

authorised to import gold and with their constituents (exporters of gold products, jewellery manufacturers and trading houses) in respect of the underlying sale/purchase and loan transactions in gold with them. The tenor of such contracts, however, should not exceed six months.

2. Banks may use exchange-traded and over-the-counter hedging products available overseas to manage the price risk. However, while using products involving options, it needs to be ensured that there is no net receipt of premium, either direct or implied.

28.6.5 Vostro Accounts

1. The aggregate limit for temporary overdrawals in *vostro* account of overseas branches/correspondents is ₹ 5 crore in aggregate for meeting normal business requirements.

28.7 Present Structure of Foreign Exchange Market

The Indian market is not yet very deep and broad, and is characterised by uneven flow of demand and supply over different periods. The market is also characterised by a few major players, and lumpy public sector demands, particularly on account of payments for oil imports and servicing of public debt. In this situation, RBI has been prepared to make sales and purchases of foreign currency in order to even out lumpy demand and supply in the relatively thin foreign exchange market and to smoothen jerky movements. However, such interventions are not governed by a predetermined target or band around the exchange rate.

With the institution of the market determined exchange rate on March 1, 1993 and large capital inflows during 1993-95, RBI has undertaken several measures to widen and deepen the foreign exchange market. At present, there are 96 banks authorised to deal in foreign exchange, referred to as authorised dealers (ADs). Of these, most foreign banks and bigger Indian banks actively quote two-way prices. The banks deal among themselves directly or through the foreign exchange brokers presently numbering 47. Besides banks, term lending institutions have been given restricted dealing licences. Foreign Exchange Dealers Association of India (FEDAI) sets ground rules for fixation of commercial and other charges and involves itself in matters of mutual interest of ADs. The market trades freely in spot and forward exchange contracts, and to a limited extent in derivatives. The efficiency/liquidity of the market is often gauged in terms of bid/offer spreads. Wider spreads are an indication of an illiquid or a one-way market.

In India, the foreign exchange market is a three-level structure consisting of: (a) Reserve Bank of India (RBI) at the top, (b) authorised dealers licensed by the RBI, and (c) customers (exporters, importers, companies, and other foreign exchange earners). In addition to these main market players, there are foreign exchange money changers who bring buyers and sellers together, but are not permitted to deal in foreign exchange on their own account.

Dealings in the foreign exchange market include transactions between authorised dealers and the exporters/importers and other customers, transactions among authorised dealers themselves, transactions with overseas banks and transactions between authorised dealers and the RBI.

The mode of exchange rate determination is of paramount importance to the development of foreign exchange market. There is no single exchange rate regime which can be considered appropriate for all countries, at all times. Though the choice of an exchange rate regime is country-specific and contingent on macroeconomic policies, there is a growing consensus globally in favour of a flexible/floating rate regime.

28.7.1 Market Segments: The Indian foreign exchange market is a decentralised multiple dealership market comprising two segments—the spot and the derivatives market. In the spot market, currencies are traded at the prevailing rates and the settlement or value date is two business days ahead. The two-day period gives adequate time for the parties to send instructions to debit and credit the appropriate bank accounts at home and abroad.

The derivatives market encompasses forwards, swaps and options. Though forward contracts exist for maturities up to 1 year, majority of forward contracts are for 1 month, 3 months, or 6 months. Forward contracts for longer periods are not common because of the uncertainties involved and related pricing issues.

A swap transaction in the foreign exchange market is a combination of a spot and a forward in the opposite direction.

The spot market is the dominant segment of the Indian foreign exchange market. The derivative segment of the foreign exchange market is assuming significance and the activity in this segment is gradually rising.

28.7.2 Market Players: Players in the Indian foreign exchange market include: (a) authorised dealers (ADs), mostly banks who are authorised to deal in foreign exchange, (b) foreign exchange brokers who act as intermediaries, and (c) customers—individuals and corporates who need foreign exchange for their transactions. Though customers are major players in the foreign exchange market, for all practical purposes they depend upon ADs and brokers. In the spot foreign exchange market, foreign exchange transactions were earlier dominated by brokers. However, the situation has changed with the evolving market conditions and as of now the transactions are dominated by ADs. Brokers continue to dominate the derivatives market.

The RBI intervenes in the market essentially to ensure orderly market conditions. The RBI undertakes sales/purchases of foreign currency in periods of excess demand/supply in the market.

Foreign Exchange Dealers' Association of India (FEDAI) plays a special role in the foreign exchange market for ensuring smooth and speedy growth of the foreign exchange market in all its aspects. All ADs are required to become members of the FEDAI and execute an undertaking to the effect that they would abide by the terms and conditions stipulated by the FEDAI for transacting foreign exchange business. The FEDAI is also the accrediting authority for the foreign exchange brokers in the inter-bank foreign exchange market.

The licences for ADs are issued to banks and other institutions, on their request, under Section 10(1) of the Foreign Exchange Management Act, 1999. ADs are divided into different categories.

All scheduled commercial banks—which include public sector banks, private sector banks and foreign banks operating in India—belong to category I of ADs.

All upgraded full-fledged money changers (FFMCs) and select regional rural banks (RRBs) and co-operative banks belong to category II of ADs.

Select financial institutions such as EXIM Bank belong to category III of ADs.

All merchant transactions in the foreign exchange market have to be necessarily undertaken directly through ADs. However, to provide depth and liquidity to the inter-bank segment, ADs have been permitted to utilise the services of brokers for better price discovery in their inter-bank transactions.

The customer segment of the foreign exchange market comprises major public sector units, corporates and business entities with foreign exchange exposure. It is generally dominated by select large public sector units such as Indian Oil Corporation (IOC), Oil and Natural Gas Commission (ONGC), Bharat Heavy Electrical Limited (BHEL), Steel Authority of India Limited (SAIL), Maruti Udyog and also the Government of India (for defence and civil debt service) as also big private sector corporates like Reliance Group, Tata Group and Larsen and Toubro, among others.

In recent years, foreign institutional investors (FIIs) have emerged as major players in the foreign exchange market.

28.8 Sources of Supply and Demand of Foreign Exchange

The major sources of supply of foreign exchange in the Indian foreign exchange market are receipts on account of exports and invisibles in the current account and inflows in the capital account such as foreign direct investment (FDI), portfolio investment, external commercial borrowings (ECBs) and non-resident deposits. In India, the Government has no foreign currency account, and thus the external aid received by the Government comes directly to the reserves and the RBI releases the required rupee funds. Hence, this particular source of supply of foreign exchange is not routed through the market and as such does not impact the exchange rate.

Demand for foreign exchange emanates from imports and invisible payments in the current account, amortisation of ECBs (including short-term trade credits) and external aid, redemption of NRI deposits and outflows on account of direct and portfolio investment.

28.8.1 Derivative Market Instruments: Derivatives play a crucial role in developing the foreign exchange market as they enable market players to hedge against underlying exposures and shape the overall risk profile of participants in the market. Banks in India have been increasingly using derivatives for managing risks and have also been offering these products to corporates. In India, various informal forms of derivatives contracts have existed for a long time though the formal introduction of a variety of instruments in the foreign exchange derivatives market started only in the post-reform period, especially from mid-1990s. The foreign exchange derivative products that are now available in Indian financial markets can be grouped into three broad segments, viz. forwards, options (foreign currency rupee options and cross currency options) and currency swaps (foreign currency rupee swaps and cross currency swaps).

The most widely used derivative instruments are the forwards and foreign exchange swaps (rupee-dollar).

28.9 Foreign Exchange Dealers' Association of India

FEDAI was set up in August 1958 as a regulatory body, assuming at inception, primarily, the role of Exchange Banks' Association. The FEDAI members are all authorised dealers (Category I) in foreign exchange (101 members as of April 2017), who are required to be members of the FEDAI and abide by its Rules and guidelines, as per licensing norms of Reserve Bank.

In the formative years, the FEDAI's principal preoccupation was ensuring a level playing field in the foreign exchange market domain in India, by laying down transaction-based guidelines, and transaction-based tariff norms for member banks. The FEDAI's role has subsequently evolved very substantially, with a facilitatory side also emerging strongly. While, with considerable deregulation in the market, the FEDAI dissociated completely from laying down tariff norms for the members from September 1999 onwards, there was a quantum jump in its advisory and facilitatory activities.

Guidelines and rules for forex business (other than prescription of tariff norms), continue to be among the FEDAI's main activities. These include announcement of several daily, weekly, monthly and quarterly market-related numbers, which are primarily used by member banks for revaluation of portfolio, mark-to-market exercise, quoting of rates in NRI deposits, etc., and are also available to the public at large for information.

Additionally, training of bank personnel in various areas of foreign exchange business, advising/assisting members in settling issues among themselves and dealings with customers, piloting of new products/innovations on behalf of members with regulators, representing member banks at Government/Reserve Bank/other bodies, representing members on International Chambers of Commerce (ICC)'s Commission on Banking Techniques and Practices, Paris (which inter alia frames rules like Uniform Customs and Practice for Documentary Credit (UCP 500–now superseded by UCP 600), accreditation of forex brokers, laying down a Code of Conduct between member banks and brokers, and closely monitoring market conduct are some of the other areas where the Association has become very active over the years. FEDAI now plays a catalytic role for smooth functioning of the market through close co-ordination with the Reserve Bank, sister organisations like FIMMDA, Forex Association of India and others.

To sum up, various reforms measures initiated have resulted in significant growth of the foreign exchange market. Also, despite liberalisation of capital account and introduction of market determined exchange rate, the foreign exchange market in India remained stable during the 1990s barring a few episodes of volatility. India's exchange rate policy of managing volatility without fixed target, while allowing the underlying demand and supply conditions to determine the exchange rate, has yielded satisfactory results. Various reforms measures in the foreign exchange market have also led to the widening and deepening of the forex market in India as reflected in the substantial increase in the foreign exchange market turnover, particularly in the inter-bank segment.

True, the reforms in the forex market have yielded good results, but there are some issues which need to be addressed to enhance its stability and ensure further growth. Although the turnover in the market increased considerably over the years, it still remains small. Since the market lacks depth, the RBI has to actively intervene in the market to absorb and provide liquidity. There is, therefore, need to take steps to further develop the market so that the need for intervention by the RBI is minimised.

The market is presently skewed with a few public sector banks accounting for the major share of the merchant transactions. For development of the market on healthy lines, it is necessary to have large number of players participating in the market.

Derivatives are an important instrument of risk hedging. Although a few derivative products have been introduced, there has not been much activity in some of them, such as FRAs. There is a need to further develop a range of derivative products like forex options.

The momentous developments over the past few years are reflected in the enhanced risk-bearing capacity of banks along with rising foreign exchange trading volumes and finer margins. The foreign exchange market has acquired depth. The conditions in the foreign exchange market have also generally remained orderly. While it is not possible for any country to remain completely unaffected by developments in international markets, India was able to keep the spill over effect of the Asian crisis to a minimum through constant monitoring and timely action, including recourse to strong monetary measures, when necessary. However, the recent global financial turmoil has triggered an increased volatility in the foreign exchange market. The Indian economy is moving towards fuller capital account convertibility, albeit in a calibrated manner.

With the economy moving towards fuller capital account convertibility in a calibrated manner, focused regulation and monitoring of the foreign exchange market assumes added importance. In this context, there is a need to strengthen infrastructure, transparency and disclosure, and product range in the foreign exchange derivative markets. Strengthening the trading infrastructure, market conduct, transparency of OTC derivatives in the foreign exchange market, accounting and disclosures in line with international practices, including disclosures by non-bank corporates, needs to be done on a priority basis. The recent introduction of currency futures is a step in this regard.

In short, the foreign exchange market structure in India has undergone substantial transformation from the early 1990s. The market participants have become diversified and there are several instruments available to manage their risks. Sources of supply and demand in the foreign exchange market have also changed in line with the shifts in the relative importance in balance of payments from current to capital account. There has also been considerable improvement in the market infrastructure in terms of trading platforms and settlement mechanisms. Trading in Indian foreign exchange market is largely concentrated in the spot segment even as volumes in the derivatives segment are on the rise.

29

Payment Systems, Clearing and Settlement Infrastructure

Payment system architecture in India is based on international benchmarks, and guiding principles. The Payment and Settlement System Act, 2007 provides a comprehensive legal framework for payment and settlement services in India for subjects like authorisation of payment system operators, netting and finality of payment and settlement. The payment system objectives of having a safe, sound, cost-effective and wide distribution network are being met in so far as the large value and countrywide payment and settlement systems are concerned. The grand vision is that cash dominant economy may transit to a predominantly non-cash dominant economy with non-cash transactions primarily in electronic mode, which is the international norm. The existing payment system is being constantly reviewed to suggest an action plan for orderly growth of the payment systems.

29.1 Importance of a Sound Payment and Settlement System

The payment and settlement systems are at the core of financial infrastructure in a country. A well-functioning payment and settlement system is crucial for the successful implementation of monetary policy and maintaining the financial stability. Central banks have, therefore, always maintained a keen interest in the development of payment and settlement system as part of their responsibilities for monetary and financial stability. In India, the development of a safe, secure and sound payment and settlement system has been the key policy objective. In this direction, the RBI, apart from performing the regulatory and supervisory functions, has also been making efforts to promote functionality and modernisation of the payment and settlement systems on an ongoing basis.

A safe and efficient payment system is a prerequisite for smooth functioning of the financial markets. The conduct of monetary policy in an effective manner requires safe and efficient payment and settlement systems to facilitate transfer of funds and securities between the central bank and other participants in the financial system. An efficient and stable payment and settlement system is also a pre-condition for inter-bank money markets and other short-term credit markets through which monetary policy is transmitted. In addition, developments in the payment and settlement systems that affect the speed and realisation/availability of funds for further deployment can influence the overall demand for money in the economy.

By linking financial institutions together for the purpose of transferring monetary claims and settling payment obligations, payment and settlement system becomes a channel through which financial risks are transmitted across financial institutions and markets. Well-designed and efficiently managed systems, therefore, help in maintaining financial stability by reducing uncertainty of settlement. Settlement failures which spread to other payment and settlement systems through the contagion effect not only undermine the smooth functioning of the financial markets, but can also adversely affect the public confidence in money and efficacy of the instruments used to transfer money.

Payment and settlement systems, which constitute the backbone of the financial economy, aim at minimising the systemic risk. The payment system influences the speed, financial risk, reliability and the cost of domestic and international transactions. With the significant improvements in payment and settlement systems, depth and liquidity of various segments of the financial market can be improved.

Settlement systems in India have evolved over a period of time from physical settlement systems with considerable amount of risks to the current electronic systems with central counterparty with emphasis on risk mitigation. During the early 1990s, government securities market was opaque with limited information dissemination and inefficient pricing. The securities were held in physical form requiring execution of physical transfer forms for transfer of securities in any trade leading to inefficiencies in settling the trades. Settlement of securities and funds legs were independent of each other (non-DvP), leading to considerable settlement risks. Moreover, pre-settlement comparison and confirmation of trades was not systematised. Settlement cycles were not uniform with settlements happening on T+0 and T+1 basis.

29.2 Segments of Payment System

Payment systems in India comprise electronic payment systems as well as paper-based systems. Another classification pertains to large value payment systems and retail payment systems.

The large value payment infrastructure comprises RTGS, high value clearing, and CCIL. Based on the criteria outlined by CPSS, the RTGS system and the high value clearing system have been identified as SIPS. The funds leg of the CCIL-operated clearing systems covering government securities, foreign exchange and money market settle in the RTGS system.

The retail payment systems include MICR/non-MICR cheque clearing, national electronic funds transfer (NEFT) system, electronic clearing service (ECS), cheque truncation system (CTS) and payment channels like credit/debit cards, internet and mobile phone-based products.

29.3 Large Value Payment Systems

29.3.1 Real Time Gross Settlement (RTGS) System: The Indian RTGS system was operationalised in March 2004. The system started operations with four banks and settled only inter-bank transactions. Subsequently, the system was opened for settlement of customer transactions. It was operationalised for settlement of multilateral net settlement batch (MNSB) files from September 2006.

RTGS system is owned and operated by the Reserve Bank of India (RBI). The system works on a mainframe computer. Members are provided with a participant interface (PI), using which the participants connect to the system at the RBI through the INFINET. The message flow architecture in the RTGS system uses the Y topology. The members communicate through their PI to the inter-bank funds transfer processor (IFTP) which validates all communication and also does the *strip and store* function.

Upon successful completion of a transaction and receipt of confirmation from the RTGS, the IFTP forwards the complete credit information to the beneficiary member's PI. All communication between the PI and IFTP and IFTP to RTGS uses digital signatures (public key infrastructure) to ensure security.

The membership of RTGS is open to all scheduled commercial banks (SCBs), primary dealers (PDs) and others, as may be decided by the RBI. The SCBs are provided with Type A membership, primary dealers Type B and clearing houses Type D membership.

Except Type A members, customer-based transactions cannot be submitted by other members. Type D members are permitted to submit only net settlement batches for settlement under the RTGS system. Other banks and financial institutions can participate as customers of the direct members.

RTGS operations are governed by the RTGS Membership Regulations, 2004 and RTGS (Membership) Business Operating Guidelines, 2004. The members of the system agree to abide by these regulations and guidelines and any subsequent amendments to these documents.

The settlement of RTGS transactions takes place in the books of the RBI. For this purpose, members have to open a 'RTGS Settlement Account' with the RBI at Mumbai. This account is to be funded at the beginning of each RTGS processing day from the member's current account with the RBI, and at the end of the day, the balance in the settlement account is transferred back to the current account of the member.

Members are provided with collateralized intra-day liquidity (IDL) facility to tide over their IDL mis-matches. This facility is provided to Type A and Type B members only. The IDL facility utilised by the members has to necessarily be reversed by them at the end of RTGS day. Failure to do so attracts penal action.

In addition to IDL, the system provides many features for effective liquidity management by the members. These include message release method, queuing management and queue visibility. The Indian RTGS has adopted the FIFO rule for queuing. The system has a centralised queuing arrangement with priorities assigned by the system participant. The participant/system operator can change the priority of messages/revoke the messages in the queue. The system operator would alter the queue only in extreme situations. At the end of the day, all pending unsettled messages are cancelled by the system. The system has a multilateral offsetting algorithm to resolve any gridlock situations that may arise. This process can be configured to be invoked manually or automatically by the system. Since it is mainly a large-value funds transfer system, a floor of ₹ 2 lakh has been prescribed for minimum value of transactions that can be settled through RTGS.

There has been a substantial increase in the volume of transactions settled through

RTGS. The inter-bank clearing at all the RBI centres have been migrated to the RTGS system. Further, multilateral net settlements from CCIL, viz. rupee leg of US dollar-Indian rupee settlement, funds leg of government securities settlement and funds leg of CBLO, and the retail net settlement systems operated by National Clearing Cell, Mumbai (MICR cheque clearing, high value clearing, NEFT and ECS) are settled in RTGS as multilateral net settlement batch (MNSB) files. The liquidity management operations of the RBI are also settled through the RTGS system.

29.4 Retail Payment Systems

The retail payment systems in India consist of the paper-based clearing systems, electronic clearing systems and those systems relating to payment cards (credit and debit).

29.4.1 Paper-based Systems (Cheques): Cheques as payment instruments are the most popular mode of non-cash payment in India. The clearing and settlement of cheques drawn on different banks require the coming together of the banks in that area for transfer of instruments and the final settlement of funds. This process is facilitated by the clearing houses at these centres. As on May 31, 2014 there were 1,396 operational clearing houses. Of these, at 66 centres, the clearing and settlement processes have been automated by the introduction of MICR technology-based sorter machines. 80 percent of the total cheque clearing volume and value are accounted for by these centres. The clearing and settlement cycle is completed in two days—on day 1, the cheques are presented at the clearing house and on day 2, the funds settlement and return clearing are accounted for.

Paper-based systems still constitute the major part of retail payment systems in India. Steps taken by the Reserve Bank to improve the availability of this facility have resulted in an increase in the number of clearing houses from 860 in 2001 to 1,396 as on May 31, 2014. Further, in order to increase the spread of computerised clearing houses, magnetic media-based clearing system (MMBCS) technology is also being implemented in cities and towns where the process is carried out manually at present.

The introduction of cheque truncation system (CTS) was yet another step for increasing the efficiency of retail payment system. Truncation is the process of stopping the flow of the physical cheque issued by a drawer at some point with the presenting bank enroute to the drawee bank branch. In its place, an electronic image of the cheque is transmitted to the drawee branch by the clearing house, along with relevant information like data on the MICR band, date of presentation, presenting bank, etc.

The Reserve Bank implemented the CTS in the National Capital Region (NCR), New Delhi, Chennai and Mumbai with effect from February 1, 2008, September 24, 2011 and April 27, 2013 respectively. After migration of the entire cheque volume from MICR system to CTS, the traditional MICR based cheque processing has been discontinued in the country. Based on the advantages realised by the stakeholders and the experienced gained from the roll-out in these centres, it was decided to operationalise CTS across the country. The new approach envisioned as part of the national roll-out is the grid-based approach. Under this approach, the entire cheque volume in the country which was earlier cleared through 66 MICR cheque processing locations is consolidated into the three grids in New Delhi, Chennai and Mumbai. Each grid provides processing and clearing services to all the banks under its respective jurisdiction.

Under grid-based cheque truncation system clearing, all cheques drawn on bank branches falling within in the grid jurisdiction are treated and cleared as local cheques.

29.4.2 Electronic Retail Payment Instruments: The electronic retail payment systems in India are National Electronic Funds Transfer (NEFT) system and the electronic clearing service (ECS).

A. National Electronic Funds Transfer (NEFT): Electronic Funds Transfer (EFT) system was introduced in the mid-1990s. EFT facilitates transfer of funds from one bank account to another. In the beginning EFT system was permitted only for government transactions and RBI-initiated payments. NEFT is an electronic message-based payment system, and was introduced by the Reserve Bank of India in November 2005 to replace the EFT system which was public key infrastructure (PKI)-enabled and the settlements were effected on a decentralized mode.

NEFT is more secure, nation-wide retail electronic payment system to facilitate funds transfer by the bank customers, between the networked bank branches in the country. This has facilitated the availability of electronic payment modes at more centres. There are 12 daily settlements during weekdays.

The banks are to credit the accounts of the customers for the first four settlements on the same day and for the fifth and sixth settlements, the customers' accounts are to be credited not later than T+1 (next working day).

As on January 7, 2017, NEFT was available at 1,34,363 branches all over the country with 178 participating banks.

In order to popularise the e-payments in the country, the RBI, on its part, waived the service charges to be levied on the member banks, till March 31, 2009, in respect of the real time gross settlement (RTGS) and NEFT transactions. The RBI also provides, free of charge, intra-day liquidity to the banks for the RTGS transactions.

The service charges to be levied by banks from their customers for RTGS and NEFT have, however, been deregulated and left to the discretion of the individual banks. While some of the banks have rationalised their service charges and a few have made it even cost-free to the customers, there are also certain banks that have fixed unreasonably high service charges for providing these services to their customers—even though the RBI provides these services to the banks free of charge.

B. Electronic Clearing Services (ECS): ECS is a retail payment system which facilitates bulk payments that can be classified as one-to-many and receipts that are many-to-one. The two components of this system are ECS (Credit) and ECS (Debit). This facility is now available at 91 major centres.

- **ECS (Credit):** It facilitates the bulk payments whereby the account of the institution remitting the payment is debited and the payments remitted to beneficiaries' accounts. This facility is mostly used for making multiple payments, like payment of dividend to investors, payment of salaries of employees by institutions etc. For this purpose, the company or entity making the payment has to have the bank account details of the individual beneficiaries.

- **ECS (Debit):** It facilitates the collection of payments by utility companies. In this system the account of the customers of the utility company in different banks are debited and the amounts are transferred to the account of the utility company. The company providing this facility has to receive the mandate to collect funds from its customer. On receipt of the mandate, the company advises the consumer's bank to debit the payment due from the account on the due dates.

Settlement in this system currently takes place on T+0 basis and the cycle gets completed on T+1 basis. The clearing and settlement transactions through ECS occur at the respective centres. A centralised facility is available at the RBI, Mumbai to receive the ECS (Credit) files meant for credit at the other 14 RBI centres.

29.4.3 Deficiencies in Retail Payment Systems: The deficiencies in retail payments mainly pertain to the inefficient outstation cheque collection process. In this regard, it is difficult to prescribe a standard time-frame for collection in view of large disparities at various centres, in terms of their location, availability of infrastructure, communication facilities, etc. In respect of metropolitan cities, State capitals and A class cities, most banks have a policy of collecting instruments within a period of 7 to 10 days. In respect of other cities including States in the North-Eastern region, most banks have declared in their policies that the instruments will be collected within a maximum period of 14 days.

The usage of ECS has seen rapid increase. The main deficiency in ECS system has been the decentralised model of transaction processing in the system. While a centralised ECS has been provided, this is available only at the RBI centres. To address this deficiency, a National Electronic Clearing Platform was implemented in September 2008.

The benefits of electronic payment infrastructure are not yet trickling down to the lower end of the customer segment which still largely uses services like money order and informal channels for transferring money of small value which has much higher cost and time lag for transferring money. There is a need to develop solutions using newer technologies which would allow all segments of the society to gain access to the benefits offered by these facilities.

In order to popularise the e-payments in the country, the RBI, on its part, waived the service charges levied on the member banks till March 31, 2009, in respect of the RTGS and NEFT transactions. The RBI also provides, free of charge, intra-day liquidity to the banks for the RTGS transactions. The service charges to be levied by banks from their customers for RTGS and NEFT have, however, been deregulated and left to discretion of the individual bank. While some of the banks have rationalised their service charges and a few have made it even cost-free to the customers, there are also certain banks that have fixed multiples slabs or unreasonably high service charges, at times linked to the amount of the transaction, for providing these services to their customers, even though the RBI provides these services to the banks free of charge.

See also section 29.9 of this chapter.

29.5 Reforms Pertaining to Clearing and Settlement

The area of clearing and settlement has witnessed substantial progress in Indian securities market over the last decade as a result of the various reforms initiated by the regulatory authorities. Implementation of advanced information technology, at every stage, has played a crucial role in the entire process. Some of the key developments, in this regard are as under:

1. Screen-based trading.
2. Dematerialisation and electronic transfer of securities.
3. Introduction of rolling settlement.
4. Compression of settlement cycle to T+2.
5. Multilateral netting.
6. Delivery versus payment.
7. Robust risk management.
8. Emergence of clearing corporation to assume counterparty risk.
9. Real time gross settlement/electronic fund transfer facility.
10. Limited straight-through processing (STP).
11. Cheque truncation system (CTS).

29.6 Central Counterparties

29.6.1 Clearing Corporation of India Limited (CCIL): CCIL was incorporated on April 30, 2001 to provide clearing and settlement services in government securities, foreign exchange and money market instruments. The RBI took the initiative of setting up the CCIL with State Bank of India (SBI), Industrial Development Bank of India (IDBI), Life Insurance Corporation of India (LIC), ICICI Bank Ltd., Bank of Baroda and HDFC Bank Ltd. as its core promoters. This initiative was taken recognising the need for upgrading the country's financial infrastructure in respect of clearing and settlement of debt instruments and forex transactions. CCIL currently provides guaranteed settlement facility for government securities clearing, clearing of collateralised borrowing and lending obligations (CBLO) and foreign exchange clearing.

CCIL-operated systems include the following:

A. Government Securities Segment: During 1996-2002, a quasi-DvP system was in place with the book-entry system in government securities not directly linked with the funds accounts, with no mechanism to prevent a gridlock in the system. In 2002, CCIL was constituted by the banks to play the role of a CCP and for providing a settlement guarantee mechanism. The government securities settlement system has evolved since then and transactions are now settled on a net basis. Settlement through CCIL has the following advantages: (a) assurance of settlement to the members on the settlement date, (b) reduction in counterparty exposure, (c) operational efficiency, and (d) improved liquidity.

CCIL provides guaranteed settlement of all secondary market outright sales and repo transactions in government securities by the process of novation. All trades reported on the RBI's NDS platform or contracted on the online anonymous, trading platform NDSOM, are accepted by CCIL for settlement after the necessary validations. These trades are settled on a

DvP-III basis, i.e. the funds leg and the securities leg are settled on a net basis.

B. CBLO Segment: The CBLO is a money market product developed by CCIL and launched on January 20, 2003. The product was initially developed with a view to providing entities that have been phased out from the unsecured inter-bank call money market with an avenue for their funds operations. A repo variant, CBLO enables borrowing/lending of funds of various maturities up to one year, fully backed by collaterals in the form of central government securities/treasury bills. CCIL provides guaranteed settlement facility for trades in this instrument as a central counterparty. The funds leg of the trades in this instrument is settled in the current account maintained by these entities with the RBI. The borrowing and lending takes place through an electronic anonymous order matching platform. CBLO operates in a straight-through processing (STP)- enabled environment, seamlessly encompassing dealing to settlement.

The CBLO market has now become the preferred option for participants in the money market. The volume in this market is now significantly higher than the combined volumes in the call and the repo market.

C. Forex Segment: CCIL provides a guaranteed settlement facility for all US dollar-Indian Rupee inter-bank Cash, Tom, Spot and forward transactions. The matched and accepted forward deals are guaranteed for settlement from S-2 day (two days previous to settlement) and the Spot, Tom, Cash deals are guaranteed for settlement from the trade date as the CCIL becomes the central counterparty to every accepted trade through the process of novation. The rupee-leg of the transaction is settled through the member's current account with the RBI and the US dollar leg through CCIL's account with the Settlement Bank at New York.

CCIL also provides continuous-linked settlement (CLS) settlement services for banks in India by availing of third party services of a settlement bank. Banks participating in this segment of CCIL report their cross-currency trades to the settlement bank directly or through CCIL. The settlement is made through the nostro accounts of CCIL with the settlement bank in CLS settlement currencies.

The settlement of forex transactions by CCIL has resulted in a reduction in counterparty exposure, increased operational efficiency and overall lower operational costs. Forex settlement volumes in CCIL have been rising consistently through the years and have witnessed substantial growth since it commenced operations.

29.6.2 National Securities Clearing Corporation Ltd (NSCCL): See section 26.8 of chapter 26 of this book.

29.7 Government Securities Settlement System

The infrastructure for the government securities settlement systems in India is provided by the RBI. The Public Debt Office (PDO) in the RBI functions as the depository. The PDO has well-laid-down guidelines for opening subsidiary general ledger accounts (SGL) for recording all purchase and sales transactions in government securities. Secondary market transactions in government securities are settled in the books of the RBI for both securities leg and funds leg on delivery versus payment (DvP) basis.

A series of measures taken by the RBI has changed the way the government securities settle currently in India:

- **July 1995: Introduction of Delivery versus Payment (DvP):** The system was DvP I, wherein securities and funds were settled on a gross basis. Through this, settlement risk has been greatly reduced.

- **February 2002: Establishment of Clearing Corporation of India (CCIL):** Acting as a central counterparty through novation, the CCIL provides guaranteed settlement and has put in place risk management systems to limit settlement risk and operates a settlement guarantee fund backed by lines of credit from commercial banks. The netting of funds by CCIL reduces the liquidity requirements of the market and thereby liquidity risk of the system. All the transactions in government securities market, concluded or reported on NDS and NDS-OM have to be necessarily settled through the CCIL.

- **February 2002: Introduction of Negotiated Dealing System (NDS):** Besides enabling electronic dealing and transparency in the system, the NDS-enabled paperless settlement of transactions in government securities with electronic connectivity to CCIL and the DvP settlement system at the Public Debt Office through electronic SGL transfer form. All entities having SGL Accounts with the RBI were advised to join the NDS-CCIL system by March 31, 2003.

- **May 2002: Introduction of Compulsory Holding of Government Securities in Demat Form:** Compulsory holding of government securities in demat form for the RBI-regulated entities was introduced to prevent possibility of fraudulent transactions in government securities held in physical form. This improved the efficiency of security settlements by reducing the time taken and aided in simplification of settlement procedures.

- **March 2004: Introduction of Real Time Gross Settlement System (RTGS):** Introduction of RTGS system was an important measure in improving the stability of settlements in all inter-bank transactions including the government securities. The netted settlement files are also currently being submitted on RTGS for settlement. The system has integrated module for IDL against government securities. Towards the end of 2006, the total solution release (TSR) of RTGS has been implemented in which the security settlement system (SSS) has been integrated facilitating *on-demand* IDL facility for the market participants.

- **May 2005: Introduction of Standardised Settlement Cycle of T+1:** The settlement cycle for all outright OTC and NDS-OM trades in government securities was standardised to T+1 cycle for better fund management and risk management by the participants.

29.8 Role of RBI in Payment and Settlement System

Central banks world-wide are involved in payment and settlement systems in a number of ways. They provide settlement accounts, oversee core payment arrangements, and operate, provide and use various payment services.

In India, RBI regulates and supervises payment and settlement systems with the objective of promoting safety and efficiency by monitoring the existing and planned systems, assessing them against the stated objectives and, where necessary, inducing change. The oversight of payment and settlement systems has become more distinct and formal in recent years as part of a growing concern with financial stability as also with the increasing role of private participants in financial transactions. The increasing attention by the RBI also reflects the large increase in the value of transfers cleared and settled, the increasing centralisation of transactions around a small number of key systems and the growing technological complexity.

29.8.1 Vision Document for Payment Systems, 2005-08: In the recent period, the RBI has taken a number of initiatives to strengthen the institutional, technological and procedural framework for the payment and settlement systems. To carry forward these initiatives in an integrated and cohesive manner, a Vision Document for 2005-08 was prepared after taking into consideration the feedback from the various stakeholders such as banks, technology solution providers, members of public and other experts in the field. The Vision Document set out the roadmap for implementing the vision for payment and settlement systems within the next three years. The key themes of the action plans identified in the Vision Document are safety, security, soundness and efficiency (Triple-S and E). While safety in payment and settlement systems relates to risk reduction measures, security implies confidence in the integrity of the payment systems. All payment systems are envisaged to be on a sound footing with adequate legal backing for operational procedures and transparency norms. Efficiency enhancements are envisaged by leveraging the benefits of technology for cost effective solutions.

The main action points for Payment and Settlement Systems, 2005-08 as set out in the Vision Document are indicated below:

A. Action Points during 2005-06

1. Pursuing with Indian Banks' Association and major banks for setting up of a national level entity which will operate all retail payment systems in the country.
2. Operationalising National Settlement System for all clearings at four metro centres by December 2005.
3. Finalising the proposed electronic funds transfer (EFT) regulations.
4. Implementing Stage-2 of RTGS System, i.e., integrated accounting system (IAS)-RTGS rollout during which all inter-bank transactions at all major centres would be settled on RTGS platform and paper-based inter-bank clearing will be closed.
5. Pursuing with RTGS participants to cover all their networked branches under RTGS framework paving way for RTGS-based customer related transactions at about ten thousand branches in the country.
6. Implementing image-based cheque truncation system (CTS) at the National Capital Region (NCR) on a pilot basis.
7. Preparing minimum standard of operational efficiency at MICR cheque processing centre (CPC).
8. Making available EFT facility at 500 capital market intensive centres as identified by

BSE and NSE.

9. Setting up customer facilitation centre (CFC) at the RBI for various segments of national payment systems.

10. Public disclosure from each payment service provider of its standards, terms and conditions under which the payment will be effected and also compensation policy and procedure for any deficiency in services including the setting up of CFC.

11. Drafting the Red Book on payment systems in India.

12. Drafting a comprehensive legislation on payment system.

B. Action Points during 2006-07

1. To complete the tasks initiated during 2005-06.

2. To extend MICR clearing to 20 additional identified centres.

3. To ensure that every cheque issued follows MICR format and standards.

4. To implement EFT systems at a national level through the new retail payment institution.

5. To take all payment systems in India compliant with the core principles for systemically important payment systems (SIPS).

6. To increase the reach of payment services by means of tie-up and collaboration with other large coverage entities such as the post offices.

7.   To facilitate government payments and receipts through electronic mode.

C. Action Points during 2007-08

1. Creating off-city back-up arrangements for large value national payment systems such as RTGS and G-Sec clearing.

2. Making fully functional the new organisation for retail payment systems with all such payment under its umbrella.

3. Regulating various payment systems.

4. Ensuring cheque truncation based clearing at Mumbai, Chennai and Kolkata.

5. Covering National Settlement System at all major clearing houses/clearing organisations in the country.

29.8.2 Board for Regulation and Supervision of Payment and Settlement Systems (BPSS): In order to provide focused attention to the payment and settlement systems, the RBI constituted the BPSS as a Committee of its Central Board. The Reserve Bank of India (Board for Regulation and Supervision of Payment and Settlement Systems) Regulations, 2005 were notified in the Gazette of India on February 18, 2005. The BPSS is headed by the Governor of the RBI with the Deputy Governor in-charge of payment and settlement systems as the Vice-Chairman and the other Deputy Governors and two members of the Central Board of the RBI as members. Functions and powers of the BPSS include the following.

1. Formulating policies relating to the regulation and supervision of all types of payment and settlement systems.

2. Setting standards for existing and future systems.

3. Authorising the payment and settlement systems.

4. Determining criteria for membership.

The National Payments Council, which was set up in 1999, has been designated as a Technical Advisory Committee of the BPSS. To assist the BPSS in performing its functions, a new department, the Department of Payments and Settlement Systems (DPSS), was set up in the RBI in March 2005.

The Board at its meetings had emphasised, *inter alia*, the following.

1. Payment system services in India should be taken to a level comparable with the best in the world.
2. Appropriate legal infrastructure may be created as early as possible.
3. A plan be drawn up to "leapfrog" from cash to electronic modes of payment, wherever possible.
4. Cheque clearing system would have to be made more efficient through cheque truncation system.
5. Usage of the real time gross settlement (RTGS) system be increased both in terms of opening additional branch outlets and more number of transactions being put through.

29.8.3 Vision Document for Payment Systems, 2012-15: The main focus of the Vision Document for Payments Systems, 2012-15 is to provide a thrust to modern electronic payments that are safe, simple and low-cost for use by all. The document aims at increasing the share of electronic payment transactions and taking measures towards moving to a less cash society and customer convenience.

The focus of cheque clearing operations in the coming years would be consolidation, rationalisation, centralisation, through the implementation of grid-based CTS solution (which is Information Technology Act compliant) across the country by NPCI. The grid-based CTS will usher in a standardised cheque clearing scenario across the country. The issuance of CTS 2010 compliant cheques will facilitate this process. Introduction of user/customer friendly features and increasing the number of settlement cycles in NEFT would be further examined.

29.9 Recent Measures to Promote Electronic Retail Payments

29.9.1 Benefits of Electronic Payments: These are as under:

A. Common Man: (a) Reduced cash and hence more safety, (b) faster payment, (c) reduced number of visits to bank, and (d) interest earning on money in the bank.

B. Vendors: (a) Transactions settled quickly, (b) getting rid of coins and change, (c) larger transactions made easy, (d) improved accounting and book keeping, (e) no need to keep large amounts of cash.

29.9.2 National Payments Corporation of India (NPCI): NPCI is an umbrella organization for all retail payments system in India. It was set up with the guidance and support of the Reserve Bank of India (RBI) and Indian Banks' Association (IBA).

The RBI, after setting up the Board for Regulation and Supervision of Payment and Settlement Systems (BPSS) in 2005, released a vision document incorporating a proposal to set up an umbrella institution for all the Retail Payment Systems in the country. The core objective was to consolidate and integrate the multiple systems with varying service levels into nation-wide uniform and standard business process for all retail payment systems. The other objective was to facilitate an affordable payment mechanism to benefit the common man across the country and help financial inclusion.

IBA's untiring efforts during the last few years helped to turn this vision into a reality. NPCI was incorporated in December 2008 and the Certificate of Commencement of Business was issued in April 2009. It was incorporated as a Section 25 company under Companies Act, 1956 (now Section 8 of Companies Act 2013) and is aimed to operate for the benefit of all the member banks and their customers. The authorized capital is pegged at ₹ 300 crore and paid-up capital is ₹ 100 crore. The aim is to create infrastructure of large dimension and operate on high volumes resulting in payment services at a fraction of the present cost structure.

NPCI has ten promoter banks, namely State Bank of India, Punjab National Bank, Canara Bank, Bank of Baroda, Union Bank of India, Bank of India, ICICI Bank, HDFC Bank, Citibank and HSBC.

From a single service of switching of inter-bank ATM transactions, the range of services has grown to cheque clearing, immediate payments service (24x7x365), automated clearing house, electronic benefit transfer and a domestic card payment network named RuPay to provide an alternative to international card schemes. As in January 2016, over 247 million Indians owned RuPay cards. During the week following the demonetization, RuPay card usage increased by 118.6 percent.

BPSS at its meeting held on September 24, 2009 had given an in-principle approval to issue authorization to NPCI for operating various retail payment systems in the country and granted Certificate of Authorization for operation of National Financial Switch (NFS) ATM Network with effect from October 15, 2009. NPCI had deputed its officials to IDRBT Hyderabad and had taken over NFS operations on December 14, 2009. Membership regulations and rules had been framed for enrolling all banks in the country as members. This was done so that when the nation-wide payment systems are launched, all would get included on a standardized platform.

29.9.3 Committee to Review the Framework Related to Digital Payments: Ministry of Finance, Government of India had constituted this Committee on Digital Payments to review the payment systems in the country and to recommend appropriate measures for encouraging digital payments. The Committee (Chairman: Ratan P. Watal) was constituted on August 23, 2016 with the following terms of reference:

1. To study and recommend need for charges, if any, in the regulatory mechanism and any legislation, relevant for the purpose of promotion of payments by digital modes.
2. To study and recommend ways for leveraging Unique Identification Number or any other proof of identity for authentication of card/digital transactions and setting up of a Centralised KYC Registry.
3. To study introduction of single window system of Payment Gateway to accept all types of cards/digital payments of Government receipts.
4. To study feasibility and framing rules for creating a payments history of all digital payments and create necessary linkages between payments transaction history and

credit information.

5. To study and recommend various measures to incentivize transactions through cards and digital means.
6. To study global best practices in payments including initiatives taken by various Governments/Government Agencies.
7. To identify market failure(s), if any, along with suitable interventions that may be implemented to promote payment by card/digital means.
8. To identify regulatory bottlenecks, if any, and suggest changes to promote payment by card/digital means.
9. To study and make recommendations on any other matter related to promotion of payments through cards and digital means.

The Committee submitted an Interim Report to the Ministry of Finance on November 21, 2016. Towards finalization of the report, the Committee engaged extensively with all stakeholders and technology groups including Reserve Bank of India (RBI), State Governments, Comptroller and Auditor General of India, payment companies, technology companies and the academia. The Committee submitted its Final Report to the Finance Minister on December 9, 2016.

The Committee, inter alia, recommended a medium-term strategy for accelerating growth of digital payments in India with a regulatory regime which is conducive to bridging the *digital divide* by promoting competition, open access and inter-operability in payments. The Committee recommended inclusion of financially and socially excluded groups and assimilation of emerging technologies in the market, while safeguarding security of digital transactions and providing level playing to all stakeholders and new players who will enter this new transaction space. It suggested inter-operability of the payments system between banks and non-banks, upgradation of the digital payment infrastructure and institutions and a framework to reward innovations and for leading efforts in enabling digital payments. This Committee was seized of the developments following the decision of the Government to cancel legal tender character of currency of high denominations. The Committee calibrated its recommendations accordingly and provided a suitable framework for smooth and speedy transition towards a digital payments economy.

29.9.4 Credit/Debit Cards: In recent years advancements in banking technology, progress in mobile banking and innovative technologies to facilitate digital payments have enabled large number of small denomination transactions to be handled smoothly in electronic mode. The Government of India has taken policy decisions to encourage cashless/electronic transactions. In its endeavour on moving towards electronic payments, the Central Government has announced a number of incentives.

A credit card is a payment card issued to users (cardholders) to enable the cardholder to pay a merchant for goods and services, based on the cardholder's promise to the card issuer to pay them for the amounts so paid plus other agreed charges. The card issuer (usually a bank) creates a revolving account and grants a line of credit to the cardholder, from which the cardholder can borrow money for payment to a merchant or as a cash advance.

A debit card is a plastic payment card that can be used instead of cash when making purchases. It is similar to a credit card, but unlike a credit card, the money comes directly from the user's bank account when performing a transaction.

There has been phenomenal increase in the number of credit cards issued by the banks in India during the last few years. The number of outstanding credit cards at end-October 2016 stood at 2.73 crore.

While the increasing usage of the credit cards is a welcome development in as much as it reduces reliance on currency for settlement of transactions, it also entails certain additional elements of operational risk and can be a potential source of customer complaints.

In order to ensure orderly growth of the card segment of consumer credit and protect the interests of banks/non-banking financial companies (NBFCs) and their customers, the RBI constituted a Working Group on Regulatory Mechanism for Cards (Chairman: R. Gandhi).

Based of the recommendations of the Working Group, draft guidelines on credit cards were framed by the RBI in June 2005 for all commercial banks/NBFCs with regard to their credit card operations.

The draft guidelines delineated the broad parameters that banks/NBFCs should, at the minimum, take into account with regard to the following:

1. Issue of cards with respect to clear mentioning of most important terms and conditions (MITCs).
2. Interest rates and other charges on customers.
3. Corrective mechanism on account of wrongful billing.
4. Use of direct sale agents and other agents for outsourcing various credit card operations.
5. Protection of customer rights especially in respect of right to privacy, customer confidentiality and fair practices in debt collection.
6. Redressal avenues of customer grievances.
7. Internal control and monitoring systems of the banks/NBFCs for such card operations.

The draft guidelines further stipulated that each bank/NBFC must have a well-documented policy and a *fair practices code* for credit card operations. The *fair practices code* for credit card operations released by the IBA in March 2005 could also be used by banks/NBFCs. The bank/NBFCs code should, at the minimum, however, incorporate the relevant guidelines contained in the draft guidelines released by the RBI.

29.9.5 ATM Networks: The main advantage of an ATM network is that it obviates the need for having bank-specific multiple ATM installations in the same geographical area, thereby reducing the entailed costs for the banks but without compromising on the reach of the banks to their customers.

Over the years, the relative growth in off-site ATMs has been much more than that of on-site ATMs. As a result, by end April 2017, off-site ATMs accounted for approximately 47.19 percent (98,073) of the total ATMs in the country. With the policy initiative to enable non-bank entities to set up and operate ATMs—White Label ATMs (WLAs)—the proportion of off-site ATMs is likely to grow further.

The National Financial Switch (NFS) network started its operations on August 27, 2004. NFS is one of the several shared ATM networks which inter-connect the ATM switches of the banks together and thus enable inter-operability of the ATM cards issued by any bank across the entire network. The Board for Regulation and Supervision of Payment and Settlement systems (BPSS) approved in-principle to issue authorisation to National Payments Corporation of India (NPCI) for operating various retail payment systems in the country. Reserve Bank of India also issued authorisation to NPCI to take over the operations of National Financial Switch (NFS) from the Institute of Development and Research in Banking Technology (IDRBT) on October 15, 2009. NPCI took over NFS operations from December 14, 2009. Use of the ATMs connected through any of the ATM networks in the country became cost free for the customers from April 1, 2009.

As at end-April 2017, the number of ATMs in the country stood at 2,07,813.

29.9.6 Digital Wallet: *Digital wallet* refers to an electronic device that allows an individual to make electronic transactions. This can include purchasing items online with a computer or using a smartphone to purchase something at a store. An individual's bank account can also be linked to the digital wallet. He may also have his driver's license, health card, loyalty card(s) and other ID documents stored on the phone. The credentials can be passed to a merchant's terminal wirelessly via near field communication (NFC). Increasingly, digital wallets are being made not just for basic financial transactions but to also authenticate the holder's credentials. For example, a digital wallet could potentially verify the age of the buyer to the store while purchasing alcohol. The system has already gained popularity in Japan, where digital wallets are known as "wallet mobiles".

A digital wallet has both a software and information component. The software provides security and encryption for the personal information and for the actual transaction. Typically, digital wallets are stored on the client side and are easily self-maintained and fully compatible with most e-commerce websites. A server-side digital wallet, also known as a thin wallet, is one that an organization creates for and about you and maintains on its servers. Server-side digital wallets are gaining popularity among major retailers due to the security, efficiency, and added utility it provides to the end-user, which increases their satisfaction of their overall purchase. The information component is basically a database of user-input information. This information consists of your shipping address, billing address, payment methods (including credit card numbers, expiry dates, and security numbers), and other information.

Digital wallet systems enable the widespread use of digital wallet transactions among various retail vendors in the form of mobile payments systems and digital wallet applications.

A client-side digital wallet requires minimal set-up and is relatively easy to use. Once the software is installed, the user begins by entering all the pertinent information. The digital wallet is now set up. At the purchase or check-out page of an e-commerce site, the digital wallet software has the ability to automatically enter the user information in the online form. By default, most digital wallets prompt when the software recognizes a form in which it can fill out; if one chooses to fill out the form automatically, the user will be prompted for a password. This keeps unauthorized users away from viewing personal information stored on a particular computer.

A. Application of Digital Wallets: Consumers are not required to fill out order forms on each site when they purchase an item because the information has already been stored and is automatically updated and entered into the order fields across merchant sites when using a digital wallet. Consumers also benefit when using digital wallets because their information is encrypted or protected by a private software code; merchants benefit by receiving protection against fraud.

Digital wallets are available to consumers free of charge, and they are fairly easy to obtain. For example, when a consumer makes a purchase at a merchant site that is set up to handle server-side digital wallets, he types his name and payment and shipping information into the merchant's own form. At the end of the purchase, the consumer is asked to sign up for a wallet of his choice by entering a user name and password for future purchases. Users can also acquire wallets at a wallet vendor's site.

Although a wallet is free for consumers, vendors charge merchants for wallets. Some wallet vendors make arrangements for merchants to pay them a percentage of every successful purchase directed through their wallets. In other cases, digital wallet vendors process the transactions between cardholders and participating merchants and charge merchants a flat fee.

B. Advantages for E-commerce Sites: Many online shoppers abandon their order due to frustration in filling in forms. The digital wallet combats this problem by giving users the option to transfer their information securely and accurately. This simplified approach to completing transactions results in better usability and ultimately more utility for the customer.

Digital wallets can also increase the security of the transaction since the wallet typically does not pass payment card details to the website (a unique transaction identifier or token is shared instead). Increasingly this approach is a feature of online payment gateways, especially if the payment gateway offers a *hosted payment page* integration approach.

29.7 Aadhaar-enabled Payment System (AEPS): AEPS is a bank led model which allows online interoperable financial inclusion transaction at PoS (Micro-ATM) through the Business Correspondent of any bank using the Aadhaar authentication.

The four Aadhaar enabled basic types of banking transactions are as follows:
1. Balance enquiry.
2. Cash withdrawal.
3. Cash deposit.
4. Aadhaar-to-Aadhaar funds transfer.

The only inputs required for a customer to do a transaction under this method are the following:
1. IIN (Identifying the bank to which the customer is associated).
2. Aadhaar number.
3. Fingerprints captured during the enrolment

A. Objectives: These are as under:
1. To empower a bank customer to use Aadhaar as his identity to access his respective Aadhaar enabled bank account and perform basic banking transactions like balance enquiry, cash deposit, cash withdrawal, remittances that are intra-bank or inter-bank in

nature, through a Business Correspondent.

2. To sub-serve the goal of Government of India and Reserve Bank of India (RBI) in furthering Financial Inclusion.
3. To sub-serve the goal of RBI in electronification of retail payments.
4. To enable banks to route the Aadhaar initiated inter-bank transactions through a central switching and clearing agency.
5. To facilitate disbursements of Government entitlements like MGNREGA, social security pension, handicapped old age pension etc. of any Central or State Government bodies, using Aadhaar and authentication thereof as supported by UIDAI.
6. To facilitate inter-operability across banks in a safe and secured manner.
7. To build the foundation for a full range of Aadhaar-enabled banking services.

AEPS is a new payment service offered by the National Payments Corporation of India to banks, financial institutions using Aadhaar. This is known as Aadhaar-enabled Payment System and may also be referred to as AEPS.

Aadhaar is a unique identification number issued by the Unique Identification Authority of India (UIDAI) to any resident of India.

Any resident of India holding an Aadhaar number and having a bank account may be a part of the Aadhaar-enabled Payment System. Also, the customer needs to have a bank account for availing AEPS.

Customer should have an Aadhaar (Unique ID as issued by UIDAI) number linked with any bank account (bank should be a part of AEPS network) where customer has an account. The registration process shall be as per the procedures laid down by the bank providing AEPS service.

A customer may visit a business correspondent (BC) customer access point. The BC [1] using the point of sale (micro-ATM) device will be able to process transactions like cash withdrawal, cash deposit, balance enquiry and fund transfer by selecting the transaction of their choice. The customer needs to provide his Aadhaar Number and his bank name or bank IIN number. [2]

A point of sale-PoS (Micro-ATM) device is used to facilitate customers to make cash deposit, cash withdrawal, fund transfer and balance enquiry. The PoS device may be a micro-ATM.

29.8 Unified Payment Interface (UPI) of India: UPI is a payment system which facilitates the fund transfer between two bank accounts. This payment system works on the mobile platform. Sending money through the UPI app is as easy as sending a message. The customer is not required to give bank account details for the funds transfer through the UPI payment system.

A. Benefits of UPI: What is UPI App: These are as under:

1. UPI transfers the fund immediately. No restriction of holiday or working hours. The bank strike will also not affect the UPI payments.
2. Customer does not require the bank account number and IFSC code of the recipient.
3. Customer can transact from many bank account through a single UPI app.
4. Customer is not required to wait up to 24 hours to send money to a new payee. Anyone

would get money immediately.

5. Customer can send bills and get money once the client approves it.

6. Customer can use the cash on delivery without paying cash to the delivery boy. Just approve the bill and the delivery boy would get confirmation.

Although IMPS method transfers fund immediately (24x7) yet UPI has some advantages.

To send the money through the UPI, the user does not need to know about the bank of the recipient. It is necessary in the case of IMPS. To use the IMPS, the customer needs the bank account number and IFSC code of the recipient.

Only through the UPI, the customer can ask for the payments through the banking channel. In fact, one touch would complete the payment. One cannot pay for online shopping through the IMPS. But UPI gives the easiest way of online payment.

B. Virtual Payment Address (VPA): The UPI payment system does not use the bank account details of the recipient. But, there should be an accurate identification of the money recipient. Ultimately, all this convenience is fruitful if the money goes in right hands.

Therefore, every user of the UPI apps must have a unique ID. This unique ID is called as the virtual payment address (VPA). In fact, the App provider bank would allot the VPA to each user. The user can choose the VPA similar to the mail address. One can give this VPA to anyone to receive the money. The app would itself keep storing the VPAs of the persons to whom you have transferred the money. It is like saving contacts in email.

UPI payment system works only through the mobile application. Thus, you need a smartphone and internet data pack.

There are several UPI apps. You can choose any of them. Each bank can launch its UPI-based app. Banks can also incorporate UPI features into their existing mobile application. In fact, most of the banks have incorporated UPI in their existing mobile application.

UPI has made the fund transfer very easy. But it is not a mobile wallet. Unlike the mobile wallet, you are not required to credit money into the UPI app.

Rather, the every fund transfers take place through your bank account. UPI app just acts as the link between you and your account. In other words, it has made the bank account transaction much easy and cheap.

Therefore, to establish the link between you and your account, you have to connect UPI app to your bank account. This is a one-time process. It is done when you download a new UPI app.

While connecting to the bank account, you have to authenticate it through the card details and OTP. Once your UPI app gets connected to a bank account, you can easily transfer funds to any person.

The UPI payment system is revolutionary. It makes the non-cash payment a very easy affair. Moreover, the NPCI is coming with new features of UPI. Soon the UPI 2.0 would be launched which has more flexibility, easy and wide reach. You should adopt this method of payment because it also reduces the black economy.

29.9 Unstructured Supplementary Service Data (USSD): *99# Banking: Mobile banking has brought the bank account in your hand. Today, you can check bank-balance, get a mini statement and transfer fund through the mobile banking. But, what if you do not have a smart phone or you do not have the internet? The answer to this problem is the USSD based mobile banking. Just dial *99# and see the magic. You can do all those things which are available to a person with smartphone and 3G data. Almost every bank supports *99# USSD mobile banking service.

You get the mobile balance by dialling a certain code. Similarly, the recharge vendor uses certain codes to access mobile services. These are, in fact, USSD codes. The code which directly communicates with the server of telecom company is called as the USSD. This code starts with * (asterisk) and ends with # (hash).

As USSD code connects to the telecom operator's server, it also connects to bank's server. Hence, it gives you access to your bank account and performs some transaction. The entry to your bank account is given on the basis of registered mobile number. Thus, you must use registered mobile number to dial the USSD code.

The connection to the server of your bank goes through the servers of telecom companies. The NPCI handles all the technicality of this USSD service.

A special number *99# is fixed to access the banking services. This number works across the banks. This system of banking transaction is termed as the NUUP.

National Unified USSD Platform (NUUP) is an innovative service developed by NPCI and launched by the Indian government in 2014. The service allows the banks and telecom service providers to work together seamlessly. The services of NUUP are based on the USSD method.

USSD is a technology normally used in the field of telecommunication. It is available on all GSM enabled handsets. You do not need an internet connection to use the services of this method. It uses voice connectivity only.

NUUP uses USSD to perform various financial, non-financial and value added services. You can not only check your balance and see mini statement but also send money. There are some more options such as show MMID, generate OTP and change M-PIN.

A. How to Use USSD Code for Banking: First of all, you need to register your mobile number to your bank account. Visit your branch to get your mobile number registered. If your mobile number is already registered then you can directly dial the *99#. Follow these steps for USSD banking:

Step 1: Dial *99# with your registered number and wait for 3-5 seconds.

Step 2: Enter the three letter abbreviation of your bank name or first four-letter of bank IFSC or first two digits of bank's numeric code and hit send or call button.

Step 3: You will see some options for the services. It can be different for different banks. These options are as under:

1. Account balance.
2. Mini statement.
3. Send money using MMID.
4. Send money using IFSC.
5. Send money using Aadhaar number.
6. Show MMID.

7.   Change M-PIN.
8.   Generate OTP.
From here, the process will be different for every service.

29.10 RuPay: RuPay is an Indian domestic card scheme conceived and launched by the National Payments Corporation of India (NPCI). It was created to fulfil the Reserve Bank of India's desire to have a domestic, open loop, and multilateral system of payments in India. In India, 90 percent of credit card transactions and almost all debit card transactions are domestic. However, the cost of transactions was high due to monopoly of foreign gateways like Visa and MasterCard. In recent years, the usage of credit and debit cards (called plastic money) has increased manifold. It was thought that if this process of transactions is made India-centric, cost can come down drastically. RuPay facilitates electronic payment at all Indian banks and financial institutions, and competes with MasterCard and Visa in India. NPCI maintains ties with Discover Financial to enable the card scheme to gain international acceptance.

RuPay is a portmanteau of the words *ru*pee and *pay*ment. The colours used in the logo are an allusion to the tricolour national flag.

RuPay card was launched on March 26, 2012. NPCI entered into a strategic partnership with Discover Financial Services (DFS) for RuPay Card, enabling the acceptance of RuPay Global Cards on Discover's global payment network outside of India.

RuPay cards are accepted at all ATMs across India under National Financial Switch, and under the NPCI's agreement with DFS, RuPay cards are accepted on the international Discover network. According to the data published by National Payments Corporation of India, there are around 145,270 ATMs and more than 875,000 point of sale (PoS) terminals in India under the RuPay platform. In addition to the ATMs and PoS terminals, RuPay cards are accepted online on 10,000 e-commerce websites.

RuPay cards are accepted at all PoS terminals in India. To enable this, RuPay has certified 29 major banks in India to accept the RuPay card at their respective PoS terminals located at different merchant locations.

29.11 Bharat Interface for Money (BHIM): It is a Mobile App developed by National Payments Corporation of India (NPCI) based on the Unified Payment Interface (UPI). It was launched by Prime Minister Shri Narendra Modi in New Delhi on December 30, 2016. Named after Dr. Bhimrao Ambedkar, it is intended to facilitate e-payments directly through banks and as a part of the drive towards cashless transactions in the wake of demonetization of high value currency notes in November 2016.

This UPI App supports all Indian banks which use that platform, which is built over the *immediate payment service* infrastructure and allows the user to instantly transfer money between the bank accounts of any two parties. It can be used on all mobile devices.

To sum up, several steps have been taken by the RBI in recent years to improve customer service of commercial banks. In the context of the rapidly evolving financial landscape, RBI has also been suitably reorienting its regulatory and supervisory framework to meet the needs of the common man. It has also been the endeavour of RBI to improve credit delivery and customer service by banks. RBI has simultaneously focussed on financial inclusion and extension of banking services to the unbanked areas of the economy. RBI has taken a host of measures in recent years aimed at providing customer service at reasonable cost. These measures include enhancing customer protection and disclosures, code of ethics and grievance redressal, among others. RBI's broad approach to financial inclusion aims at *connecting people* with the banking system and not just credit dispensation; giving people access to the payments system; and portraying financial inclusion as a viable business model and opportunity. RBI has been initiating measures to improve the outreach of banks and their services, and promote financial inclusion in less developed states and union territories.

As is well-known, the financial sector has witnessed a quantum jump in the availability of technological solutions for delivery of financial services, and the RBI too has launched several payment system products for improving the efficiency of the payment system.

To sum up, a smooth and efficient payment and settlement infrastructure plays an important role in maintaining stability in the financial sector. Significant progress has been made in improving the payment systems infrastructure in India with the introduction of RTGS, operation of high value cheque clearing system (HVCCS), setting up of Clearing Corporation of India Limited (CCIL) as the central counterparty in the government securities, foreign exchange and collateralised borrowing and lending obligation (CBLO) segments as also setting up Central Counterparties (CCPs) for the settlement of equities and derivatives. The legal framework for payment and settlement systems has also been strengthened by the recent notification of the Payment and Settlement Systems Act and Rules. This has made India largely compliant with international standards and codes in this area.

Though there have been improvements in legal infrastructure in the financial sector like setting up of debt recovery tribunals (DRTs) and the enactment of the Securitisation and Reconstruction of Financial Assets and Enforcement of Security Interests (SARFAESI) Act, the major concern is that despite the robust insolvency laws the time taken for completion of liquidation proceedings is one of the highest in the world and the recovery rate one of the lowest.

Endnotes

1. Business Correspondent (BC) is an approved bank agent providing basic banking service using a MicroATM (terminal) to any bank customer wishing to avail their bank BC service.
2. IIN identifies the bank with which a customer has mapped his Aadhaar number. IIN is a six digit number. In most banks BC customer service points, this number would be represented on the terminal by the banks logo or name.

30

Integration of Financial Markets

Integrated financial markets are a key element in the transmission process and hence for the smooth conduct of monetary policy. Financial integration also leads to a better diversification of risks and makes a positive contribution to financial stability by improving the capacity of economies to absorb shocks. On the other hand, fully integrated financial markets also pave the way for shocks to propagate more quickly among market participants, which could necessitate appropriate safeguards. To mitigate the risks and maximise benefits from financial integration, it is imperative that the financial markets are developed further. Enhanced co-operation among various regulatory authorities is also important for ensuring effective corrective action in an increasingly integrated environment. Further, it is necessary to establish further linkages amongst the various components of financial infrastructure—the trading, payment, clearing, settlement and custodian systems.

Financial markets in India have come a long way and are getting increasingly integrated domestically and globally. Reform measures in terms of free pricing, removal of barriers to flows and broad-based participation have yielded results in terms of fairly high degree of integration of the money market, the government securities market and the foreign exchange market, although in varying degrees. The money market and the foreign exchange market are reasonably well integrated, which is reflected in the high correlation coefficients between various money market rates and forward premia. The inter-linkage between the domestic money and international markets has also increased as is reflected in the increasing importance of interest rate differentials in the determination of forward premia. In general, the interest rate differential between the domestic money and international markets motivates market participants to shift funds between the markets. Thus, interest arbitrage links the domestic and international money markets and the forward markets.

30.1 Integration of Financial Markets: Conceptual Framework

30.1.1 Meaning: Integration of financial markets is a process of unifying markets and enabling convergence of risk-adjusted returns on the assets of similar maturity across the markets. The process of integration is facilitated by an unimpeded access of participants to various market segments. Financial markets all over the world have witnessed growing integration within as well as across boundaries, spurred by deregulation, globalisation and advances in information technology. Central banks in various parts of the world have made concerted efforts to develop financial markets, especially after the experience of several financial crises in the 1990s.

Expectedly, financial markets tend to be better integrated in developed countries. At the same time, deregulation in developing countries has led to removal of restrictions on pricing of various financial assets, which is one of the pre-requisites for market integration.

Financial market integration encompasses a complex interplay of various factors such as policy initiatives, structure and growth of financial intermediaries, organic linkages among market participants and the preference of savers and investors for financial instruments. The study of integration of financial markets must keep in view the heterogeneity of markets, dimensions of integration, measurement issues and perceived benefits and risks of integration.

Financial market integration at the theoretical level has been postulated in several ways. The most popular economic principles of financial integration include the law of one price, term structure of interest rates, parity conditions such as purchasing power parity, covered and uncovered interest parity conditions, capital asset price model and arbitrage price theory.

30.1.2 Heterogeneous Nature of Financial Markets: Various financial market segments are not uniform as they trade in a variety of instruments which differ in terms of risk and liquidity. Financial markets are heterogeneous due to following reasons:

1. Some market segments are national, whereas others are international in nature, depending on where financial transactions occur among participants within a country's geographic boundary or across the border. Generally, money and credit market segments involving participation of banks and other financial institutions operating within a country's boundary are national in character. Conversely, foreign exchange markets dealing with cross-border transactions and stock markets with cross-listings of securities and participation of foreign institutional investors are international in nature.

2. Financial markets differ in terms of depth and liquidity. For instance, money market instruments are more liquid, while bonds in the capital markets are less liquid.

3. Financial markets differ in terms of economic nature of instruments catering to various needs of economic agents. For instance, a distinction can be made between saving, investment, credit and derivative instruments.

4. Financial markets are differentiated in terms of risk profile of instruments such as government bonds, which do not involve default and credit risks, and corporate bonds, which are relatively more risky in nature. Integration of market segments, thus, reflects an investor's attitude towards risk and the trade-off between risk and return on assets.

5. Market participants in different financial markets could be different such as banks, non-bank financial institutions, including mutual funds, insurance companies, mortgage institutions and specialised long-term financial institutions.

30.1.3 Dimensions of Financial Market Integration: Broadly, financial market integration occurs in three dimensions, nationally, regionally and globally. From an alternative perspective, financial market integration could take place horizontally and vertically. In the horizontal integration, inter-linkages occur among domestic financial market segments, while vertical integration occurs between domestic markets and regional/international financial markets.

A. Domestic Financial Integration: It entails horizontal linkages of various segments, reflecting portfolio diversification by savers, investors and intermediaries. Under horizontal integration, market interest rates typically revolve around a basic reference rate, which is defined as the price of a short-term low-risk financial instrument in a competitive and liquid market. Domestic markets may be closely integrated because intermediaries operate simultaneously in various market segments; for instance, commercial banks operate in both the saving (deposit) and loan markets.

B. Regional Financial Integration: It occurs due to ties between a given region and the major financial centre serving that region. Economic integration might be easier to achieve at a regional level due to network externalities and the tendency of market makers to concentrate in certain geographical centres. Furthermore, regional financial integration can be an important means of developing local financial markets, for instance, through peer pressure to strengthen institutions and upgrade local practices.

C. Global Financial Integration: It refers to the opening up of domestic markets and institutions to the free cross-border flow of capital and financial services by removing barriers such as capital controls and withholding taxes. A deeper dimension of global integration entails removing obstacles to movement of people, technology and market participants across border. Global integration is promoted through harmonisation of national standards and laws, either through the adoption of commonly agreed minimum standards or the mutual recognition of standards.

30.1.4 Measures of Financial Integration: Indicators of financial integration can be classified into *de jure* and *de facto* measures.

The existence of legal restrictions on trade and capital flows across border as well as market segments is the most frequently used *de jure* indicators. However, these indicators have several shortcomings as restrictions may not be binding, or they are not respected. They may not cover a specific aspect of all possible impediments to financial integration.

De facto indicators of financial integration are usually based either on prices or quantities. The commonly used price-based measures for gauging price equalisation and convergence of market segments include cross-market spreads, correlation among various interest rates, tests of common trend in the term structure of interest rates and volatility transmission. Interest rate spreads between the official short-term rate and a benchmark short-term market instrument on the one hand, and various other market interest rates on the other, are used for measuring price convergence and effectiveness of policy. Price-related measures also include covered and uncovered interest rate parity as well as asset price correlations between countries. There are, however, serious practical problems in using prices to measure regional or global financial integration, particularly in developing countries. This is because prices may move together because of a common external factor or because of similar macroeconomic fundamentals and not because of market integration. Moreover, prices may be affected by differences in currency, credit and liquidity risks, implying different price movements even if there is a substantial degree of financial integration.

30.1.5 Benefits and Risks of Financial Integration: Though financial integration provides several benefits, it also involves various risks. The benefits and costs of financial market integration depend on the degree of domestic financial market integration, international financial integration and financial development. Evaluating the benefits and risks of financial market integration is a complex issue, particularly in an economy with open capital account.

A. Benefits: The benefits of global integration depend on size, composition, and quality of capital flows. Global financial integration involves direct and indirect or collateral benefits. Analytical arguments supporting financial openness revolve around main considerations such as the benefits of international risk sharing for consumption smoothing, the positive impact of capital flows on domestic investment and growth, enhanced macroeconomic discipline and increased efficiency as well as greater stability of the domestic financial system associated with financial openness. International financial integration could positively affect total factor productivity. Financial openness may increase the depth and breadth of domestic financial markets and lead to an increase in the degree of efficiency of the financial intermediation process by lowering costs and excessive profits associated with monopolistic and cartelised markets, thereby lowering the cost of investment and improving the resource allocation.

B. Risks: Financial market integration also poses some risks and entails costs. A major risk is that of contagion, which was evident in the case of East Asian crisis and the recent global financial turmoil. Increased domestic and international integration accentuates the risk of contagion as problems in one market segment are likely to be transmitted to other markets with the potential to cause systemic instability.

In the context of globalisation, potential costs include: (a) high degree of concentration of capital flows, (b) misallocation of flows which may hamper their growth effects and exacerbate domestic distortions; (c) loss of macroeconomic stability, (d) pro-cyclical nature of short-term capital flows and the risk of abrupt reversals, (e) a high degree of volatility of capital flows which relates in part to herding and contagion effects, and (f) risks associated with foreign bank penetration.

Direct investment tends to be less volatile than other forms of capital flows. Volatility of capital flows translates into exchange rate instability (under flexible exchange rate) or large fluctuations in official reserves (under a pegged exchange rate regime). Nominal exchange rate volatility may hamper expansion of exports if appropriate hedging techniques are not available to exporters. Large capital inflows can also lead to rapid monetary expansion, inflationary pressures, real exchange rate appreciation and widening of current account deficits.

The nature of optimal integration is highly country-specific and contextual. Financial integration needs to be approached cautiously, preferably within the framework of a plausible roadmap that is drawn up embodying the country-specific context and institutional features. On balance, there appears to be a greater advantage in well-managed and appropriate integration into the global process, which implies not large-scale but more effective interventions by the authorities.

30.2 Need for Integration of Domestic Financial Markets

Integration of financial markets assumes importance due to the following reasons:

1. Efficient and integrated financial markets constitute an important vehicle for promoting domestic savings, investment and consequently economic growth.
2. Financial market integration, by enhancing competition and efficiency of intermediaries in their operations and allocation of resources, contributes to financial stability.
3. Integrated markets serve as a conduit for authorities to transmit important price signals.
4. Integrated financial markets induce market discipline and informational efficiency.
5. Market integration promotes the adoption of modern technology and payment systems to achieve cost effective financial intermediation services.
6. Integrated markets lead to innovations and cost effective intermediation, thereby improving access to financial services for members of the public, institutions and companies alike.
7. Financial market integration fosters the necessary condition for financial sector of a country to emerge as an international or a regional financial centre.

An important objective of reforms in India has been to integrate the various segments of the financial market for bringing about a transformation in the structure of markets, reducing arbitrage opportunities, achieving higher level of efficiency in market operation of intermediaries and increasing efficacy of monetary policy in the economy. Efficient allocation of funds across the financial sector and uniformity in the pricing of various financial products through greater inter-linkages of financial markets has been the basic emphasis of monetary policy.

In the domestic sphere, integration of markets has been pursued through the following measures:

1. Strengthening competition.
2. Financial deepening with innovative instruments.
3. Easing of restrictions on flows or transactions.
4. Lowering of transaction costs.
5. Enhancing liquidity.

Financial markets in India have also increasingly integrated with the global financial system as a result of calibrated and gradual capital account liberalisation in keeping with the underlying macroeconomic developments, the state of readiness of the domestic financial system and the dynamics of international financial markets.

Until the early 1990s, India's financial sector was tightly controlled. Interest rates in all market segments were administered. The flow of funds between various market segments was restricted by extensive micro-regulations. There were also restrictions on participants operating in different market segments. Banks remained captive subscribers to government securities under statutory arrangements. The secondary market of government securities was dormant. In the equity market, new equity issues were governed by several complex regulations and restrictions. The secondary market trading of such equities lacked transparency and depth. The foreign exchange market remained extremely shallow as most transactions were governed by inflexible and low limits under exchange regulation and prior approval requirements. The exchange rate was linked to a basket of currencies. Although the financial sector grew considerably in the regulated environment, it could not achieve the desired level of efficiency. Compartmentalisation of activities of different types of financial intermediaries eliminated the scope for competition among existing financial intermediaries.

Financial markets reform initiated in the early 1990s focused on removal of structural bottlenecks, introduction of new players/instruments, free pricing of financial assets, relaxation of quantitative restrictions, improvement in trading, clearing and settlement practices and greater transparency. Other policy initiatives in the money, the foreign exchange, the government securities and the equity markets were aimed at strengthening institutions, greater transparency, encouraging good market practices, effective payment and settlement mechanism, rationalised tax structures and enabling legislative framework. Dismantling of various price and non-price controls in the financial system has facilitated the integration of financial markets.

Broadly, India's domestic financial market comprises the money market, the credit market, the government securities market, the equity market, the corporate debt market and the foreign exchange market. The channels of integration among various market segments differ. For instance, the Indian money and the foreign exchange markets are intrinsically linked in view of the presence of commercial banks and the short-term nature of both markets. The linkage is established through various channels such as banks borrowing in overseas markets, providing hedging facilities to corporates, accepting foreign currency deposits and acting as conduit for making payments for overseas merchant transactions. The linkage between the call money and the government securities markets exists, as at times, large positions in government securities are funded through short-term borrowings. The foreign exchange market and the equity markets are linked through the operations of foreign institutional investors. The emerging linkages among the money, the government securities and the foreign exchange markets have at times necessitated the use of short-term monetary measures by the RBI for meeting demand-supply mismatches to curb volatility.

30.3 Measures Taken for Integration of Financial Markets in India

Broadly, integration of financial markets in India has been facilitated by various measures in the form of free pricing, widening of participation base in markets, introduction of new instruments and improvements in payment and settlement infrastructure.

30.3.1 Free Pricing: Free pricing in financial markets has been facilitated by various measures. These have included, *inter alia,* the following:

1. Freedom to banks to decide interest rate on deposits and credit.
2. Replacement of administered interest rates on government securities by an auction system.
3. Abolition of the system of *ad hoc* Treasury Bills in April 1997 and its replacement by the system of ways and means advances (WMAs) with effect from April 1, 1997.

4. Shift in the exchange rate regime from a single-currency fixed-exchange rate system to a market-determined floating exchange rate regime.
5. Gradual liberalisation of the capital account.
6. Freedom to banks to determine interest rates (subject to a ceiling) and maturity period of foreign currency non-resident (FCNR) deposits (not exceeding three years).
7. Use derivative products for hedging risk.
8. In 1992, the Capital Issues (Control) Act, 1947 was repealed and with this ended all controls related to raising of resources from the market. Since then the issuers of securities can raise capital from the market without requiring any consent from any authority, either for making the issue or for pricing it.

30.3.2 Widening Participation: This has been achieved with the adoption of following measures:

1. Enhanced presence of foreign banks in line with India's commitment to the World Trade Organization (WTO) under GATS, strengthened domestic and international markets inter-linkages, apart from increasing competition.
2. Participation in the call market was gradually widened by including non-banks such as financial institutions, non-banking financial companies, primary/satellite dealers, mutual funds and corporates (through primary dealers). The process of transformation of the call money market into a pure inter-bank market which commenced from May 2001, was completed in August 2005.
3. Foreign institutional investors (FIIs) have been allowed to participate in the Indian equity market and set up 100 percent debt funds to invest in government (Central and State) dated securities in both the primary and secondary markets. This provided a major thrust to the integration of domestic markets with international markets.
4. Linkage between the domestic foreign exchange market and the overseas market (vertical integration) has been facilitated by allowing banks/authorised dealers (ADs) to borrow and invest funds abroad (subject to certain limits), and to lend in foreign currency to companies in India for any productive purpose, giving them the choice to economise on interest cost and exchange risk. Exporters also have the ability to substitute rupee credit for foreign currency credit.
5. Indian companies have been permitted to raise resources from abroad through American/global depository receipts (ADRs/GDRs), foreign currency convertible bonds (FCCBs) and external commercial borrowings (ECBs), thus, facilitating integration of domestic capital market with international capital market. The RBI allowed two-way fungibility of ADRs/GDRs in February 2002.
6. Corporates have been allowed to undertake active hedging operations by resorting to cancellation and rebooking of forward contracts, booking forward contracts based on past performance, using foreign currency options and forwards, and accessing foreign currency-rupee swap to manage longer-term exposures arising out of external commercial borrowings.
7. Integration of the credit market and the equity market has been strengthened by application of capital adequacy norms and allowing public sector banks to raise

capital from the equity market up to 49 percent of their paid-up capital.

30.3.3 New Instruments: These have included the following:

1. Repurchase agreement (repo) has introduced as a tool of short-term liquidity adjustment. The liquidity adjustment facility (LAF) is open to banks and primary dealers. The LAF has emerged as a tool for both liquidity management and also signalling device for interest rates in the overnight market. Several new financial instruments such as inter-bank participation certificates (1988), certificates of deposit (June 1989), commercial paper (January 1990) and repos (December 1992) have been introduced. Collateralised borrowing and lending obligation (CBLO) and market repos have also emerged as money market instruments.

2. New auction-based instruments were introduced for 364-day, 182-day, 91-day and 14-day Treasury Bills, the zero coupon bond and government of India dated securities. In the long-term segment, floating rate bonds (FRBs) benchmarked to the 364-day Treasury Bills yields and a 10-year loan with embedded call and put options exercisable on or after 5 years from the date of issue have been introduced.

3. Derivative products—such as forward rate agreements and interest rate swaps— were introduced in July 1999 to enable banks, FIs and PDs to hedge interest rate risks. A rupee-foreign currency swap market has been developed. ADs in the foreign exchange market have been permitted to use cross-currency options, interest rate and currency swaps, caps/collars and forward rate agreements (FRAs) in the international foreign exchange market, thereby facilitating the deepening of the market and enabling participants to diversify their risk.

30.3.4 Institutional Measures: These have included the following:

1. Institutions such as Discount and Finance House of India (DFHI), Securities Trading Corporation of India (STCI) and PDs have been allowed to participate in more than one market, thus strengthening the market inter-linkages.

2. The Clearing Corporation of India Ltd. (CCIL) was set up to act as a central counter-party to all trades involving foreign exchange, government securities and other debt instruments routed through it and to guarantee their settlement.

30.3.5 Technology, Payment and Settlement Infrastructure: Measures taken in this regard have included the following:

1. The delivery-versus-payment (DvP) system, the negotiated dealing system (NDS) and subsequently, the advanced negotiated dealing system-order matching (NDS-OM) trading module and the real time gross settlement system (RTGS) have brought about immense benefits in facilitating transactions and improving the settlement process, which have helped in the integration of markets.

2. In the equity market, the floor-based open outcry trading system has been replaced by electronic trading system in all the stock exchanges.

Various segments of financial markets have become better integrated in the reform period, especially from the mid-1990s. As reforms in the financial markets progressed, linkages amongst various segments of market and between domestic and international markets improved.

30.4 Segment-wise Integration

30.4.1 Integration of the Government Securities Market: The existence of a well-developed government securities market is a pre-requisite for a market-based monetary policy and for facilitating financial market integration. The government securities market is also required to develop a domestic rupee yield curve, which could provide a credible benchmark for pricing of securities in other markets. The government securities market is increasingly getting integrated with other market segments as is reflected in the close co-movement of interest rates.

30.4.2 Integration of the Credit Market: The integration of the credit market with other money market segments has become more pronounced in recent years. Sustained credit demand has led to higher demand for funds, exerting some pressure on liquidity. This has been reflected in the decline in investment of banks in government securities and higher activity in all the money market segments such as inter-bank call money, collateralised borrowing and lending obligation (CBLO) and market repo rates.

30.4.3 Integration of the Foreign Exchange Market: The degree of integration of the foreign exchange market with other markets is largely determined by the degree of openness. At the cornerstone of the international finance, integration through foreign exchange market is characterised with the purchasing power parity (PPP) doctrine. According to the PPP, in the absence of restrictions on cross border movements of goods and services and assuming no transactions costs, commodity prices expressed in any single currency should be the same all over the world. In other words, the path of the nominal exchange rate should be guided by the developments in the domestic prices of goods and services vis-à-vis prices of the major trading partners.

30.4.4 Stock Market Integration: The equity market has relatively low and negative correlation with other market segments. The low correlation of the equity market with risk free instruments is indicative of greater volatility of stock returns and the existence of large equity risk premium. The large risk premium occurs when equity price movements cannot be rationalised with standard inter-temporal optimisation models of macroeconomic fundamentals such as consumption and savings. This can be on account of different participants in the equity and other financial markets. For instance, the common participation by banks in the money, the government, the foreign exchange and the credit markets ensures fairly high correlation among these segments. The exposure of banks to the capital market remains limited on account of restrictions due to prudential regulation.

30.5 Regional Financial Integration (Asia)

After the South East Asian crisis of 1997, the geographic scope of cooperation initiatives is expanding across sub-regions of Asia. Asian economies have embarked on various initiatives for regional monetary and financial cooperation.

30.5.1 SEANZA and SEACEN [1]: SEANZA and SEACEN are the oldest initiatives in central bank cooperation in Asia. The SEANZA, formed in 1956, promotes cooperation among central banks by conducting intensive training courses for higher central banking executive positions with the objective to build up knowledge of central banking and foster technical cooperation among central banks in the SEANZA region. The SEACEN provides a forum for member central bank governors to be familiar with each other and to gain deeper understanding of the economic conditions of the individual SEACEN countries. It initiates and facilitates co-operation in research and training relating to the policy and operational aspects of central banking, i.e., monetary policy, banking supervision and payments and settlement systems.

30.5.2 Asian Clearing Union (ACU): ACU—an arrangement of central banking cooperation—is successfully functioning since 1974 for multilateral settlement of payments for promoting trade and monetary cooperation among the member countries. [2] Since 1989, the ACU has also included a currency swap arrangement among its operational objectives.

30.5.3 EMEAP: A more explicit central banking cooperation has been existing in the form of EMEAP since 1991. [3] The ongoing work of EMEAP seeks to further strengthen policy analysis and advice within the region and encourage co-operation with respect to operational and institutional central banking issues. EMEAP central banks have actively coordinated on issues relating to financial markets, banking supervision and payment and settlement systems. The Asian Bond Fund (ABF) initiative of the EMEAP Group has been one of the major initiatives aimed at broadening and deepening the domestic and regional bond markets in Asia. The initiative has been in the form of ABF1 and ABF2. In the near term, the ABF2 Initiative is expected to help raise investor awareness and interest in Asian bonds by providing innovative, low-cost and efficient products in the form of passively managed bond funds. More and more similar kinds of index-driven private bond funds are rapidly emerging in Asia. At present, India does not contribute in the ABF. The informal meeting organised by Asia Cooperation Dialogue (ACD) is, however, attended by participant central banks including India, to discuss promotion of supply of Asian Bonds. The Government of India has given a commitment on participation in the ABF2 to the tune of US$ 1 billion.

30.5.4 SAARCFINANCE: SAARCFINANCE, established in September 1998 is a regional network of the SAARC Central Bank Governors and Finance Secretaries which aims at strengthening the SAARC with specific emphasis on international finance and monetary issues. [4] India has been very actively participating in SAARCFINANCE activities.

30.5.5 ASEAN+3: The countries of ASEAN—Brunei Darussalam, Cambodia, Indonesia, Laos, Malaysia, Myanmar, the Philippines, Singapore, Thailand and Vietnam—and India have entered into a Framework Agreement on comprehensive economic cooperation. The ASEAN has embarked on a process to expand economic cooperation with its neighbours in the north, namely China, Japan and South Korea -(ASEAN+3). As far as India's association with ASEAN community is concerned, currently India is not a full-fledged part of the ASEAN network but holds a regular summit with the ASEAN. However, in the years ahead, it is envisaged that ASEAN+3+3 network [5] would help India to share and cooperate on various financial issues as the present network of ASEAN+3 has been consistently engaging in economic policy dialogue of unprecedented scope and depth.

30.5.6 Chiang Mai Initiative: Another instance of central banking cooperation in Asia exists in the form of reciprocal currency or swap arrangements under the Chiang Mai Initiative. [6] The ASEAN Swap Arrangement (ASA) was created primarily to provide liquidity support to countries experiencing balance of payments difficulties. The Finance Ministers of ASEAN+3 announced this initiative in May 2000 with the intention to cooperate in four major areas, *viz*. monitoring capital flows, regional surveillance, swap networks and training personnel.

The clearest evidence of Asian countries' desire to forge closer economic relationships is the proliferation of Free Trade Agreements (FTAs). By 2006, there were more than 30 FTAs under negotiation in East Asia alone. Increasingly, these agreements are also deeper, extending to areas beyond just tariff reduction. An example is the recently signed India-Singapore comprehensive economic cooperation agreement, which covers not only trade in goods, but also services, investments and cooperation in technology, education, air services and human resources.

Regional integration in Asia has improved significantly due to liberalisation measures, formation of several regional cooperation agreements and stronger economic activity in the region. The sharp increase in intra-regional trade indicates that regional economies are better integrated. Regional financial integration is manifested in the price co-movements in the stock, the money and the bond markets. Stock markets in the Asian region are better correlated than the bond and the money markets.

30.6 International Financial Integration

In the wake of globalization, capital has become more mobile across national boundaries as nations are increasingly relying on savings of other nations to supplement the domestic savings. Technological developments in electronic payment and communication systems have substantially reduced the arbitrage opportunities across financial centres, thereby aiding the cross border mobility of funds. Changes in the operating framework of monetary policy, with a shift in emphasis from quantitative controls to price-based instruments such as the short-term policy interest rate, brought about changes in the term structure of interest rates. This has contributed to the integration of various financial market segments. Harmonisation of prudential regulations in line with international best practices, by enabling competitive pricing of products, has also strengthened the market integration process.

Development of financial markets is required for the purpose of not only realising the hidden saving potential and effective monetary policy, but also for expanding the role and participation of a country in the process of globalization, regional and international integration. With growing openness, global factors come to play a greater role in domestic policy formulation, leading to greater financial market integration.

A key feature of global financial integration since early 1980s is the shift in the composition of capital flows to developing and emerging market economies. Private sector flows have outpaced official flows due to increasing liberalisation. Moreover, a shift has occurred in terms of components, from the dominance of debt flows in the 1970s and the 1980s to foreign direct investment (FDI) and portfolio flows since the 1990s. FDI flows have been determined by several push and pull factors, including strong global growth, soft interest rates in home countries, lessening of risks in developing countries, greater business and consumer confidence, rising corporate profitability, large scale corporate restructuring, sharp recovery of asset prices and rising commodity prices. Trade and FDI openness has encouraged domestic institutional and governance reforms promoting trade and investment further. The hope of better risk sharing, more efficient allocation of capital, more productive investment and ultimately higher standards of living for all have also propelled the drive for stronger regional connections of financial systems across the world. In terms of overall financial flows, Asia has benefited from the surge in net capital flows to emerging markets in recent years.

Greater international financial market integration exposes domestic markets to certain risks and contagion. For instance, global financial imbalances, growing sophistication of financial market participants and the proliferation of complex and highly leveraged financial instruments, including credit derivatives and structured products such as collateralised debt obligations, can heighten volatility in the financial markets. Thus, with growing international integration, there would be a need to be vigilant about the risk profile of financial intermediaries and their vulnerability to abrupt market price shocks. This underlines the need for appropriate risk management strategies as also greater coordination and information sharing among central banks to prevent the transmission of adverse developments abroad to the domestic economy and markets.

With growing financial globalisation, it is important for India to develop financial markets to manage the risks associated with large capital flows. The Report of the Committee on Fuller Capital Account Convertibility, 2006 (Chairman: S.S. Tarapore) observed that in order to make a move towards the fuller capital account convertibility, it needs to be ensured that different market segments are not only well-developed but also that they are well-integrated.

As a result of policy measures undertaken since the early 1990s, India's trade and financial integration has grown with the global economy. The increasing openness of the Indian economy to the external sector in recent years characterises its expanding economic relationships with the rest of Asia. In recent years, the Asian economies are emerging as major trading partners of India.

In tandem with trade openness, India's capital account has witnessed a structural transformation since the early 1990s, with a shift in the composition from official flows to market-oriented private sector flows. From 1950 to 1980, trade balance was financed by capital account balance comprising mainly the official flows. During the 1980s, the dependence on official flows moderated sharply with private debt flows in the form of external commercial borrowing and non-resident Indian (NRI) deposits emerging as the key components of the capital account.

Following the shift in emphasis from debt to non-debt flows in the reform period, foreign investment comprising direct investment and portfolio flows emerged as predominant component of capital account.

To sum up, since early 1990s, there has been a rapid increase in the pace of globalisation, led by growing participation of developing and emerging economies. Financial integration has outpaced trade integration. Cross-border flows of real and financial capital have increased sharply, reflecting the decline in the degree of home bias in capital markets.

The domestic credit market is also getting increasingly integrated with the international capital market as large and creditworthy borrowers have been raising large resources by way of external commercial borrowings. Such corporates are, therefore, less constrained by domestic credit conditions. Raising of resources by banks, the major players in the credit market, by way of external commercial borrowings, *albeit* within limits, has also integrated the domestic and international credit markets. The money market and the government securities market are also integrated as changes in money market rates are quickly transmitted to government securities yields. The linkage between the money market and the credit market also exists even as some stickiness has been observed in the lending interest rate structure. The inter-linkages between the credit market and the bond market are also growing through asset securitisation by banks.

However, the inter-linkages between the equity market on the one hand, and the money, the foreign exchange and the government securities markets on the other, are still weak. The term money market and the private corporate debt market are missing links in the Indian financial markets. There is not much activity in the public issue segment of the corporate debt market, despite availability of good infrastructure, a vibrant equity market and a reasonably developed government securities market. In the corporate debt market, the issuers prefer the private placement segment, which lacks transparency and deprives the retail investor from participating in the debt market.

Regional integration has served as a major catalyst to the global integration process since early 1990s. East and Southeast Asian economies, in particular, have achieved substantial integration. Apart from Asia's growing integration with the rest of the world, increasing integration within Asia also reflects the growing intra-regional trade and financial flows. The stock markets in Asia are more integrated than the money and the bond markets. In the region, Japan, Hong Kong and Singapore serve as the nodal centres for other stock markets. India's trade and financial links with Asia are also growing amidst recent initiatives taken to promote regional cooperation. Emerging Asia has become the *growth centre* of the world due to shifting of production base to the region. This is likely to stimulate greater financial integration in the region.

At the regional level, India's trade links with Asia are growing at a rapid pace, spurred by trade links with China and Southeast Asian countries. Also, India's financial integration with the Asian region has occurred through the linkage of regional stock markets and through modest correlation of bond and money markets.

A key feature of global financial integration since early 1980s has reflected in the shift in the composition of capital flows to developing and emerging market economies, especially from official to private flows. India's financial integration within the region and with the international financial markets is likely to increase in future in view of its robust growth prospects. However, if benefits are to be maximised from a more integrated economy, efforts are needed towards a greater sophistication of financial markets and financial market instruments that allow risks to be shared more broadly and capital to flow into the most productive sectors.

India's integration with the world economy has increased significantly in terms of trade openness and financial integration. Tariff liberalisation and removal of non-tariff barriers have contributed to India's trade integration at global and regional levels. India's capital account has witnessed a structural transformation during the reform period with cross-border non-debt creating private capital flows, emerging as a major component. India is now a major destination for global portfolio equity flows suggesting growing confidence of foreign investors in the Indian economy and financial markets.

Integration among various market segments has grown, especially in the recent period. Growing integration among various financial market segments has been accompanied by lower volatility of interest rates. Financial market integration reflects a dynamic interaction among various parameters such as liquidity, safety and risk, foreign exchange market development, private sector activity, and macroeconomic fundamentals. Alternatively, financial integration exhibits interaction among financial intermediaries, the Government, the private sector and the external sector.

Endnotes

1. The SEANZA refers to South East Asia, New Zealand and Australia. The SEACEN refers to South East Asia Central Banks.
2. At present, its membership includes eight members including India, Islamic Republic of Iran, Nepal, Pakistan and Sri Lanka being the founder members (Myanmar, Bangladesh and Bhutan joined later).
3. Members are the central banks of Australia, China, Hong Kong, Indonesia, Japan, Korea, Malaysia, New Zealand, the Philippines, Singapore and Thailand.
4. SAARCFINANCE members are India, Pakistan, Sri Lanka, Bangladesh, Bhutan, Maldives and Nepal. It is a permanent body, which got formal recognition of SAARC at the 11th SAARC Summit, held in Kathmandu, Nepal in January 2002.
5. India, Australia and New Zealand are included in ASEAN+3+3.
6. Under this Initiative, the total resources available are currently estimated to be around US$ 75 billion (up from less than US$ 40 billion in May 2005), reflecting the renegotiation of most Bilateral Swap Agreements (BSAs).

31

Credit Rating Practices

The importance of credit rating, as a tool to evaluate credit risk, has increased in recent years. Credit ratings are extensively used by investors including large institutional investors like banks, mutual funds, financial institutions and provident funds while making their lending decisions. This is evident from the fact that increasing number of debt issuance in the private placement markets has been rated even if it is not a mandatory requirement. The credit rating agencies regularly disseminate information on new/outstanding ratings through print media. The list of rated entities and latest rating actions can also be accessed from the website of credit rating agencies. Established rating agencies also periodically publish data regarding the default statistics and rating migrations.

Credit ratings measure a borrower's creditworthiness and provide an international framework for comparing the credit quality of issuers and rated debt securities. Rating agencies allocate three kinds of ratings: issuer credit ratings, long-term debt, and short-term debt. Issuer credit ratings are amongst the most widely watched. They measure the creditworthiness of the borrower including its capacity and willingness to meet financial needs. The top credit rating issued by the main agencies—Standard & Poor's, Moody's and Fitch IBCA—is AAA or Aaa. This is reserved for a few sovereign and corporate issuers. Ratings are divided into two broad groups—investment grade and speculative (junk) grade.

Credit rating agency means a body corporate which is engaged in, or proposes to be engaged in, the business of rating of securities offered by way of public or rights issue.

Credit-rating in India is relatively new, compared to the developed economies. The first rating agency, CRISIL, was set up in 1987. Credit-rating was made mandatory for commercial papers and debentures from 1991—when ICRA, India's second credit-rating agency was established. Since then, the rating industry has grown significantly in terms of rated debt issued and subscribed, both at the corporate and retail levels (primarily fixed deposits).

The importance of credit rating agencies in India as information providers, which had been increasing, came to greater focus with the adoption of Basel II framework. The rating agencies in India face two constraints which impact their default statistics. One, they have a small base of rated entities. Two, they lack the geographical diversification benefits which the international rating entities enjoy. The processes and methodologies adopted by rating agencies in India are generally in alignment with those of the international rating agencies. Moreover, despite the above two constraining factors, their default statistics may not be out of sync with the Basel trigger ratios. The domestic rating agencies are equipped to scale up their resources, when required, to cater to a higher demand for ratings consequent upon implementation of Basel II.

At present, the ratings in India are issue-specific and not issuer-specific. The rating agencies, therefore, are also working out methodologies for undertaking issuer ratings. It is, therefore, expected that with the implementation of Basel II in India, the proportion of rated entities is likely to increase over a period, providing the appropriate basis for risk discrimination in the system.

The rating system is required to undergo a validation process consisting of a formal set of activities, instruments and procedures for assessing the accuracy of the estimates of all material risk components and the regular operation, predictive power and overall performance of the IRB system adopted. In the validation process, the bank has to, on an ongoing, iterative basis, verify the reliability of the results generated by the rating system and its continued consistency with regulatory requirements, operational needs and developments in the reference market.

Achieving these objectives requires the performance of quantitative and qualitative analyses, the breadth and depth of which is modulated in accordance with the type and scope of the portfolios examined, the overall complexity of the bank, and the reliability of the environment under analysis. The validation instruments and methods need to be periodically reviewed and adjusted in order to ensure that they remain appropriate in a context of continually evolving market variables and operating conditions. The validation process shall not consist solely of a statistical comparison of actual risk measures against the related *ex ante* estimates, but will also involve analysis of all the components of the IRB system, including operational processes, controls, documentation, IT infrastructure, as well as an assessment of their overall consistency.

The validation process involves verifying compliance with the quantitative and organisational requirements for the rating systems. Specifically, this should include the following:

1. Assessment of the model development process, with particular reference to the underlying logical structure and the methodological criteria supporting the risk parameter estimates.
2. Performance analyses of the rating system.
3. Parameter calibrations, benchmarking and stress tests verification that the rating system is actually used in the various areas of operations. The results of the validation process should be adequately documented and periodically submitted to the internal control functions and the governing bodies and should specifically address any problem areas.

Non-availability of adequate information, lack of separate departments for bond rating in different type of industries and subjective analysis of qualitative factors are some of the main problems which obstruct the smooth functioning of the working of the rating agencies in India. The objective operationalisation of subjective parameters, development of an independent database for industry-specific information, periodic organisation of training programmes and seminars by financial experts to improve the skills of rating analysts and establishment of private rating agencies to increase the competition and their efficiency which could go a long way for improving the functioning of the rating system.

Table 31.1 lists leading credit rating agencies in India.

Table 31.1: Credit Rating Agencies in India

S. No.	Agency	Location
1.	CRISIL Ltd.	Mumbai
2.	India Ratings and Research Pvt. Ltd. (*formerly Fitch Ratings India Pvt. Ltd.*)	Mumbai
3.	ICRA Ltd.	New Delhi
4.	Credit Analysis and Research Ltd. (CARE)	Mumbai
5.	Brickwork Ratings India Private Ltd.	Bengaluru
6.	SMERA Ratings Ltd.	Mumbai
7.	Infomerics Valuation and Rating Pvt. Ltd.	New Delhi

Source: Securities and Exchange Board of India (SEBI).

Credit rating standards followed by Indian credit rating agencies seem to be rather lax, showing greater consideration for the *issuers* need than for the *investors* interests. They are not sufficiently forward looking, resulting in frequent downgrades, not long after the original issue. For this reason, the rating agencies have not been able to win the confidence of investors. This is partly due to competition among the rating agencies. There is a need for regular data on default rates of financial instruments rated by different credit rating agencies and also on migration to lower rating grades.

Part IV

Traditional and Innovative Financial Instruments

32

Principal Direct Financial
Instruments of the Capital Market

The maturity and sophistication of financial system depends upon the prevalence of a variety of financial instruments to suit the varied investment requirements of heterogeneous investors so as to enable it to mobilize savings from as wide section of the investing public as possible. Since early 1990s, the Indian financial system has witnessed tremendous growth in financial product innovation by corporates as well as financial institutions.

Capital market instruments fall into two broad groups: (i) direct instruments, and (ii) derivates instruments (discussed in the next chapter). Direct instruments include the following:

1. Ordinary (or equity) shares.
2. Preference shares.
3. Debentures.

While the ordinary and preference shares represent ownership instruments, debentures and innovating debt instruments are creditorship securities.

32.1 Ordinary Shares

Ordinary shares represent ownership capital and their owners—ordinary shareholders—share the reward and risk associated with ownership of corporate enterprises. They are called ordinary shares in contrast with preference shares which carry certain prior rights with regard to income and redemption.

There are certain concepts associated with ordinary shares. Authorised equity represents the maximum amount that a company can raise from the ordinary shareholders. It can be changed in the prescribed manner. The portion of the authorized capital offered by the company to investors is the issued capital. Subscribed share capital is that part of the issued capital which has been subscribed by the investors. The actual amount paid by the shareholders is the paid-up capital. The issued, subscribed and paid-up capitals are generally the same.

Ordinary shares typically have a face value in terms of the price of each share, the most popular denomination being ₹ 10. However, companies are permitted to issue such shares without a face value. The price at which the ordinary shares are issued is the issue price. The issue price for new companies is generally equal to the face value. It may be higher for existing companies, the difference being the share premium. The book value of ordinary shares refers to the paid-up capital plus reserves and surplus (net worth) divided by the number of outstanding shares. The price at which ordinary shares are traded in the stock market is their market value.

Ordinary shares have some special features in terms of the rights and claims of their holders: (a) residual claim to income/assets, (b) right to control, (c) pre-emptive rights, and (d) limited liability.

Ordinary shareholders have a residual claim to the income of the company. They are entitled to the remaining income/profits of the company after all outside claims are met. The amount actually received by the shareholders in the form of dividend depends on the decision of the board of directors. The directors have the right to decide what portion of the earning will be distributed to the shareholders as cash dividend and what portion will be ploughed back as retained earnings, which the shareholders may receive later in the form of capital appreciation/bonus shares.

The ordinary shareholders' claim in the assets of the company is also residual in that their claim would rank after the claims of the creditors and preference shareholders in the event of liquidation. If the liquidation value of assets is insufficient, their claims may remain unpaid.

As owners of the company, ordinary shareholders have the right to control the operations of, participate in the management of, the company. Their control is, however, indirect. The major policies/decisions are approved by the board of directors and the board-appointed management carries out the day-to-day operations. The shareholders have the legal right/power to elect the board of directors as well as vote on every resolution placed in various meetings of the company.

The ordinary shareholders exercise their right to control the company through voting in the meetings of the company. According to the most commonly used system of voting in India, namely majority rule voting, each share carries one vote. As a result, shareholders/groups holding more than 50 percent of the outstanding equity shares are able to elect all the directors of their choice.

The ordinary shareholders of a company enjoy pre-emptive rights in the sense that they have a legal right to be offered, by the company, the first opportunity to purchase additional issues of equity capital in proportion to their existing holdings.

Although ordinary shareholders share the ownership risk, their liability is limited to the extent of their investment in the share capital of the company.

32.2 Preference Shares

Preference shares are a unique type of long-term capital market instruments in that they combine some of the features of ordinary shares as well as some features of debentures.

1. As a hybrid form of financial instrument, they are similar to debentures insofar as they carry a fixed rate of dividend.
2. They rank higher than ordinary shares as claimants to the income/assets of the company.
3. Generally, preference shareholders do not have voting rights.
4. They do not have a share in residual earnings/assets.
5. Dividend on preference shares is paid out of divisible/after tax profit.

6. Payment of preference dividend depends on the discretion of the management, i.e. it is not an obligatory payment and non-payment does not force insolvency/liquidation.
7. Irredeemable types of preference shares have no fixed maturity date.

Preference shares have a prior claim over ordinary shares both on the income and assets of the company. In other words, preference dividend must be paid in full before payment of any dividend on ordinary shares. In the event of liquidation, the whole of preference share capital must be paid before anything is paid to the ordinary shareholders. Thus, preference shares stand midway between debentures and ordinary shares as regards claims on the income and assets of the company. Stated in terms of risk perspective, preference shares are less risky than ordinary shares but more risky than debentures.

32.3 Debentures

Debentures represent creditorship securities and debentures holders are long-term creditors of the company. As a secured instrument, it is a promise to pay interest and repay principal at stipulated times.

The payment of interest and repayment of principal is a contractual obligation enforceable by law. Failure/default leads to bankruptcy of the company. The claim of debenture holders on income and assets ranks paripassu with other secured debt and higher than that of shareholders—preference as well as ordinary shares.

Convertible debentures give the holders the right (option) to convert them into equity shares on certain terms. They are entitled to a fixed income till the conversion option is exercised and share the benefits associated with equity shares after the conversion.

32.4 Types of Orders

In the stock market, when prices of the well-traded securities are quoted, full prices are seldom indicated. The various kinds of order given by various traders are explained below.

32.4.1 Market Order: Market order is the most common type of order and simply involves an instruction to buy or sell at the prevailing price in the market. It represents the best price one can get at a point of time. Small orders can be conveniently executed at the market rate but if the size of the order is larger than the volume which is currently available in the dealing pit, then executions might not all be at the same price because the dealer would have to bid up or offer down until desired volumes are secured. Thus, large orders *at market* have a tendency to move against those who give them. No wonder then that large orders may be placed by market participants who wish to move the market in a particular direction.

32.4.2 Limit Order: A limit order is an order to buy or sell at a specified price, or a price better than that. Thus, a limit order is exemplified when a client may give a broker a price limit above which he should not buy or below which he should not sell. Also, there is a time limit for which it may be given. This kind of an order puts more responsibility on the dealer since he has to be aware of his limits orders once the limit is reached. A limit order kind of order is feasible when it is considered that there is sufficient market force in the opposite direction at current prices. This has the advantage that it is far less likely to push prices in an adverse direction.

32.4.3 Stop-Loss Order: A stop-loss order is aimed at closing out positions when a particular price level is traded. It is this kind of an order when a client orders his broker to sell a share or some other security, if its market price falls to a certain level below the current price. Thus, once the specified price is reached or penetrated, the order becomes the market order. Stop-loss orders are a good means of protecting profits or limiting losses while waiting for the market to recover.

32.4.4 Stop-Limit Order: A stop-limit order is said to be placed when, for example, a client can place a stop order at a particular level with a limit beyond which the market would cease to be chased.

32.4.5 Fill or Kill Order: This is an order to a broker to buy or sell a security or derivative immediately. If the order is not executed at once, it is treated as withdrawn. This type of an order is often used by a party wishing to take out a large bid/offer but, in case of a failure, it does not wish to be viewed as a possible large counter party in the market.

32.4.6 Market if Touched (MIT): It is a limit order which automatically becomes a market order once a predetermined price is reached.

32.4.7 Good Till Cancelled (GTC): This is a client's order to buy or sell, usually at a specified price, which remains valid until its execution or cancellation.

32.4.8 Day Order or Good for the Day: As the name implies, this means the limits or stop order would lapse at the end of the day (of dealing) if it has not been executed during the day.

33

Financial Derivatives: Emergence and Popularity

33.1 Emergence of Complex Financial Products

In recent years, complex financial products such as asset-backed securities, derivatives, credit-default swaps (CDSs) and collateralised debt obligations (CDOs) have proliferated in developed countries. These products have become highly popular with banks and financial institutions as they allow them to hedge their risks and manage their regulatory and economic capital more efficiently.

Although various structured products have enabled the transfer of risks and enhanced the liquidity of instruments, the recent turmoil in the US sub-prime mortgage market and related developments connected with complex derivatives have also brought to the fore the risks posed by these instruments.

The emergence of the market for derivative products, most notably forwards, futures and options, can be traced back to the willingness of risk-averse economic agents to guard themselves against uncertainties arising out of fluctuations in asset prices. By their very nature, the financial markets are marked by a very high degree of volatility. Through the use of derivative products, it is possible to partially or fully transfer price risks by locking-in asset prices. As instruments of risk management, derivatives generally do not influence the fluctuations in the underlying asset prices. However, by locking-in asset prices, derivative products minimize the impact of fluctuations in asset prices on the profitability and cash flow situation of risk-averse investors.

Derivative products initially emerged as hedging devices against fluctuations in commodity prices and commodity-linked derivatives remained the sole form of such products for a long time. The financial derivatives came into spotlight in post-1970 period due to growing instability in the financial markets. However, since their emergence, financial derivatives have become very popular and by 1990s, they accounted for about two-thirds of total transactions in derivative products. In recent years, the market for financial derivatives has grown tremendously both in terms of variety of instruments available, their complexity and also turnover.

In India also financial products such as mortgage-backed securities (MBS) and asset-backed securities (ABS) are in existence. Besides the securitised products, the Indian forex and rupee derivative markets have also developed significantly over the years.

In respect of forex derivatives involving rupee, residents have access to foreign exchange forward contracts, foreign currency-rupee swap instruments and currency options—both cross currency and foreign currency-rupee. As stated in the Annual Policy Statement for the year 2008-09, the Reserve Bank of India (RBI) announced the introduction of currency futures in the eligible exchanges for which the broad framework was announced in August 2008. In future, some more innovative and complex products might emerge. These products may pose several regulatory and supervisory challenges.

33.2 Meaning of Derivatives

Derivative in mathematics means a variable derived from another variable. The term *derivative* indicates that it has no independent value, i.e. its value is entirely *derived* from the value of the underlying asset. The underlying asset can be security, commodity, bullion, currency, live stock or anything else. In other words, derivative means a forward, future, option or any other hybrid contract of pre-determined fixed duration, linked for the purpose of contract fulfilment to the value of a specified real or financial asset of an index of securities. Similarly, in the financial sense, a derivative is a financial product, which has been derived from a market for another product. Without the underlying product, derivatives do not have any independent existence in the market.

Derivative instruments are defined by the Indian Securities Contracts (Regulation) Act, 1956 to include: (i) a security derived from a debt instrument, share, secured/unsecured loan, risk instrument or contract for differences, or any other form of security, and (ii) a contract that derives its value from the prices/index of prices of underlying securities.

In other words, derivatives are financial instruments/contracts whose value depends upon the value of an underlying. Since their value is essentially derived out of an underlying, they are financial abstractions whose value is derived mathematically from the changes in the value of the underlying.

The International Monetary Fund (IMF) defines derivatives as, "financial instruments that are linked to a specific financial instrument or indicator or commodity and through which specific financial risks can be traded in financial markets in their own right. The value of a financial derivative derives from the price of an underlying item, such as an asset or index. Unlike debt securities, no principal is advanced to be repaid and no investment income accrues".

Derivatives have come into being because of the existence of risks in business. Thus, derivatives are means of managing risks. The parties managing risks in the market are known as *hedgers*. Some people/organizations are in the business of taking risks to earn profits. Such entities represent the *speculators*. The third players in the market, known as the *arbitragers,* take advantage of the market mistakes.

In recent years, derivatives have become increasingly important in the field of finance. While futures and options are now actively traded on many exchanges, forward contracts are popular on the over-the-counter (OTC) market.

33.3 Reasons for the Popularity of Derivatives

Financial derivatives have become popular due to the following reasons:
1. Increased volatility in asset prices in financial markets.
2. Increased integration of national financial markets with the international markets.
3. Marked improvement in communication facilities and sharp decline in their costs.

4. Development of more sophisticated risk management tools, providing economic agents a wider choice of risk management strategies.

5. Innovations in the derivatives markets, which optimally combine the risks and returns over a large number of financial assets, leading to higher returns, reduced risk as well as transaction costs as compared to individual financial assets.

In the class of equity derivatives, futures and options on stock indices have gained more popularity than on individual stocks, especially among institutional investors, who are major users of index-linked derivatives. Even small investors find these useful due to high correlation of the popular indices with various portfolios and ease of use. The lower costs associated with index derivatives vis-à-vis derivative products based on individual securities is another reason for their growing use.

33.4 Variants (or Types) of Derivative Contracts

Derivative contracts have several variants. The most common variants are forwards, futures, options and swaps.

33.4.1 Forwards/Forward Contracts: A forward contract is a customised contract between two entities, where settlement takes place on a specific date in the future at today's pre-agreed price. A forward contract is an agreement to buy or sell an asset on a specified date for specified price. One of the parties to the contract assumes a long position and agrees to buy the underlying asset on a certain specified future date, for a certain specified price. The other party assumes a short position and agrees to sell the asset on the same date for the same price. Other contract details like delivery date, price and quantity are negotiated bilaterally by the parties to the contract.

Forward contracts are normally traded outside stock exchanges. They are popular on the over the counter (OTC) market.

The salient features of forward contracts are as follows:

1. They are bilateral contracts and hence exposed to counter party risk.
2. Each contract is customer designed, and, hence, is unique in terms of contract size, expiration date and the asset type and quality.
3. The contract price is generally not available in public domain.
4. On the expiration date, the contract has to be settled by delivery for the asset.
5. If a party wishes to reverse the contract, it has to compulsorily go to the same counterparty, which often results in a high price being charged.

Forward contracts are very useful in hedging and speculation. A typical hedging application may pertain to an exporter who expects to receive payment in US dollars, 2 months later. He is exposed to the risk of exchange rate fluctuations. By using the currency forward market to sell dollars forward, he can lock-on a rate today and reduce his uncertainty. Likewise, an importer who is required to make a payment in US dollars 2 months hence can reduce his exposure to exchange rate fluctuations by buying dollars forward.

33.4.2 Futures/Future Contracts: Future contracts are special types of forward contracts in the sense that the former are standardised exchange-traded contracts. Future contract markets are designed to solve the problems that exist in forward markets. A future contract is an agreement between two parties to buy or sell an asset at a certain time in future, at a certain price. However, unlike forward contracts, future contracts are standardized and stock exchange-traded. To facilitate liquidity in the future contracts, the exchange specifies certain standard features for the contract. It is a standardized contract with a standard underlying instrument, a standard quantity and quality of the underlying instrument that can be delivered, and a standard timing of such settlement. A future contract may be offset prior to maturity by entering into an equal and opposite transaction. The standardized items in a future contract are the following:

1. Quantity of the underlying.
2. Quality of the underlying.
3. Date/month of delivery.
4. Units of price quotation and minimum price change.
5. Location of settlement.

33.4.3 Options: Options are fundamentally different from forward and future contracts. An option gives the holder of the option the right to do something. The holder does not have to necessarily exercise this right. In contrast, in a forward or future contract, the two parties commit themselves to doing something. Whereas it costs nothing (except margin requirements) to enter into a future contract, the purchase of an option requires an up front payment.

Options are of two types: calls options and put options. Calls options give the buyer the right but not the obligation to buy a given quantity of the underlying asset, at a given price on or before a given future date. Put options give the buyer the right, but not the obligation to sell a given quantity of the underlying asset at a given price on or before a given date.

A. Warrants: Options generally have lives of up to 1 year, the majority of options traded on options exchanges having maximum maturity of 9 months. Longer-dated options are called *warrants* and are generally traded over-the-counter.

B. LEAPS: The acronym LEAPS means Long-term Equity Anticipation Securities. These are options having a maturity of up to 3 years.

C. Baskets: Basket options are options on portfolios of underlying assets. The underlying asset is usually a moving average or a basket of assets. Equity index options are a form of basket options.

33.4.4 Swaps: Swaps are private agreements between two parties to exchange cash flows in the future according to a pre-arranged formula. They can be regarded as portfolios of forward contracts. Following are the two commonly used swaps:

A. Interest Rate Swaps: These entail swapping of only the interest-related cash flows between the parties in the same currency.

B. Currency Swaps: These entail swapping of both principal and interest between the parties, with the cash flows in one direction being in a different currency than those in the opposite direction.

33.4.5 Swaptions: Swaptions are options to buy or sell a swap that will become operative at the expiry of the options. Thus, swaption is an option on a forward swap. Rather than have call options and put options, the swaptions market has receiver swaptions and payer swaptions.

33.5 Participants in the Derivatives Market

The following three broad categories of participants, viz. hedgers, speculators, and arbitrageurs trade in the derivatives market.

33.5.1 Hedgers: Hedgers face risk associated with the price of an asset. They use future or option markets to reduce or eliminate this risk. In other words, hedgers are those who wish to protect their existing exposures and essentially are safety-driven.

33.5.2 Speculators: They bet on future movements in the price of an asset. Future and option contracts can give them an extra leverage; that is, they can increase both the potential gains and potential losses in a speculative venture. Speculators are willing risk takers who are expectation-driven.

33.5.3 Arbitrageurs: They are in business to take advantage of a discrepancy between prices in two different markets. If, for example, they see the futures price of an asset getting out of line with the cash price, they will take offsetting positions in the two markets to lock-in a profit. Arbitragers are traders and market-makers who deal in buying and selling derivatives contracts hoping to profit from price-differentials between different markets. A market maker is one who provides two-way quotes for a given product and thereby runs a position in that product.

33.6 Economic Role of Derivatives

Derivative markets perform three essential economic functions:
1. Risk management.
2. Price discovery.
3. Transactional efficiency.

The first function refers to the ability of traders to offset financial risks through derivatives. The principal benefit of the derivatives market is that it provides the opportunity for risk management through hedging. [1] Derivatives are innovations in risk management not in risk itself.

The second refers to the better allocation of resources in an economy that is created by the wide availability of an equilibrium price which serves as a measure of value.

The third function alludes to increased efficiency of transacting through derivatives. Derivative markets reduce the costs of trading and raising capital, thereby enhancing their risk management and price discovery functions.

Derivatives have played a major role in the development of financial markets and their integration across several economies, especially in developed countries. Derivatives serve to achieve a more complete financial system because previously fixed combinations of the risk properties of loans and financial assets can be bundled and unbundled into new synthetic assets. For instance, structured products or synthetic derivatives could be created by adding elementary assets or underlying assets such as bonds, equities and borrowing and lending instruments with a combination of derivative products such as put and call options. Repackaging risk properties in this way can provide a more perfect match between an investor's risk preferences and the effective risk of the portfolio or cash-flow. Derivatives allow individual risk elements of an asset to be priced and traded individually, thus ensuring an efficient price system in the asset markets.

The economic functions performed by derivatives market can be summarised as under:

1. Derivatives market helps to increase savings and investment in the long-run. Transfer of risk enables market participants to expand their volume of activity.

2. Derivatives trading acts as a catalyst for new entrepreneurial activity. Derivatives have a history of attracting many bright, creative, well educated people with an entrepreneurial attitude.

3. Prices in an organized derivatives market reflect the perception of the market participants about the future and lead the prices of underlying to the perceived future level.

4. Prices of derivatives converge with the prices of the underlying at the expiration of the derivatives contract. In fact, derivatives help in the discovery of the future as well as current prices.

5. Derivatives market helps to transfer risks from those who have them but may not like them to those who have an appetite for them.

6. Derivatives, due to their inherent nature are linked to the underlying cash markets. With the introduction of derivatives, the underlying market witnesses higher trading volumes because of participation by more players who would not otherwise participate for lack of an arrangement to transfer risk.

7. Speculative trades shift to a more controlled environment of derivatives market. In the absence of an organized derivatives market, speculators trade in the underlying cash markets. Margining, monitoring and surveillance of the activities of various participants become extremely difficult in these kinds of mixed markets.

33.7 History of Derivatives

The first future contracts are generally traced to the Yodoya rice market in Osaka, Japan around 1650. These were evidently standardized contracts, which made them much like today's futures, although it is not known if the contracts were marked to market daily and/or had credit guarantees.

Probably the next major event, and the most significant as regards the history of US future markets, was the creation of the Chicago Board of Trade in 1848. Due to its prime location on Lake Michigan, Chicago was developing as a major centre for the storage, sale, and distribution of Midwestern grain. Due to the seasonality of grain, Chicago's storage facilities were unable to accommodate the enormous increase in supply that occurred following the harvest. Similarly, its facilities were underutilized in the spring. Chicago spot prices rose and fell drastically. A group of grain traders created the *to-arrive* contract, which permitted farmers to lock-in the price and deliver the grain later. This allowed the farmer to store the grain either on the farm or at a storage facility nearby and deliver it to Chicago months later. These *to-arrive* contracts proved useful as a device for hedging and speculating on price changes. Farmers and traders soon realized that the sale and delivery of the grain itself was not as important as the ability to transfer the price risk associated with the grain. The grain could always be sold and delivered anywhere else at any time. These contracts were eventually standardized around 1865, and in 1925 the first future clearing house was formed. From that point on, future contracts were pretty much of the form we know them today.

In the early 19th century, famed New York financier Russell Sage began creating synthetic loans using the principle of put-call parity. Sage would buy the stock and a put from his customer and sell the customer a call. By fixing the put, call, and strike prices, Sage was creating a synthetic loan with an interest rate significantly higher than usury laws allowed.

Interestingly, futures/options/derivatives trading was banned numerous times in Europe and Japan and even in the US in the state of Illinois in 1867 though the law was quickly repealed. In 1874, the Chicago Mercantile Exchange predecessor, the Chicago Produce Exchange, was formed. It became the modern day Merc in 1919. Other exchanges had been popping up around the country and continued to do so.

In 1922, the US Federal Government made its first effort to regulate the futures market with the Grain Futures Act. In 1936, options on futures were banned in the US. All the while options, futures and various derivatives continued to be banned from time to time in other countries.

The 1950s marked the era of two significant events in the futures market. In 1955, the US Supreme Court ruled in the case of Corn Products Refining Company that profits from hedging were treated as ordinary income. This ruling stood until it was challenged by the 1988 ruling in the Arkansas Best case. The Best decision denied the deductibility of capital losses against ordinary income and effectively gave hedging a tax disadvantage. Fortunately, this interpretation was overturned in 1993.

In 1972 the Chicago Mercantile Exchange, responding to the now-freely floating international currencies, created the International Monetary Market, which allowed trading in currency futures. These were the first future contracts that were not on physical commodities. In 1975, the Chicago Board of Trade created the first interest rate futures contract, one based on Ginnie Mae (GNMA) mortgages. While the contract met with initial success, it eventually died. In 1975, the Merc responded with the Treasury bill futures contract. This contract was the first successful pure interest rate futures. In 1982, the Kansas City Board of Trade launched the first stock index futures, a contract on the Value Line Index. The Chicago Mercantile Exchange quickly followed with their highly successful contract on the S&P 500 index.

1973 marked the creation of both the Chicago Board Options Exchange and the publication of perhaps the most famous formula in finance, the option pricing model of Fischer Black and Myron Scholes. These events revolutionized the investment world in ways no one could imagine at that time. The Black-Scholes model, as it came to be known, set up a mathematical framework that formed the basis for an explosive revolution in the use of derivatives. In 1983, the Chicago Board Options Exchange decided to create an option on an index of stocks. Though originally known as the CBOE 100 Index, it was soon turned over to Standard and Poor's and became known as the S&P 100, which remains the most actively traded exchange-listed option.

The 1980s marked the beginning of the era of swaps and other over-the-counter (OTC) derivatives. Although OTC options and forwards had previously existed, the generation of corporate financial managers of that decade was the first to come out of business schools with exposure to derivatives. Soon virtually every large corporation, and even some that were not so large, were using derivatives to hedge, and in some cases, speculate on interest rate, exchange rate and commodity risk. New products were rapidly created to hedge the now-recognized wide varieties of risks. As the problems became more complex, Wall Street turned increasingly to the talents of mathematicians and physicists, offering them new and quite different career paths and unheard-of money. The instruments became more complex and were sometimes even referred to as *exotic*.

In 1994, the derivatives world was hit with a series of large losses on derivatives trading announced by some well-known and highly experienced firms, such as Procter and Gamble and Metallgesellschaft. One of America's wealthiest localities, Orange County, California, declared bankruptcy, allegedly due to derivatives trading, but more accurately, due to the use of leverage in a portfolio of short-term Treasury securities. England's venerable Barings Bank declared bankruptcy due to speculative trading in future contracts by a 28 year old clerk in its Singapore office. These and other large losses led to a huge outcry, sometimes against the instruments and sometimes against the firms that sold them. While some minor changes occurred in the way in which derivatives were sold, most firms simply instituted tighter controls and continued to use derivatives.

33.8 International Experience of Derivatives

As we watch efforts going into the creation of India's exchange-traded derivatives industry, comparisons with other countries are useful. In all OECD countries, derivatives are a crucial and vibrant part of the financial system.

The most interesting and important experience is that of China, a fascinating case study of the merits and demerits of a relatively unregulated start of derivatives trading. In the early 1990s, a plethora of unregulated derivatives exchanges came up in China. Many of these exchanges lacked the key institution of the clearing house as counterparty, and most of them featured rampant market manipulation where insiders in the exchange management earned abnormal profits at the expense of outside market participants.

Many observers have cited China's experience with 50 exchanges as an example of how poorly-regulated and hasty growth of derivatives markets may be problematic. However, the other side of the picture is now clear: the experience with these 50 exchanges got the Chinese markets off the ground, and generated the necessary know-how amongst exchange staff, regulators and users. In the end, China has derivatives exchanges which have significant trading volumes on a world scale.

Another important example is that of Mexico, which is in the same time zone as

Chicago: the derivatives exchanges of Chicago have done a thorough job of launching numerous derivative products based on Mexican underlying. This has made the creation of exchanges in Mexico much harder.

Taiwan is another interesting case. Taiwan is like India in terms of enormous delays which have beset the creation of a domestic derivatives exchange. In January 1997, markets in Chicago and Singapore started trading futures on a Taiwanese market index.

Exchanges such as the Chicago Mercantile Exchange (CME), Chicago Board of Trade (CBOT), Chicago Board Options Exchange (CBOE), American Stock Exchange, Sydney Futures Exchange, Hong Kong Futures Exchange and Singapore International Monetary Exchange (SIMEX) have all launched emerging market initiatives, whereby they aim to trade derivatives of underlying from emerging markets.

The US is an example of a clumsy regulatory approach, where an agency named the CFTC regulates futures while the traditional securities markets regulator, the SEC, regulates options on securities. This artificial distinction has no economic rationale, and has served to distort the development of the markets.

What are the problems which bedevil the growth of derivative markets across emerging markets in general? One source of difficulty is poor infrastructure, particularly in clearing and settlement.

In India, a major initiative in clearing for derivatives was National Securities Clearing Corporation (NSCC) which was created by National Stock Exchange (NSE). NSCC was the first effort in clearing where the clearing corporation becomes the *legal counterparty* to both legs of every transaction, and thus eliminates counterparty risk.

To sum up, derivatives is an area where a *unified* picture of the entire securities industry—spanning equity, debt, foreign exchange, commodities and real estate—is enormously useful. The functioning of the derivatives industry emphasizes that a futures is a futures, regardless of the underlying on which the futures is being traded. The great derivatives exchanges of the world simultaneously trade derivatives on all of equity, debt, foreign exchange, commodities and real estate. In this sense, the basic policy issues faced in the derivatives area (market manipulation, strength of the clearing house and competition between exchanges worldwide) are universal to all major markets.

Endnote

1. Hedging is the process of stabilizing the value (including cash flows) of a given portfolio by neutralizing adverse market movements.

34

Forwards, Futures and Options

34.1 Forwards/Forward Contracts

A forward contract is a particularly simple derivative. A deal for the purchase or sale of a commodity, security or other asset can be in the spot or forward markets. A spot or cash market is the most commonly used for trading. A majority of day to day transaction are in the cash market, where we pay cash and get the delivery of the goods. In addition to a cash purchase, another way to acquire or sell assets is by entering into a forward contract. In a forward contract, the buyer agrees to pay cash at a later date when the seller delivers the goods.

A forward contract is an agreement to buy or sell an asset on a specified date for a specified price. One of the parties to the contract assumes a long position and agrees to buy the underlying asset on a certain specified future date for a certain specified price. The other party assumes a short position and agrees to sell the asset on the same date for the same price. Other contract details like delivery date, price and quantity are negotiated bilaterally by the parties to the contract. The forward contracts are normally traded outside the exchanges.

34.1.1 Salient Features of Forward Contracts: These are as under:

1   They are bilateral contracts and hence exposed to counter party risk.
2   Each contract is custom designed, and hence is unique in terms of contract size, expiration date and the asset type and quality.
3   Contract price is generally not available in public domain.
4   On the expiration date, the contract has to be settled by delivery of the asset.
5   If the party wishes to reverse the contract, it has to compulsorily go to the same counterparty, which often results in high prices being charged.

Usually no money changes hands when forward contracts are entered into, but sometimes one or both the parties to a contract may like to ask for some initial, good-faith deposits to insure that the contract is honoured by the other party.

A forward contract is settled at maturity. The holder of the short position delivers the asset to the holder price. A forward contract is worth zero when it is first entered into. Later it can have position or negative value, depending on movements in the price of the asset.

However, forward contracts in certain markets have become much standardised, as in the case of foreign exchange, thereby reducing transaction costs and increasing transaction volumes. This process of standardisation reaches its limit in the organised futures market.

34.1.2 Advantages of Forwards: Forward contracts are very useful in hedging and speculation. A typical hedging application would be that of an exporter who expects to

receive payment in dollars 3 months later. He is exposed to the risk of exchange rate fluctuations. By using the currency forward market to sell dollars forward, he can lock-on to a rate today and reduce his uncertainty. Similarly, an importer who is required to make a payment in dollars 2 months hence can reduce his exposure to exchange rate fluctuations by buying dollars forward.

In a forward contract the price at which the underlying commodity or assets will be traded, is decided at the time of entering into the contract. The essential idea of entering into the forward contract is to peg the price and thereby avoid the price risk. Thus, by entering in the forward contract, one is assured of the price at which one can buy/sell goods or other assets. Manufacturers using a certain raw material whose price is subject to variation, can avoid the risk of price moving adversely by entering into a forward contract and plan their operations better. Similarly, by entering into a forward contract, a farmer can ensure the price he can get for his crops and not worry about what price would prevail at the time of maturity of the contract. Of course, at the time of maturity of contract, if the market price of the commodity is greater than the price agreed, then the buyer stands to gain. The opposite would hold when the market price is lower than the agreed price.

If a speculator has information or analysis, which forecasts an upturn in a price, then he can go long on the forward market instead of the cash market. The speculator would go long on the forward, wait for the price to rise, and then take a reversing transaction to book profits. Speculators may well be required to deposit a margin upfront. However, this is generally a relatively small proportion of the value of the assets underlying the forward contract. The use of forward markets supplies leverage to the speculator.

34.1.3 Problems of Forward Contracts: Forward contracts have been in existence for quite some time. The organized commodity exchanges, on which forward contracts are traded, probably started in Japan in the early 18th century, while the establishment of the Chicago Board of Trade (CBOT) in 1848 led to the start of a formal commodity exchange in the US.

A forward contract is evidently a good mean of avoiding price risk, but it entails elements of risk in that a party to the contract may not honour its part of the obligation. Thus, each party is at risk of default. There is another problem. Once a position of buyer and seller takes in a forward contract, an investor cannot retreat except through mutual consent with the party or by entering into an identical contract and taking a position that is the reverse of earlier position. Alternatives are by no means easy. With forward contract entered on a one-to-one basis and with no standardization, the forward contract has virtually no liquidity. This problem of credit risk and no liquidity associated with forward contracts led to the emergence of future contracts. Future contracts are the refined version of forward contracts.

Forward markets world-wide are afflicted by several problems:
1. Lack of centralisation of trading.
2. Illiquidity.
3. Counter party risk.

In the first two of these, the basic problem is that of too much flexibility and generality. The forward market is like a real estate market in that any two consenting adults can form contracts against each other. This often makes them design terms of the deal which are very convenient in that specific situation, but makes the contract non-tradable. Counter party risk arises from the possibility of default by any one party to the transaction. When one of the two sides to the transaction declares bankruptcy, the other suffers. Even when forward markets trade standardised contracts, and hence avoid the problem of illiquidity, still the counterparty risk remains a very serious issue.

34.2 Futures/Future Contracts

Future markets are designed to solve the problems that exist in forward markets. A future contract is an agreement between two parties to buy or sell an asset at a certain time in future at a certain price. However, unlike forward contracts, the future contracts are standardised and exchange traded. To facilitate liquidity in the future contracts, the exchange specifies certain standard features of the contract. It is a standardised contract with standard underlying instrument, a standard quantity and quality of the underlying instrument that can be delivered and a standard timing of such settlement.

A future contract may be offset prior to maturity by entering into an equal and opposite transaction. The standardised items in a future contract are as under:
1. Quantity of the underlying.
2. Quality of the underlying.
3. Date and the month of delivery.
4. Units of price quotation and minimum price change.
5. Location of settlement.

Future contracts are normally traded on an exchange. To make trading possible, the exchange specifies certain standardized features of the contract. As the two parties to the contract do not necessarily know each other the exchange also provides a mechanism, which gives the two parties a guarantee that the contract will be honoured.

34.2.1 Distinction between Futures and Forwards: Forward and future contracts are different in following respects.

A. Standardization: A forward contract is a tailor-made contract between the buyer and the seller where the terms are settled in mutual agreement between the parties. On the other hand, a future contract is standardized in regards to the quality, quantity, place of delivery of the asset etc. Only the price is negotiated. Forwards are popular on the over the counter (OTC) market. Futures are traded on an organised stock exchange. Exchange-traded derivatives tend to be more standardised and offer greater liquidity than OTC contracts, which are negotiated between counterparties and tailored to meet the needs of the parties to the contract. Exchange-traded derivatives also offer centralised limits on individual positions and have formal rules for risk and burden sharing.

B. Liquidity: There is no secondary market for forward contracts while future contracts are traded on organized exchanges. Accordingly, future contracts are usually much more liquid than the forward contracts. Forwards have customised contract terms, and therefore they are less liquid. Futures have standardised contract terms, and hence they are more liquid.

C. Conclusion of Contract: A forward contract is generally concluded with a delivery of the asset in question whereas the future contracts are settled sometimes with delivery of the asset and generally with the payment of the price differences. One who holds a contract can always eliminate his/her obligation by subsequently selling a contract for the same asset and same delivery date, before the conclusion of contract one holds. In the same manner, the seller of a future contract can buy a similar contract and offset his/her position before maturity of the first contract. Each one of these actions is called offsetting a trade.

D. Margins: A forward contract has zero value for both the parties involved so that no collateral is required for entering into such a contract. There are only two parties involved. But in a futures contract, a third party called Clearing Corporation is also involved with which margin is required to be kept by both parties. In other words, forwards require no margin payments. Futures require margin payments.

E. Profit/Loss Settlement: The settlement of a forward contract takes place on the date of maturity so that the profit/loss is booked on maturity only. On the other hand, the future contracts are marked-to-market daily so that the profits or losses are settled daily. In other words, in the case of forwards, settlement happens at the end of the period. Futures follow daily settlement.

Thus, future contracts are a significant improvement over forward contracts as they eliminate counterparty risk and offer more liquidity.

Future contracts represent an improvement over the forward contracts in terms of standardization, performance guarantee and liquidity. A future contract is a standardized contract between two parties where one of the parties commits to sell, and the other to buy, a stipulated quantity of a commodity, currency, security, index or some other specified item at an agreed price on a given date in the future.

Future contracts are traded on commodity exchanges or other future exchanges. People can buy or sell futures like other commodities. When an investor buys a future contract on an organized future exchange, he is in fact assuming the right and obligation of taking the delivery of the specified underlying item on a specified date. Similarly, when an investor sells a contract, to take a short position, one assumes the right and obligation to make the delivery of the underlying asset. There is no risk of non-performance in the case of trading in the future contracts. This is because a clearing house or a clearing corporation is associated with the futures exchange, which plays a pivotal role in the trading of futures. A clearing house takes the opposite in each trade, so that it becomes the buyer to the seller and vice versa. When a party takes a short position in a contract, it is obliged to sell the underlying commodity in question at the stipulated price to the clearing house on maturity of the contract. Similarly, an investor who takes a long position on the contract can seek its performance through the clearing house only.

It is noteworthy that while a clearing house guarantees the performance of the future contracts, the parties in the contracts are required to keep margins with it. The margins are taken to ensure that each party to a contract performs its part. The margins are adjusted on a daily basis to account for the gains or losses, depending upon the situation. This is known as marking-to-market and involves giving a credit to the buyer of the contract, if the price of the contract rises, debiting the seller's account by an equal amount. Similarly, the buyer's balance is reduced when the contract price declines and the seller's account is accordingly updated.

It is not necessary to hold on to a futures contract until maturity and one can easily close out a position. Either of the parties may reverse their position by initiating a reverse trade, so that the original buyer of a contract can sell an identical contract at a later date, cancelling, in effect, the original contract. Thus, the exchange facilitates subsequent selling (buying) of a contract so that a party can offset its position and eliminate the obligation. The fact that the buyer as well as the seller of a contract is free to transfer his interest in the contract to another party makes such contracts highly liquid in nature. In fact, most of the future contracts are cancelled by the parties, by engaging into reverse trades: the buyers cancel a contract by selling another contract, while the seller does so by buying another contract. Only a very small portion of them is held for actual delivery.

34.2.2 History of Futures: Future contracts, especially those which involve agricultural commodities, have been traded for long. In US, for instance, such contracts began on the Chicago Board of Trade (CBOT) in the 1860s. Subsequently, contracts began to trade on commodities involving precious metals like gold, silver etc. However, significant changes have taken place in recent years with the development of financial future contracts. They represent a very significant financial innovation. Such contracts encompass a variety of underlying asset-security, stock indices, and interest rates and so on. The beginnings of financial futures were made with the introduction of foreign currency future contracts on the International Monetary Markets (IMM) in 1972. Subsequently, interest rate futures—where a contract is on an asset whose price is dependent solely on the level of interest rates—were introduced.

An important development took place in the world of future contracts in 1982 when stock index futures were introduced in US, after strong initial opposition to such contracts. A future contract on a stock index has been a revolutionary and novel idea because it represents a contract based not on a readily deliverable physical commodity or currency or other negotiable instrument. It is instead based on the concept of a mathematically measurable index that is determined by the market movements of a pre-determined set of equity stocks. Such contracts are now very widely traded the world over.

34.2.3 Introduction of Futures in India: The first derivative product introduced in the Indian securities market was *index futures* in June 2000. In India, the *stock futures* were first introduced on November 9, 2001.

The Indian capital market has grown quite well since the early 1990s. In the boom period of 1992 and thereafter, even the common man was attracted to the stock market. The stock market was considered a profitable investment opportunity. Before July 2001, various stock exchanges including the Bombay Stock Exchange (BSE), National Stock Exchange (NSE) and Delhi Stock Exchange, provided carry forward facilities through the traditional *badla* system. By means of this system the purchase or sale of a security was not postponed till a particular future date; instead the system only provided for the carry forward of a transaction from one settlement period (seven days) to the next settlement period for the payment of a fee known as *badla* charges.

In the *badla* system, due to limited settlement period and no future price discovery, a speculator could manipulate prices, thus causing loss to small investors and ultimately eroding investors' confidence in the capital market. Hence, the necessity of futures trading in the capital market was emphasized. In the absence of an efficient futures market, there was no price discovery and therefore prices could be moved in any desired direction. Recent developments in the capital market culminated in a ban on *badla* from July 2001.

In the absence of futures trading, certain operators—either on their own or in collusion with corporate management teams—at times manipulated prices in the secondary market, causing irreparable damage to the growth of the market. The small and medium investors, who are the backbone of the market and whose savings come to the market via primary or secondary routes shied away. As the small investors avoided the capital market, the downturn in the secondary market ultimately affected the primary market because people stopped investing in share for fear of loss or liquidity. Introducing futures in major shares along with index futures helped to revive the capital market. This not only provided liquidity and efficiency to the market, but also helped in future price discovery.

34.2.4 Futures and Stock Indices: For understanding stock index futures a thorough knowledge of the composition of indexes is essential. Choosing the right index is important in choosing the right contract for speculation or hedging. For speculation, the volatility of the index is important whereas for hedging the choice of index depends upon the relationship between the stocks being hedged and the characteristics of the index.

Choosing and understanding the right index is important as the movement of stock index futures is quite similar to that of the underlying stock index. Volatility of the future indexes is generally greater than spot stock indexes.

Every time an investor takes a long or short position on a stock, he also has hidden exposure to the Nifty or Sensex. This is so because most often stock values fall in tune with the entire market sentiment and rise when the market as a whole is rising.

Retail investors will find the index derivatives useful due to the high correlation of the index with their portfolio/stock and low cost associated with using index futures for hedging.

34.2.5 Index Futures: A future contract is an agreement between two parties to buy or sell an asset at a certain time in the future at a certain price. Index futures are all future contracts where the underlying is the stock index (Nifty or Sensex) and helps a trader to take a view of the market as a whole.

Index futures permit speculation and if a trader anticipates a major rally in the market, he can simply buy a future contract and hope for a price rise on the future contract when the rally occurs.

34.2.6 Settlements in the Futures Market: All trades in the futures market are cash settled on a T+1 basis and all positions (buy/sell) which are not closed out are marked-to-market. The closing price of the index futures is the daily settlement price and the position is carried to the next day at the settlement price.

The most common way of liquidating an open position is to execute an offsetting future transaction by which the initial transaction is squared up. The initial buyer liquidates his long position by selling identical future contract. In index futures the other way of settlement is cash settled at the final settlement. At the end of the contract period the difference between the contract value and closing index value is paid.

34.3 Options

An option is a contract which gives the buyer the right, but not the obligation, to buy or sell specified quantity of the underlying assets, at a specific (strike) price on or before a specified time (expiration date). The underlying may be a commodity like wheat or rice or financial instrument like equity stock or bonds etc. Options are basically of two types: call options and put options.

34.3.1 Call Options: A call option is an option to buy a stock at a specific price on or before a certain date. In this way, call options are like security deposits. If, for example, Mr. Wilson wants to rent a certain property, and leaves a security deposit for it, the money would be used to insure that he would, in fact, rent that property at the price agreed upon when he returns. If Mr. Wilson never returns, he would lose his security deposit, but he would have no other liability.

Call options usually increase in value as the value of the underlying instrument rises. When you buy a call option, the price you pay for it, called the option premium, secures your right to buy that certain stock at a specified price called the strike price. If you decide not to use the option to buy the stock, and you are not obligated to, your only cost is the *option premium*.

34.3.2 Put Options: Put options are options to sell a stock at a specific price on or before a certain date. In this way, put options are like insurance policies. If you buy a new car, and then buy auto insurance on the car, you pay a premium and are, hence, protected if the asset is damaged in an accident. If this happens, you can use your policy to regain the insured value of the car. In this way, the put option gains in value as the value of the underlying instrument decreases. If all goes well and the insurance is not needed, the insurance company keeps your premium in return for taking on the risk.

With a put option, you can *insure* a stock by fixing a selling price. If something happens which causes the stock price to fall, and thus, *damages* your asset, you can exercise your option and sell it at its *insured* price level. If the price of your stock goes up, and there is no *damage*, then you do not need to use the insurance, and, once again, your only cost is the premium.

Buying put options is buying insurance. To buy a put option on Nifty is to buy insurance which reimburses the full extent to which Nifty drops below the strike price of the put option. This is attractive to many people, and to mutual funds creating *guaranteed return products*. The Nifty index fund industry will find it very useful to make a bundle of a Nifty index fund and a Nifty put option to create a new kind of a

Nifty index fund, which gives the investor protection against extreme drops in Nifty. Selling put options is selling insurance, so anyone who feels like earning revenues by selling insurance can set himself up to do so on the index options market.

Like forwards and futures, options represent another derivative instrument and provide a mechanism by which one can acquire a certain commodity or other asset in order to make profit or cover risk for a price. The options are similar to the future contracts in the sense that they are also standardized but are different from them in many ways. Options, in fact, represent the rights.

An option is the right, but not the obligation, to buy or sell a specified amount (and quality) of a commodity, currency, index, or financial instrument, or to buy or sell a specified number of underlying future contracts, at a specific price on or before a given date in future. Like other contracts, there are two parties to an option contract: the buyer who takes a long position and the seller or writer, who takes a short position. The option contract gives the owner a right to buy/sell a particular commodity or other asset at a specific pre-destined price by a specified date. The price involved is called exercise or strike price and the date involved is known as expiration. It is important to understand that such a contract gives its holder the right, and not the obligation to buy/sell. The option writer, on the other hand, undertakes upon himself the obligation to sell/buy the underlying asset if that suits the option holder. There is a wide variety of underlying assets including agricultural commodities, metals, shares, indices and so on, on which options are written.

Further, like future contracts, options are also tradable on exchanges. The exchange-traded options are standardized contracts and their trading is regulated by the exchanges that ensure the honouring of such contracts. Thus, in case of options as well, a clearing corporation takes the other side in every contract so that the party with the long position has a claim against the clearing corporation and the one with short position is obliged to it. However, buying or selling of future contracts does not require any price to be paid, called premium. The writer of an option receives the premium as a compensation of the risk that he takes upon himself. The premium belongs to the writer and is not adjusted in the price if the holder of the option decides to exercise it. This price is determined on the exchange, like the price of a share, by the forces of demand and supply. Further, like the share prices, the option prices also keep on changing with passage of time as trading takes place.

One difference between future and option trading may be noted. Whereas both parties to a future contract are required to deposit margins to the exchange, only the party with the short position is called upon to pay margin in case of options trading. The party with the long position does not pay anything beyond the premium.

34.3.3 Options in Historical Perspective: Options were traded in the US and UK during the 19th century but confined mainly to the agricultural commodities. Earlier, they were declared illegal in UK in 1733 and remained so until 1860 when the Act declaring them illegal was repealed. In the US, options on equity stocks of the companies were available on the over the counter (OTC) market only, until April 1973. They were not standardized and involved the intra-party risk. In India, options on stocks of companies, though illegal, were traded for many years on a limited scale in the form of *teji* and *mandi*, and related transactions. As such, this trading was a very risky proposition to undertake.

In spite of the long time that has elapsed since the inception of options, they were, until not very long ago, looked down upon as mere speculative tools and associated with corrupt practices. Things changed dramatically in the 1970s when options were transformed from relative obscurity to a systematically traded asset which is an integral part of financial portfolios. In fact, the year 1973 witnessed some major developments. Black and Scholes published a seminal paper explaining the basic principal of options pricing and hedging. In the same year, the Chicago Board Options Exchange (CBOT) was created. It was the first registered securities exchange dedicated to options trading. While trading in options existed for long, it experienced a gigantic growth with the creation of this exchange. The listing of options meant orderly and thicker markets for this kind of securities. Options trading is now undertaken widely in many countries besides the US and UK. In fact, options have become an integral part of the large and developed financial markets.

34.3.4 Advantages of Option Trading:

A. Risk Management: Put options allow investors holding shares to hedge against a possible fall in their value. This can be considered similar to taking out insurance against a fall in the share price.

B. Time to Decide: By taking a call option the purchase price for the shares is locked-in. This gives the call option holder until the expiry day to decide whether or not to exercise the option and buy the shares. Likewise, the taker of a put option has time to decide whether or not to sell the shares.

C. Speculation: The ease of trading in and out of an option position makes it possible to trade options with no intention of ever exercising them. If an investor expects the market to rise, he may decide to buy call options. If expecting a fall, he may decide to buy put options. Either way the holder can sell the option prior to expiry to take a profit or limit a loss. Trading options has a lower cost than shares, as there is no stamp duty payable unless and until options are exercised.

D. Leverage: Leverage provides the potential to make a higher return from a smaller initial outlay than investing directly. However, leverage usually involves more risks than a direct investment in the underlying shares. Trading in options can allow investors to benefit from a change in the price of the share without having to pay the full price of the share.

E. Income Generation: Shareholders can earn extra income over and above dividends by writing call options against their shares. By writing an option they receive the option premium upfront. While they get to keep the option premium, there is a possibility that they could be exercised against and have to deliver their shares to the taker at the exercise price.

F. Strategies: By combining different options, investors can create a wide range of potential profit scenarios.

34.3.5 Distinction between Futures and Options: Options are different from futures in several respects. At a practical level, the option buyer pays for the option in full at the time it is purchased. After this, he only has an upside. There is no possibility of the options position generating any further loss to him—other than the funds already paid for the option. Contrarily, futures are free to enter into but can generate very large losses. This feature makes options attractive to many occasional market participants who do not have time to monitor their futures positions.

More generally, options offer *non-linear payoffs* whereas futures only have *linear payoffs*. By combining futures and options, a wide variety of innovative and useful payoff structures can be created.

34.3.6 Pricing Options: Black-Scholes Formulae: An option buyer has the right but not the obligation to exercise on the seller. The worst that can happen to a buyer is the loss of the premium paid by him. His downside is limited to this premium, but his upside is potentially unlimited. This optionality is precious and has a value, which is expressed in terms of the option price. Just like in other free markets, it is the supply and demand in the secondary market that drives the price of an option.

There are various models which help us get close to the true price of an option. Most of these are variants of the celebrated Black-Scholes model for pricing European options. Today most calculators and spread-sheets come with a built-in Black-Scholes options pricing formula so to price options we do not really need to memorise the formula.

Options have existed—at least in concept—since antiquity. It was not until publication of the Black-Scholes (1973) option pricing formula that a theoretically consistent framework for pricing options became available. That framework was a direct result of work by Robert Merton as well as Fisher Black and Myron Scholes. In 1997, Scholes and Merton won the Nobel Prize in economics for this work. Black had died in 1995, but otherwise would have shared the prize.

The factors affecting the option price are the following:
1. Spot price of the underlying.
2. Exercise price.
3. Risk-free interest rate.
4. Volatility of the underlying.
5. Time to expiration.
6. Dividends on the underlying (stock or index).

Interestingly, before Black and Scholes came up with their option pricing model, there was a widespread belief that the expected growth of the underlying ought to affect the option price. Black and Scholes demonstrate that this is not true. The significance of the Black and Scholes model is that like any good model, it tells us what is important and what is not. It does not promise to produce the exact prices that show up in the market, but certainly does a remarkable job of pricing options within the framework of assumptions of the model. Virtually all option pricing models, even the most complex ones, have much in common with the Black-Scholes model.

Black and Scholes start by specifying a simple and well-known equation that models the way in which stock prices fluctuate. This equation called geometric brownian motion, implies that stock returns will have a lognormal distribution, meaning that the logarithm of the stock's return will follow the normal (bell-shaped) distribution. Black and Scholes then propose that the option's price is determined by only two variables that are allowed to change: time and the underlying stock price. The other factors, namely the volatility, the exercise price, and the risk-free interest rate do affect the option's price but they are not allowed to change. By forming a portfolio consisting of a long position in stock and a short position in calls, the risk of the stock is eliminated. This hedged portfolio is obtained by setting the number of shares of stock equal to the approximate change in the call price for a change in the stock price. This mix of stock and calls must be revised continuously, a process known as delta hedging.

Black and Scholes then turn to a little-known result in a specialised field of probability known as stochastic calculus. This result defines how the option price changes in terms of the change in the stock price and time to expiration. They then reason that this hedged combination of options and stock should grow in value at the risk-free rate. The result then is a partial differential equation. The solution is found by forcing a condition called a boundary condition on the model that requires the option price to converge to the exercise value at expiration. The end result is the Black and Scholes model.

34.4 Currency Futures

Globalisation and integration of financial markets, coupled with the progressively increasing cross-border flow of funds, have transformed the intensity of market risk, which, in turn, has made the issues relating to hedging of such risk exposures very critical. The economic agents in India currently have a menu of over the counter (OTC) products, such as forwards, swaps and options, available to them for hedging their currency risk and the markets for these are quite deep and liquid. However, in the context of growing integration of the Indian economy with the rest of the world, as also the continued development of financial markets, a need has been felt to make available a wider choice of hedging instruments to the market participants to enable them to cope better with their currency risk exposures.

34.4.1 The Origin: The origin of futures can be traced back to 1851 when the Chicago Board of Trade (CBOT) introduced standardized forward contracts which were being traded in non-standard bilateral form for the preceding three years. In comparison, the birth of currency futures is of a recent origin and was a sequel to the breakdown of the Bretton Woods system. The resultant currency volatility provided a business opportunity for launching futures contracts in foreign currencies. The Chicago Mercantile Exchange (CME) first conceived the idea of a currency futures exchange and it launched the same in 1972 amidst considerable scepticism, since traditionally futures market had traded agricultural commodities and not financial instruments. The CME commissioned Professor Milton Friedman to write a paper on currency futures in order to gain credibility in the market. Professor Milton Friedman stated, "Changes in the international financial structure will create a great expansion in the demand for foreign cover. It is highly desirable that this demand be met by as broad, as deep, as resilient a futures market in foreign currencies as possible in order to facilitate foreign trade and investment. Such a wider market is almost certain to develop in response to the demand. The major open question is where. The US is a natural place and it is very much in the interests of the US that it should develop here". The CBOT saw this as a competitive challenge, as also an opportunity to launch other financial futures and proposed trading options and futures on stocks.

34.4.2 The Rationale: The rationale for establishing currency futures market is manifold. Both residents and non-residents are exposed to currency risk when residents purchase foreign currency assets and non-residents purchase domestic currency assets. If the exchange rate remains unchanged from the time of the purchase of the asset to its sale, no gains and losses are made out of currency exposures. But if domestic currency depreciates (appreciates) against the foreign currency, the exposure would result in gain (loss) for residents purchasing foreign assets and loss (gain) for non-residents purchasing domestic asset. In this backdrop, unpredicted movements in exchange rates expose investors to currency risks. Currency futures enable them to hedge these risks. Nominal exchange rates are often random walks with or without drift, while real exchange rates over long-run are mean reverting. As such, it is possible that over a long-run, the incentive to hedge currency risk may not be large.

However, financial planning horizon is much smaller than the long-run, which is typically inter-generational in the context of exchange rates. As such, there is a strong need to hedge currency risk and this need has grown manifold with fast growth in cross-border trade and investments flows. The argument for hedging currency risks appear to be natural in case of assets, and applies equally to trade in goods and services, which result in income flows with leads and lags and get converted into different currencies at the market rates. Empirically, changes in exchange rate are found to have very low correlations with foreign equity and bond returns. This in theory should lower portfolio risk. Therefore, sometimes argument is advanced against the need for hedging currency risks. But there is strong empirical evidence to suggest that hedging reduces the volatility of returns and indeed considering the episodic nature of currency returns, there are strong arguments to use instruments to hedge currency risks.

Currency risks could be hedged mainly through forwards, futures, swaps and options. Each of these instruments has its role in managing the currency risk. The main advantage of currency futures over its closest substitute product, viz., forwards which are traded over the counter (OTC) lies in price transparency, elimination of counterparty credit risk and greater reach in terms of easy accessibility to all. Currency futures are expected to bring about better price discovery and also possibly lower transaction costs. Apart from pure hedgers, currency futures also invite arbitrageurs, speculators and noise traders who may take a bet on exchange rate movements without an underlying or an economic exposure as a motivation for trading.

From an economy-wide perspective, currency futures contribute to hedging of risks and help traders and investors in undertaking their economic activity. There is a large body of empirical evidence which suggests that exchange rate volatility has an adverse impact on foreign trade. Since there are first order gains from trade which contribute to output growth and consumer welfare, currency futures can potentially have an important impact on real economy. Gains from international risk sharing through trade in assets could be of relatively smaller magnitude than gains from trade. However, in a dynamic setting these investments could still significantly impact capital formation in an economy and as such currency futures could be seen as a facilitator in promoting investment and aggregate demand in the economy, thus promoting growth.

34.4.3 The Basics: A futures contract is a standardized contract, traded on an exchange, to buy or sell a certain underlying asset or an instrument at a certain date in the future, at a specified price. Where the underlying asset happens to be a commodity, the futures contract is termed as *commodity futures* whereas in cases where the underlying happens to be a financial asset or instrument, the resultant futures contract is referred to as *financial futures*.

A currency futures contract, also called an FX future, is a type of financial futures contract where the underlying is an exchange rate. In other words, it is a futures contract to exchange one currency for another at a specified date in the future at a price (exchange rate) that is fixed on the last trading date. The buyer or seller in a futures market locks into an exchange rate for a specific value date or delivery date. In other words, currency futures are used primarily as a price setting mechanism rather than for physical exchange of currencies. The future date is called the delivery date or final settlement date. The pre-set price is termed as future price, while the price of the underlying asset on the delivery date is termed as the settlement price. The future price normally converges towards the spot price on the settlement date. The futures contract gives the holder the right to buy or sell, in contrast to the option contract which gives the holder the right, but not the obligation to buy or sell the underlying.

Thus, both the parties of the futures contract must fulfil their contractual obligations on the settlement date. However, such contracts do provide options to deliver the underlying asset or settle the difference in cash. The holder of a contract could exit from his commitment prior to the settlement date by either selling a long position or buying back a short position (offset or reverse trade). The futures contracts are exchange traded derivatives and the exchange's clearing house acts as counterparty to all contracts, sets margin requirements etc.

34.5 Forward Markets Commission (FMC)

FMC was merged with SEBI in September 2015. FMC was the chief regulator of forwards and futures markets in India. Headquartered in Mumbai,, it was overseen by the Ministry of Consumer Affairs, Food and Public Distribution, Government of India.

Established in 1953 under the provisions of the Forward Contracts (Regulation) Act, 1952, it consisted of 2 to 4 members, all appointed by the Government of India. The Commission allowed commodity trading in 22 exchanges in India, of which 6 were national.

Just at the time the FMC was established, the Government felt that derivative markets increased speculation which led to increased costs and price instabilities. Therefore, options and futures trading was prohibited altogether in 1953.

The industry was pushed underground and the prohibition meant that development and expansion came to a halt. As futures and options markets began to develop in the rest of the world, Indian derivatives markets were left behind. The apprehensions about the role of speculation, particularly in the conditions of scarcity, prompted the Government to continue the prohibition well into the 1980s.

This left the country with a large number of small and isolated regional futures markets. The futures markets were dispersed and fragmented, with separate trading communities in different regions with little contact with one another. The exchanges generally were yet to embrace modern technology or modern business practices.

Next to the officially approved exchanges, there were many *hawala* markets. Most of these unofficial commodity exchanges operated for many decades. Some unofficial markets traded 20 to 30 times the volume of the *official* futures exchanges. They offered not only futures, but also option contracts. Transaction costs were low, and they attracted many speculators and smaller hedgers. Absence of regulation and proper clearing arrangements, however, meant that these markets were mostly *regulated* by the reputation of the main players.

Responsibilities and functions of Forward Markets Commission (FMC) were as follows:

1. To advise the Central Government in respect of the recognition or the withdrawal of recognition from any association or in respect of any other matter arising out of the administration of the Forward Contracts (Regulation) Act, 1952.
2. To keep forward markets under observation and to take such action in relation to them, as it may consider necessary, in exercise of the powers assigned to it by or under the Act.
3. To collect and, whenever the Commission thinks it necessary, publish information regarding the trading conditions in respect of goods to which any of the provisions of the Act is made applicable, including information regarding supply, demand and prices, and to submit to the Central Government, periodical reports on the working of forward markets relating to such goods.
4. To make recommendations generally with a view to improving the organization and working of forward markets.
5. To undertake the inspection of the accounts and other documents of any recognized association or registered association or any member of such association whenever it considers it necessary.

Derivative Instruments in India

India has introduced different equity derivatives in a phased manner. This phased approach was adopted in India with index futures being introduced in June 2000, index options in June 2001 and individual stock options in July 2001.

35.1 L.C. Gupta Committee on Derivatives Trading in India

Securities and Exchange Board of India (SEBI) set up a 24-member committee under the Chairmanship of L.C. Gupta on November 18, 1996 to develop appropriate regulatory framework for derivatives trading in India. The Committee submitted its report on March 17, 1998 prescribing necessary preconditions for introduction of derivatives trading in India. The committee recommended that derivatives should be declared as *securities* so that regulatory framework applicable to trading of *securities* could also govern trading of derivatives. [1]

35.1.1 Regulatory Objectives: The Committee outlined the goals of regulation in Paragraph 3.1 of its Report which is reproduced below.

"The Committee believes that regulation should be designed to achieve specific, well-defined goals. It is inclined towards positive regulation designed to encourage healthy activity and behaviour. It has been guided by the following objectives:

A. Investor Protection: Attention needs to be given to the following four aspects:

- **Fairness and Transparency:** The trading rules should ensure that trading is conducted in a fair and transparent manner. Experience in other countries shows that in many cases, derivative brokers/dealers failed to disclose potential risk to the clients. In this context, sales practices adopted by dealers for derivatives would require specific regulation. In some of the most widely reported mishaps in the derivatives market elsewhere, the underlying reason was inadequate internal control system at the user-firm itself so that overall exposure was not controlled and the use of derivatives was for speculation rather than for risk hedging. These experiences provide useful lessons for us for designing regulations.

- **Safeguard for Clients' Moneys:** Moneys and securities deposited by clients with the trading members should not only be kept in a separate clients' account but should also not be attachable for meeting the broker's own debts. It should be ensured that trading by dealers on own account is totally segregated from that for clients.

- **Competent and Honest Service:** The eligibility criteria for trading members should be designed to encourage competent and qualified personnel so that investors/clients are served well. This makes it necessary to prescribe qualification for derivatives brokers/dealers and the sales persons appointed by them in terms of a knowledge base.

- **Market Integrity:** The trading system should ensure that the market's integrity is safeguarded by minimising the possibility of defaults. This requires framing appropriate rules about capital adequacy, margins, clearing corporation etc.

B. Quality of Markets: The concept of *quality of markets* goes well beyond market integrity and aims at enhancing important market qualities, such as cost-efficiency, price-continuity, and price-discovery. This is a much broader objective than market integrity.

C. Innovation: While curbing any undesirable tendencies, the regulatory framework should not stifle innovation which is the source of all economic progress, more so because financial derivatives represent a new rapidly developing area, aided by advancements in information technology".

35.1.2 Derivative Products:

A. Interest and Currency Futures: The Committee stated in Paragraph 1.24: "There are inter-connections among the various kinds of financial futures [equity, interest rate and currency], because the various financial markets are closely inter-linked, as the recent financial market turmoil in East and South-East Asian countries has shown. The basic principles underlying the running of future markets and their regulation are the same. Having a common trading infrastructure will have important advantages. The Committee, therefore, feels that the attempt should be to develop an integrated market structure".

B. Single Stock Derivatives: The Committee advocated a phased introduction of different equity derivatives in India in Paragraph 2.17 of its report: "The consensus in the Committee was that stock index futures would be the best starting point for equity derivatives in India. The Committee has arrived at this conclusion after careful examination of all aspects of the problem, including the survey findings and regulatory preparedness. The Committee would favour the introduction of other types of equity derivatives also, as the derivatives market grows and the market players acquire familiarity with its operations. Other equity derivatives include options on stock index or on individual stocks. There may also be room for more than one stock index futures. It is bound to be a gradual process, shaped by market forces under the over-all supervision of SEBI".

The Committee was not much inclined towards the fourth type of equity derivatives (individual stock futures) given its then limited popularity globally: "The fourth type, viz. individual stock futures, was favoured much less. It is pertinent to note that the US does not permit individual stock futures. Only one or two countries in the world are known to have futures on individual stocks". (Paragraph 2.3)

35.1.3 Use of Derivatives by Mutual Funds:
The Committee recommended that mutual funds should be permitted to use derivatives for hedging and portfolio rebalancing: "Mutual funds should be allowed to use financial derivatives for hedging purposes (including anticipated hedging) and portfolio re-balancing within a policy framework and rules laid down by their Board of Trustees who should specify what derivatives are allowed to be used, within what limits, for what purposes, for which schemes, and also the authorisation procedure". (Paragraph 7.10)

35.1.4 SEBI Related Issues:
The Committee very rightly emphasised the need for

SEBI to build competencies in the area of derivatives: "SEBI should immediately create a special Derivatives Cell because derivatives demand special knowledge. It should encourage its staff members to undergo training in derivatives and also recruit some specialised personnel.

A Derivatives Advisory Council may also be created to tap the outside expertise for independent advice on many problems which are bound to arise from time to time in regard to derivatives. (Paragraph 4.11[b])

35.2 Amendment of Securities Contract Regulation Act (SCRA)

In pursuance of the recommendations of the L.C. Gupta Committee, SCRA was amended in December 1999 to include derivatives within the ambit of *securities* and the regulatory framework was developed for governing derivatives trading. The Act also made it clear that derivatives shall be legal and valid only if such contracts are traded on a recognised stock exchange, thus precluding OTC derivatives. The government also rescinded in March 2000, the three-decade old notification, which prohibited forward trading in securities.

Derivatives trading commenced in India in June 2000 after SEBI granted the final approval to this effect in May 2000. SEBI permitted the derivatives segments of two stock exchanges NSE and BSE, and their clearing house/corporation to commence trading and settlement in approved derivative contracts. To begin with, SEBI approved trading in index future contracts based on S&P CNX Nifty and BSE-30 (Sensex) index. This was followed by approval for trading in options which commenced in June 2001 and the trading in options on individual securities commenced in July 2001. Future contracts on individual stocks were launched in November 2001. Trading and settlement in derivative contracts is done in accordance with the rules, by-laws, and regulations of the respective exchanges and their clearing house/corporation duly approved by SEBI and notified in the official gazette.

35.3 Measures to Protect the Rights of Investors in the Derivatives Market

Investors' money has to be kept separate at all levels and is permitted to be used only against the liability of the investor and is not available to the trading member or clearing member or even any other investor.

A trading member is required to provide every investor with a risk disclosure document which will disclose the risks associated with the derivatives trading so that investors can take a conscious decision to trade in derivatives.

Investors get the contract note duly time stamped for receipt of the order and execution of the order. The order is executed with the identity of the client and without client ID order is not accepted by the system. The investors can demand the trade confirmation slip with their respective ID in support of the contract note. This protects them from the risk of price favours, if any, extended by the Member.

In the derivatives market all money paid by the investors towards margins on all open positions is kept in trust with the clearing house/clearing corporation and in the event of default of the trading or clearing member the amounts paid by the client towards margins are segregated and not utilized towards the default of the member. However, in the event of default of a member, losses suffered by the investors, if any, on settled/closed out position are compensated from the investors' protection fund, as per the rules, by-laws and regulations of the derivative segment of the exchanges.

35.4 Recent Developments in the Derivatives Market

The derivatives market got a shot in the arm with the Government deciding to treat income from derivatives trading as a non-speculative income.

The decision to treat income from derivative trading as a non-speculative income will contribute to an increase in trading volume in the derivative market since it provides for setting off of derivative income/loss against normal income/loss.

FIIs are permitted to submit appropriate collateral, in cash or otherwise when trading in domestic derivatives. According to market players, this will bring about flexibility and encourage FIIs to take greater exposure through the derivative contracts.

Local players already had the flexibility of submitting collaterals; such as bank guarantee or shares or deposit receipt, in place of cash or along with cash, for meeting their margin obligations.

35.5 Credit Derivatives

The credit derivatives are gaining increasing popularity in many countries. Since the early 1990s, there has been proliferation of different types of credit derivatives in several countries.

A credit derivative is a contract (derivative) to transfer the risk of the total return on a credit asset falling below an agreed level, without transfer of the underlying asset. This is usually achieved by transferring risk on a credit reference asset. Early forms of credit derivatives were financial guarantees. Credit derivatives are designed to allow independent trading/hedging of credit risk. It is also possible to transfer and/or transform credit risk through securitisation. Credit derivative is a logical extension of two of the most significant developments in financial markets, viz., securitisation and derivatives.

35.5.1 Forms of Credit Derivatives

Credit derivatives are instruments that transfer a part or all of the credit risk of an obligation (or a pool of obligations), without transferring the ownership of the underlying asset(s). This is usually achieved by transferring risk on a credit reference asset. Three common forms of credit derivatives are credit default swap (CDS), total return swap (TRS) and credit linked note (CLN).

A. Credit Default Swap (CDS): A CDS consists of swapping, usually on an ongoing basis, the risk premium inherent in an interest rate on a bond or a loan in return for a cash payment that is made in the event of default by the debtor. The CDS has become the main driver of the credit derivatives market, offering liquid price discovery and trading on which the rest of the market is based. It is an agreement between a protection buyer and a protection seller, whereby the buyer pays a periodic fee in return for a contingent payment by the seller upon a credit event happening in the reference entity. The contingent payment usually replicates the loss incurred by creditor of the reference entity in the event of its default. It covers only the credit risk embedded in the asset, risks arising from other factors, such as interest rate movements, remain with the buyer.

B. Total Return Swap (TRS): A TRS (also known as total rate of return swap) is a contract between two counterparties, whereby they swap periodic payments for the period of the contract. Typically, one party receives the total return (interest payments plus any capital gains or losses for the payment period) from a specified reference asset, while the other receives a specified fixed or floating cash flow that is not related to the creditworthiness of the reference asset, as with a vanilla interest rate swap. The payments are based upon the same notional amount. The reference asset may be any asset, index or basket of assets. The TRS is simply a mechanism that allows one party to derive the economic benefit of owning an asset without use of the balance sheet, and which allows the other to effectively buy protection against loss in value due to ownership of a credit asset.

While the CDS provides protection against specific credit events, the TRS protects against the loss of value irrespective of cause, whether default and widening of credit spreads, among others.

C. Credit Linked Note (CLN): A CLN is an instrument whose cash flow depends upon a credit event, which can be a default, credit spread, or rating change. The definition of the relevant credit events must be negotiated by the parties to the note. A CLN, in effect, combines a credit-default swap with a regular note (with coupon, maturity, redemption). Given its regular-note features, a CLN is an on-balance sheet asset, unlike a CDS.

35.5.2 Significance of Credit Derivatives: Credit derivative markets are most active where credit quality measurement and rating systems are transparent and have widespread adoption as in North America and Europe. In addition, the demand for structured credit products in Asia and the Middle East has been growing. The rapid pace of growth and widespread participation in the credit derivatives market in several countries has transformed the financial landscape. Credit derivatives have significance for both banks and investors in mitigating credit risk. For instance, a commercial bank can use credit derivatives to manage the risk of its loan portfolio and an investment bank can use credit derivatives to manage the risks it incurs when underwriting securities. Investors—such as an insurance company, asset manager, or hedge fund—can use credit derivatives to align its credit risk exposure with its desired credit risk profile.

Credit derivatives in international markets have effectively helped to enhance the efficiency of the financial system by providing to both bank and non-bank financial institutions access to a broader range of risk-return combinations and a wider pool of underlying risks and enhancing the liquidity of corporate bond markets. The information revealed through credit derivative mechanism is very useful for supervision and market surveillance.

35.5.3 Benefits of Credit Derivatives: Banks and the financial institutions derive at least three main benefits from credit derivatives:

1. Credit derivatives allow banks to transfer credit risk and hence free up capital, which can be used for other productive purposes.
2. Banks can conduct business on existing client relationships in excess of exposure norms and transfer away the risks. For instance, a bank which has hit its exposure limits with a client group may have to turn down a lucrative guarantee deal. However, with credit derivatives, the bank can take up the guarantee and maintain its exposure limits by transferring the credit risk on the guarantee or previous exposures. This allows bank to maintain client relationships.
3. Banks can construct and manage a credit risk portfolio of their own choice and risk appetite unconstrained by funds, distribution and sales effort.

35.5.4 Risks Involved in Credit Derivatives: Credit derivatives pose risk management challenges of their own. Credit derivatives can transform credit risk in intricate ways that may not be easy to understand. Complex credit derivatives rely on complex models, leading to model risk. Credit rating agencies interpret this complexity for investors, but their ratings can be misunderstood, creating rating agency risk. The settlement of a credit derivative contract following a default can have its own complications, creating settlement risk. Apart from these risks, the credit risk remains the core risk in the credit derivative segment. The use of credit derivative instruments has changed the underlying borrower-lender relationship and established new relationships between lenders that become risk shedders and the new risk takers. This new relationship has the potential for market failure due, for instance, to asymmetric information. The growth of hedge funds, particularly credit-oriented hedge funds, has accelerated market development and credit risk dispersion. While credit derivative markets increasingly facilitate the primary transfer of credit risk, secondary market liquidity is still lacking within some segments, creating the potential for market disruptions. As such, these markets are subject to increased attention from supervisors and policymakers and raise some supervisory concerns.

In short, the use of credit derivatives raises the following concerns:
1. Some of the credit derivatives, which are being used, are at their infancy and need to mature. Introduction of such products, therefore, may be potentially destabilising.
2. The measurement and management of credit risk is much more complicated than market risk.
3. Documentation risk is an important aspect of credit derivatives.
4. Certain incentive issues arise with the use of credit derivatives. This is because such instruments typically change the underlying borrower-lender relationship and establish new relationships between lenders that become risk shedders and the new risk takers. This new relationship has the potential for market failure due, for instance, to asymmetric information.

35.5.5 Credit Derivatives and Sub-prime Crisis of 2007: The role that credit derivatives played in the 2007 sub-prime crisis is well-known. The macroeconomic environment with a prolonged period of low interest rates, high liquidity and low volatility led to underestimation of risks by financial institutions, breakdown of credit and risk management practices in many financial institutions, and shortcomings in financial regulation and supervision. Banks, especially in the US, increasingly turned to *originate and distribute model* in which they bundled and sold standardised mortgages as securities. Though favourable credit ratings were obtained for most of these bundled securities by carefully structuring their priority in receiving cash flow from servicing of the original portfolio, many of these were in reality sub-prime securities. As housing prices in the US declined, the defaults rose in several leading international banks. The kind of problems witnessed in the US sub-prime mortgage market can also surface in other types of lending such as leveraged loans and consumer credit. Furthermore, such problems may not confine to industrial countries, but can surface in other emerging economies as well where financial institutions take excessive risks in the wake of weak lending practices, and where regulatory and supervisory frameworks are found to be inadequate.

The unbridled proliferation of complex credit derivatives and excessive risk transfer by adoption of the originate-to-distribute model is recognised as one of the root causes of the current financial crisis. The recent credit turmoil has also underscored the importance of liquidity risk arising from off-balance sheet commitments, implicit or explicit, of the credit intermediaries.

While the development of markets for credit derivatives and asset securitization products can play a critical role in furthering economic growth, this requires to be pursued in a gradual manner by sequencing reforms and putting in place appropriate safeguards before introducing such products.

35.6 Credit Derivatives in India

The credit market refers to the market where financial instruments that embrace credit risk are traded. In addition to traditional instruments, such as loans and advances, corporate bonds, and commercial papers the credit market now includes securitised products in which various credit risks have been pooled as well as credit derivatives whose underlying assets encompass credit risks.

As a financial system which is dominated by bank intermediation, credit has traditionally been the main source of funds to various sectors in the Indian economy, and loans and advances continue to be the preferred part of asset books of banks. However, the implementation of risk management guidelines and the requirement for providing a capital charge for credit risk in the balance sheet has given banks an incentive to look for innovative methods of transferring credit risk from their books.

While simple techniques for transferring credit risk, such as financial guarantees, collateral and credit insurance have long been prevalent in the Indian banking industry, the recent innovative instruments in credit risk transfer are yet to make an impact. However, in recent years the risk management architecture of banks in India has strengthened and they are on the way to becoming Basel II compliant, providing adequate comfort level for the introduction of credit derivatives.

The Reserve Bank in its Annual Policy announced in April 2007 mentioned that as part of the gradual process of financial sector liberalization in India, it was considered appropriate to introduce credit derivatives in a calibrated manner. Furthermore, the amendment to the Reserve Bank of India Act, 1934 had provided legality to OTC (over the counter) derivative instruments, including credit derivatives.

Although derivative instruments were introduced in July 1999 in the money/foreign exchange market in the form of forward rate agreements (FRAs) [2] and interest rate swaps (IRS), [3] credit derivatives are yet to be introduced. The RBI's Annual Policy Statement 2007-08 announced the introduction of credit derivatives in India in a calibrated manner. In view of certain adverse developments in the international financial markets, especially credit markets, resulting from recent financial turmoil, it was widely felt that time is not opportune to introduce the credit derivatives in India for the present. As such, the RBI announced on June 19, 2008 its decision to keep in abeyance the issuance of the final guidelines on introduction of credit derivatives in India.

35.7 Traders and Trading System of Derivatives
35.7.1 Traders in Derivatives Market:
A. Hedgers: Hedgers are the traders who wish to eliminate the risk (of price change) to which they are already exposed. They may take a long position on, or short sell, a commodity and would, therefore, stand to lose should the prices move in the adverse direction. The trader can sell future (or forward) contracts with a matching price, to hedge.

Stocks carry two types of risk: company specific and market risk. While company risk can be minimized by diversifying your portfolio, market risk cannot be diversified but has to be hedged.

Hedging involves protecting an existing asset position from future adverse price movements. In order to hedge a position, a market player needs to take an equal and opposite position in the futures market to the one held in the cash market.

How does one measure the market risk? Market risk can be known from Beta which measures the relationship between movement of the index to the movement of the stock. The beta measures the percentage impact on the stock prices for 1 percent change in the index. Therefore, for a portfolio whose value goes down by 11 percent when the index goes down by 10 percent, the beta would be 1.1. When the index increases by 10 percent, the value of the portfolio increases 11 percent. The idea is to make beta of your portfolio zero to nullify your losses.

B. Speculators: If hedgers are the people who wish to avoid the price risk, speculators are those who are willing to take such risk. These are the people who take position in the market and assume risks to profit from fluctuations in prices. In fact, the speculators consume information, make forecasts about the prices and put their money in these forecasts. Depending on their perceptions, they may take long or short positions on futures and/or options, or may hold spread positions (simultaneous long and short positions on the same derivatives).

Speculators are those who do not have any position on which they enter in futures and options market. They only have a particular view on the market, stock, commodity etc. In short, speculators put their money at risk in the hope of earning profit from an anticipated price change. They consider various factors such as demand, supply, market position, open interests, economic fundamentals and other data to take their positions.

C. Arbitrageurs: Arbitrageurs thrive on market imperfections. An arbitrageur profits by trading a given commodity, or other item, that sells for different prices in different markets. This becomes possible by simultaneous purchase of securities in one market where the price is low and sale in another market, where the price is comparatively higher.

This is done when the same securities are being quoted at different prices in the two markets. Arbitrageurs derive advantage from difference in prices of securities prevailing in the two markets.

An arbitrageur is basically risk averse. He enters into those contracts were he can earn riskless profits. When markets are imperfect, buying in one market and simultaneously selling in other market gives riskless profit. Arbitrageurs are always in the look out for such imperfections.

In the futures market one can take advantages of arbitrage opportunities by buying from lower priced market and selling at the higher priced market. In index futures arbitrage is possible between the spot market and the futures market.

35.7.2 Trading System:

A. National Exchange for Automated Trading (NEAT-F&O): Futures and options trading system of NSE— called NEAT-F&O trading system—provides a fully automated screen-based trading for index futures and options, stock futures and options and futures on interest rate on a nationwide basis as well as an online monitoring and surveillance mechanism. It supports an order driven market and provides complete transparency of trading operations. It is similar to that of trading of equities in the cash market segment.

The software for the F&O market has been developed to facilitate efficient and transparent trading in futures and options instruments. Keeping in view the familiarity of trading members with the current capital market trading system, modifications have been introduced in the existing capital market trading system so as to make it suitable for trading futures and options.

B. Trading Mechanism: The NEAT-F&O system supports an order driven market, wherein orders match automatically. Order matching is essentially on the basis of security, its price, time and quantity. All quantity fields are in units and price in rupees. The lot size on the futures and options market is 50 for Nifty. The exchange notifies the regular lot size and tick size for each security traded on this segment from time to time. Orders, as and when they are received, are first time stamped and then immediately processed for potential match. When any order enters the trading system, it is an active order. If it finds a match, a trade is generated. If a match is not found, then the orders are stored in different books. Orders are stored in price-time priority in various books in the following sequence: (a) best price, and (b) within price, by time priority.

C. Entities in the Trading System: There are four entities in the trading system:

1. **Trading Members:** Trading members are members of NSE. They can trade either

on their own account or on behalf of their clients including participants. The exchange assigns ID to each trading member. Each trading member can have more than one user.

2. **Clearing Members:** Clearing members are members of NSCCL. They carry out risk management activities and confirmation/inquiry of trades through the trading system.

3. **Professional Clearing Members:** Professional clearing members are clearing members who are not trading member. Typically, banks and custodians become professional clearing members and clear and settle for their trading members.

4. **Participants:** A participant is a client of trading members like financial institutions. These clients may trade through multiple trading members but settle through a single clearing member.

D. Corporate Hierarchy: In the F&O trading software, a trading member has the facility of defining a hierarchy amongst users of the system. This hierarchy comprises corporate manager, branch manager and dealer.

1. **Corporate Manager:** The term *corporate manager* is assigned to a user placed at the highest level in a trading firm. Such a user can perform all the functions such as order and trade-related activities, receiving reports for all branches of the trading member firm and also all dealers of the firm. Additionally, a corporate manager can define exposure limits for the branches of the firm. This facility is available only to the corporate manager.

2. **Branch Manager:** The branch manager is a term assigned to a user who is placed under the corporate manager. Such a user can perform and view order and trade-related activities for all dealers under that branch.

3. **Dealer:** Dealer is a user at the lower level of the hierarchy. A dealer can perform trade-related activities only for himself and does not have access to information on other dealers under either the same branch or other branches.

35.7.3 Order Types and Conditions

The system allows the trading members to enter orders with various conditions attached to them as per their requirements. These conditions are broadly divided into the following three categories:

A. Time Conditions:

- **Day Order:** A day order, as the name suggests, is an order which is valid for the day on which it is entered. If the order is not executed during the day, the system cancels the order automatically at the end of the day.

- **Immediate or Cancel (IOC):** An IOC order allows the user to buy or sell a contract as soon as the order is released into the system, failing which the order is cancelled from the system. Partial match is possible for the order, and the unmatched portion of the order is cancelled immediately.

B. Price Conditions:

- **Stop-loss:** This facility allows the user to release an order into the system, after the market price (last traded price) of the security reaches or crosses a threshold price, e.g. if for stop-loss buy order, the trigger is 1027, the limit price is 1030 and the market (last traded) price is 1023, then this order is released into the system once the market price reaches or exceeds 1027. This order is added to the regular lot book with time of triggering as the time stamp, as a limit order of 1030. For the stop-loss sell order, the trigger price has to be greater than the limit price.

C. Other Conditions:

- **Market Price:** Market orders are orders for which no price is specified at the time the order is entered (i.e. price is market price). For such orders, the system determines the price.
- **Limit Price:** Price of the order after triggering from stop loss book.
- **Pro:** Pro means that the orders are entered on the trading member's own account.
- **Cli:** Cli means that the trading member enters the orders on behalf of a client.
- **Trigger Price:** It is the price at which an order gets triggered from stop-loss book. Several combinations of the above are allowed thereby providing enormous flexibility to the users.

35.7.4 Market Watch: The purpose of market watch is to allow continuous monitoring of contracts or securities that are of specific interest to the user. It displays trading information for contracts selected by the user. The user also gets a broadcast of all the cash market securities on the screen. This function is also available if the user selects the relevant securities for display on the market watch screen. Display of trading information related to cash market securities is in *read only* format, i.e. the dealer can only view the information on cash market but cannot trade in them through the system. This is the main window from the dealer's perspective.

The following windows are displayed on a trader's workstation screen.

1. Title bar.
2. Ticker window of futures and options market.
3. Ticker window of underlying (capital) market.
4. Tool bar.
5. Market watch window.
6. Inquiry window.
7. Snap quote.
8. Order/trade window.
9. System message window.

35.7.5 Placing Orders on the Trading System: While entering orders on the trading system—for both futures and the options market—members are required to identify orders as being proprietary or client orders. Proprietary orders should be identified as *Pro* and those of clients should be identified as *Cli*. Apart from this, in the case of *Cli* trades, the client account number should also be provided. The futures and options market is a zero sum game, i.e. the total number of long in contracts always equals the total number of short in contracts. The total number of outstanding contracts (long/short) at any point in time is called the *open interest*. This open interest figure is a good indicator of the liquidity in the contract. Based on studies carried out in international exchanges, it is found that open interest is maximum in near month expiry contracts.

35.7.6 Eligibility Criteria for Securities/Indices Traded in F&O
A. Eligibility Criteria for Stocks:

- The stock is chosen from amongst the top 500 stocks in terms of average daily market capitalisation and average daily traded value in the previous 6 months on a rolling basis.
- A stock's median quarter-sigma order size over the last 6 months should not be less than ₹ 1 lakh. For this purpose, a stock's quarter-sigma order size should mean the order size (in value terms) required to cause a change in the stock price equal to one-quarter of a standard deviation.
- The market wide position limit in the stock should not be less than ₹ 50 crore. The market wide position limit (number of shares) is valued taking into account the closing prices of stocks in the underlying cash market on the date of expiry of contract in the month. The market wide position limit of open position (in terms of the number of underlying stock) on futures and option contracts on a particular underlying stock should be lower of 20 percent of the number of shares held by non-promoters in the relevant underlying security i.e. free-float holding.

If an existing security fails to meet the eligibility criteria for 3 months consecutively, then no fresh month contract will be issued on that security.

However, the existing unexpired contracts can be permitted to trade till expiry and new strikes can also be introduced in the existing contract months.

For unlisted companies coming out with initial public offering, if the net public offer is ₹ 500 crore or more, then the exchange may consider introducing stock options and stock futures on such stocks at the time of its listing than in cash market.

B. Eligibility Criteria for Indices: The exchange may consider introducing derivative contracts on an index if the stocks contributing to 80 percent weightage of the index are individually eligible for derivative trading. However, no single eligible stock in the index should have a weightage of more than 5 percent in the index. The above criteria is applied every month, if the index fails to meet the eligibility criteria for 3 months consecutively, then no fresh month contract would be issued on that index.

C. Eligibility Criteria for Stocks for Derivatives Trading on Account of Corporate Restructuring: The criteria in this case are as under:

1. All the following conditions shall be met in the case of shares of a company undergoing restructuring through any means for eligibility to reintroduce derivative contracts on that company from the first day of listing of the post- restructured company's stock in the underlying market:
- Futures and options contracts on the stock of the original (pre-restructure) company were traded on any exchange prior to its restructuring.
- Pre-restructured company had a market capitalisation of at least ₹ 1,000 crore prior to its restructuring.
- Post-restructured company would be treated like a new stock and if it is, in the opinion of the exchange, likely to be at least one-third the size of the pre-restructured company in terms of revenues, or assets, or (where appropriate) analyst valuations.
- In the opinion of the exchange, the scheme of restructuring does not suggest that the

post-restructured company would have any characteristic (for example extremely low free float) that would render the company ineligible for derivatives trading.

2. If the above conditions are satisfied, then the exchange takes the following course of action in dealing with the existing derivative contracts on the pre-restructured company and introduction of fresh contracts on the post- restructured company:

- In the contract month in which the post-restructured company begins to trade, the exchange introduces near month, middle month and far month derivative contracts on the stock of the restructured company.

- In subsequent contract months, the normal rules for entry and exit of stocks in terms of eligibility requirements would apply. If these tests are not met, the exchange shall not permit further derivative contracts on this stock and future month series shall not be introduced.

To sum up, financial derivatives are of recent origin in India, barring trade-related forward contracts in the forex market. Over the counter (OTC) as well as exchange-traded derivatives have been introduced, marking an important development in the structure of financial markets in India. Forward contracts in the forex market have also been liberalised. OTC derivatives, viz. interest rate swaps (IRS) and forward rate agreements (FRAs) were introduced in July 1999. The IRS and FRA were introduced with a view to deepening the money market as also to enable banks, primary dealers and financial institutions to hedge interest rate risks.

Endnotes

1. SEBI also set up a group in June 1998 under the chairmanship of Professor J.R. Varma, to recommend measures for risk containment in derivatives market in India. The report, which was submitted in October 1998, worked out the operational details of margining system, methodology for charging initial margins, net worth of brokers, deposit requirements and real-time monitoring requirements.

2. The FRA is an off-balance sheet contract between two parties under which one party agrees on the start date for trade and the party that agrees, would lodge a notional deposit with the other for a specified sum of money for a specified period of time (the FRA period) at a specified rate of interest (the contract rate). The party that has agreed to make the notional deposit has, thus, sold the FRA to the other party who has bought it.

3. The IRS is a contract between two counter-parties for exchange interest payment for a specified period based on a notional principal amount. The notional principal is used to calculate interest payments, but is not exchanged. Only interest payments are exchanged.

Bibliography

Acharya, Viral V., Hemal Khandwala and T. Sabri Öncü (2013), "The Growth of a Shadow Banking System in Emerging Markets: Evidence from India", *Journal of International Money and Finance*, 39, 207-230.

Ahluwalia, M.S. (2011), "Second Generation Reforms in the Banks: Major Issues", paper presented at the Bank Economists' Conference, January, New Delhi.

Banerji, S., K. Gangopadhyay, I. Patnaik and A. Shah (2012), "New Thinking on Corporate Debt in India", mimeo.

Bank for International Settlements, "Supervision of Financial Conglomerates: A Report by the Tripartite Group of Bank, Securities and Insurance Regulators", July 1995.

Basu, Priya (2005), "A Financial System for India's Poor", *Economic and Political Weekly*, No. 37.

Basu, Priya (2005), "Rural Finance Access Survey (RFAS)", World Bank and the National Council of Applied Economic Research (NCAER).

Beatrize, Armendariz and Jonathan Morduch (2007), "Economics of Microfinance", Prentice Hall of India Pvt. Ltd.

Bhatt, Nitin and Y.S.P. Thorat (2001), "India's Regional Rural Banks: The Institutional Dimension of Reforms", *Journal of Microfinance*, Vol. 3, No. 1.

Bhavani, T.A. and N.R. Bhanumurthy (2012), "Financial Access in Post-Reform India", Oxford University Press, New Delhi.

Binswanger, Hans P., Shahidur R. Khandker and Mark R. Rosenzweig (1993), "How Infrastructure and Financial Institutions Affect Agricultural Output and Investment in India", *Journal of Development Economics*, 41: 337-366.

Chattopadhyay, S.K. (2010), "RBI Working Paper on Financial Inclusion in India: A Case Study of West Bengal", Working Paper Series, September, RBI.

European Central Bank, "Report on Electronic Money", August 1998.

Financial Action Task Force (FATF) (2013), "Anti-money Laundering and Terrorist Financing Measures and Financial Inclusion".

Fisher, Thomas and M.S. Sriram (2000), "Beyond Micro-credit: Putting Development Back into Micro-finance", Vistaar Publications.

Gopinath, S. (2005), "Recent Development in Forex, Money and Government Securities Markets: Account and Outlook", *RBI Bulletin*, August.

Government of India, "Banking Committee Report", 1972.

——Planning Commission, "Five Year Plans".

——Ministry of Finance, "Budget Papers" (various years).

——Ministry of Finance, "Economic Survey" (various issues).

——Ministry of Law, Justice, and Company Affairs, "Constitution of India".

Greening, H. and Bikki Randhwa (1999), "A Framework for Regulating Microfinance Institutions", World Bank.

Gupta, Sanjeev Kumar (2011), "Financial Inclusion: IT as Enabler", Reserve Bank of

India Occasional Papers 31, No. 2.

Halan, Monika, Renuka Sane and Susan Thomas (2013), "Estimating Losses to Customers on Account of Mis-selling Life Insurance Policies in India", No. 2013-007, Indira Gandhi Institute of Development Research, Working Paper Series.

International Monetary Fund, "World Economic Outlook", September 2005.

——"Currency Crises: The Role of Monetary Policy", *Finance and Development,* March 1998.

——"Guidelines for Public Debt Management", 2001.

——"Global Financial Stability Report", 2005.

Jadhav, Narendra (2003), "Central Bank Strategies, Credibility and Independence: Global Evolution and the Indian Experience", RBI Occasional Papers.

——(2005), "Monetary Policy, Financial Stability and Central Banking in India", New Delhi: Macmillan India Ltd.

Jadhav, Narendra, Partha Ray, D. Bose and Indranil Sen Gupta (2003), "The Reserve Bank of India's Balance Sheet: Analytics and Dynamics of Evolution", RBI Occasional Papers.

Jalan, Bimal, "Finance and Development: Which Way Now?", *RBI Bulletin*, January 2001.

——"Development and Management of Forex Markets: A Central Banking Perspective", *RBI Bulletin*, February 2001.

——"Strengthening Indian Banking and Finance: Progress and Prospects", Speech delivered at the Bank Economists' Conference at Bangalore, December 27, 2002.

Johri and Jauhari (1994), "Role of Computers in Banking Operation Systems", Himalaya Publishing House, New Delhi.

Kalpana, K. (2005), "Shifting Trajectories in Micro Finance Discourse", *Economic and Political Weekly*, Vol. XL, No. 51.

Kashyap, Anil K., Raghuram Rajan and Jeremy C. Stein (2002), "Banks as Liquidity Providers: An Explanation for the Co-existence of Lending and Deposit-taking", *The Journal of Finance*, No. 1, 33-73.

Kaveri, V.S. (2001), "Loan Default and Profitability of Banks", *IBA Bulletin,* January.

Kohli, S.S. (2001), "Indian Banking Industry: Emerging Challenges", *IBA Bulletin*, March.

Kulkarni, R.V. (2000), "Changing Face of Banking from Brick and Mortar Banking to E-Banking", *IBA Bulletin,* January.

Malhotra, R.N. (1990), "Evolution of Financial System", Nineteenth Frank Moraes Memorial Lecture, Chennai, September.

Martinez, Jose de Luna and Thomas A. Rose (2003), "International Survey of Integrated Financial Sector Supervision", World Bank Policy Research Working Paper 3096.

Merton, R.C. (2005), "Financial Innovation and Economic Performance", *Journal of Applied Corporate Finance*, Vol. 4, Issue 4, 12-22.

Metzer, S.R. (2000), "Strategic Planning for Future Bank Growth", *The Banker's Magazine,* July-August.

Mohan, Rakesh (2003), "Transforming Indian Banking: In Search of a Better

Tomorrow", *RBI Bulletin*.

——(2004), "Ownership and Governance in Private Sector Banks in India", *RBI Bulletin*.

——(2004), "Financial Sector Reforms in India: Policies and Performance Analysis", *RBI Bulletin*, October.

——(2004), "A Decade of Reforms in Government Securities Market in India and the Road Ahead", *RBI Bulletin*, November.

——(2005), "Human Development and State Finances", *RBI Bulletin*, December.

Nair, C.K.G. (2012), "Financial Sector Reforms: Refining the Architecture", in R. Malhotra (ed.), 'A Critical Decade: Policies for India's Development', Oxford University Press, New Delhi.

Nair, T. and Ajay Tankha (2013), "Microfinance India: State of the Sector Report 2013", Sage Publications, New Delhi.

Puhazhendhi, V. and K.J.S. Satyasai (2001), "Microfinance for Rural People: An Impact Study", NABARD, Mumbai.

Rajan, R. and L. Zingales (1998), "Financial Dependence and Growth", *American Economic Review,* Vol. 88.

Rajaraman, Indira (2005), "Financing Rural Infrastructure in Developing Countries", *Applied Econometrics and International Development,* Vol. 5.

Rangarajan, C. (1988), "Issues in Monetary Management", Presidential Address at the Indian Economic Conference, Calcutta, December.

——(1993), "Autonomy of Central Banks", Tenth Kutty Memorial Lecture, Calcutta, September.

——(1997), "Activating Debt Markets in India", *RBI Bulletin*, October.

——(1997), "Dimensions of Monetary Policy", Anantharamakrishnan Memorial Lecture, Chennai, February.

——(2001), "Some Critical Issues in Monetary Policy", *Economic and Political Weekly*, June 16.

——(2008), "Report of the Committee (Chairman: C. Rangarajan) of Financial Inclusion", Planning Commission, Government of India.

Rao, K.S. (2009), "Micro Credit Engine for Inclusive Growth", *The Indian Banker*, September, Vol. 4, No. 9, 40-43.

Reddy, Y.V. (1997), "Financial Sector Reforms and RBI's Balance Sheet Management", *RBI Bulletin*, December.

——(2005), "Banks and Corporates as Partners in Progress", *RBI Bulletin*, November.

——(2005), "The Road Map for Fixed Income and Derivatives Markets", *RBI Bulletin*, March.

——(2005), "Globalisation of Monetary Policy and Indian Experience", *RBI Bulletin*, June.

——(2005), "Monetary Co-operation in Asia", *RBI Bulletin*, October.

——(2005), "Implications of Global Financial Imbalances for the Emerging Market Economies", *RBI Bulletin*, November.

——(2004), "Financial Stability: Indian Experience", Speech at Zurich University Zurich, Switzerland.

Reserve Bank of India, "Functions and Working of RBI", Fourth Edition (1983).

——"Reserve Bank of India: Fifty Years (1935-85)", 1985.

——"Report of the Committee to Review the Working of the Monetary System in India (Chairman: Sukhamoy Chakravarty)", 1985.

——"Report of the Working Group on the Money Market (Chairman: N. Vaghul)", 1987.

——"Report of the Committee on Financial System (Chairman: M. Narasimham)", 1991.

——"Report of the Committee to Enquire into the Irregularities in Securities Transactions of Banks and Financial Institutions (Chairman: R. Janakiraman)", 1992.

——"Report of the High Level Committee on Balance of Payments (Chairman: C. Rangarajan)", 1993.

——"Report of the Expert Group on Foreign Exchange Market in India (Chairman: O.P. Sodhani)", 1995.

——"Report of the Committee on Capital Account Convertibility (Chairman: S.S. Tarapore)", 1997.

——"Payment Systems in India", 1998.

——"Report of the Committee on Banking Sector Reforms (Chairman: M. Narasimham)", 1998.

——"Report of the Informal Advisory Committee on Ways and Means Advances to State Governments (Chairman: B.P.R. Vithal)", 1998.

——"Report of the Technical Committee on State Government Guarantees (Chairperson: Usha Thorat)", May 1999.

——"Report on Repurchase Agreements (REPO)", 1999.

——"Core Principles of Effective Banking Supervision", 1999.

——"Report of the Advisory Group on Transparency in Monetary and Financial Policies (Chairman: M. Narasimham)", 2000.

——"Report of the Working Group on Internet Banking (Chairman: S.R. Mittal)", 2001.

——"Report of the Working Group on Consolidated Accounting and Other Quantitative Methods to Facilitate Consolidated Supervision", December 2001.

——"Reserve Bank of India: Functions and Working", Reserve Bank Staff College, Chennai, 2001.

——"Report of the Working Group on Electronic Money", 2002.

——"Risk-Based Supervision Manual", 2003.

——"Report of the Group to Study the Pension Liabilities of the State Governments (Chairman: B. K. Bhattacharya)", 2003.

——"Report of the Advisory Committee on Ways and Means Advances to State Government (Chairman: C. Ramachandran)", 2003.

——"Report of the Working Group on Instruments of Sterilisation (Chairman: Usha Thorat)", 2003.

——"Report of the Working Group on Monitoring of Systemically Important Financial Intermediaries (Financial Conglomerates), 2004.

——"Committee on Flow of Credit to Agriculture and Related Activities from the Banking System (Chairman: V.S. Vyas)", 2004.

——"Report of the Internal Technical Group on Forex Market", 2005.

——"Report of the Technical Group on Money Market", May 2005.

——"Report of the Internal Technical Group on Central Government Securities Market", July 2005.

——"History of the Reserve Bank of India" (Volume III), 2005.

——"Report on Trend and Progress of Banking in India (2004-05)", 2005.

——"Banking Structure in India: The Way Forward", Discussion Paper, 2013.

——"Report on Currency and Finance" (various years).

——"Handbook of Statistics on Indian Economy" (various years).

——"Bulletins".

——"Occasional Papers".

——"Supplement on Finances of State Governments".

——"Annual Report" (various issues).

Radhakrishna, R. (2007), "Report of the Expert Group on Agricultural Indebtedness", Ministry of Finance, Government of India.

Rajan, Raghuram (2009), "A Hundred Small Steps: Report of the Committee on Financial Sector Reforms", Planning Commission, Government of India, Sage Publications, New Delhi.

Sarangi, Umesh Chandra (2010), "Report of the Task Force on Credit Related Issues of Farmers", Ministry of Agriculture, Government of India.

Sarkar, A.N. and Jagjit Singh (2006), "Savings-led Micro Finance to Bank the Unbankables: Sharing of Global Experience", *Global Economic Review*, July, Vol. 7, No. 2.

Sarma, M. (2008), "Index of Financial Inclusion", ICRIER Working Paper, August.

Sen, Amartya, (2000), "Development as Freedom", Anchor Books, New York.

Shetty, S.L. (2003), "Credit Flows to Rural Poor", mimeo, EPW Research Foundation, Mumbai.

Sinha, Saurabh (1998), "Micro Credit: Impact, Training and Sustainability", *Institute of Development Studies* (IDS), Vol. 29, No. 4, October, University Sussex, U.K.

Srikrishna, B.N. (2013), "Report of the Financial Sector Legislative Reforms Commission", Volume I, Ministry of Finance, Government of India.

Srinivasan, N. (2012), "Microfinance India: State of the Sector Report 2011", Sage Publications, New Delhi.

Stern, Nicholas H. (2001), "Building a Climate for Investment, Growth and Poverty Reduction in India", 16th Exim Bank Commencement Day Annual Lecture, Mumbai.

Tarapore, S.S. (1990), "Domestic Debt Management Policy and Monetary Control", 18th SEANZA Central Banking Course Lectures, Reserve Bank of India, Mumbai.

——(1996), "The Government Securities Market: The Next Stage of Reform", Valedictory Address at the Conference on Government Securities Market, Securities Trading Corporation of India, April.

Tara, S. Nair (2005), "The Transforming World of Indian Micro Finance", *Economic and Political Weekly*, April 23.

Thingalaya, N.K. (2000), "The Other Side of Rural Banking", BIRD Publication, Lucknow.

Thorat, U. (2010), Keynote address at a panel session on "Setting New Paradigm in Regulation" at the FICCI-IBA Conference on 'Global Banking: Paradigm Shift'.

——(2002), "Developing Bond Markets to Diversify Long-Term Development Finance: Country Study of India", *Asia-Pacific Development Journal*, June.

Thorat, Y.S.P. (2011), "Report of the Working Group on Outreach of Institutional Finance, Co-operatives, and Risk Management", Planning Commission, Government of India.

Trivedi, Pratima (2008), "Financial Inclusion: A Must for Financial Stability", *Vinimaya*, Vol. XXIX (2), 59-64.

Umapathy, Deeptha, Parul Agarwal and Santadarshan Sadhu (2012), "A Scoping Study of Financial Literacy Training Programmes in India".

UNCDF (2006), "Building Inclusive Financial Sectors for Development", UNCDF, May.

Valpy, FitzGerald (2006), "Financial Development and Economic Growth: A Critical View", Background paper for World Economic and Social Survey, 2006, Oxford University, U.K.

World Bank, "Improving Access to Finance for India's Rural Poor", The World Bank, 2008.

—— "Finance for All: Policies and Pitfalls in Expanding Access", World Bank, Washington, 2008.

——"Measuring Financial Inclusion", Policy Research Working Paper, 6025, World Bank, Washington D.C., 2011.

——"Financial Access: The State of Financial Inclusion through the Crisis", Consultative Group to Assist the Poor (CGAP), 2010.

Websites

Ministry of Finance, Government of India
Ministry of Corporate Affairs, Government of India
Reserve Bank of India (RBI)
Securities and Exchange Board of India (SEBI)
National Bank for Agriculture and Rural Development (NABARD)
Insurance Regulatory and Development Authority (IRDA)
Pension Fund Regulatory and Development Authority (PFRDA)
Niti Aayog
World Bank
International Monetary Fund (IMF)
Bank for International Settlements (BIS)

Index